Liver	All rich ___ ___ sparerib ___ luncheon meats; brains, sweetbreads, kidney, tongue, etc.
Duck (no skin)	Fat poultry and skin; goose
Shellfish (shrimp, clams, etc.)	
	No more than 3 egg yolks a week including those used in cooking
Cheeses made from partially skimmed milk	Sweet cream; sour cream; whole milk; butter; whole milk cheeses; nondairy cream substitutes (which usually contain coconut oil); chocolate milk; ice cream; whole milk yogurt
Olives and avocados (both high in monounsaturated fat)	Vegetables prepared in sauces of unknown ingredients
Olive oil may be used occasionally for flavor, but it is low in polyunsaturates and does not take the place of recommended oils	Ordinary margarines; solid fats and shortenings, such as butter, lard, and Crisco; meat fat, salt pork fat; coconut oil
	Canned cream soups; canned soups made with butter or hydrogenated oils; cream soups of unknown ingredients
Egg noodles	Butter rolls, egg breads; commercial biscuits, muffins, doughnuts, sweet rolls; cheese breads; prepared cake mixes; all commercially prepared baked goods unless you are sure they do not contain saturated fats, whole milk, cream, etc.
	Coconut and coconut oil; whole milk puddings; milk sherbets; filberts; cashews; macadamia nuts
	Potato chips and other deep-fried snacks

Live High on Low Fat

Live High on Low Fat

by Sylvia Rosenthal

New Enlarged Edition

with a Foreword by
Jeremiah Stamler, M.D.

J. B. Lippincott Company
Philadelphia and New York

U.S. Library of Congress Cataloging in Publication Data

Rosenthal, Sylvia Dworsky, birth date
  Live high on low fat.

  Includes index.
  1. Low-fat diet. 2. Menus. I. Title.
RM237.9.R6 1975   641.5′638   75-8938
ISBN-0-397-01060-5

To T. R., who has made me
one of the most fortunate of wives

Contents

Foreword
by Jeremiah Stamler, M.D.

Professor and Chairman, Department of Community Health and Preventive Medicine, and Harry W. Dingman Professor of Cardiology, Northwestern University Medical School

This book is a fitting sign of the times. It betokens the urgency of the coronary heart-disease problem in the United States today and the necessity for large-scale efforts to grapple with it.

This book is unique in that its author is neither nutritionist nor physician. She is an intelligent, gifted woman whose husband, a physician, was stricken by a heart attack. Stimulated by this harsh circumstance, she learned that it may be possible to prevent repeat attacks—and first attacks as well—by dietary means. As this book eloquently testifies, she proceeded to become a past master of the science and fine art required to "Live High on Low Fat." In this labor of love, she had the good fortune to be aided by the late Dr. Norman Jolliffe and his colleagues of the Anti-Coronary Club, New York City Department of Health.

Books like this are urgently needed. Atherosclerotic coronary heart disease has been the twentieth-century epidemic afflicting Americans. As everyone knows from personal experience, it strikes down persons in the prime of life, as well as the elderly. However, government statistics released in the early 1970's indicated a drop in the coronary death rate among men and women. This was the first decrease noted in over a decade and suggests that years of public health efforts to change the American life-style that increases coronary risk have begun to show results.

The average healthy middle-aged American man—women are much less susceptible—has about one chance in five of developing atherosclerotic coronary heart disease before age sixty-five and about one chance in fifteen of dying from it before age sixty-five. Within recent years, statistics from the United States Department of Health, Education, and Welfare indicate that over one third of all deaths in men aged forty-five to fifty-four have been caused by this one disease. In about 35 percent of cases, the first attack is acutely fatal within four to six weeks of onset. Many of the deaths occur suddenly; people drop dead. Of those surviving the first attack, 20 to 40 percent (depending upon the circumstances of the acute attack) are destined to die in the next five years if reliance is placed solely upon the older approaches to treatment.

These few statistics alone are enough to emphasize the need for continuing our efforts, particularly to achieve primary prevention—that is, the prevention of the disease from ever occurring clinically. A few additional facts further highlight this need. A large group of middle-aged American men—more than 20 percent, in fact—have a very high risk of developing coronary disease in the prime of life, much higher than the average man. These men are susceptible or coronary-prone because of such abnormalities as hypercholesterolemia (a high level of the fatty material, cholesterol, in their blood), high blood pressure, overweight, diabetes, excessive cigarette smoking, and sedentary living habits. Men with two or more of these abnormalities in combination have a very high risk of premature heart attacks, as high as one chance in two or two chances in three—or worse. These men, numbering in the millions in the United States today, are particularly in need of timely preventive measures.

Fortunately, it is now possible, thanks to the research successes of recent years, to offer hope in the face of these dire statistics. It is now possible to treat the abnormalities associated with increased risk of atherosclerotic coronary heart disease. They can be corrected in whole or part, and controlled, by modern medical means. This is true for high blood cholesterol, high blood pressure, overweight, diabetes, excessive cigarette smoking, lack of exercise, etc. Therefore, a mood of restrained cautious optimism has become widespread among the expert researchers in this field. It may be possible, as the Statement by the American Heart Association emphasized, to prevent heart attacks—and strokes as well.

Modern nutritional science is one cornerstone of this new preventive approach. For it has been shown that high blood cholesterol, overweight, and (to a limited degree) high blood pressure and diabetes can be brought under control by dietary means. High blood cholesterol, for example, can be readily lowered at least 15 to 20 percent in most cases. And the available statistics warrant the prediction that this change alone might lead to a 25 to 50 percent fall in the rate of heart attacks in middle-aged men. Encouraging data are already available on the salutary effects of controlling overweight, high blood pressure, diabetes, and heavy cigarette smoking.

A cardinal consideration is the need for a *permanent change* in habits. Short-lived efforts—the frequent American pattern of going on a diet and then going off—are futile. A *sustained correction*—for years—of high blood cholesterol, overweight, etc., must be achieved if anything is to be accomplished in the way of preventing heart attacks.

The dietary approaches required to attain these goals have been worked out in great detail, as this book amply illustrates. In the language of nutrition, they involve diets moderate in total calories, total fats, polyunsaturated fatty acids, monounsaturated fatty acids, and carbohydrates; *low in saturated fatty acids and cholesterol*; and high in all essential nutrients (proteins, amino acids, vitamins, minerals). In terms of foodstuffs this means:

Emphasizing the low-fat dairy products (skim milk, buttermilk, cottage cheese) and de-emphasizing the high-fat products (sweet cream, sour cream, ice cream, whipped cream, cheeses, butter).

Emphasizing the lean cuts of meat and poultry and de-emphasizing the fat cuts, by trimming off fat before cooking, cooking so as to get rid of fat (broiling, rotisserieing, roasting with discarding of drippings, letting stews and soups stand in the refrigerator overnight and skimming off congealed fat); the use of vegetable oils in braising meats, etc.; moderation of the meat portion size (four to six ounces, not twelve to sixteen!).

Emphasizing fish and seafood; de-emphasizing eggs.

Emphasizing vegetable oils and polyunsaturated soft margarines and de-emphasizing solid table spreads (butter, ordinary margarines) and solid shortenings (lard, suet, hydrogenated vegetable fats).

Emphasizing fruit desserts (citrus and noncitrus) and de-emphasizing commercial cakes, pastries, shortcakes, cookies, and pies.

Emphasizing green and yellow vegetables and legumes (peas, beans).

Emphasizing moderation in the use of starches (potatoes, rice, spaghetti, breads, cereals), carbohydrate-rich spreads (jellies, jams, honey, marmalade), and alcoholic beverages.

Mrs. Rosenthal's book spells out in rich detail precisely what this means in terms of day-to-day eating. It should therefore receive a hearty welcome in millions of American homes where a desire exists to take the simple, reasonable steps needed to change dietary patterns in an attempt to prevent heart attacks. Anyone scanning the pages and pages of delightful and tempting recipes in *Live High on Low Fat* must be convinced that pleasure lies ahead along this way of good hope for the prevention of heart attacks. Indeed, one of the major merits of this book is its demonstration that one of the pleasures of the good life— the pleasure of good eating—can and should remain with us as we continue our efforts to further diminish the contemporary epidemic of premature heart attacks.

Live High on Low Fat

1

Speaking of Cholesterol

This new edition of *Live High on Low Fat* contains everything I have learned and done during the last twenty years of planning and preparing meals that would please my family and at the same time exert a benign influence on their well-being and—more specifically—on their cholesterol levels. It has been a rewarding experience, for apparently whatever it is I have done has worked. And judging from the hundreds of letters I have received over the years from readers, it has worked for others as well.

While in the process of revising and reorganizing this book, the thought crossed my mind that just as it takes a crisis or upheaval in public life to initiate a wave of reform, so it is in our private lives. In our case, the crisis was my husband's coronary heart attack and the reform centered mainly around the kitchen.

This crisis goes back about twenty years to when the word "cholesterol" was still a term that belonged to doctors and laboratory technicians. It had not yet found its way into layman's language. I had heard it, of course— one can't have been a doctor's wife for over a quarter of a century without exposure to bits and pieces of scientific jargon and medical terminology. It had as much significance for me, however, as a mathematical equation relating to nuclear physics. I did not, as the psychiatrists say, relate—not until the coronary episode.

I will skip over that period with all haste, leaving room for just one wifely comment. Of all the various kinds of patients in the world—good, bad, cooperative, and otherwise—sick doctors are in a class by themselves. They are the *worst* kind. In their defense, though, I suppose we could admit that firsthand knowledge of assorted complications is of questionable comfort when it is your own symptoms that are under consideration.

Happily, however, there came the period of convalescence and with it time to visit with friends and colleagues and leisure to catch up on the reams of medical literature that flood doctors' offices and spill over into their homes. It was just at that time that a series of reports of investigations by scientists from various parts of the world was beginning to trickle into the medical literature. These reports called attention to an interesting correlation between diet and the incidence of heart disease. Our national diet in the United States is high in fat—from 40 to 50 percent of total calories, a large part of them from meat and dairy fats. It is also high in cholesterol. Some populations in Asia, Africa, and Latin America have barely a third as much fat and cholesterol intake and a correspondingly lower coronary disease rate. It appeared that the richer the country, the more likely it was to have a high rate of coronary heart disease.

It was noticed that in World War II the coronary disease mortality in Norway dropped greatly during the German occupation. This was associated not only with decreased consumption of fatty food, difficult to obtain in those stringent times, but also with bomb damage to the plants that manufactured the hard or saturated fats.

There were obvious inferences to be drawn from studies done on Japanese living in Japan, Hawaii, and California in relation to coronary heart disease. In each case, the death rate of this ethnic group paralleled that of the community in which the people lived. The coronary death rate was lowest in Japan, where little dairy fat is consumed, and highest in California, where the usual American diet, high in saturated fat, prevailed.

This was but a small part of the data which made an impressive case for a change in our cooking routines, although I must confess to a few pangs at abandoning a recipe file bulging with all sorts of mouth-watering dishes that—and I don't mean to sound immodest—had earned our household a reputation among our friends for distinguished food. On the other hand, how can a *roux* made with country-fresh butter stand up against such dismal reports as those showing that over half of all deaths among Americans are caused by cardiovascular disease, and that in the United States today coronary heart disease has the macabre distinction of being the leading cause of death, if there is the slightest possibility that the ingredients in the *roux* may be a contributing factor? With my concern selfishly centered on the one cardiac patient whose well-being obscured all else, I resolved to be unimpressed by what Escoffier might have done if he were handed some dried skim milk instead of heavy cream— particularly since Escoffier is dead and we aren't.

Nevertheless, at that moment I anticipated a dim future for our kitchen. Visions of sugarplums did not dance in my head. What did was something more like pale chicken and pale fish. The memory of my dismay makes me empathetic with the first reactions of other people whose doctors recommend an eating program stripped of what the patients had considered a way of life. Having to change the habits of a lifetime can be unsettling, but on the other hand some lifetime habits need to be changed.

I am reminded of a dinner party at our home in our B.C. (Before Cholesterol) period. Among our guests was a cardiologist—a peppery old gentleman. On second thought, perhaps he wasn't so old, but twenty-five or thirty years ago anyone who had passed the half-century mark seemed—well, mature. I don't remember our menu, but in view of my then habits, it might very well have started with a crab bisque (lots of cream and crab meat); continued with a beef Stroganoff or perhaps a well-marbled, rare roast beef, special stuffed potatoes (lots of butter and cheese), asparagus with hollandaise (lots of egg yolks and butter), avocado in the salad and a ripe, melting Brie along the way; and ended with a smashing crescendo furnished by an obscenely rich chocolate cream torte (lots of Maillard's sweet chocolate, heavy cream, and many eggs).

Everyone purred with repletion and pleasure during coffee—that is, everyone except the peppery old gentleman, whose professional instincts were superior to his manners. He fixed me with a baleful eye and practically snarled, "That's no way to feed people!" In my ignorance I hadn't the slightest idea of what had evoked his ire—or, indeed, what he was talking about. Much, much later, I understood. He was right. That *is* no way to feed people—not with the specter of atherosclerosis waiting in the wings.

Atherosclerosis, or hardening of the arteries, is a disease in which arteries are narrowed and hardened by deposits of minute globules containing a waxy substance called cholesterol, which is present in some foods we eat and is also manufactured by the body. When the blood vessels become clogged with this substance, the flow of blood to the heart and brain is restricted, resulting in heart attacks and strokes. In spite of some gaps and tangled threads in the fabric of evidence pointing up the villain in this physiological process, the bulk of informed scientific opinion is now in agreement that a leading factor predisposing toward atherosclerosis is a high cholesterol content in the blood.

To attempt to reduce the tremendously complicated disease process of atherosclerosis to a few well-rounded phrases is an impossible task, even for doctors' wives, who are an intrepid lot, medically. Unhampered by formal training and proper degrees, we are walking repositories of a long string of diagnoses and quasi-medical terms that we can unleash at the drop of a symptom. Whereas our husbands, cautious, inhibited souls that they are, require a history, clinical examination, and laboratory tests before arriving at an opinion, we are restrained by no such technicalities. Fortunately, nobody listens to doctors' wives except other doctors' wives, who are automatically safeguarded by the doctors.

And so, properly humble and mindful of the failings of the ladies who dwell on the fringes of legitimate medicine, I shall not attempt to distill the physiological principles of serum cholesterol levels in relation to body metabolism and fat intake in twenty-five words or less. I am not a scientist, and this is not a scientific treatise.

For us, the cooks, it is enough to know what we are trying to do—reduce the intake of cholesterol and saturated fats and increase polyunsaturated fats; why we are doing it—a high ratio of polyunsaturated fats over saturated fats generally reduces the blood cholesterol; and how to go about it—follow the diet pattern and the recipes in the following pages.

It has been found that the serum cholesterol level will

also be lowered when the cholesterol intake is reduced and the total fat intake is limited to from 15 to 20 percent, or less, of the total calories. However, this stringent limitation imposes a considerable hardship and deprivation on a dieter—except for a confirmed vegetarian, perhaps—and thus is less desirable from a practical and realistic standpoint than the method of increasing the polyunsaturated fatty acids over the saturated ones.

Fats are composed of three types of fatty acids, depending upon their chemical composition: saturated, which have the effect of raising the cholesterol level in the blood; polyunsaturated, which tend to lower it; and monounsaturated, which are neutral in their effect, neither raising nor lowering it to any extent. Olive oil is a good example of the last-named.

All three types of fatty acids are usually present in any single food, but in varying proportions. For practical purposes, foods containing large amounts of saturated fatty acids are called saturated and those containing large amounts of polyunsaturated acids are referred to as polyunsaturated.

Polyunsaturated fats are usually liquid oils of vegetable origin such as corn, cottonseed, soybean, and safflower (see Approximate Composition of Common Food Fats in the back of the book). They contain large quantities of linoleic acid, an essential nutrient that must be supplied by food because the body cannot make it. Fish, grains, and some nuts—particularly walnuts—are high in polyunsaturates.

Saturated fats are usually solid and of animal origin—the fats in meat, whole milk, sour cream, sweet cream, cheeses made from whole milk, butter, solid shortenings such as ordinary margarines, lard, and hydrogenated vegetable shortenings such as Crisco and Spry. Coconut oil is very highly saturated. These items and all products made with them are the ones we seek to limit.

The process of hydrogenation that converts liquid vegetable oils into a solid state is, unfortunately, a double-edged sword. While this method converts the fat into a creamy solid that looks attractive and keeps well, it also changes the polyunsaturated qualities of the liquid oil into saturated ones, thereby removing it from our orbit. Most soft margarines—that is, the ones packaged in half-pound tubs—contain more liquid oil than the margarines of the same manufacture that are packaged in firm bars. Consequently, the soft margarines are more unsaturated.

Cholesterol is a fatlike substance found in all animal products. It is present in considerable amounts in egg yolks, animal organs (liver, brains, sweetbreads, etc.), and in shellfish (see Cholesterol Content of Some Foods in the back of the book). It is not present in foods of plant origin, such as fruits, vegetables, cereal grains, legumes, and nuts. However, the cholesterol content of an individual's diet is just one of a number of factors that influence the amount of cholesterol in the blood.

Like most new medical concepts, the dietary theory that forms the basis of this book did not come into popular acceptance at once. It had its disciples and detractors. But in 1962 the American Heart Association, after many years of scrupulous observation and carefully controlled studies in various parts of the world, issued a statement in relation to it. It declared, in part, "Reduction or control of fat under medical supervision with reasonable substitution of polyunsaturated for saturated fat is recommended as a possible means of preventing atherosclerosis and decreasing the risk of heart attacks and strokes." A rather cautious statement, to be sure, but just three years later—in 1965—the AHA came out unabashedly with the recommendation that all Americans cut down on saturated fats and cholesterol and adopt "the prudent diet."

What started with a whisper developed into a chorus as many of the country's most prestigious medical and nutritional organizations issued unequivocal statements on the importance of a lowered cholesterol and the need for a better diet to combat heart disease. It has been repeatedly demonstrated that a fat-modified diet can effect a reduction in serum cholesterol. In recent years, there has also been strong evidence that a change of diet can reverse the process of atherosclerosis to some extent—that changing from a high-cholesterol to a low-cholesterol diet can lead to a regression of atherosclerotic lesions in man. In other words, it is never too late.

Nor is it ever too early. Many pediatricians and cardiologists are now recommending that infants be placed on antiatherosclerotic diets shortly after birth, since the earlier any disease prevention program begins, the more effective it can be. There is a strong body of opinion to the effect that lowering cholesterol levels in children may prevent premature heart attacks in adult life. Our daughter's children have been on skim milk since they were four months old, on the advice of their pediatrician (with nary a suggestion from the grandparents).

A three-year study conducted by an Arizona pediatrician with a group of his young private patients who were kept on a low-cholesterol, low-saturated fat diet modified for the age group showed no difference between the growth, development, and body chemistry of this group and a similar age group of nondieting children, except that the former had a lowered serum cholesterol.

Whether infants grow up with a life-style committed to a high-saturated fat, high-cholesterol diet is determined to some measure by what they are exposed to in their homes. If they are given a good example by parents, young people can be educated to good nutrition habits that could conceivably lay the cornerstone for longer, healthier lives—a kind of cultural osmosis.

Many parents make the mistake of forcing milk, meat, and eggs on their young people because these are protein foods. Unfortunately, they are also high in saturated fat and cholesterol. Frequently as much as 75 percent of the calories in the popular hamburger eaten at the corner lunch counter are fat, and most of it highly saturated! What most people consider plain cake, cookies, and Danish pastry are chockablock with saturated fat.

It would be irresponsible to suggest that, as a result of a low-fat, low-cholesterol regime, one could be assured of the usual fairy-tale ending "and they lived happily ever after." The human organism is not simple, and the ultimate answer to the complex problem of what causes heart disease has not yet been determined. Certainly no doctor will take issue with the fact that the best way anyone has yet discovered to reach a rich old age is to come from a line of ancestors who lived to be 100 and left huge trust funds for their descendants.

However, among the factors known to influence the incidence of coronary heart disease—diet, heredity, cigarette smoking, stress, sedentary living, overweight, hormone imbalance—diet is surely one of the most amenable to control. As long as these imperfect wrappings with which we are gifted are the only ones we shall ever be privileged to call our own, it seems to me that it would be exceedingly silly and shortsighted not to give them every advantage that an enlightened medical science has developed.

You may have noticed that males occupy a predominant place in most heart studies. The explanation for this may be found in actuarial tables. For some not too clearly understood reason, the female sex hormones confer a degree of immunity on women up to the time of menopause. After the menopause they gain equality with the males—a Pyrrhic victory, to be sure—and the coronary rate between the sexes becomes the same.

Meanwhile, the battle being fought in the laboratories by dedicated researchers continues. The years ahead will undoubtedly expose some new villains in the cause of heart disease and uncover new questions. And while no one would suggest that the final word on atherosclerosis has yet been written, neither would anyone deny that our present knowledge gives us firmly documented justification for control of dietary fats.

We have never considered our eating program in the nature of a "diet." That word, particularly in a population like ours, which is never out of earshot of a steady bombardment of nutritional propaganda and Cassandralike pronouncements of the dire results of overweight (unfortunately substantiated by statistics), has an unpleasant connotation of deprivations, stringencies, and omissions. Nothing could be further from the truth in this case. This is a method of cooking that can please the whole family. It can produce fascinating table fare in endless variety. It offers adventures in tastes and textures of food that might previously have been lost, drowned in blobs of whipped cream or rich taste-disguising sauces.

There are a few adjustments the cook will have to make, of course—but mostly in point of view. Some foods are to be emphasized, others relegated to places of less importance in our meal planning. We now have the advantage of increased knowledge and the availability of many excellent commercial products in which fats have been reduced. Consider the case of butter, for example. When we went off the hard-fat standard in 1956, doing without butter seemed a minor hardship. I can't think of more than two or three people we know who are using butter today. Also, at that time one sometimes had to visit a number of stores before one could find a container of skim milk. In the first edition of this book, I included a recipe for making yogurt with skim milk. It is no longer necessary to make it at home, unless from choice, for it is now possible to buy low-fat yogurt anywhere. There was no imitation ice cream available in many parts of the country a few years ago; today frozen-food sections of every supermarket are replete with ice milk. The same is true of low-fat cottage cheese. Food processors still have a long way to go, however, and we hope that one day they will switch to using polyunsaturated oils in the preparation of all their prepackaged items.

Many people mistakenly think that this dietary constitutes a reducing program. This could hardly be so, for fats are fats, with the same caloric values, whether they are manufactured by a cow or from corn. On the other hand, meal planning that consistently avoids the concentrated calories in cream, rich desserts, fat meats, and the like will automatically serve as a balance wheel to maintain weight at an even level. As Exhibit A, I offer my husband's waistline. The ten pounds he lost during his coronary illness—one of the few fringe benefits of that episode—have stayed lost. A praiseworthy record, in view of his enthusiasm for eating and his rather sedentary routine.

No volume concerned with diet and its effect on health would be complete without emphasis on the importance of keeping the weight within normal limits. With all media of communication constantly barraging the public to "watch its waistline in the interest of longer life and better health," to say nothing of improved appearance, it seems unlikely that there could be anyone still unaware of the dangers of overweight. It should be noted that the combination of overweight and high blood pressure is a high-risk factor in coronary heart disease.

Just as it is a rare man or woman who does not know that excessive body weight can shorten life expectancy, it would be equally unusual to find someone similarly unacquainted with the concentrated calories lurking in starches, sugars, and fats. For most people who want to reduce, a simple modification of food intake, assiduously adhered to over a period of weeks, days, or months, will bring about the desired result. An extensive weight loss should always be undertaken with medical supervision.

This is one situation where information is not enough, however, as evidenced by the oversize doctors one occasionally meets. Knowledge may be Power, but it is no substitute for the firm resolve to lessen food intake that constitutes the only successful weapon for victory over excess poundage.

In his book *Reduce and Stay Reduced,* Dr. Norman Jolliffe fashioned a wonderfully descriptive phrase: "empty calories." This sums up the goodies in the candy jar or the sweet nothings that we sometimes busy ourselves with. Lacking vitamins, proteins, minerals, guaranteed not to bring a sparkle to the eye, a glow to the skin, a spring to the step, these "empty calories" are good only for bumps and bulges. If the victims of overweight could decide once and forever that the momentary satisfaction derived from eating "empty calories" is too big a price to pay for the unpleasant consequences of excess weight, both physical and aesthetic, they would be on their way to better health. There is no gainsaying the fact that the overweight person with a high cholesterol runs a greater risk of heart attack than his leaner brother whose cholesterol is within normal limits.

I believe that my family was never sharply aware of the moment of departure from our former cooking era with its unlimited use of saturated fats. If some items ceased coming to the table, others equally interesting and eye-appealing took their places. I improvised, adapted, experimented, and produced a succession of dishes as varied and flavorful as I knew how.

This, I think, is the solution to the problem of successful meal planning that may be obliged to sidestep some previously used ingredients no longer suitable for our eating program. Don't let any of the gaps show! With the huge variety of foods that we can produce, all within the proper structure of a polyunsaturated master plan, our cooking horizons are practically unlimited.

2

Design for Living

There is nothing complex or difficult about a diet that will effectively lower serum cholesterol in most people. It contains almost all the usual food products. The subtleties of food choices and preparation that make the difference between a desirable polyunsaturated and saturated ratio in a meal can be known mainly to the cook—not to the diner, for a good dinner is a good dinner!

The framework for our eating program was borrowed from the book of rules established by the New York City Health Department's famous Diet and Coronary Heart Disease Study. This study, better known as the Anti-Coronary Club, was begun in 1957 to research the relationship between diet and coronary heart disease. Out of their list of admonitions, precepts, foods allowable, and those forbidden developed the Prudent Diet. My contribution consists of translating their dos and don'ts into kitchen procedures, made practicable and tempting with ingredients and measurements.

My revered mentor, Dr. Norman Jolliffe, the distinguished authority on nutrition who was Director of the Bureau of Nutrition at that time, was chiefly responsible for the study project. It involved a carefully selected group of men between the ages of forty and fifty-nine who volunteered to follow the Prudent Diet and meet regularly with a team of doctors, nurses, and nutritionists for consultation and follow-up that included blood tests to determine serum cholesterol levels. In 1959 another group of volunteers who remained on their usual diet, known as the control group, was established for the purpose of comparison with the experimental group regarding serum cholesterol changes and incidence of coronary heart disease.

The results are now well known. The 1967 findings on this study show that the Prudent Diet significantly lowered and sustained a drop in serum cholesterol levels when compared with the control group. And more important, the experimental group with the lowered serum cholesterol experienced a significantly decreased incidence of coronary heart disease—about one third less—when compared with the control group.

RECOMMENDED FOODS

The Prudent Diet recommends the use of adequate amounts of protein at each meal in the form of low-fat cottage cheese, skim milk, lean poultry, egg whites, well-trimmed lean meats, legumes, and/or fish in all forms—fresh, canned, pickled, frozen, dried, or smoked. Fish is high in polyunsaturates and may be eaten three times a day. Young broilers, preferably skinned, and lean veal may be served often.

MEATS

Beef, pork, and lamb are a different story. This whole family is restricted to a total maximum of four meals a week, with portions not to exceed four to six ounces. In the course of a week, you will have fourteen lunches and dinners. We simplify our scorekeeping with a fish, poultry, or cottage cheese program at lunch, which leaves only seven meals to account for. It is helpful to plan the seven main courses at the beginning of each week to avoid being caught short with only a steak in your freezer when you have already reached your full quota with the pot roast you had for two meals, the leg of lamb, and the pork loin. Taking a bird's-eye view of the week's rations is a simple procedure to which you can easily become accustomed. There is still a world of lovely choices for the main course, even if they don't revolve around individual twelve-ounce steaks. In the chapter on meats you will find cooking techniques designed to eliminate as much of the fat from meat as possible.

EGGS

Most cardiologists and nutritionists feel the fewer eggs the better. Three a week should be the limit for adults. Dr. Jeremiah Stamler's view "that eggs should be restored to their original function, i.e., making of chickens," may not win him the Man of the Year Award from the Chicken Farmers League, but it is a widely held opinion among authorities in the field of atherosclerosis. The egg whites are pure protein and you may have as many as you wish, but the egg yolk prices itself out of our dietary reach because of the large amounts of *both* cholesterol and saturated fat it contains. It can claim the dubious honor of being higher in cholesterol than any other item of food except brains. The daily two-egg breakfast is surely not for households interested in maintaining a lowered blood cholesterol level.

People with a deep and abiding passion for eggs will still be able to include a poached, fried, or scrambled egg from time to time. But to stay within the limit of three, they must take into account the fractions of eggs they eat in baked and cooked foods. While one portion of a two-egg cake may represent only one-quarter or one-fifth of an egg, which by itself is negligible, these segments can add up.

Some egg substitute products are now available. Fleischmann makes a cholesterol-free egg substitute called Egg Beaters, available in the frozen-food sections of most supermarkets. When defrosted, Egg Beaters can be scrambled or used in baking and many forms of cooking. Tillie Lewis makes a product called Eggstra which contains 80 percent less cholesterol and roughly half the calories of fresh eggs. Available in most supermarkets, it comes in powdered form and is ready to use when dissolved in water.

POWDERED EGG WHITE

Even though I have no sympathy with the perfidious quality of egg yolks, it does trouble my housewifely conscience to keep chucking them out. The answer to this dilemma is powdered egg white, which, when dissolved in water, performs the same as fresh egg white. The powder will last for years if kept in an airtight container in a cool, dry place, away from moisture.

It can be ordered by mail (minimum order is 2 pounds) from Henningsen Foods, Inc., 2 Corporate Park Drive, White Plains, New York 10604. For the equivalent of 1 egg white, add 4 teaspoons of egg white powder to 2 tablespoons of water and beat with a wire whisk until dissolved. It is ready to use at once and can be whipped into a satisfactory meringue.

SUBSTITUTING FOR EGG YOLKS

Very often two egg whites may be used in place of one whole egg in baking and cooking. The white has about the same coating, binding, and leavening properties as the yolk but, since it lacks the fat, flavor, and some of the thickening properties of the yolk, it will not always substitute for it satisfactorily. Much depends upon the function of the yolk in the recipe, and no general rule for its substitution can be given that will assure good results. It is necessary to experiment with individual recipes to judge.

If you have been in the habit of baking cakes that use four to six or more eggs, abandon them. You can make excellent cakes with one or two eggs, or even none, as you will see from the recipes.

Yolk-thickened sauces should likewise be abandoned in favor of the cream sauces on page 331. These sauces may also be made with cornstarch, using the same method and the same ingredients, but only half as much cornstarch as flour.

MILK

Whole milk is permitted for coffee only. Otherwise, restrict milk to the nonfat varieties, such as fresh skim milk or skim milk reconstituted from nonfat milk solids, fat-free buttermilk, or evaporated skimmed milk. Since the important vitamins, minerals, and proteins are contained in the nonfat portions of the milk, you are giving up mainly the butterfat, a splendid thing to forgo. And in line with the present informed opinion, this includes most children and teenagers as well.

Since most commercial buttermilk is artificially cultured, check carefully to make sure that what you are buying is made from skim milk and not whole milk. I see both kinds in my markets. It is a simple matter to make your own buttermilk, however. Fill a quart container with 3 cups of water and add the contents of a premeasured 1-quart package of dry skim-milk powder. Shake well to dissolve, then add 1 cup of buttermilk and a pinch of salt and stir until blended. Cover the jar and place in a warmish place in the kitchen—near the stove pilot light, for instance—for twenty-four hours. Stir well and you will find yourself with a quart of low-fat buttermilk. Chill in the refrigerator. You can keep this going indefinitely, using the last cup to start a new batch.

Powdered skim milk, or nonfat milk solids, is a wonderfully satisfactory product when reconstituted, both for drinking and cooking. A box of it on your pantry shelf affords all the conveniences of a lactating cow in your back yard, with none of the responsibilities. If your family is not enthusiastic about drinking milk, use more of it in cooking. They will probably welcome it in the form of cream soups, cream sauces, and puddings. Skim milk may be substituted for whole milk or cream in any recipe, in the same proportion. Where a richer or creamier product is desired, add an extra tablespoon or two of powdered milk to one cup of skim milk.

Cans of evaporated skimmed milk are another fine cooking aid. I try always to have a supply of them on hand for use, undiluted, in sauces, soups, and puddings. Many people like it for coffee, but I can't pass judgment on that, for we drink ours black. However, you might try it.

Whipped topping made from dry skim milk (page 374) may be substituted for whipped cream in the same amount in chiffon pies or frozen puddings.

Perhaps this would be a propitious moment for a warning against the whipped cream, sour cream, and coffee cream substitutes presently around. One of the whipped cream substitutes heralds the news that it contains no milk or milk products. But if you take the time to read the label, you will see that it contains hydrogenated oil, which translates into saturated fat and will not do for our purposes. The coffee cream and sour cream substitutes must be equally suspect. They make much of the fact that they are free of butterfat and contain only vegetable oil. A letter to the manufacturer of a popular coffee cream substitute revealed the truth of that statement—except that, unfortunately, the vegetable oil was coconut oil, the most highly saturated of all oils. Sweet cream would probably be less damaging than this product. The only coffee cream substitute I know of at this writing that meets our standards of polyunsaturation (there may be others) is a product called Poly Perx, manufactured by Mitchell Foods, Inc., of Fredonia, New York.

Be very selective when shopping for any of these milk or cream substitutes. If the label leaves you in doubt, do take the trouble to write to the manufacturer.

VEGETABLE OILS AND TABLE SPREADS

Time was when anyone wanting a polyunsaturated margarine had to buy it at a drugstore. There was just one brand available and, if memory serves me right, it didn't taste any worse than some of the other nostrums dispensed by the pharmacist. Processors have made a good deal of progress, and we are now offered a wide choice of polyunsaturated margarines that can fulfill a household's need for a shortening and table spread.

The special margarines—particularly the soft ones that come in tubs—contain substantially higher levels of polyunsaturated fatty acids than the standard margarines. But no margarine can contain as much of the essential fatty acids as are present in liquid oil. The process of hydrogenation that converts the liquid oil into a solid state also reduces the linoleic fatty acid content. Linoleic acid is one of the most prevalent polyunsaturated fatty acids in food fats and one of the most valuable in lowering blood cholesterol. Also, the composition of liquid oils remains constant, whereas the formulas of margarines can be variable. Some margarine manufacturers have been known to suddenly change the composition of their product, substituting a less polyunsaturated oil than the one originally used, thereby making the product less desirable from our standpoint. And so to introduce into the diet the optimum amount of linoleic acid, I use liquid oil almost exclusively in cooking and baking.

In discussing the use of liquid vegetable oils in the

kitchen, I find myself sounding like a television commercial. But there you are—the oils are easy to measure, require no creaming, are less costly than some of the other shortenings, do not change the flavor of the food, and give excellent results, all bonuses for a product that contains cholesterol-reducing properties. Among the predominantly polyunsaturated oils, in descending order of their degree of polyunsaturates, are safflower (the most highly unsaturated of all oils), soybean, corn, cottonseed, and sunflower.

People are sometimes concerned on hearing that when vegetable oil is heated, it loses its polyunsaturated qualities and becomes saturated. These fears can be allayed; I have been assured by nutritionists and biochemists that, at ordinary cooking temperatures, there is no significant loss in polyunsaturates. A marked decrease in polyunsaturates occurs only when the oil is heated until it foams and smokes and becomes dark and smelly. There is no ill effect on oils used in baking, for they are protected by the other ingredients. However, oil should never be reused because repeated heatings do have an undesirable effect on the polyunsaturate levels.

Olive oil is monounsaturated and will neither raise nor lower cholesterol. But since our objective is to increase our intake of polyunsaturates *over* saturates, the monounsaturate can exert a negative influence on the ratio. For the same reason we avoid avocado, which is extremely high in monounsaturated fat.

When selecting a margarine, do not be misled by the fact that a product is advertised as being made from 100 percent corn, soybean, or safflower oil. The statement may be true, but it is also meaningless; for unless the oil is in liquid form, it cannot be effective. Food labeling requires that the ingredients be listed in the order of their importance in the product, with the predominant ingredient appearing first. If liquid oil is the first mentioned in the list of ingredients, the margarine is suitable. You may have noticed that diet margarine, or imitation margarine, lists water first. The product contains half the calories of regular margarine, but it is also lower in polyunsaturated fat. It can be used as a table spread, but it is not suitable for cooking (as you may have discovered) because of its high water content.

ADAPTING YOUR OWN RECIPES

In cooking, liquid oils may be substituted in any recipe calling for melted shortenings, in a lesser quantity than that required for hard shortenings.

Standard baking recipes that call for hard fats will not generally give as good results when liquid oils are substituted. Use only recipes specially designed for liquid fats, unless you wish to experiment a bit with the balance of the other ingredients to achieve your usual results.

Use the following table as a guide to the amount of oil required to substitute for melted hard fats in cooking:

Melted Hard Fats	Oil
1 tablespoon	1 tablespoon
2 tablespoons	1½ tablespoons
¼ cup (4 tablespoons)	3 tablespoons
⅛ pound	3 tablespoons
⅓ cup	4 tablespoons
½ cup (¼ pound)	6 tablespoons
¾ cup	½ cup plus 2 tablespoons
1 cup	⅔ cup plus 1 tablespoon
2 cups (1 pound)	1½ cups

CHEESE

The butterfat content of cheese ranges from about 1 to 50 percent of its total calories, depending on whether the starting material was skim milk, whole milk, cream, or a combination of these. Consequently, the choice of cheese calls for careful discrimination on the part of cholesterol-conscious people.

However, the situation has improved considerably. We are now offered a wide choice of good-tasting low-fat cottage cheeses. Cottage cheese is made from skim milk and is an eminently desirable food, high in protein, low in fat, and worthy of the overworked adjectives "delicious" and "nutritious." The regular creamed cottage cheese is required by law to contain at least 4 percent fat, but the low-fat creamed cottage cheese has only about 1.8 percent fat. Skim milk and pot-style cottage cheeses contain 0.3 percent fat. Low-fat cottage cheese can play an important part in our diet, starting the day as a spread for the breakfast toast, combining with fruit or vegetables for lunch, accompanying salad at dinner, or furnishing substance for the late-night hungry time.

Farmer cheese can be used as a substitute for cream cheese in canapés or sandwiches. (The midget farmer cheeses have about 8 percent fat, but this is an improvement over cream cheese, as much as 50 percent of the calories of which are in fat.) It can be mashed and softened with skim milk to make it more spreadable.

There are two Cheddar-type cheeses that we find most useful for eating (grilled sandwiches, etc.) and in cooking. One is Cheezola, a filled pasteurized cheese in which the milk fat has been replaced by corn oil. The other is Count Down, a 99 percent fat-free pasteurized cheese. Both may be ordered by mail from Fisher Cheese Company, Wapakoneta, Ohio 45895.

The cheeses made "partially from skim milk" must be viewed with skepticism, since we have no way of knowing how much is "partially." Some of these part skim milk cheeses have been laboratory tested for butterfat, and the results in many cases showed little, if any, difference between them and the regular cheeses. For the most part, unless you have more information about a cheese than the "partly skim milk" stamped on the rind, you would do well to use it most sparingly.

For au gratin dishes, we use an import from Switzerland called sapsago cheese. It is a combination of a skim milk cheese and herbs and is suitable only for grating. It comes already grated and also in a small, thimble-shaped cube form, which must be kept under refrigeration and should be allowed to come to room temperature before you grate it. I sometimes combine the grated sapsago with grated Parmesan, or I may use a tablespoon or so of grated Parmesan by itself. A small amount of Parmesan goes a long way; and with a tablespoon of it divided among four or six portions, the amount of fat per portion is negligible.

OUT-OF-BOUNDS

Actually, very little is prohibited in the Prudent Diet Pattern, as you can see. Certain foods are limited in quantity, but the large choice of acceptable ones amply compensates.

The red flag with FORBIDDEN waves unequivocally over the following, however: butter, ordinary margarines and shortenings, lard, sweet cream, sour cream, ice cream, cream cheese, most hard or dessert cheeses, and foods containing any of these items in large quantities, such as commercially prepared cakes and pastries. Butter rolls, commercial biscuits, muffins, doughnuts, sweet rolls, packaged popcorn, potato chips, and French fried potatoes should be avoided. French fried potatoes cooked in polyunsaturated oil are acceptable. Coconut and coconut oil are highly saturated and rank high on our Don't list.

Chocolate is now acceptable—good news for chocolate lovers. Recent experiments indicate that chocolate does *not* raise blood cholesterol.

The prohibition on commercial bakery products may represent a deprivation for some families; but where people are willing to do their own baking, this need not be a problem. The assortment of breads, cakes, yeast doughs, and pastries that can come out of our kitchens can be a gratifying experience, bringing satisfaction to the cook and pleasure to the people who eat them.

Of the prepared cake mixes, only the angel food cake fulfills our requirements. A glance at the list of ingredients on the boxes will tell you why. The presence of butterfat, whole milk, and hydrogenated shortenings is clearly indicated on all packaged foods, so please, please, READ THE LABELS, including the fine print. Bear in mind that "vegetable oil" or "vegetable fat" on the list of ingredients generally means coconut oil. The time you take for a careful look at the list of ingredients of every can and package you buy is well spent.

SEASONINGS

In these days of tested recipes and graduated measuring cups, anyone who can read, is willing to make an effort, has an adventuresome spirit—in the kitchen, that is—and is equipped with functioning taste buds can acquire cooking skills. The last is important. Family preferences in types and degrees of seasonings vary, and foods themselves are variable—some lemons are sourer than others, for example. No recipe can be all things to all people, and only the cook can determine if it is a soupçon of sugar or a pinch of a spice or an herb that is needed to make the dish just right for the family. Taste while you are cooking, after you have seasoned, and just before serving. It won't make you fat either. Chubby cooks got that way from eating, not tasting.

This is not a low sodium book; we do use salt, but sparingly. We prefer to rely for variety of flavors on wines and herbs. Households restricted in the use of salt will know how to adapt many of the recipes.

The condiment shelves of grocery markets and department stores offer a wide variety of seasonings that will add interest and piquancy to your food. Lawry's seasoned salt is one of my favorites, and I use it often in place of plain salt. I also recommend to your attention the MBT broth powders, which I use, dissolved, in place of water or stock. I find them less salty than bouillon cubes, and they dissolve easily. The MBT chicken broth powder and instant mix for vegetable broth are particularly flavorful, and the amount of fat they contain is negligible.

A reasonable facsimile of butter taste can be given foods, particularly sauces and baked goods, with imitation butter flavoring. Many people seem to like this product. Durkee is one brand, and there are also others.

A little thought, effort, and small expense will supply your pantry with adequate first aid for ailing dishes. Often just a bit of the meat glaze called Bovril, a teaspoon of Worcestershire sauce or Kitchen Bouquet, a pinch of dry mustard, or a quarter-teaspoon of an herb are all you need to rescue a sauce from undistinguished mediocrity. With proper supplies on hand, you can always taste, judge, and correct.

PLANNING THE FAMILY'S MEALS

The general outline for the family's meals is based on average nutritional needs. Calories may vary according to age, activity, and personal characteristics of family members:

1. A source of protein at each meal, including meats, poultry, fish, eggs, low-fat cottage cheese, peanut butter, grain products, and legumes such as dried peas, beans,

and nuts. Meats should be lean, and poultry and fish emphasized.

2. Four or more servings of vegetables, fruits, and fruit juices a day. This includes citrus fruits, tomatoes, cabbage, strawberries, cantaloupe, and a dark green or yellow vegetable, such as broccoli, kale, spinach, pumpkin, or sweet potato. Include potatoes and a variety of other vegetables for additional vitamins and minerals.

3. Skim milk or skim milk products daily for both children and adults, including low-fat buttermilk, low-fat yogurt, low-fat cottage cheese, and evaporated skim milk, some of which can be used in cooking.

4. Whole grain and enriched breads and cereals.

Cooking fats, sweets, and nuts may be added according to the total calorie allowance.

DINING OUT

This diet pattern presents no difficulties in restaurant dining. The most limited menu will offer acceptable choices: simple grilled fish, meat, or poultry; vegetable dishes ordered without butter or cream sauces; sandwiches such as chicken, turkey, and tuna fish; clear soups; salads (commercial mayonnaise is acceptable); fruits and gelatin desserts.

Speaking of restaurants reminds me that my husband wanted to be sure that I mentioned the "lunch business," which he seems to consider as great a boon to ailing man as antibiotics. In order to carry out his doctor's order for a noontime rest period when he first returned to work after his coronary bout, we hit upon the expedient of his taking lunch from home. (What did you *think* doctors carried in those little black bags?) In this way he avoided the midday restaurant rush, was assured a purely unsaturated sandwich, and found time for rest and meditation. The noontime siestas are a long-gone memory, but the sandwiches linger on. A number of our friends have instituted the same practice, for which their wives may or may not thank me, depending upon how they feel about making a sandwich almost before the sun rises.

To leave ourselves a margin for error and an unguarded, mad moment with perhaps a miniature pizza at somebody's cocktail party, we keep our saturated fat consumption at home even under the minimum suggested by the Prudent Diet. Beef and lamb are generally saved for company, as are fancy desserts. After all, it is possible to control what happens in our kitchens, whereas on the outside we may be victims of circumstance, to use a lame excuse.

We bypass most pork products and all beef so marbled with fat that it cannot be trimmed. This includes rib roast beef. The presence of these foods at dinner parties need not be disconcerting, however. Angels with flaming swords are not likely to appear if you perform your guestly duties by eating. It would be worse, I think, to embarrass your hosts and yourself with a pointed refusal. Take small portions, no seconds, and leave the visible fat on your plate.

Hosts generally don't mind substituting a simple fruit for a rich dessert. Almost everyone has a spare orange in the refrigerator. In these allergy-conscious days, I notice more and more people asking about food preferences when they extend dinner invitations. I am never loath to suggest chicken, butterless vegetables, and anything for dessert as long as it's fruit.

Let us remember that success with this diet does not depend upon following any one rule, such as "no cream" or "no butter" or "cooking with corn oil or a polyunsaturated margarine." Rather, it depends upon the realization that both animal fat and vegetable oil must be balanced. Removing all visible fat from meat will not negate the effects of a richly marbled piece of meat, although it will help. The effect of frequent overlarge servings of meat will not be counteracted by polyunsaturated oil or special margarines. Close attention to the choice and preparation of foods will not ensure complete success if the polyunsaturated oil in the diet is neglected.

To sum up briefly, a diet that is generally effective in lowering serum cholesterol contains all the usual food products. In addition to ordinary breads, cereals, fruits, vegetables, and low-fat beverages, there should be two servings a day of lean meat, poultry, or fish, with beef, lean pork, or lamb not more than four times a week. Polyunsaturated vegetable oils such as corn, cottonseed, soybean, and safflower should replace hard fats in cooking. Special margarines may be used for table spreads. Up to three egg yolks a week are permitted. (A Summary for Cholesterol Watchers appears in the back of the book.)

This cooking program should not be considered as an interlude or a temporary expedient, later to be replaced by former habits of hard fats, cream, and the like. You may find, as we have, that your tastes have changed and you couldn't go back to them under any circumstances. It becomes a way of life, a permanent approach to the art of cooking and healthful eating. In our house, we have found the physical benefits as well as the intellectual satisfaction of knowing that we are pursuing the right course rewarding indeed.

3

The Losing Battle

It is mind-boggling to ponder the number of words that have been written about dieting since men and women first took a good look at themselves and perhaps didn't like what they saw. Among the earliest pundits to point out that eating too much can be dangerous was Hippocrates, the father of medicine. This was nearly 2,500 years ago. Since that time, the trickle of words about dieting has swelled into a flood, and what started as a matter of superficial concern and interest has grown into an obsession. Millions of copies of several hundred diet books now on bookstore shelves are sold each year. Miracle diets sweep the country like so many tidal waves and, after a period of wild notoriety nourished by high hopes, followed by blasted expectations, fade into obscurity, only to be replaced in a short time by another magic formula that is guaranteed to melt pounds. In spite of these recurrent oscillations on the nutritional front, the fact remains that no nationwide decrease in obesity has been observed.

I leave the solution of this weighty problem to my betters (who still haven't batted a thousand). My approach is simply to nibble away at a tiny corner of it from the modest viewpoint of what the factotum of the household can do to help.

Twentieth-century living in an affluent society presents no end of challenges. We are constantly being seduced by supermarkets with their diabolically beguiling food displays; by the wistful emptiness of home freezer compartments crying to be filled; by the persuasive tones of television announcers tantalizing our gastric juices with the lure of the Utopia awaiting our first bite of the ice cream bombe, the chocolate-marshmallow-coconut delight, or whatever it is they are being paid to sell; and lastly, by the mechanics of television watching itself.

Of all the crimes of which television has been accused, from causing eyestrain to impairing the morals of minors and heading them toward juvenile delinquency, perhaps the most valid is its contribution to the widespread (this takes on the significance of a descriptive adjective) overweight that prevails among teenagers and adults. The incessant nibbling that so often accompanies the viewing can turn an hour-long program into a dangerous health hazard. However, blaming the television industry for self-inflicted paunches and jowls is neither a constructive approach nor a solution to the problem if it exists in our homes.

I claim no authority in the field of dieting except that born out of firsthand experience for lo, these many years. I have intimate knowledge of all the ruses used to duck the stringencies of self-denial, since at one time or another I have used every one of them: the artful dodge ("I'll start next Monday"); the rationalization ("I need the food energy"); the excuse ("My face gets haggard"); the self-delusion ("The cleaner shrank the dress"); and the downright deceit ("I really don't eat much"). With all the righteous zeal of a reformed criminal, I now take a dim view of such proceedings.

Naturally, the first line of defense in the struggle against excess poundage must be stationed at the point where the assault usually begins—at the dining table. Since we housewives are generally the persons responsible for meal planning and preparation, it falls to our lot to translate the usual weight-losing allowance of 1,200 calories for women or 1,600 calories for men into as attractive fare as possible. It may be just as well that this job *is* relegated to the ladies, since statistics indicate less overweight among them than among the men.

One of the obstacles to overcome in a restricted diet is an appearance of meagerness about a meal. This causes many people, particularly men, to feel put upon and deprived. Serve the meals with a full complement of courses that make them look complete. Clear soups, vegetable juices, bulky salads dressed with lemon juice, generous portions of low-calorie vegetables to make up for limited portions of meat and starches, and for desserts interesting arrangements of fresh fruit in preference to the more caloric canned varieties, impart a sense of lavishness not reflected in the total calories. If the main-course portions are a bit smaller than they used to be, serve them on a luncheon-size plate instead of the large dinner size so they won't look squinchy.

Save a calorie wherever you can in your cooking. These little savings have a way of adding up to your family's advantage. Sweeten sauces, fruits, and puddings with artificial sweeteners instead of sugar; avail yourself of the water-packed and dietetic canned products; use the low-calorie prepared puddings, such as D-Zerta brand, to satisfy the yearning for something sweet.

Acquaint yourself with calorie tables. Consider that there are about 60 calories in 4 ounces of unsweetened pineapple juice and 25 in a like amount of tomato juice; 45 calories in 2 ounces of white wine and 150 in the same amount of Scotch; 375 calories in an average serving of apple pie and 75 in a small raw apple. The inference is obvious. In the back of this book is a complete calorie table with which you can tot up the caloric value of every recipe in the book. Add up the calories of each ingredient and divide the total by the number of people who will share the recipe.

Coated cooking utensils such as Teflon, which require no greasing, can be most valuable when all fats must be restricted to expedite weight loss. The no-calorie spray products such as Pam that prevent food from sticking during cooking are also helpful.

An accurate bathroom scale is a must for a weight-watching family. Clothes may shrink or stretch, and waistlines fluctuate during the course of a day, but the arrow on the scale inexorably points to the truth. Weighing once or twice a week at the same time of day and under the same conditions can encourage a conscientious dieter, or mutely reprimand a miscreant.

The very real hardship that a restricted diet inflicts on some people, I think, is beyond the understanding of those who have small appetites or are uninterested in food. The doctors and nutritionists who come into contact with would-be and should-be dieters are softly sympathetic with these sufferers from medically imposed hunger. They are also aware that unless a person has great motivation and determination, he needs more than just a printed diet slip along with an encouraging slap on the back and a parting admonition.

Dieters need the help and encouragement of their families in addition to an understanding of themselves. They must know whether the little cake at which they are casting sheep's eyes will satisfy their "sweet hunger" or whether it will set off a chain reaction that will make them want to devour everything in sight.

Anyone who is on a diet should try to avoid coming to the dinner table in a ravenous state. A small cup of bouillon or coffee, or a few ounces of tomato juice with some celery stalks or carrot sticks, eaten half an hour before dinner, can take the edge off a hunger that might otherwise drive caution to the winds.

Provision must also be made for the evening hours (with or without TV) when idleness, boredom, and frustration combine to produce a state of being hungry-in-the-head that drives wanderers in the direction of the refrigerator looking for something to do. They find it, too. This moment of madness can keep clothing seams bulging forever. Those people chronically addicted to the habit might find it helpful if they would save their dessert from dinner to eat at the time when food resistance is low.

Eating one's meals in low gear, waltz time, or however you would describe a slow tempo, is also helpful. Small bites, much chewing, and lots of conversation between bites can save hundreds of calories each day. I have noticed that people who eat very slowly are seldom overweight.

But no matter how helpful a family tries to be, the burden of a successful weight-watching regime must rest with the dieter himself. No amount of cajoling, pampering, or weighed and measured menus offered at home can atone for eating excesses indulged in at lunchtime or when no one is looking. The best we can do (outside of applying a muzzle and chaining the culprit to the bedpost—a procedure generally frowned upon) is to continue to provide proper meals, refrain from nagging, and pray that one day the light will dawn. Sometimes it does.

Once the felicitous state of normal weight has been achieved, eternal vigilance must be the watchword: one eye on your scale and the other on your conscience. This is not so formidable as it sounds because all habits, whether good or bad, become automatic after a while, and sound nutritional practices are no exception. Happily, this dietary, with its avoidance of the concentrated calories in dairy products and large meat portions, is a great force for good in maintaining proper weight.

You may have to experiment a bit before you find the proper formula for eating that keeps the pounds from creeping up. Perhaps it will be something as simple as avoiding bread and rolls at dinner or limiting cake and pie desserts. In our case, we have found that the cleaner never shrinks our clothes as long as we keep our desserts simple on family nights and avoid eating between meals. With the exception of some fresh fruit or a drink, our rule is Never. It is with not the slightest sense of deprivation that we watch our friends guzzling blinis, hamburgers, or cake at an after-theater restaurant, because they won't be any happier in half an hour whether they ate it or not and they may very well hate themselves in the morning.

Crash diets, liquid diets, high carbohydrate diets, and appetite-depressing drugs among dozens of other panaceas have all had their vogue. While perhaps some of them have their advantages in certain situations, medical men are profoundly concerned with their ineffectiveness in establishing sound eating habits that will maintain weight at a healthful level. Nothing takes the place of self-discipline. And self-discipline doesn't come in bottles—unfortunately.

4
Breakfast

Based on a modest and unscientific survey of breakfast habits, I have come to the conclusion that most people like variety in their foods, but not when they first get up in the morning. On second thought, I don't know why I should be surprised by this. Judging by ourselves, our breakfasts, with perhaps a few minor variations, are entirely predictable, except for weekend mornings. Maybe we seek the familiar sight of the same menu to give us the reassurance we need to face the rigors of another day, or perhaps we are not quite up to the unexpected in the first cold glare of the early morning light.

In any event, the reason is not important. It is a simple matter to vary a breakfast menu—pancakes instead of toast, waffles instead of pancakes, a whole sliced orange in place of orange juice, Wheatena substituted for oatmeal, and so on. The enormous variety of breakfast cereals available (not the sweet ones, please) surely offers enough choice to please any palate. The essential consideration for most people is that there *be* a breakfast; that it be adequate enough to provide energy and nourishment to carry through to lunch; that the choice of foods be consistent with the aims of our eating program.

The hastily gulped cup of coffee or tea before going off to work, implemented at the ten o'clock coffee break with a Danish pastry or sweet bun ("empty calories" and saturated fat), is a poor substitute for a meal that should provide us with the nutrients and energy-producing foods we require. A proper breakfast includes fruit, fresh or stewed, or juice; a protein food such as cereal, cottage cheese, or skim milk; and bread or toast plus a hot beverage. If this sounds like a formidable undertaking to the non-breakfast eaters, perhaps we could translate it into orange juice, a toasted English muffin or plain toast topped with a generous frosting of low-fat cottage cheese, and the usual coffee or tea.

You may still have an occasional ounce of well-cooked Canadian bacon with the occasional egg if you will remember to include it in the planning of your week's meat ration. Many people find the cholesterol-reduced and cholesterol-less egg substitute a welcome addition to their morning meal.

Pancakes are a simple matter to prepare, and made-in-advance batter keeps splendidly in the refrigerator. There are a number of acceptable ready-mixes for those who prefer to use them, such as Aunt Jemima's and the Tillie Lewis Low Calorie Pancake Mix, to mention just two. Just be sure to read the labels on the boxes. The list of ingredients will tell you exactly what you need to know. If it includes hydrogenated oils, whole milk, butter, etc., replace the box on the shelf and look further.

Whenever you bake muffins or biscuits, squirrel away a few for future breakfasts. They keep nicely in plastic bags in the freezer and take only a few minutes to warm up when needed.

Don't let your family be one of the group that saves its breakfast eating for weekends. The habit pays a poor dividend. Make sure that each member of the household starts the day with a well-balanced, nutritionally adequate meal.

BUTTERMILK CHIFFON PANCAKES

We make the pancakes quite small—no more than 2 inches in diameter. Five or six make an adequate portion. It is convenient to keep a covered jar of the batter (minus the egg white) in the refrigerator. Then you need only add the beaten egg white and the pancakes are ready to go. The batter keeps well and even improves with standing.

1⅓	cups flour, sifted	1½	cups skim buttermilk
1	tablespoon sugar	¼	cup oil
½	teaspoon salt	2	egg whites, stiffly
¾	teaspoon baking soda		beaten

Place a griddle over low heat. It is ready when a drop of water bounces off.

Sift the flour, sugar, and salt together. Stir the baking soda into the buttermilk, add to the flour mixture, and stir just enough to dissolve the flour. Overbeating makes pancakes tough. Stir in the oil. Fold in the egg whites.

When the griddle is hot enough, drop the batter from the tip of a spoon onto the ungreased griddle and cook until the cakes puff up and bubbles begin to break. Turn just once and cook the other side. Serve with warmed maple syrup or fruit preserves.

Serves 4

DELICIOUS BUTTERMILK WAFFLES

Wrap the leftover waffles in aluminum foil or a plastic bag. They freeze very well and can be quickly heated in the toaster.

2 cups all-purpose flour
1 teaspoon baking powder
½ teaspoon salt
2 teaspoons baking soda
2 cups skim buttermilk
¼ cup oil
3 egg whites, stiffly beaten

Sift together the flour, baking powder, and salt. Dissolve the soda in the buttermilk, add to the flour mixture, and mix well. Add the oil and beat until smooth. Strain into a bowl or a pitcher through a wire strainer. Fold in the egg whites. Bake in a hot waffle iron until golden brown, using about ½ cup of batter for each waffle. Serve with warmed maple syrup or fruit preserves.

Makes 10 to 12

COTTAGE CHEESE PANCAKES

1 cup low-fat cottage cheese
2 egg whites, beaten until frothy
6 tablespoons flour
3 tablespoons sugar
1 tablespoon oil
Pinch salt
Cinnamon and sugar or Braised Apple Slices

In a medium-sized bowl, combine the cottage cheese, egg whites, flour, sugar, oil, and salt. Don't try to make the batter smooth; the cottage cheese lumps can remain with no damage.

Lightly oil a griddle and heat until a drop of water bounces off. For each pancake, pour enough batter to make it about 3 inches across. When nicely browned, flip over to the other side and repeat. Sprinkle lightly with cinnamon and sugar or serve with Braised Apple Slices (below).

Makes 14 to 16

BRAISED APPLE SLICES

4 firm tart apples	Pinch of ground
4 tablespoons oil	cloves
1½ tablespoons brown	1 heaping tablespoon
sugar	orange marmalade or
	apricot preserves

These also give a good account of themselves as a dinner dessert. Peel the apples and cut in two. Remove the cores and slice the apples into wedges about ⅜ inch thick. Place the oil in a bowl, add the apple slices, and toss well to coat them in oil. Heat a heavy skillet and place the apple slices in it. You won't need any additional oil. Sprinkle with the brown sugar and cloves. Cover the skillet and cook for 10 minutes over medium heat. Stir in the fruit preserves and cook the apples, uncovered, for another 10 minutes, or until tender but not mushy, turning them frequently. Remove the apples with a slotted spoon. Serve warm.

Serves 4

GRIDDLECAKES

1⅔ cups skim milk	1½ teaspoons baking
1 egg, lightly beaten	powder
2½ tablespoons oil	½ teaspoon baking soda
1½ cups flour, unsifted	½ teaspoon salt
1½ tablespoons sugar	

Lightly oil a griddle. It is ready when a drop of water bounces off.

In a small bowl, mix together the milk, egg, and oil. In a larger bowl, combine the dry ingredients.

Add the liquids to the flour mixture and beat with a rotary beater until all the flour is moistened and the large lumps disappear. Don't try to get all the lumps out—the cooking will take care of them.

You will need about ¼ cup of batter for each griddlecake. Pour onto the heated griddle and cook until bubbles form and break and the edges seem cooked. Turn and cook until the other side is nicely browned.

Serve with warmed maple syrup or honey.

Makes about 12

BAKED KIPPERED HERRING

I always try to keep a few cans of kippers on hand. They are excellent for either breakfast or lunch. To heat them, place the can in a flat skillet with a cover, add enough water to cover the top of the can, and boil, covered, for 15 minutes. The kippers will come out of the can heated through and ready to eat. Drain them well, arrange on a platter, sprinkle with chopped parsley, and serve with lemon wedges.

For a more substantial kipper, get the large smoked ones at your fish store. Kippers are apt to be . . . redolent (this is a euphemism for a more descriptive word) while cooking, but you will find that wrapping them in aluminum foil helps somewhat (as does an air freshener in the kitchen).

4 kippers
⅓ cup oil
　Dash Tabasco
1 teaspoon
　Worcestershire sauce

Juice of ½ lemon
2 tablespoons chopped parsley

Soak the kippers for 10 minutes in hot water. Drain well. Preheat the oven to 400°. Line a baking dish with aluminum foil, leaving plenty of lap so you can make a tight package of the kippers. Arrange the kippers on the foil, dribble half the oil over them, and bring the edges of the foil together, crimping them securely. Bake for 15 to 20 minutes, or until they are thoroughly heated.

Meanwhile, heat the remaining oil in a small saucepan. Add the Tabasco and Worcestershire sauce, lemon juice, and parsley. Remove the kippers from the foil package, place on a warmed platter, pour the hot oil mixture over them, and serve.

Serves 4

5
Hors d'Oeuvres and Appetizers

The business of the hors d'oeuvres and appetizer course is to prickle the appetite and whet the palate, although sometimes its effect is to deaden one and dull the other. Hors d'oeuvres or appetizers that are too substantial, too starchy, too sweet, or just too much in quantity can take the edge off the diner's appetite for the good things to come.

In these calorie-conscious days, people are generally quite happy with a platter of crisp, chilled raw vegetables with perhaps a sauce to dunk them in. Celery stalks, carrot sticks, slices of finocchio, pickled mushrooms, marinated artichoke hearts, cherry tomatoes, raw cauliflowerets, strips of cucumber or zucchini—there's a wide choice to keep your guests busy while they're sipping their aperitifs.

Out of the increasing informality that pervades our entertaining in these do-it-yourself days has emerged the American custom of Dunks and Dips. Perhaps you remember the time of the tortured sardine wearing a colored cream cheese rosette on its nose, ensconced on a slab of soggy bread. That day has passed. Except for unwieldy gatherings so large that the canapés must circulate because the guests cannot, or for the occasions when professional kitchen help is brought in, the order of the day for informal entertaining seems to be a mound of some good-tasting mixture surrounded by toast or pumpernickel with which the guests can make their own canapés. You will find a number of suggestions in the following pages for various mixtures as well as for the little tidbits, both hot and cold, that some occasions demand.

MELBA TOAST

This homemade melba toast retains its crispness, which makes it particularly nice for table use and cocktail spreads. Any kind of thin-sliced bread may be used. If you are going to use it for hors d'oeuvres, remove the crusts and cut each slice into four quarters before baking. For dinner use, leave the crusts on and divide each slice into two triangles before placing in the oven.

Place the cut slices on a cookie sheet and bake at 300° for 20 or 25 minutes until they are golden. The time required varies with the thickness and freshness of the bread. It isn't necessary to turn the slices—just keep an eye on them so they won't get too brown.

MIDDLE EASTERN MELBA TOAST

I hope you are able to buy in your area the type of bread known as Middle Eastern bread—I'm told it is available country-wide. It is now a supermarket item in our neck of the woods. It is called "pita" and is a round flat bread consisting of two crusts with no dough in the middle. It makes a splendid melba toast for dips. It can also serve as a warm bread with salads or appetizer courses.

Cut each pita into four quarters and with a pointed knife separate the upper and lower crusts. Each pita will yield eight pieces. Spread the pieces with polyunsaturated margarine and, if desired, a sprinkling of grated Parmesan cheese and sesame seeds. Curry fanciers might like to mix a tiny bit of curry powder with the margarine and omit the Parmesan and sesame seeds. Toast the pita sections under the broiler until golden. They brown quickly, so watch them carefully and remove when done. Serve warm.

COTTAGE CHEESE SAVORY SPREAD

1½ cups low-fat cottage cheese
2 tablespoons oil
4 anchovy fillets, drained
1 tablespoon caraway seeds
1 tablespoon chopped capers
1 tablespoon chopped chives
1 teaspoon paprika
1 teaspoon prepared mustard
Parsley sprigs
3 pimiento-stuffed olives, sliced

Whip the cottage cheese with a beater until smooth and fluffy. Add the oil and blend well. Mash the anchovies and work into the cheese. Mix in the caraway seeds, capers, chives, paprika, and mustard. Chill in a small bowl until ready to serve. Garnish the top with parsley and the stuffed olive slices. Serve with Melba Toast (page 51), crackers, or thin pumpernickel.

Yields 1¾ cups

CHEESE BALL

A normally bland cheese becomes a colorful spicy concoction with an interesting flavor.

8 ounces farmer cheese
1 tablespoon anchovy paste
1 tablespoon crushed capers
1 tablespoon lemon juice
2 tablespoons sweet paprika
1 tablespoon caraway seeds
1 tablespoon finely minced onion
1 teaspoon prepared mustard
Finely chopped parsley

Mix together in a bowl all the ingredients except the parsley until smooth and creamy. Form into a ball and roll in the parsley to cover completely. Refrigerate for a few hours before serving. Serve with crackers or Melba Toast (page 51).

Serves 10 or more

GARBANZO (CHICK-PEA) DIP

This specialty from the Middle East, where it is known as *hummus*, is traditionally served with *pita*, the Middle Eastern bread referred to earlier in this chapter. It is also suitable as a dip for raw vegetables.

1 1-pound-4-ounce can chick-peas
3 tablespoons oil
½ teaspoon sesame seeds
½ teaspoon salt
  Freshly ground pepper
1 large clove garlic, minced
2 tablespoons chopped parsley
4 tablespoons lemon juice
  Paprika
  Parsley sprigs

Drain the chick-peas thoroughly. Whir in a blender with the oil, sesame seeds, salt, pepper, garlic, chopped parsley, and lemon juice until smooth and creamy. Transfer to a bowl and chill in the refrigerator. To serve, place in a serving bowl surrounded by Middle Eastern Melba Toast (page 51) or by celery and carrot sticks. Garnish the dip with a light sprinkling of paprika and parsley sprigs.

Yields 1½ cups

POOR MAN'S CAVIAR (EGGPLANT ORIENTALE)

This is another Middle East specialty that is an interesting and tasteful dip.

2 medium-sized eggplants
2 tomatoes
2 cloves garlic, crushed
½ cup snipped fresh dill
⅓ cup parsley, chopped
1 medium-sized onion, chopped
¼ cup lemon juice or vinegar
  Salt and freshly ground pepper

Bake the unpeeled eggplants in a 350° oven until very soft (about 1¼ to 1½ hours).

Plunge the tomatoes into boiling water for a few seconds and slip off the skins. Cut the tomatoes in half (parallel to the stem end) and discard the seeds. Chop coarsely.

Scoop out the eggplant pulp and combine with all the remaining ingredients except the salt and pepper. Place in a blender and blend at low speed until the mixture is spreadable and retains texture but is not liquefied. Chill. Before serving, season to taste with salt and pepper. Serve in a bowl surrounded by Middle Eastern Melba Toast (page 51) or thin black bread.

Serves 12 or more as appetizer

CODFISH ANTIPASTO

A snowy-white mound with an unusual flavor.

½ pound salt codfish	Freshly ground pepper
6 tablespoons oil	¼ teaspoon basil
6 tablespoons skim milk	2 tablespoons lemon
1 clove garlic, crushed	juice
2 teaspoons parsley, finely chopped	Sprigs of parsley or watercress

Soak the salt codfish overnight, changing the water a few times. Drain, cover with cold water, and slowly bring to a boil. Cook for 5 minutes or until the fish flakes easily. Drain well.

Place in a blender with the oil, milk, garlic, parsley, pepper, basil, and lemon juice. Blend at low speed until the mixture is smooth and spreadable but not liquefied. Pack in a small round bowl and refrigerate for 2 hours or more. Unmold on a round plate and surround it with melba toast or pumpernickel bread. Garnish with a few sprigs of parsley or watercress.

Serves 6

SARDINE SPREAD

1 3¾-ounce can boneless and skinless sardines	2 tablespoons lemon juice Dash Tabasco
8 ounces farmer cheese	1 teaspoon dried dill
1 tablespoon Worcestershire sauce	Chopped parsley

Drain the sardines well and mash. Combine with the cheese, Worcestershire sauce, lemon juice, Tabasco, and dill. Mash together with a fork until all are combined. Pack in a small bowl and refrigerate. Serve garnished with a sprinkling of chopped parsley, accompanied by melba toast or crackers.

Serves 6

RAW VEGETABLE DIP

The choice of raw vegetables can be dictated by what is in your refrigerator crisper, what are your personal preferences, and what your greengrocer happened to have in stock. Celery, carrots, cherry tomatoes, cauliflowerets, broccoli, zucchini, cucumber, string beans, finocchio, etc.—all are suitable. This dip is a most agreeable accompaniment for the vegetables.

1 cup mayonnaise	1½ teaspoons prepared mild mustard
3 tablespoons plain low-fat yogurt	3 tablespoons lemon juice
½ teaspoon curry powder	

Combine all the ingredients and mix until smooth. Serve in a bowl surrounded by raw vegetables, attractively cut and arranged.

Serves 8

COCKTAIL NIBBLES

Tidbits for the nibblers who might otherwise busy themselves with potato chips or other less desirable foods.

5 tablespoons oil	1 teaspoon seasoned salt
4 teaspoons Worcestershire sauce	1 cup walnut halves
Scant ½ teaspoon garlic powder or onion powder (optional)	2 cups each of Wheat Chex, Rice Chex, and Corn Chex

Heat the oven to 250°. In a large, flat pan—a jelly roll pan, for instance—place the oil with the Worcestershire sauce and seasonings over low heat. Add the nuts and cereals and mix until all the pieces are coated with the oil. Place in the oven for 1 hour, stirring every 15 minutes. Spread on brown paper or absorbent paper towels to cool. Store in airtight containers.

Yields 7 cups

PECANS DELUXE

These meringue-covered nuts are fine cocktail nibbles. You'll want large splendid pecan halves to start with. We get ours from one of those mail-order places that specializes in pecans. We order them in quantity and keep them in the freezer, both shelled and unshelled. They last for ages, and, like all special things (and people), are nice to have around the house.

1 egg white	2 teaspoons skim milk
½ teaspoon salt	1 heaping cup large
1 teaspoon sugar	pecan halves

Beat the egg white until stiff. Combine the salt and sugar and fold into the meringue. Beat in the milk. Add the pecans to the mixture and coat well. Place carefully on a cookie sheet lined with aluminum foil. Leave a small space between the nuts so they don't stick together. Place in a preheated 300° oven. After 20 minutes turn the nuts carefully. They stick a bit, so you may have to coax them gently. Bake another 20 minutes. Reduce the heat to 275°, shake the pan to turn the nuts, and bake 10 minutes longer.

Yields 1½ cups

SMOKED SALMON CANAPÉS

¼ pound farmer cheese	¼ pound smoked salmon,
½ teaspoon prepared	thinly sliced
white horseradish	Lemon juice
4 thin slices	2 black olives, sliced
pumpernickel	into crescents
	Chopped parsley

We prefer the Nova Scotia salmon. It is bland and delicate and not salty.

Mash the cheese with the horseradish. If the cheese seems too stiff, soften with a little skim milk and mix well to make it creamy. Spread the slices of bread with the cheese mixture. Cover with the salmon slices. Cut each slice of bread into quarters. Sprinkle with the lemon juice and garnish with a black olive crescent and a sprinkling of the parsley. Serve with a pepper mill for those who like a sprinkling of black pepper with the salmon.

Makes 16

SALMON ENDIVE CANAPÉS

People who count calories are always pleased with this version of the salmon canapé.

1 large cluster of Belgian endive	Tiny sweet pickles (cornichons) or sliced gherkins
¼ pound thin-sliced smoked salmon	Capers
Lemon juice	Freshly ground black pepper (optional)

Separate the endive leaves. Cut the smoked salmon into strips that will fit on the endive. Sprinkle the salmon lightly with lemon juice. Place a strip of salmon on each of the leaves and garnish with cornichons or gherkins and a few capers, judiciously arranged. A few grinds of black pepper may be sprinkled on each hors d'oeuvre, if desired.

Serves 4 or 5

CUCUMBER ROUNDS

1 large cucumber	Pinch garlic powder
¼ cup low-fat cottage cheese, drained	Dash Tabasco
¼ teaspoon celery seeds	½ teaspoon minced parsley
1 teaspoon minced onion	Pimiento strips

Wash the cucumber and leave the skin on unless it is heavily waxed—in which case, off with it. Cut the cucumber into ¼-inch slices. Crisp the cucumber rounds in ice water for an hour or so. Mix together the cottage cheese, celery seeds, onion, garlic powder, and Tabasco and chill until ready to serve.

Drain and dry the cucumber rounds. Top each with a generous mound of the cheese mixture. Garnish with the parsley and two small pimiento strips, crossed.

Serves 4

PICKLED MUSHROOMS

For me, the sight of lovely fresh, white, uniformly sized mushrooms is a clarion call for spices, vinegar, and oil. The pickled mushrooms are splendid as an hors d'oeuvre or in a salad.

1 pound fresh white mushrooms	1 teaspoon salt Freshly ground pepper
1 cup oil	½ teaspoon oregano
3 tablespoons wine vinegar	½ teaspoon rosemary, crushed
3 tablespoons lemon juice	½ teaspoon dry mustard Pinch sugar
5 scallions, chopped	

Cut the stems from the mushrooms and reserve for another use. Wash the mushrooms well and wipe dry. Combine the remaining ingredients and mix well. Taste the dressing and correct the seasoning. Place the mushrooms in a large glass jar with a cover and pour in the dressing. Shake the jar well so that the mushrooms are well bathed in the dressing. Cover the jar and refrigerate for at least 12 hours. Shake the jar from time to time. Don't worry about there not being enough dressing to cover; the mushrooms reduce in bulk after a while and duck down nicely in the marinade.

As a shortcut, I sometimes use the Good Seasons Garlic Dressing. Prepare the dressing according to the directions on the package and pour at once over the mushrooms. Marinate as in the preceding paragraph.

To serve, drain the mushrooms well and serve on picks.

Serves 12 or more as hors d'oeuvre

TUNA HORS D'OEUVRE

1 7-ounce can chunk-style tuna fish, well drained and mashed
1 tablespoon lemon juice
1 teaspoon dry mustard
1 teaspoon minced onion
¼ teaspoon celery seeds
3½ tablespoons mayonnaise
1 egg white, unbeaten
½ cup cornflake crumbs
3 tablespoons sesame seeds

Combine the tuna fish with all the remaining ingredients except the sesame seeds. Mix thoroughly and form into small balls the size of cherries. Roll the balls lightly in the sesame seeds and broil about 4 inches from the heat for 5 minutes, until they are heated through and the sesame seeds are lightly browned. Turn once during broiling. Serve hot.

Makes 18 to 20 hors d'oeuvres

HOT CLAM MERINGUES

Simply superb and superbly simple. You can put most of the ingredients together ahead of time and add the beaten egg white at the last minute.

½ cup minced clams, well drained
1½ tablespoons mayonnaise
1 tablespoon bread crumbs
¼ teaspoon salt
¼ teaspoon dry mustard
½ teaspoon Worcestershire sauce
½ teaspoon dried green onions or chives
½ teaspoon horseradish
1 egg white, stiffly beaten

Mix together all the ingredients except the egg white. Taste for seasoning. Fold in the egg white and mound on small squares of melba toast. Place under the broiler for 3 or 4 minutes, or until the tops are nicely browned and puffy. Serve hot.

Makes 20

ASPARAGUS ROLLED SANDWICH

This hot cocktail bit is a great favorite. Few people seem to recognize that it's just plain bread that forms the outer crust, since I am so often asked for the recipe for the pastry.

¼	pound farmer cheese	1	teaspoon chopped parsley
½	teaspoon white horseradish	10	slices white bread
1	tablespoon chili sauce	10	small asparagus tips
	Pinch dry mustard		Oil for frying
1	teaspoon Worcestershire sauce		

In a bowl, mash the cheese. If it seems a little dry, add a bit of skim milk, but don't make it watery. Add the horseradish, chili sauce, mustard, Worcestershire sauce, and parsley. Mix well until fairly smooth.

Remove the crusts from fresh sliced white bread (such as Arnold's) and roll out with a rolling pin, making the slices as flat as possible. Spread the slices with the cheese mixture. Place an asparagus tip (cut the same length as the bread) along an outer edge. Roll up and press closed firmly; the cheese will make the end of the bread adhere. Roll in waxed paper and refrigerate until ready to fry.

Warm ¼ inch of oil in a skillet over low heat. Fry just a few rolls at a time so you can rotate them in the oil and brown them evenly. They cook quickly (3 or 4 minutes). As they are done, remove with a slotted spoon and drain on absorbent paper. Add more oil as needed. Keep the finished rolls warm in a 250° oven. Cut in half and serve.

Makes 20

CURRIED CHICKEN PUFFS

These little bite-sized puffs are delicious and impressive. You can make the puffs the day before you use them.

Fill them early in the day you are going to serve them and pop them in the oven to warm as your company settles down with their before-dinner drink. The two eggs make such a large quantity that the amount of yolk in each is negligible.

½ cup boiling water   ½ cup all-purpose flour
¼ cup oil   2 eggs
¼ teaspoon salt

Preheat the oven to 400°.

In a medium-sized saucepan, heat the water and oil to the boiling point. Add the salt and flour all at once and stir vigorously until the flour is absorbed and the mixture leaves the sides of the pan. Remove from the fire and add the unbeaten eggs, one at a time, beating vigorously after the addition of each egg. The mixture will become spongy and shiny and, with a little prodding from the beating spoon, form into a mound, leaving the sides of the pan.

Lightly oil a flat cookie sheet. Drop mounds of batter by the half teaspoonful about 1 inch apart. Make them as round as you can and keep them small. This amount should yield 30 or more puffs. Bake for 10 minutes, then lower the heat to 375° and bake another 20 minutes. They are done when they are doubled in size and are firm and crusty to the touch. Take one from the oven for a test: if it retains its shape and does not fall, consider them done. Remove from the oven and pierce the side of each with a sharp knife to let out any steam that might make the inside damp.

When ready to use, cut open on one side near the top and fill with the chicken mixture. Just before serving, reheat in a 350° oven for 5 or 6 minutes.

Makes 30 or more

Curried Chicken Filling

3 tablespoons   1 tablespoon chopped
   mayonnaise   parsley
½ teaspoon curry powder   Squirt lemon juice
¼ teaspoon dry mustard   1 cup cooked finely
                                 minced chicken

Combine the mayonnaise with the curry powder, mustard, parsley, and lemon juice. Toss with the chicken, mixing well. Taste for seasoning. Fill the puffs with the mixture and refrigerate until ready to use.

HOT SARDINE CANAPÉ

Half this recipe will do as a family first course with tomato juice.

4 slices white bread
2 tablespoons oil
2 3¾-ounce cans
boneless and skinless
sardines, drained
1 tablespoon
mayonnaise

1 teaspoon lemon juice
Dash Tabasco
¼ teaspoon dry mustard
Freshly ground pepper
Paprika

Remove the crusts from the bread and cut each slice into thirds. Heat the oil in a skillet and lightly brown both sides of the bread oblongs. Drain on absorbent paper towels.

Mash the sardines and moisten with the mayonnaise. Add the lemon juice, Tabasco, mustard, and pepper. Spread on the toasted bread, dust with paprika, and place under the broiler for 5 or 6 minutes, or until heated through.

Makes 12

BROILED ARTICHOKE HEARTS

1 14-ounce can artichoke
hearts
16 melba toast rounds
4 tablespoons oil
2 teaspoons lemon juice
½ teaspoon salt

Freshly ground pepper
1 small clove garlic,
minced
Salt
1 tablespoon sesame
seeds

Use water-packed artichokes for this—not oil-packed. The 14-ounce cans generally contain between 8 and 10 artichoke hearts. Drain the artichokes and split in half. Place each half, cut side up, on a toast round.

Combine the oil, lemon juice, ½ teaspoon salt, pepper, and garlic and mix well. Pour this mixture over the artichokes, getting it between the leaves. Dust lightly with salt and sprinkle with the sesame seeds. Place the toast rounds on a cookie sheet and bake for 10 minutes in a 350° oven, or until they are heated through. Place them under the broiler for a few minutes to brown the tops lightly.

Makes 16 hors d'oeuvres

BROILED MUSHROOMS ARTURO

12 large mushrooms	Dash Tabasco
3 tablespoons oil	1 tablespoon
1 small onion	Worcestershire sauce
⅓ cup walnuts	½ teaspoon salt
1 teaspoon basil	1 tablespoon grated
3 tablespoons cornflake crumbs	Parmesan cheese

Wipe the mushrooms with a damp cloth and dry well. Remove the stems and set aside. Brush the mushroom caps with a little of the oil. Chop the stems, onion, and nuts coarsely. In a medium-sized skillet, heat 2 tablespoons of the oil and sauté the mixture for 5 minutes. Add the basil, cornflake crumbs, Tabasco, Worcestershire sauce, and salt. Stuff the mushrooms with the mixture and sprinkle with the Parmesan cheese. Oil a shallow baking dish and heat under the broiler for a couple of minutes. Place the filled mushrooms in the heated baking dish and put under the broiler for 5 minutes, or until completely heated.

Serves 6 to 8

CAPONATA
(EGGPLANT APPETIZER)

This versatile and flavorful Italian antipasto may be served in a bowl flanked by melba toast or crackers so that your guests can make their own hors d'oeuvres. It may also be served hot or cold as a first course at the table, or even as a vegetable course with beef or veal.

1 large eggplant	2 tablespoons capers
6 tablespoons oil	6 stuffed green olives, sliced
2 tablespoons pine nuts	
1 large onion, coarsely chopped	6 pitted black olives, sliced
1 clove garlic, crushed	⅓ cup wine vinegar
4 tablespoons tomato sauce	1 tablespoon sugar
	1 teaspoon salt
½ cup celery, chopped	Freshly ground pepper
½ cup green pepper, diced	Lemon wedges

Cut the unpeeled eggplant into slices ½ inch thick. Cut the slices into ½-inch cubes. In a large, heavy skillet, heat the oil and add as much of the eggplant as will fit in a single layer. Over high heat, fry the cubes quickly, turning frequently. When they are completely brown, remove with a slotted spoon and place in a bowl. Continue with the rest of the cubes until all are done, adding more oil if needed. Reduce the heat and fry the pine nuts slowly until golden. Add the nuts to the eggplant. Pour off any oil that has accumulated in the bowl and discard. (Eggplant has a way of absorbing oil, as you may have noticed.)

Cook the onion in the skillet until golden. Add the garlic, tomato sauce, celery, and green pepper and simmer, covered, for 15 to 20 minutes, or until the vegetables are tender. Add a little water or tomato sauce if the sauce cooks down. Return the eggplant to the skillet and add the capers and olives. In a small saucepan heat the vinegar and sugar together and add to the eggplant. Add the salt and pepper. Simmer the mixture 10 minutes longer, stirring frequently so it doesn't stick. Taste and correct the seasoning.

If serving caponata cold, chill for a few hours, or, better still, overnight, but serve at room temperature on a bed of lettuce. Garnish with lemon wedges.

Serves 6 to 8

FRUITS AND FRUIT AND VEGETABLE JUICES

Fruits and juices serve admirably as an appetizer course. My only reservation, and this could be a personal thing, has to do with sweetened fruits and juices that can sate the palate rather than tantalize it—which is why I prefer to save a fruit mélange for the close of dinner rather than the beginning. A half grapefruit, carefully dissected between the membranes so you don't have to battle it with a dull teaspoon, is a fine start for a meal. You might like to dribble a bit of sherry over it, tuck a fresh strawberry in the center, and brown it under the broiler. A slice of melon with a segment of fresh lime or lemon, or some assorted tiny melon balls in your prettiest compote dishes, will get your meal off to a good start.

Most fruit juices combine well with others. Unsweetened grapefruit juice mixed with pineapple or cranberry juice makes a refreshing drink. Experiment with a few mixtures of your own for variety.

Chilled V-8 and tomato juice are favorites in our house among the vegetable juices. We prefer the tomato juices that come from California. They have a rich texture and flavor that, in our opinion, make them superior to others.

On the following pages are some appetizer ideas that we like.

HERRING SALAD

This tangy salad was one of the reasons for our periodic visits to a well-known German restaurant at the other end of town until I decided it was easier to make the salad than the trip.

1 cup herring	Freshly ground black
⅔ cup cooked beets	pepper
1 cup raw apple, peeled	1 tablespoon sugar
½ small sour pickle	1 tablespoon (or more)
⅔ cup cooked potato	mayonnaise
3 tablespoons wine	White of hard-boiled
vinegar	egg
1 tablespoon sherry	Parsley sprigs

You may use either regular salt fillet of herring or a jar of herring tidbits in wine sauce, drained. The latter will make it less sharp. Dice the herring, beets, apples, pickle, and potato in ¼-inch cubes and mix together. Add the vinegar, sherry, pepper, sugar, and mayonnaise and toss lightly. Taste and correct the seasoning. Chill for a few hours in the refrigerator.

Serve at room temperature on individual plates on crisp lettuce. Sprinkle each portion with the white of a hard-boiled egg rubbed through a sieve and garnish with parsley sprigs. Accompany with thinly sliced pumpernickel.

Serves 6

ITALIAN ANTIPASTO

This can be served on a single large round platter and passed or arranged on individual plates.

2	tomatoes, thinly sliced	1	teaspoon capers
1	14-ounce can artichoke hearts, drained	1	teaspoon chopped chives
	French dressing	¼	teaspoon basil
4	hard-boiled eggs	8	sardines
6	anchovy fillets	2	celery hearts, split
½	cup low-fat cottage cheese, beaten until smooth	4	halves sweet pimiento
		4	green olives
		4	black olives
1	7-ounce can tuna fish, drained	4	lemon wedges sprinkled with chopped parsley
1	tablespoon mayonnaise		Watercress

Marinate the tomatoes and artichoke hearts in French dressing, separately. Split the eggs lengthwise in half and discard the yolks. Mash the anchovy fillets and add to the cottage cheese. Mix well and mound the egg whites with this mixture.

Place the tuna fish in the center of a serving dish. Spread the mayonnaise lightly over the tuna fish and sprinkle with the capers. Arrange around the tuna fish, in rows radiating from the center, the tomatoes sprinkled with the chives and basil, sardines, celery hearts, pimiento, artichoke hearts, olives, and stuffed eggs. Garnish the platter with the lemon wedges and watercress. Serve with thin Italian breadsticks.

Serves 4

ASPARAGUS APPETIZER

1 can asparagus tips (18–24 asparagus)
6 large choice tomato slices
French dressing

½ teaspoon sweet basil (dried) or 1 tablespoon fresh basil
½ teaspoon oregano
4 stuffed olives, sliced
Watercress

Use three or four asparagus tips for each tomato slice. Trim the asparagus the same size as the tomato slices and marinate the tips in French dressing for half an hour or so. When ready to serve, place a slice of tomato on each plate, sprinkle with the basil and oregano, cover with the asparagus tips and a bit of the French dressing, and decorate with the olives. Garnish with watercress.

Serves 6

SALMON CORNUCOPIAS

½ cup mayonnaise
1 tablespoon prepared horseradish (or more, depending on taste)
Freshly ground pepper
¼ teaspoon dry mustard

6 large slices smoked salmon
6 thin lemon slices
1 small can asparagus tips (12–18 asparagus)
1 tablespoon chopped parsley

Combine the mayonnaise, horseradish, pepper, and mustard. Horseradish varies in strength, so taste the mixture and use your own judgment as to whether or not you need more.

Spread a heaping tablespoon of this mixture on each salmon slice and roll into a cornucopia. Place each cornucopia on an individual plate, with the pointed end resting on a slice of lemon. Arrange 2 or 3 asparagus tips in the open end of each cornucopia. Sprinkle with the parsley. Serve with thinly sliced pumpernickel bread. Pass the pepper mill.

Serves 6

SMOKED BROOK TROUT WITH HORSERADISH SAUCE

This is less a recipe than a suggestion for an interesting appetizer course with which you may not be familiar or perhaps just need to be reminded of. A delightful young couple who were introduced to this delicacy at our home were so enchanted with it that they immediately bought a smoker and now do their own—from scratch, which includes catching the trout. If you are in this category, don't bother to read any further. I have never smoked a trout, or even fished for one.

I buy the smoked trout from my friend the fish man. The trout weigh about a pound each, more or less. A half will do as an appetizer portion. I have the center bone removed for my guests' convenience, but insist that the skin be left on for the appearance. Serve the fillets with a wedge of lemon and a lettuce cup filled with horseradish sauce.

Horseradish Sauce

½ cup mayonnaise
⅓ cup plain low-fat yogurt
1-2 tablespoons horseradish, depending on strength

1 teaspoon mustard
2 teaspoons lemon juice
Salt and pepper

Blend all the ingredients until smooth, using a fork or a wire whisk. Taste for seasoning and correct. Chill until ready to use.

Serves 4 or 5

ESCABECHE OF FISH

Of Spanish and Provençal origin, escabeche of fish features a slightly different method of preparation. The fish is first cooked, then marinated in a tangy dressing and served cold. It provides an interesting appetizer course.

A variety of fishes may be used. Small ones such as smelts, small mackerel, or fresh sardines, or about 1½-inch-thick slices of preferably heavy dark fish such as bluefish or king mackerel, may be used. Portion-sized pieces of salmon or fresh tuna also do well.

2	pounds fish	½	pound mushrooms, sliced
⅓	cup lime or lemon juice	1	clove garlic, crushed
½	cup flour		Dash of Tabasco
1	teaspoon salt	½	bay leaf
	Freshly ground pepper	¾	cup white vinegar
1	teaspoon sweet paprika	¼	cup water
⅓	cup oil	½	teaspoon dried thyme
2	large onions, chopped	3	parsley sprigs
1	medium-sized carrot, cut in thin crosswise slices	½	teaspoon salt
			Freshly ground pepper

Marinate the fish in the lime or lemon juice for 15 minutes. Remove and pat dry. Place the flour on a square of waxed paper and combine with the teaspoon of salt, pepper, and the paprika. Dredge the fish in the seasoned flour. In a heavy skillet heat the oil and cook the fish quickly, turning to brown both sides. Place the fish in a large shallow glass or enamel dish.

Using the same skillet with the oil remaining in it, sauté the onions and carrot until softened. Add the mushrooms and cook another 2 minutes. Pour off and discard any excess oil that remains in the pan. Add the remaining ingredients and bring to a boil. Boil briskly for 10 minutes and pour the marinade over the fish. Cover and refrigerate 24 hours. Serve cold.

Serves 6 to 8

TUNA COQUILLE

Time was when we made this with crab meat, but between the cost and cholesterol associated with it, we are most content with using tuna these days. We serve it in baking shells, and it makes a very nice first course.

1	7-ounce can tuna fish	1	teaspoon
1½	tablespoons oil		Worcestershire sauce
1½	tablespoons flour	1	tablespoon grated
¾	cup skim milk		Parmesan cheese
½	teaspoon salt	½	teaspoon lemon juice
	Freshly ground		
	pepper		

Drain the tuna fish well and flake it, breaking up the large lumps. In a small saucepan, heat the oil, add the flour, and stir over low heat until it bubbles. Add the milk slowly, stirring with a wire whisk, and cook, stirring constantly, until the sauce is thickened and smooth. Stir in the salt, pepper, Worcestershire sauce, and cheese and mix well. Add the lemon juice. Mix in the tuna fish. Divide the mixture among 3 oiled baking shells or ramekins and heat in a 350° oven for 10 minutes. Run under the broiler for a few minutes to brown the tops. Serve hot.

Serves 3

EGGPLANT, ARMENIAN STYLE

This bland, pleasant-tasting concoction is a Middle East specialty. The orthodox recipe calls for charring the eggplant and peppers under or over direct heat, but I find that baking is simpler, requiring less attention and giving satisfactory results.

1	large eggplant	3	tablespoons parsley,
2	small green peppers		finely chopped
1	small onion, finely	1	teaspoon salt
	chopped		Freshly ground pepper
1	large tomato, cut into	2	tablespoons oil
	small pieces	2	tablespoons wine
			vinegar

Wash the eggplant and green peppers and place them on a sheet of aluminum foil in a preheated 350° oven. Bake until soft (the eggplant will need about 1 hour; the peppers, about 40 minutes). While they are baking, prepare the onion, tomato, and parsley. When the peppers and eggplant are cool enough to handle, scoop out the eggplant pulp and chop. Core and chop the peppers. Mix all the ingredients together. Taste for seasoning and correct. Chill in the refrigerator. Serve in lettuce cups.

Serves 6

EGGPLANT APPETIZER

Another version of a cold eggplant preparation, low in calories and high in flavor.

1 small eggplant	⅛ teaspoon dried dill
½ cup celery, finely chopped	¼ teaspoon oregano
⅓ cup pimiento, finely chopped	½ teaspoon salt
1 small clove garlic, minced	Freshly ground pepper
2 tablespoons parsley, minced	2 tablespoons oil
	2 teaspoons wine vinegar

Cover the eggplant with salted boiling water and cook for 20 minutes, or until tender. Drain and cool, then peel and cut into strips about 2 inches long and ½ inch wide. The eggplant should yield approximately 2 cups. Add the remaining ingredients and mix well. Taste to see if you want any additional seasonings. Chill overnight in the refrigerator. Serve cold in lettuce cups.

Serves 6

ARTICHOKES VINAIGRETTE

The flowery artichoke is splendid for calorie-cholesterol-conscious citizens. Not only is it pleasant to eat, but the act of eating it is a time- and motion-consuming operation, which can be an added bonus, since it uses up a considerable part of the meal period with a minimum number of calories. Most children seem to like artichokes, too, perhaps because artichokes are one of the few foods that allow finger eating to be good manners.

Artichokes do nicely as an appetizer course or a main course for lunch. When the choke is removed, they can be filled with a variety of ingredients—meat, fish, mushrooms, vegetables—and served hot or cold. Standard Operating Procedure in our house is cold artichokes accompanied by a tangy vinaigrette dressing served in small individual bowls. When buying, look for firm, heavy artichokes with tightly closed petals.

4 artichokes	¼ cup lemon juice or
Boiling water	vinegar
1 teaspoon salt	French Dressing

Wash the artichokes. With a sharp knife, trim off the stem end of each artichoke flush with the bottom petal bases so that it will stand upright firmly. Pull off any tough outer petals at the base. Place the artichoke on its side and slice a good ½ inch or more from the top. With scissors, shorten the rest of the leaves neatly and evenly, cutting them to about ⅔ of their original height.

Place the artichoke bases down in a deep kettle so they fit snugly together. Cover with boiling water, add the salt and lemon juice or vinegar, and cook, covered, for 30 to 45 minutes. Start testing for doneness after 30 minutes by piercing the bottom of the artichoke with a small, sharp-pointed knife; if it encounters no resistance, the artichoke is done. The cooking time varies according to the size and age of the artichoke, but I find that generally half an hour is enough. Artichokes should not be overcooked or they will fall apart. If the water level gets low during the cooking, add boiling water so that the boiling process is never interrupted.

When done, remove from the water with kitchen tongs or two long-handled spoons. Place upside down and allow to drain for 10 minutes, by which time they will be cool enough to handle.

To remove the choke, spread the center leaves of the artichoke and twist out the center cone. It should come out nicely in one piece. With a pointed teaspoon, scoop out the fuzzy choke that lies on the artichoke bottom and rub the bottom with a lemon segment to prevent darkening. Chill in the refrigerator. Serve cold with French Dressing (page 326).

Serves 4

STUFFED ARTICHOKES

4 cooked artichokes
4 tablespoons oil
1 clove garlic, minced
1 cup stale ¼-inch
  bread cubes
2 tablespoons minced
  parsley
4 shallots, finely
  chopped
6 water chestnuts,
  thinly sliced

8 small mushrooms,
  thinly sliced
1 tablespoon Parmesan
  cheese
½ teaspoon oregano
½ teaspoon salt
  Freshly ground pepper
2 tablespoons lemon
  juice

Prepare the artichokes as in the preceding recipe, but undercook them a bit. Something like 25 minutes in the boiling water should do it.

In a medium-sized skillet, heat 3 tablespoons of the oil and add all the remaining ingredients except the lemon juice and half of the mushroom slices that you will use for garnish. Mix well and place over low heat for 5 minutes. Carefully pack into the 4 artichokes and between the leaves. Arrange in a pan that will hold the artichokes snugly upright. Drizzle the artichokes with the remaining tablespoon of oil and the lemon juice. Place a scant ½ inch of hot water in the bottom of the pan and bake for 10 minutes in a 350° oven, or until the artichokes are heated through. Garnish with mushroom slices.

Serves 4

Note: Individual cooked artichoke leaves make very nice bases for hors d'oeuvres also. Detach the leaves after the artichokes have been cooked and place a small mound of cold fish salad or chicken salad over the eating portion of the leaf. You then have the nice juicy morsel of the artichoke along with whatever you have seen fit to place on it.

ONION PIE

We came across this delicious concoction in Nice, where it is known by its proper name, *pissaladière*. Both its name and ingredients suggest the Italian *pizza*, and I have no idea whether it predated or followed it. At any rate, it is fine, hearty eating and can serve as a substantial cocktail course or the beginning of a light meal that needs bolstering. It can do also as the main event of a supper. The traditional recipe calls for a bread dough, but to lighten the burden of the cook, I have allowed Mr. Pillsbury to furnish the crust.

2	pounds onions, thinly sliced	12	cherry tomatoes, cut in half
⅓	cup oil	5	black olives, sliced in thin crescents
½	teaspoon Bovril	½	teaspoon basil
1	bay leaf	1	teaspoon Parmesan cheese
1	package Pillsbury crescent rolls		
2	2-ounce cans flat anchovy fillets, well drained		

Medium-sized yellow onions usually run around 4 to 5 to the pound, so you will need from 8 to 10. Don't worry about using an extra onion; it can only improve the end result. Use a good, heavy pot to cook the onions, since they will simmer about an hour and should be completely done, but not browned or charred. Heat the oil, add the onions, and mix well. Mix in the Bovril and add the bay leaf. Cover and cook over very low heat for 1 hour, stirring from time to time. After the first 30 minutes, discard the bay leaf.

While the onions are simmering, lightly oil a 10-inch glass pie plate and line it with the dough triangles. Fit the widest end of the triangle to the outside lip of the pie dish. Seven of the triangles should cover, with the eighth used for the gap in the center. Press all the seams tightly together.

Drain the cooked onions well through a strainer and reserve the liquid. Spread the drained onions evenly over the dough. Arrange the anchovy fillets over the top in lattice style. Place a half cherry tomato, cut side up, in each lattice square and garnish with the olives. Sprinkle a little basil on each tomato and sprinkle a little Parmesan cheese over all. Dribble 2 or 3 tablespoons of the reserved onion liquid over the top. Place in a preheated 400° oven and bake for 40 minutes. Serve warm. (The pie can be kept in a warm oven for half an hour or so without damage.)

Serves 8 to 10

HEARTS OF PALM APPETIZER

Hearts of palm are native to Brazil and are available in this country in cans. They look somewhat like the stalk of very thick white asparagus and have a smooth texture and a bland, pleasant flavor. They can be served hot or cold and are a fine salad ingredient. As a cold appetizer they do nicely sliced, marinated in Russian dressing, and served on a bed of watercress or lettuce. One of our favorite neighborhood Brazilian restaurants makes a specialty of the following hot appetizer (here tailored to fit our needs):

1 14-ounce can hearts of palm	Freshly ground pepper
2 tablespoons oil	¼ teaspoon dry mustard
2 tablespoons flour	½ teaspoon dried dill
1 cup skim milk	1 tablespoon dry sherry
1 package MBT chicken broth powder	1 tablespoon Parmesan cheese

Drain the hearts of palm and slice crosswise into ½-inch slices. In a small saucepan, heat the oil and add the flour, stirring until it begins to bubble. Reduce the heat and stir in the milk, beating with a wire whisk. Add the remaining ingredients and cook until the sauce is thickened and smooth. Add the sliced hearts of palm and heat through. Serve hot.

Serves 4

MUSHROOMS TRIFOLATI

Our affable host on the occasion of our dining at a lovely restaurant outside of Rome (the former home of Mussolini's lady friend) suggested that we order "Funghi Trifolati," since they are a popular Roman dish—akin to spoon bread in the South, perhaps. The maitre d' was genial and frustratingly vague about the recipe, but our host, true to his word, after consultations with cooks of his acquaintance filled us in on the missing ingredients via transatlantic mail.

1 pound mushrooms	1 small clove garlic,
6 tablespoons oil	crushed
1 clove garlic	2 tablespoons minced
4 anchovy fillets, crushed	parsley
4 bread triangles	2 tablespoons lemon juice

Trim the stem end of the mushrooms. Wash the mushrooms and wipe dry. Slice the stems and caps thinly. Heat 3 tablespoons of the oil with the garlic clove in a heavy skillet. When the garlic is browned, remove it and add the mushrooms. Cook over high heat, stirring often. After about 5 minutes, there will be a goodly amount of mushroom liquid in the pan. Stir a few tablespoons of this into the anchovies, making a thick paste. Add this paste to the mushrooms, mixing thoroughly. Cook another 5 minutes, or until the liquid is absorbed.

While the mushrooms are cooking, prepare the toast. Heat the crushed garlic clove in the 3 remaining tablespoons of oil, then remove the garlic. Fry the bread triangles on both sides until lightly browned. Drain on absorbent paper.

Add the parsley and lemon juice to the mushroom mixture and toss lightly. Serve immediately on the toast triangles.

Serves 4

FRIED MUSHROOMS

Add to the recipe for Mushrooms Trifolati two small tomatoes, peeled and cut into chunks, and ½ teaspoon chopped mint leaves. Omit the parsley. Serve on toast.

HADDOCK RING MOLD

In our B.C. (Before Cholesterol) period I used to make this with crab meat, but the haddock has enough merit not to be considered a substitute. Actually, cooked haddock falls into large flakes that people sometimes mistake for crab meat. The tangy aspic, made from chili sauce, is interesting and a bit different. If the occasion warrants, you might consider garnishing it with some cooked shrimps. One or two shrimps per portion aren't likely to send cholesterol levels soaring.

5	cups water	1	carrot, scraped and cut in chunks
¼	cup lemon juice		
½	teaspoon salt	1	bay leaf
1	onion, quartered	6	peppercorns
1	stalk celery with leaves	1½	pounds haddock fillets

Aspic

3	tablespoons unflavored gelatin	¾	cup lemon juice
		¾	cup chili sauce
4	tablespoons sugar	3	tablespoons pickle relish
1	teaspoon salt		
3½	cups water		Russian Dressing

In a medium-sized kettle, combine the water, lemon juice, salt, onion, celery, carrot, bay leaf, and peppercorns and boil for 20 minutes. Cut the fish into pieces, add, reduce the heat, and simmer slowly for 10 minutes or so, covered, until it flakes easily. Remove the fish from the poaching liquid, drain well, and when cool, separate into flakes.

To make the aspic, mix together the gelatin, sugar, and salt in a small saucepan with 1¾ cups of the water. Place over low heat and stir until the gelatin is dissolved. Remove from the heat and stir in the remaining water. Stir in the lemon juice and chili sauce. Lightly oil a 6-cup ring mold and pour a thin layer of the gelatin mixture into the mold, just enough to give the aspic a smooth, shiny top when it is unmolded. Chill until firm (about 40 minutes).

Fold the pickle relish and flaked fish into the remainder of the gelatin mixture and distribute evenly. Pour into the ring mold and refrigerate. When ready to serve, unmold on a round platter lined with salad greens. Serve Russian Dressing (page 330) separately.

Serves 10 to 12

SALMON MOUSSE WITH CUCUMBER SAUCE

Salmon mousse can serve very well for a hot-weather main course, or a lunch or supper dish any season of the year, so the fact that it appears in the appetizer section shouldn't discourage you from taking it out of context. However, it makes such a satisfactory introduction to a dinner that I couldn't resist placing it in this chapter. Most salmon mousses include great quantities of whipped cream, and I can't imagine why, when they are so delicious without it.

I hope you have a fish mold for this mousse. With a slice of stuffed olive for an eye, and its delicate pink body curved around a bowl of green cucumber sauce, this bigger-than-life fish makes an impressive appearance.

2	pounds fresh or frozen salmon	1	tablespoon Worcestershire sauce
6	cups water	2	teaspoons grated onion
1	stalk celery		
1	onion, quartered	1	cup skim milk
8	peppercorns	1½	tablespoons oil
1	teaspoon salt	¼	cup cider vinegar
1	bay leaf	2	tablespoons gelatin dissolved in ⅓ cup cold water
1	tablespoon flour		
1½	tablespoons sugar		
½	teaspoon salt	2	egg whites
½	teaspoon dry mustard		Watercress

Wash the salmon and set aside. In a good-sized skillet, boil the water, celery, onion, peppercorns, salt, and bay leaf for 20 minutes. Add the salmon, reduce the heat, and simmer covered for 15 to 20 minutes, or until the salmon flakes easily. Remove from the skillet, drain, and let cool. Flake, making sure you remove all the bones. Salmon bones are tricky things, as you may know. Place the flaked salmon in a large bowl.

In the top of a double boiler, mix together the flour, sugar, salt, mustard, Worcestershire sauce, grated onion, milk, oil, and vinegar. Cook over boiling water, stirring with a wire whisk, until the mixture thickens and is perfectly smooth. Add the soaked gelatin and stir until dissolved. Add the mixture to the flaked salmon and mix well. Beat the egg whites until stiff and fold into the mixture. Taste for seasoning and correct. Lightly oil a mold, pack with the fish mixture, and chill for 5 hours. Unmold on a round platter garnished with watercress. Serve Cucumber Sauce (below) separately.

Cucumber Sauce

1 large cucumber, peeled and grated with medium grater
1 cup mayonnaise
½ teaspoon prepared mustard
1 tablespoon lemon juice
1 tablespoon snipped fresh dill or 1 teaspoon dried dill
Few drops of green vegetable coloring

Place the cucumber in a strainer and with the back of a large spoon press out the liquid. Cucumbers sometimes contain a lot of juice, which will make the sauce too watery unless it is drained. Combine the cucumber pulp with the mayonnaise, mustard, lemon juice, and dill. To intensify the color of the sauce and to provide color contrast with the salmon, add a drop or two of green vegetable coloring. Taste for seasoning and correct. Chill the sauce until ready to serve.

Serves 6 to 8 as appetizer;
4 to 6 as main course

QUICK SALMON MOUSSE

This is a quickly prepared salmon mousse that calls only for a 1-pound can of salmon and a blender.

1 cup evaporated skimmed milk, well chilled
1 1-pound can salmon
1 tablespoon unflavored gelatin
2 tablespoons lemon juice
1 small onion, sliced
½ cup boiling water
½ teaspoon dry mustard
½ cup mayonnaise
¼ teaspoon sweet paprika
1 tablespoon fresh snipped dill or 1 teaspoon dried dill

Place the milk in the freezer compartment of the refrigerator so it will be very cold. If a few ice crystals should form, so much the better.

Drain the salmon well, discard the bones and skin, and set aside. Empty the gelatin into the blender. Add the lemon juice, onion, boiling water, and mustard. Blend at high speed for 40 seconds, or until the onion is liquefied. Add the mayonnaise, about half the salmon, paprika, and dill and blend until smooth. Pour in the chilled milk and blend for another 30 seconds. Mix in the remainder of the flaked salmon with a mixing spoon. (The salmon flakes will add a little variety of texture, but if you prefer a perfectly smooth mousse, all the salmon can go into the blender in the first place.) Pour the mixture into a lightly oiled 4-cup mold or fish mold and refrigerate until firm (about 3 or 4 hours). Serve with Mayonnaise (page 329) or with Cucumber Sauce as in the preceding recipe.

Serves 6 to 8 as appetizer;
4 as main course

6
Soups and Chowders

The soul-warming virtues of a splendid bowl of soup are only a small part of what it has to offer in our low-fat scheme of things. For an eating program like ours where we wish to limit certain foods, soup can do more than please our palates, warm us on a cold winter night, and refresh us when the temperature is way up there. It can lessen the need for excessive meat portions and give even a light meal a feeling of completeness.

It might be wiser to allow the gustatory pleasures of soup to rest on their own laurels, but I think we should note that soup has so much to recommend it nutritionally that we should serve it often. Cream soups can fulfill part of the one-pint-daily skim milk needs of adults, and as for vegetable soups—consider the additional advantage of serving the vitamin-laden liquid in which the vegetables have cooked, instead of sending it down the drain!

We generally save the hearty fish stews and chowders for a main lunch or supper course. Accompanied by a toasted garlic loaf or some other hot bread, a salad, and fruit for dessert, they provide an adequate meal. Consommé, meat and vegetable broths, and cream soups make fine appetizer courses. If you have had reservations about the quality of cream soups possible within this dietary, I suspect you will have some pleasant surprises in store.

Buy canned and dehydrated soups with caution, since many of them are made with hydrogenated shortenings and butter. However, there are many acceptable ones. The list of ingredients on the wrappers will tell you what you need to know, but bear in mind the fact that "vegetable oil" on the list of ingredients too often means coconut oil.

Both canned consommé and chicken broth provide excellent bases in combination with vegetables and cream sauces for more elaborate soups. We use lots of both. Considering the ingredients and the time and effort needed to produce homemade consommé, I feel grateful to Mr. Campbell for his. Served hot and undiluted, with a splash of sherry and a thin slice of lemon floating on top, it makes an agreeable beginning for a meal. I generally have a few cans of chicken broth in the refrigerator, since having them chilled makes it easier to remove the ever-present blob of fat that floats on top.

The packaged soup mixtures consisting of a variety of dried peas and beans with mushrooms and barley are easily prepared also. They cook up to a substantial soup that you can vary with the addition of a veal knuckle or meat bone and fresh tomatoes, tomato sauce, or some chicken broth powders or bouillon cubes. For richer-tasting cream soups, use skimmed evaporated milk in place of regular skim milk.

Cold jellied soups are always welcome on a hot day. Three cups of tomato juice, beef bouillon, or chicken broth seasoned to taste with salt, pepper, and lemon juice, then mixed with 1 tablespoon unflavored gelatin that has been dissolved in half a cup of the hot liquid, will chill to a soft jelly consistency. The same Campbell's consommé that we talked about earlier already has gelatin added. Chill it in the refrigerator and serve it directly from the can, topped with a dollop of plain low-fat yogurt sprinkled with chopped chives. Very nice. One can will serve two portions adequately.

FRESH VEGETABLE SOUP

1½	pounds soup meat and bones	2	onions, sliced
1	veal knucklebone	1	bay leaf
5	cups cold water	1	cup carrots, scraped and sliced
2	teaspoons salt	3	cups canned tomatoes
6	peppercorns		

½ cup peas	½ cup rice
½ cup cut-up green beans	3 tablespoons chopped parsley
1 cup sliced celery	

In a large soup kettle, combine the soup meat and bones, water, salt, peppercorns, onions, and bay leaf. Cover and simmer slowly for 2 hours. Skim as necessary. Remove the meat and strain. Chill the soup stock overnight in the refrigerator.

The next day, remove the fat from the stock, return the stock to the soup kettle, and add all the remaining ingredients except the parsley. Simmer 1 hour or until the vegetables are tender. Sprinkle each portion with some of the parsley. The leftover soup may be frozen.

Serves 8 to 10

BORSCHT (BEET SOUP)

This delicious Russian beet soup has the added distinction of being one of the few pronounceable words around that contains five consonants in consecutive order, beginning with its third letter.

There are as many variations of borscht as Russian folk costumes, but the traditional soup always had cabbage in it.

6 fresh beets, grated, or 1 1-pound can julienne beets	2 tablespoons tomato paste
1 cup beet juice	1 1-pound can tomatoes
2 tablespoons oil	1 clove garlic, crushed
2 onions, chopped	2 teaspoons lemon juice
2 cups cabbage, finely shredded	1 teaspoon vinegar
4 cups beef stock, or 3 10½-ounce cans consommé	1 teaspoon (or more) sugar or artificial sweetener (if desired)
	1 teaspoon (or more) salt

If you are using fresh beets, cook them in 2 cups of water and reserve 1 cup of the liquid. If using canned beets, drain and measure the liquid. If less than a cup, add water to the desired amount and reserve.

In a large soup kettle, heat the oil and add the onions. Sauté over low heat until limp and golden (about 10 minutes). Add the cabbage, beets, and beef stock or consommé. Simmer slowly for 15 minutes.

Add the tomato paste, tomatoes, and garlic and cook slowly for 25 minutes. Add the beet juice, lemon juice, vinegar, and sugar or sweetener. Simmer for 5 minutes. Add the salt. Taste and correct the seasoning.

Serves 5

CLAM CONSOMMÉ

1½ cups clam juice (bottled)	Salt (if desired)
2 10½-ounce cans consommé	¼ cup dry sherry

Combine the clam juice with the undiluted consommé in a saucepan. Add salt only if you need it. Clam juices vary in degree of saltiness and it may be unnecessary to add any seasoning. Simmer for a few minutes over low heat until hot. Add the sherry and heat through.

Serves 4

FISH CHOWDER

2 pounds cod fillets	1 tablespoon Worcestershire sauce
3 tablespoons oil	½ teaspoon salt
1 large carrot, scraped and finely chopped	Freshly ground pepper
1 stalk celery, finely chopped	3 medium-sized potatoes, diced
½ medium-sized green pepper, finely chopped	2 cups skim milk
2 medium-sized onions, finely chopped	2 tablespoons flour
3 cups fish stock or 2 cups clam juice and 1 cup water	3 tablespoons water
	Chopped parsley

Wash the cod fillets, cut into 1-inch squares, and set aside.

In a good-sized soup kettle, heat the oil and cook the carrot, celery, green pepper, and onions until tender, but not browned (15 to 20 minutes).

Add to the kettle the fish stock or the clam juice and water. (If you are using cod steaks instead of fillets, make the fish stock by cooking the fish bones, head, and skin in 3 cups of lightly salted water to which you have added an onion and six or eight peppercorns. Simmer for 30 minutes and strain.) Add to the kettle the Worcestershire sauce, salt, and pepper. Add the potatoes and simmer over low heat for about 15 minutes, but stop before the potatoes get mushy. They should be a little underdone at this point, since the chowder still has a bit more cooking to come.

In a separate saucepan, heat the milk just to the boiling point and add to the soup. Mix the flour and the water until smooth and add to the soup, stirring until it becomes smooth (about 3 minutes). Add the fish, cover the kettle, and simmer slowly for another 5 minutes, or until the fish is cooked. Do not allow the soup to come to a boil. Taste for seasoning and correct. Serve in large soup bowls, and sprinkle the parsley over each portion.

Serves 8

SMOKED FISH CHOWDER

The Down Easters will tell you that if you have never eaten fish chowder made with smoked fish, you have never eaten fish chowder.

1 pound finnan haddie	Dash garlic powder
3 cups cold water	(optional)
1 carrot, scraped and finely diced	White pepper
	1 quart skim milk
1 stalk celery, finely diced	2 tablespoons flour
	1½ tablespoons fresh dill, snipped, or 1 teaspoon dried dillweed
1 large potato, finely diced	
2 tablespoons oil	
1 medium-sized onion, chopped	

Wash the finnan haddie and cut into 2 or 3 pieces. Place in a large saucepan with the water and boil for 10 minutes, or until the fish flakes easily. Drain the fish and reserve the liquid. You will need 2 cups of fish stock, so if you have more, boil to reduce to that amount. When the fish is cool enough to handle, flake and return to the stock. Add the carrot, celery, and potato. Cover and simmer slowly for about 15 to 20 minutes, or until the vegetables are tender.

In a small skillet, heat the oil, sauté the onion until it turns golden, and add to the soup mixture. Add the garlic powder if desired and white pepper. Add the milk, reserving a couple of tablespoons for the flour paste. Add the dill and simmer slowly for 10 minutes. Mix the flour with the reserved milk into a smooth paste and add to the soup, stirring until thickened and smooth. Taste for seasoning. Chances are it won't need any salt, but you decide. Serve hot.

Serves 4 or 5

LAMB AND BARLEY BROTH

2 pounds lean lamb and bones (neck of lamb is a likely cut)	2 stalks celery, diced
	1 onion, chopped
	1 small turnip, diced
2 quarts cold water	3 tablespoons barley
1 onion cut in quarters	1 teaspoon salt
¼ cup celery tops	Freshly ground pepper
6 peppercorns, bruised	1 tablespoon chopped
1 teaspoon salt	parsley
1 large carrot, diced	

Wipe the meat and bones. Place in a large kettle with the water. (The uncooked leftover bone from your butterflied leg of lamb is a useful item for the soup pot.) Add the onion, celery tops, peppercorns, and 1 teaspoon of salt. Bring to a boil slowly and simmer over low heat for 1½ hours. Skim the broth a number of times. Let cool. Strain the broth and refrigerate, preferably overnight.

Remove the fat from the broth and return the broth to the soup kettle. Add all the remaining ingredients except the parsley. Cook slowly for 1½ hours, covered, or until the vegetables are tender. Taste and correct the seasoning. Sprinkle each serving with some of the parsley.

Serves 6

LENTIL SOUP

This is a delicious, hearty soup that can be a prelude to a frugal dinner or, better still, a main lunch course.

3 quarts water	3 tablespoons oil
4 large meaty bones	2 stalks celery, diced
4 celery stalks with tops	1 onion, chopped
1 large onion	1 clove garlic, crushed
3 carrots, scraped and left whole	1 tablespoon parsley, snipped
½ pound lentils	½ cup tomato (pulp only)
2 quarts water with 1 teaspoon salt	1 teaspoon salt
	Freshly ground pepper

In a large soup kettle, combine the water, bones, celery, onion, and carrots. Cook slowly for 2 hours. Skim as necessary. Let cool. Strain the broth and refrigerate, preferably overnight. Slice the carrots and reserve.

In another large saucepan, cook the lentils in the 2 quarts of boiling salted water for 45 minutes. Drain and set aside. Using the same pot, heat the oil and cook the diced celery, onion, garlic, and parsley until the vegetables are lightly browned. Add the tomato pulp, salt, and pepper and cook 5 minutes longer, or until the tomato disintegrates.

Remove the crust of fat from the soup and combine the skimmed soup stock, vegetable mixture, and drained lentils in a large kettle. Simmer for 30 minutes, or until the lentils are completely soft. Add the carrots. Taste for seasonings and correct.

Serves 12

MINESTRONE

Minestrone is the generic term for Italian vegetable soup made with beans. Each district in Italy—Lombardy,

Tuscany, Liguria, Latium, etc.—has its own variation, and each is distinctive in its own way. This recipe is a compilation of a few, adapted with our own dietary aims in view.

The celery, zucchini, and carrot may be substituted by, or used in combination with, other vegetables such as 1 pound of fresh peas, a cup of string beans, a diced turnip, ½ pound sliced mushrooms, or a few leeks, thinly sliced.

This makes a large quantity of soup, but the leftover freezes very well.

1	cup dried beans (small white or red)	2	medium-sized tomatoes, diced
2	teaspoons salt		White pepper
1	veal knucklebone	1	clove garlic, minced
1½	tablespoons oil	½	teaspoon basil
1	large onion, thinly sliced	1	very small cabbage, thinly sliced
1	carrot, diced	½	cup elbow macaroni (small size)
1	potato, diced	2	tablespoons grated
1	zucchini, diced		sapsago or Parmesan cheese
1	teaspoon parsley, chopped		
2	stalks celery, diced		

Soak the beans overnight in 1½ quarts of cold water. Drain and place in a large soup kettle with 2½ quarts of cold water, 1 teaspoon of the salt, and the veal knucklebone. Simmer over low heat, covered, for 1 hour.

In a large skillet, heat the oil and cook the onion until golden. Add the carrot, potato, zucchini, parsley, celery, tomatoes, the remaining teaspoon of salt, pepper, garlic, and basil. Cook together for 10 minutes and add to the soup. Add the cabbage and elbow macaroni and cook for 2 hours or more, covered, until the beans and vegetables are soft. Remove the bone. Taste and correct the seasoning.

Serve hot. Sprinkle each portion with some of the cheese.

Serves 6 to 8 as main dish;
10 to 12 as first course

MUSHROOM AND BARLEY SOUP

3 tablespoons oil
½ cup pearl barley
3 quarts water
1½ pounds lean short ribs
  or 3 meaty soup bones
3 carrots, sliced
½ cup dried mushrooms

1 medium-sized onion,
  chopped
3 stalks celery, diced
4 sprigs parsley
1 teaspoon salt
Pepper

In a large soup kettle, heat the oil, add the barley, and keep turning it until it becomes lightly browned. Add the water and the meat or bones and cook over medium heat for 30 minutes, covered. Skim as needed. Add the carrots, mushrooms (cut in halves or quarters, depending upon size), onion, celery, parsley, salt, and pepper. Simmer slowly for about 2½ hours. Remove the bones and parsley sprigs and chill. When chilled, remove the fat from the soup and reheat. Taste and correct the seasonings.

Serves 12

ONION SOUP

3 tablespoons oil
4 large onions, thinly
  sliced
1 tablespoon flour
3 10½-ounce cans
  consommé
2 teaspoons lemon juice

4 tablespoons dry sherry
5 slices toasted French
  bread
2 tablespoons grated
  sapsago or Parmesan
  cheese

Heat the oil in a heavy skillet and sauté the onion rings until golden. Blend in the flour. Add the consommé and simmer over low heat for 10 minutes. Add the lemon juice and sherry. Taste for seasonings (it is unlikely any will be needed).

Sprinkle the bread with the cheese and place under the broiler until the cheese is lightly browned. Serve the soup hot with a slice of toast floating on each portion.

Serves 4 or 5

PUREE MONGOLE

1 cup green split peas
4 cups water
1 teaspoon salt
2 tablespoons oil
1 medium-sized onion,
   finely chopped

4 cups chicken broth
1 clove garlic
2 cups tomato puree
Salt
Freshly ground pepper
Crisp croutons

Dried peas no longer require overnight soaking, which is pleasant for impetuous souls who are suddenly overcome with an urge for split pea soup. Wash the peas, pick them over, and add them to the water along with 1 teaspoon of salt. Bring them to a boil and boil for 3 or 4 minutes. Remove from the heat, cover, and let stand for 1 hour. Drain.

In a small skillet, heat the oil and cook the onion until limp and golden (about 10 minutes). Add to the peas the onion, chicken broth, garlic, and tomato puree. Bring to a boil, reduce the heat, and simmer slowly, covered, for about 45 minutes, or until the peas are tender. Force through a sieve or a food mill to puree the peas. Taste for seasoning and correct. You may thin the soup with water or more chicken broth if it seems too thick. Serve the soup hot, sprinkled with croutons (page 98).

Serves 6 to 8

SWEET-AND-SOUR CABBAGE SOUP

This is one of those homely, homey soups I was brought up on. When we serve it to some of the sophisticated palates that occasionally sit at our table, it is greeted with as much enthusiasm as news of a bull market on Wall Street.

2 pounds soup meat and
   bones (marrow bones,
   beef and veal)
2 quarts cold water
1 large carrot, sliced
1 onion, coarsely
   chopped

3 stalks of celery and
   tops, cut into 2-inch
   lengths
2 teaspoons salt
   Freshly ground pepper
1 small head cabbage,
   shredded

½ cup brown sugar
2 cups canned
   tomatoes, strained

Sour salt crystal (about
the size of a green pea)

Place the meat and bones in a large soup kettle and cover with the water. Bring to the boiling point slowly and skim. Add the carrot, onion, celery, salt, and pepper. Cook, covered, over low heat for 1½ hours, or until the meat is tender. Skim frequently. Strain the broth, discarding the meat and vegetables, and refrigerate overnight.

The following day, remove all fat from the broth. Add the cabbage, brown sugar, tomato pulp, and sour salt. Simmer slowly for 1 hour. Taste and correct the seasoning—you may want it a little sweeter, or a little sourer, or perhaps both.

Serves 6 to 8

CREAM OF BEAN SOUP

2 cups navy beans
   Cold water
3 cups chicken broth
4 shallots or 2 small
   onions, chopped
1 teaspoon salt
½ teaspoon curry powder
¼ teaspoon marjoram

3 tablespoons oil
2 tablespoons flour
3 cups skim milk
½ teaspoon paprika
   Freshly ground pepper
2 tablespoons chopped
   chives

Wash the beans and soak overnight in cold water to cover. Drain. In a 3-quart kettle, heat the chicken broth to the boiling point. Add the beans, shallots or onions, salt, curry powder, and marjoram. Simmer slowly until the beans are mushy. Add more water if needed. When tender, force the bean mixture through a sieve or blend in an electric blender until smooth.

In the soup kettle, heat the oil and blend in the flour, stirring until it bubbles. Slowly add the milk, stirring with a wire whisk until smooth and thickened. Mix in the bean puree and heat through, but don't allow the mixture to boil. Add the paprika and pepper and taste and correct the seasoning. Serve hot, sprinkled with the chives.

Serves 6

CREAM OF BROCCOLI SOUP

1 10-ounce package frozen
  chopped broccoli
3 tablespoons oil
1 small onion,
  chopped
2 tablespoons flour

1 10-ounce can
  consommé
1½ cups skim milk
½ teaspoon salt
¼ teaspoon nutmeg

Cook the broccoli in the least amount of water possible only until thawed and heated through. Do not overcook. In a small skillet, heat 1 tablespoon of the oil and add the onion. Cook until well browned. In an electric blender, blend the broccoli with ¼ cup of the liquid in which it cooked and the browned onion until liquefied. Set aside.

In a medium-sized pot, heat the remaining 2 tablespoons of oil. Blend in the flour and stir until it bubbles. Slowly add the consommé, stirring with a wire whisk until thickened and smooth. Add the milk and salt, bring to a boil, reduce the heat, and simmer for 3 minutes. Mix in the broccoli puree and nutmeg and heat through. Taste and correct the seasoning. Keep warm until ready to serve, but do not allow the soup to come to a boil.

Serves 3 or 4

CREAM OF CARROT SOUP

6 carrots, scraped and
  thinly sliced
1 teaspoon dried dill
½ teaspoon salt
1 teaspoon sugar
½ cup water

2 tablespoons oil
2 tablespoons flour
3½ cups skim milk
  Salt and pepper (if
  desired)
  Chopped parsley

In a heavy saucepan, cook the carrots with the dill, ½ teaspoon of salt, sugar, and water. Cover the pan and cook over low heat until the carrots are tender (about 20 to 25 minutes). Reserve a few of the carrot slices and dice them as a garnish for the soup. Puree the remaining carrots and the liquid in which they were cooked in an electric blender and set aside.

Heat the oil and blend in the flour, stirring until it bubbles. Add the milk slowly, stirring with a wire whisk until the mixture is thickened and smooth. Mix in the carrot puree and heat gently, but do not allow to boil. Taste for seasoning; add salt and pepper if needed. To serve, add the diced carrots and sprinkle with the parsley.

Serves 4

CREAM OF CORN SOUP

2 1-pound cans corn niblets
1 10½-ounce can consommé
2 tablespoons oil
1 medium-sized onion, finely chopped
2 tablespoons flour
½ teaspoon salt
  Freshly ground pepper
2½ cups skim milk
1 teaspoon Worcestershire sauce
¼ cup dry sherry
  Chopped parsley

Drain the corn niblets and place in a blender with the consommé. Blend until smooth.

Heat the oil in a large saucepan, add the onion, and cook slowly until limp and transparent. Do not brown. Sprinkle with the flour, salt, and pepper and mix well. Stir in the liquefied corn mixture. Over low heat, add the milk slowly, stirring with a wire whisk. Add the Worcestershire sauce and simmer for 10 minutes, stirring frequently. Add the sherry and heat through. Taste and correct the seasoning. Serve hot, sprinkled with the parsley.

Serves 6

CREAM OF TOMATO SOUP

3 cups canned Italian plum tomatoes
1 teaspoon sugar
½ teaspoon salt
  Freshly ground pepper
1 14-ounce can chicken broth
½ teaspoon basil
1 small onion, chopped
1½ tablespoons flour
1½ tablespoons oil
1 13-ounce can evaporated skimmed milk
  Chopped chives

Combine the tomatoes, sugar, salt, pepper, chicken broth, basil, and onion in a large saucepan. Cook over low heat for 30 minutes, or until thickened. Break up the tomatoes with a wooden spoon during the cooking. Force the mixture through a fine strainer with the wooden spoon and return to the pot. Discard the onion and tomato seeds. Make a mixture of the flour and oil and stir into the soup over medium heat until the soup is thickened and smooth. Heat the milk in a small saucepan. To prevent the soup from curdling, remove the tomato mixture from the heat and very slowly stir in the warmed milk. Taste for seasoning and correct. Keep the soup warm but do not allow to boil. Sprinkle each portion with some of the chives.

Serves 6

CREAM OF POTATO AND LEEK SOUP

It is only my eternal striving for Truth that keeps me from classifying this as Vichyssoise. The absence of certain nameless ingredients (such as a pint and a half of heavy cream) is what holds me back—but you will never miss them. This is equally good hot or cold.

4 leeks	3 cups chicken broth
3 tablespoons oil	1 teaspoon salt
1 medium-sized onion,	White pepper
thinly sliced	2 tablespoons flour
3 medium-sized potatoes,	1 quart skim milk
peeled and sliced	Chopped chives

Trim off the roots of the leeks and cut off the top part, leaving about 2½ inches of the green part. Split them to about ⅛ inch from the root end so that you can wash out any sand that has lodged there. Slice finely the white and green parts of the leek. In a heavy cooking pot, heat the oil and cook the leeks and onion until they are transparent and begin to take on a golden color. Add the potatoes, chicken broth, salt, and pepper. Cover and cook slowly for 40 minutes.

Rub the mixture through a fine sieve or a food mill. Return the pureed mixture to the pot. Make a smooth paste with the flour and ½ cup of the milk. Add the flour mixture and remainder of the milk to the puree, stirring constantly with a wire whisk until the soup is thickened and smooth. Taste and correct the seasoning.

To be assured of a perfectly smooth, creamy soup, rub the mixture once again through a fine sieve. Keep the soup hot over low heat, but do not boil. Serve sprinkled with the chives.

Serves 6

COLD ASPARAGUS SOUP

This recipe came from Mae, who, besides being one of my favorite people, is a lady who knows her way around the kitchen. She is generally in a hurry and is highly calorie-conscious. She touches base on all counts in this soup, which can be produced with practically the speed of sound and provides an adequate lunch with no strain on either the calorie budget or the cook. In spite of the other ingredients, the predominant flavor that comes through is asparagus, which is why we have so named it.

1 15½-ounce can asparagus	2 tablespoons lemon juice
1 15½-ounce can green beans	Freshly ground pepper Dash of Tabasco
1 4-ounce can boiled onions, drained	(optional)
1 package MBT chicken broth powder	¼ cup chopped pimiento

Place in a blender the asparagus, green beans, liquid from both cans, and onions. Add the chicken broth powder, lemon juice, a few grinds of pepper, and Tabasco. Whir until liquefied. Taste for seasoning and correct. Chill in the refrigerator. To serve, sprinkle the portions with the pimiento.

Serves 6

Variations: Half a teaspoon (or more) of curry powder may be added before blending. The soup may also be topped with a dollop of plain yogurt; a sprinkling of fresh chopped chives or dill instead of the pimiento; or a few slices of mushrooms, fresh or canned.

CARROT VICHYSSOISE

According to ancient folklore, carrots were good for sick livers and were a popular item in Vichy, a spa in France whose waters were reputed to have curative powers for afflicted livers—which is the genesis of Carrots Vichy. Don't look for any connection between this and the soup under discussion. (Carrots Vichy aren't even in this chapter; you will find them under Vegetables.) And I can't promise that Carrot Vichyssoise will perform any miracles for a poorly functioning liver, but it's a fine soup on a warm day.

5 large carrots, scraped and sliced	Dash of nutmeg
1 tablespoon oil	Sprinkle of garlic powder (optional)
6 scallions or 1 medium-sized onion, chopped	⅓–½ cup skim milk
1 14-ounce can chicken broth or consommé	2 tablespoons chopped fresh chives

Cook the carrots in boiling salted water, covered, until tender. This should take about 15 minutes. Drain. In a small skillet, heat the oil and cook the scallions or onion until limp and transparent. Remove from the heat before they change color.

In the blender, place the carrots, broth or consommé, and scallions or onion and blend until liquefied. Add the nutmeg, and, if desired, the garlic powder. I haven't suggested any salt, since the broth you used may have sufficient seasoning and you don't want to overpower the delicate sweetness of the carrots, but taste the soup and decide if it needs a dash of something. Chill in the refrigerator. When ready to serve, thin the soup with the milk to the desired consistency. Sprinkle each portion with some of the chives.

Serves 4

CHILLED CUCUMBER SOUP

This rich-tasting, refreshing soup is, I think, proof that an opulent taste in food can be achieved without butter and heavy cream. The essential element in this preparation (outside of the ingredients) is the blender.

2 large cucumbers, peeled and thinly sliced	2 tablespoons oil
	1½ cups chicken broth
1½ cups skim milk	1 teaspoon salt
6 scallions, sliced	Freshly ground pepper
4 large sprigs parsley stripped from stems	Grated rind of 1 lemon
3 tablespoons flour	1 cup low-fat plain yogurt
⅓ cup celery leaves, chopped	

Combine the cucumbers, milk, scallions, parsley, flour, celery leaves, and oil in a blender. Blend until completely liquefied. Pour the soup into a large saucepan, add the chicken broth, and place over low heat, stirring constantly, until the soup is slightly thickened and heated. Do not boil. Add the salt and pepper. Chill in the refrigerator. When ready to serve, sprinkle each portion with freshly grated lemon rind and top with a dollop of the yogurt.

Serves 6

GAZPACHO

A perfect hot-weather soup of Spanish origin. In recent years the tomatoes that reach our big city markets leave something to be desired in taste, so I use a good quality California tomato juice to fortify both flavor and color. A blender simplifies the preparation of this soup, although I daresay gazpacho was made in Spain before Mr. Waring dreamed up his invention.

1 tablespoon oil	1 green pepper
2 tablespoons lemon juice	6 scallions
	1 medium-sized cucumber, peeled
2 small cloves garlic, minced	3 cups tomato juice
2 tablespoons snipped fresh dill or 1 teaspoon dried dill	½ teaspoon salt
	Freshly ground pepper
	1 teaspoon sugar
1 slice day-old bread, crumbled	1 10½-ounce can chicken broth
3 ripe red tomatoes	

Croutons
½ cucumber, cut in tiny
dice

6 scallions, finely
chopped
½ sweet red or green
pepper, cut in tiny dice

Blend together the oil, lemon juice, garlic, and dill. Add the bread and beat with a fork until fluffy. Peel, seed, and chop the tomatoes. Core the green pepper and cut up. Cut up the scallions and the cucumber. (Be cautious with the cucumber: too much can overpower the other flavors, so don't splurge with a big one.) Puree the vegetables and bread mixture through a food mill or, preferably, a blender. Add some of the tomato juice during the blending. Transfer the liquefied vegetables to a large bowl. Add the remainder of the tomato juice, salt, pepper, sugar, and chicken broth and mix well. Taste and correct the seasoning. Chill for at least 4 or 5 hours.

For the garnish, pass the croutons (see below), cucumbers, scallions, and red or green pepper, so that each guest can take what he wants to mix into the soup.

Croutons: Sauté tiny bread cubes in 2 tablespoons of oil until crisply golden on all sides. Drain on absorbent paper and dry out in a 250° oven.

Serves 6 to 8

POTAGE VERT

This soup has been a family favorite for a long time, but it presented problems when I wanted to record it for these pages, since it had no name. Squash Soup, which it is, sounds terrible, almost as bad as Green Soup, which it is also—so thank heavens for the Romance languages. This can be served hot or cold; it is delicious both ways.

1½ pounds summer
squash (about 3
medium-sized)
1 pound zucchini
(about 2
medium-sized)
1 scant cup water
1 package MBT chicken
broth powder

1–1½ cups chicken broth
Salt
Freshly ground
pepper
Garlic powder
¾ cup diced cooked
chicken

Be sure to use about a third more of yellow squash than the zucchini, which will ensure a lovely soft green color.

Wash the squashes well, leaving the skins, and remove the stem ends. Slice about 12 paper-thin slices from the ends of the zucchini and set aside for garnish. Slice the remaining squashes into ¼-inch slices and cook, covered, in a saucepan in the water seasoned with the chicken broth powder. Squashes give off a considerable amount of liquid when they cook, so use as little water as possible. When soft (about 10 minutes), put the whole business—vegetables and liquid—into the blender and blend until completely liquefied.

Transfer to a soup pot or a bowl, depending on whether you will heat or chill the soup. Add enough chicken broth to give you the consistency you want—the soup should be on the thick side, like heavy cream. Add salt, pepper, and garlic powder to taste. The amount of seasoning will depend upon the saltiness of the chicken broth, so I hesitate to be specific. To serve, either chilled or heated, add some of the diced chicken and a sprinkle of coarsely chopped zucchini slices to each portion.

Serves 6

WATERCRESS AND PEA SOUP

This soup offers a lovely medley of flavors, beginning with the pleasantly astringent and distinctive watercress taste. It may be served hot or cold. This is a must for the blender—no other way to make it.

1 bunch watercress (about 2 cups)	½ cup boiling salted water
2 cups chicken broth	Freshly ground pepper
1 10-ounce package frozen green peas	Dash of nutmeg
	⅓ cup nonfat milk solids
	White of hard-boiled egg

Wash and drain the watercress. Strip the leaves from the stems, discarding the stems. Whir through the blender with ½ cup of the chicken broth until liquefied. Place the peas in a saucepan with the ½ cup of boiling water and cook for 3 minutes, only until thawed. Whir the drained peas through the blender with ½ cup of the broth. Combine the liquefied watercress and pea puree in the saucepan, add the remainder of the broth, pepper, nutmeg, and milk solids, and heat through. The amount of salt depends upon the seasoning in the broth, so taste as you go. For cold soup, chill in the refrigerator for 4 or 5 hours.

To serve, garnish each portion with some of the hard-boiled egg white, forced through a ricer.

Serves 3 or 4

COLD QUICK BORSCHT

The bottled beet soup or borscht available in most supermarkets can be improved to make a most pleasant cold soup. With the addition of a simple ingredient it takes on a lovely creamy reddish color, refreshing to look at and to drink.

1 quart prepared beet soup	3 heaping tablespoons low-fat cottage cheese
	2 teaspoons lemon juice

Strain the beet soup, reserving the grated beets. Beat the cottage cheese with a rotary beater until it is smooth and free from lumps. Mix in the beet soup and blend well. (An electric blender does a fine job of this.) Return the grated beets to the soup, add the lemon juice, and chill.

Serves 4 or 5

7
Meats

From time to time we read of plans to raise stock on poly-unsaturated feed, thereby producing meats with a high degree of polyunsaturation. That will be a splendid thing—when it happens. But until the animals can take over the job of reducing the saturated fat in our diets, we are well advised to see to it ourselves.

Meat—particularly beef, pork, or lamb—poses one of the biggest problems for a low-fat diet because of the high proportion of saturated fat contained in most cuts. However, a combination of careful selection, proper preparation, and judicious portions can do much to deal with this.

One cannot be specific about the amount of saturated fats in various meats. It varies, depending upon the ages of the animals and what they were fed before they reached the butcher shop. Since meats don't come equipped with this kind of case history, our safest procedure is to choose the leanest cuts possible, cut off all visible fat, and cook the meat long and slowly to give the remaining fat ample opportunity to drain off. In the eating, leave all visible fat on the plate, where it is guaranteed not to affect our cholesterol level. But even all these precautions cannot eliminate the invisible fat contained within the fiber of the meat itself. It is this that limits the amount of meat we may safely eat.

Beef stands at the top of the list, not only in degree of popularity among the American public, but also, unfortunately, in the amount of saturated fat it contains. The prized black Angus can indeed be the *bête noire* of our cholesterol control program. Contrary to the usual rule about the best being none too good, less choice cuts from stock less pampered and well nourished are infinitely better for our purposes. Not for the likes of us are the roasts and steaks "richly marbled with creamy fat" extolled by food writers, or the cooking method that keeps them in the oven just long enough to remove the chill and char the outside. This may sound like a dismal prospect for rare roast beef, and indeed it is. We save our roast beef eating for occasions when we are dining out and have no choice. And, just as if I hadn't said this before, we take small portions, no seconds, and trim off the visible fat.

Veal is another matter. Since animals, like humans, tend to grow fatter as they grow older, it is easy to see why the meat from an immature animal like the calf is well suited to a low-fat dietary. It is unfortunate that there is very little of the lovely, milky-white veal around except, perhaps, in the lockers of butchers who specialize in prime meats. Unfortunately, these cuts are small comfort for people who budget. And how few of us don't! I realize it isn't very chic to talk about how much things cost, but it's hard to be chic in the face of food prices. On the other hand, the good and standard grades of veal that you are more likely to find at the neighborhood butcher or supermarket can be perfectly satisfactory with an occasional peak in quality. Try to keep a weather eye out for those peaks and take advantage of the situation when you see one.

When buying your meats, select the leanest cuts you can find. After a while, your butcher will get to know exactly what you mean by "lean." Don't be afraid that these meats will be dry and stringy when cooked. We'll make them succulent and satisfying with gravies, blended with wine, herbs, and other kitchen magic that won't outrage your arteries.

For hamburger and meat loaf, choose the leanest round steak your butcher has, and watch him while he trims it— really, really trims it—before grinding. This procedure takes hamburger out of the class of budget spreaders, but it also takes it out of the 60 to 75 percent saturated fat items.

Try to make it a rule to prepare pot roasts and stews the day before you use them—or at least the first thing in the morning. By refrigerating them for a respectable period of time, you can do a complete job of removing the crusted fat. There is an additional advantage, also, in carving roasts when cold. You can cut paper-thin slices which are more eye-filling, and consequently more satisfying, than a single thickish one. To keep meat portions within the prescribed 4- to 6-ounce limit, never hesitate to resort to harmless stratagems that help make a little look like a lot. You will find many stews and ragouts in the following pages deliberately planned to stretch limited portions of meat with large portions of vegetables and pastas.

This is to serve notice that in this volume sausages, frankfurters, salami, and most delicatessen meats will be conspicuous by their absence. It is quite possible that your cholesterol won't go shooting up like Vesuvius erupting if you succumb once in a great while, but on the other hand, with all the wonderful things in the world to eat, why waste time with the less-than-good-for-you ones? It seems to me that salamis in delicatessen store windows glare back at me with the same scorn I feel when I look at them and their pasty fat globules. And did you ever read a list of what goes into frankfurters—even the all-beef ones? It's a personal vendetta I wage, and you might do well to cultivate your own with the whole sausage family.

You may notice a discrepancy between the 4- to 6-ounce portions of meat recommended for the prudent dieter and the amounts suggested in the recipes. I have taken into account general family needs—picture serving a male teenager 4 ounces of meat! Consequently, the amounts in relation to the number of portions do not reflect ideal quantities for adults. Let your good judgment and your better self be your guide.

Dr. and Mrs. Ancel Keys, in their excellent book *Eat Well and Stay Well,* make a suggestion that I have found most helpful in limiting meat portions and that, I think, merits repeating. They recommend a filling first course such as a hearty soup or, in the Italian style, some pasta, which will satisfy the diners so that they will be content with only a small amount of meat in the course that follows. "Make the accompanying items of food as tasty as possible, offer them in generous amount," they tell us, "and the meat consumption will decrease."

BEEF

BEEF STEW

4 tablespoons oil
4 large onions
1 teaspoon salt
Freshly ground pepper
1 teaspoon sweet paprika
½ cup flour
2½ pounds chuck, well trimmed of fat and cut into 1-inch cubes
1 10½-ounce can consommé
Boiling water
1 teaspoon Bovril
1 small white turnip, scraped and cut into cubes
1 carrot, coarsely grated

3 celery stalks with leaves
1 bay leaf
10–12 small white onions, peeled and left whole
8 medium-sized carrots, scraped and cut into quarters, lengthwise
10–12 small new potatoes, peeled, or 3 or 4 old ones cut into 1-inch cubes
¼ cup chopped parsley
Flour (if needed to thicken gravy)

In a large, heavy kettle or Dutch oven, heat the oil. Peel two of the large onions, chop them coarsely, and brown in the oil. Remove them with a slotted spoon and set aside. On a square of waxed paper, combine the salt, pepper, paprika, and flour. Coat the meat cubes in the seasoned flour. Brown them in the hot oil and remove them as they are done to make room for the others. If they are too crowded in the pan, you won't be able to brown them evenly. Add more oil if the pan seems to be drying out. When all the meat cubes have been browned, pour off and discard any oil that remains in the kettle.

Return the meat cubes to the kettle with the cooked onions. Add the consommé and enough boiling water to cover the meat. Stir in the Bovril. Slice the remaining 2 large onions and add along with the turnip, grated carrot, celery, and bay leaf. Simmer over low heat, uncovered, for 1 hour.

Add the small white onions, quartered carrots, and potatoes. Continue simmering for another 35 to 45 minutes, by which time both meat and vegetables should be completely tender. If there isn't enough gravy to cover the stew, add additional consommé or water and let it cook down into the stew. Taste for seasonings and add whatever you think it needs. Discard the celery and bay leaf. Stir in the parsley.

Generally the flour used to coat the meat cubes is sufficient to thicken the gravy. The grated carrot also helps, but if the gravy seems a bit thin, make a smooth paste of a little of the gravy mixed with a tablespoon of flour and stir it into the pot.

Cool the stew and refrigerate overnight. When ready to serve, remove the fat and reheat the stew.

Serves 5 or 6

POT ROAST

This delicious pot roast is as basic in the annals of good eating as simple addition in the field of mathematics. One is not likely to improve on a lean cut of meat, thinly sliced, accompanied by vegetables bathed in a rich gravy.

2 tablespoons oil	2 carrots, coarsely grated
1 4- 5-pound beef roast (top, bottom, or eye round)	2 stalks celery, grated
	4 onions, chopped
	12 small white onions, peeled
2 cups consommé	8 whole carrots, peeled
1 clove garlic, minced	6 medium-sized potatoes, peeled
1 teaspoon salt	
Freshly ground pepper	
Bay leaf	

After you have chosen the leanest pot roast your butcher has to offer, ask him to omit the usual strip of suet. This may outrage him but be firm.

Heat the oil in a heavy kettle or a Dutch oven on the top of the stove. Sear the meat on all sides, turning as needed to ensure even browning on all surfaces.

Remove the meat from the kettle, pour off and discard any fat that has collected, and wipe the kettle dry with a paper towel. Replace the meat in the kettle and add the consommé, garlic, salt, pepper, bay leaf, grated carrot and celery, and chopped onions. Cover the pot and simmer slowly for 2 hours. You will find that the grated vegetables will make a thick, rich gravy that generally requires no thickening.

Add the whole onions, carrots, and potatoes and taste for seasoning. (You might try a pinch of sugar and perhaps some additional garlic powder.) Continue simmering until the meat is fork-tender and the vegetables are done (about an hour).

Refrigerate overnight with the gravy in a separate container. When ready to serve, remove the fat from the gravy. Slice the meat into thin slices and place in a kettle or a large skillet. Cover with the gravy and vegetables. Cover the skillet and place over low heat until the meat and vegetables are thoroughly heated. Transfer to a warm platter. Cover the meat with some of the gravy and serve the remainder in a gravy boat.

Serves 8 generously

BOEUF BOURGUIGNON

Boeuf Bourguignon, Beef in Burgundy, Beef Stew in Wine—none of these names begins to do justice to the fabulous fragrance this dish emits while cooking, and the smell is more than matched by the taste. Doubled in quantity, it's a favorite for buffets or for an informal gathering.

2½	pounds lean, trimmed beef (chuck or boneless sirloin)	3	medium-sized onions, coarsely chopped
6	tablespoons oil	1	carrot, coarsely grated
2	tablespoons flour		
1½	cups dry red wine	1	clove garlic, minced
1	teaspoon salt		
	Freshly ground pepper	4–5	shallots, sliced
½	teaspoon sugar	½	teaspoon thyme
1	teaspoon Bovril	1	bay leaf

| 1 | cup (or more) water or consommé (part of this may be Madeira wine) | 1½ | ounces brandy |

Garnish

| 2 | tablespoons oil | 1 | tablespoon lemon juice |
| ½ | pound mushrooms, sliced | 2 | tablespoons chopped parsley |

Cut the meat into 1½-inch cubes, trimming every bit of fat. Heat 4 tablespoons of the oil in a large, heavy kettle, such as a Dutch oven. Add the beef and brown well, turning each piece of meat. Don't try to do them all at once, or you won't be able to brown them evenly. Remove the pieces of meat as they are browned with a slotted spoon and set aside.

Brown the flour in the kettle over high heat, stirring to keep it smooth. Reduce the heat and slowly add the red wine, stirring with a wire whisk until the sauce is smooth and thickened. Stir in the salt, pepper, sugar, and Bovril.

In a good-sized skillet, heat the remaining 2 tablespoons of oil and cook the onions until they are transparent. Add the carrot, garlic, and shallots and cook 3 to 5 minutes longer, stirring all the while, until the vegetables are slightly brown. Add these to the large kettle along with the meat cubes, thyme, and bay leaf. Add the water or consommé (with wine if possible) to barely cover the meat.

Cover the pot and simmer slowly for 2 to 3 hours, or until the meat is deliciously tender. Half an hour before serving, add the brandy.

Shortly before serving, prepare the garnish. Heat the oil in a small skillet and cook the mushrooms for 5 minutes. Turn them a few times. Sprinkle with the lemon juice and heat through.

To serve, transfer the meat and sauce to a heated bowl. Garnish with the parsley and a border of the mushrooms. Or serve in a casserole—an earthenware one, if you have it (just to make it look as authentic as it tastes).

Serve with boiled or steamed tiny new potatoes or broad noodles.

Serves 6

ROAST FILLET OF BEEF BORDELAISE

Fillet of beef is a reasonably lean cut compared with a marbled sirloin or porterhouse, but butchers generally make up for the lack of fat by wrapping an overcoat of suet around the meat. Their reason is that the fat protects the meat from drying out and keeps it juicy. True. It also does a few other things along the way that we needn't go into. So stand firm on the omission of the overcoat. The delicious wine sauce served with the beef will amply compensate for the hard white stuff.

Oil
1 2- 2½-pound fillet of beef, trimmed of fat

Salt
Freshly ground pepper

Sauce Bordelaise

1 tablespoon oil
3 shallots, finely chopped
1 tablespoon flour
1 cup consommé

1 cup dry red wine
½ teaspoon Bovril
½ cup mushrooms, sliced
1 tablespoon oil
1 teaspoon lemon juice

Heat ⅛ inch of oil in a skillet with a heatproof handle. Sear the meat quickly on all sides. Sprinkle with salt and freshly ground pepper and place the skillet in a preheated 450° oven. Bake 25 to 35 minutes, depending upon the degree of doneness you want. (120° to 125° on a meat thermometer yields rare beef; 140° yields medium rare to medium.) Baste a few times.

While the fillet is in the oven, prepare the sauce. In a medium-sized saucepan, heat 1 tablespoon of oil and sauté the shallots until golden brown, stirring often. Blend in the flour. Slowly add the consommé, wine, and Bovril and stir over medium heat with a wire whisk until the sauce comes to a boil. Boil until reduced by a third.

In a small skillet, cook the mushrooms in 1 tablespoon of oil for 5 minutes and add the lemon juice. Mix the mushrooms into the sauce. Taste for seasoning and adjust. Keep the sauce warm over low heat until ready to use.

After the roast is done, add the pan juices from the steak to the wine sauce. Slice the fillet thin and pour the sauce over the meat. Braised celery and grilled tomato halves go nicely with this.

Serves 4 to 6

BROILED FLANK STEAK

Flank steak is another desirable cut for low-fat dieters. It is leaner than most steaks, can be easily trimmed, and must be carved in thin slices, which means smaller portions. Do opt for prime meat, if possible, because an inferior grade can be tough.

1 1½- 2-pound flank steak	⅓ cup chili sauce
1 tablespoon Dijon mustard	1 tablespoon Worcestershire sauce
	1 teaspoon lemon juice

Trim all visible fat from both sides of the steak. Sometimes one end of the steak has considerable fat; don't hesitate to lop it off. Blend together the mustard, chili and Worcestershire sauces, and lemon juice. Spread on both sides of the steak and marinate for a few hours.

Preheat the broiler to very hot. Place the steak about 4 inches from the heat and broil each side for 5 or 6 minutes. Don't overcook. It should be a little pink in the middle.

The way you carve a flank steak is important. Place the meat on a wooden carving board. With a very sharp knife, cut it across the grain at an angle—almost horizontally, not up and down—in thin slices. Pour the pan juices over it. If the steak has cooled during the carving, place it in a warm oven for a few minutes. A baked potato topped with a blob of low-fat plain yogurt and sprinkled with chopped chives goes nicely with this.

Serves 4 to 6

ORIENTAL PEPPER STEAK

1 1½-pound flank steak	1 clove garlic, minced
2 green peppers	1–2 tablespoons soy sauce
2 large tomatoes	Freshly ground pepper
2 onions	½ teaspoon powdered ginger
1 1-pound can bean sprouts or ½ pound fresh bean sprouts	½ teaspoon sugar
2 tablespoons cornstarch	1 cup consommé
½ cup cold water	2 tablespoons dry sherry
2 tablespoons oil	

Once all the ingredients are prepared the cooking goes quickly, so start by having everything ready. Trim all visible fat from both sides of the steak. Cut the steak across the grain into very thin slices, as described in the preceding recipe. (You could also use lean boneless sirloin or round steak, thinly sliced.) Remove the green pepper cores and cut the peppers into ¼-inch strips. Peel the tomatoes by plunging them into boiling water for a minute and slipping off the skins. Cut the tomatoes into bite-sized chunks. Chop the onions. If fresh bean sprouts are used, just wash and drain; if canned, drain and rinse in cold water. Soaking them in cold water for a few hours will make them crisper. Make a solution of the cornstarch and water.

In a large skillet or Chinese wok, heat the oil with the garlic. Add the meat strips and brown them quickly. This should take less than a minute. Add soy sauce (1 or 2 tablespoons depending upon the saltiness of the sauce), a few grinds of black pepper, ginger, and sugar and stir. Add the green pepper strips, tomatoes, bean sprouts, and consommé. Cover and cook 3 minutes. Add the cornstarch solution to the steak mixture and stir with a wire whisk until the sauce is thickened and smooth. Add the sherry and heat through. Do not overcook; the vegetables should be crisp and underdone. Serve with boiled rice.

Serves 4 to 6

MARINATED FLANK STEAK

Some unlikely ingredients blend together into a pleasing, piquant, and interesting flavor.

1 2- 2½-pound flank steak	1 small onion, chopped
3 tablespoons red wine vinegar	2 tablespoons chutney, chopped
1–2 tablespoons soy sauce	1 clove garlic, sliced
⅓ cup oil	1 tablespoon parsley, minced

Trim the steak of all visible fat. In a shallow porcelain or glass baking dish, combine the remaining ingredients.

Mix well and marinate the steak at least 3 hours—longer, if possible. Turn it from time to time.

Preheat the broiler. Remove the steak from the marinade, arrange on a broiler pan, and dribble a little of the marinade over the steak. Place 4 inches from the heat and broil for 5 minutes. Turn the meat with kitchen tongs, dribble a bit more marinade over the top, and broil another 5 minutes. Carve against the grain on a slant into very thin slices. If the meat cools during the carving, place in the warmed oven for a couple of minutes.

Serves 6

BEEF ORIENTAL

Very thin slices of lean sirloin or round steak give a good account of themselves in this simple preparation.

1½	pounds sirloin or round steak, sliced ⅛ inch thick	½	pound mushrooms, sliced
¼	cup flour	1½	cups consommé
½	teaspoon salt Freshly ground pepper	1	clove garlic, minced
		1	tablespoon cornstarch
3	tablespoons oil	2	tablespoons cold water
1	large onion, chopped	1	tablespoon soy sauce

Trim all fat from the meat and cut the meat into 2½-inch squares. On a square of waxed paper, combine the flour, salt, and pepper. Dredge the meat in the seasoned flour. Heat the oil in a heavy skillet and brown the meat on both sides over high heat, then remove it and set aside. Reduce the heat, add the onion and mushrooms, and cook gently until the onion becomes limp (about 5 minutes). Pour off any excess fat in the pan and add the consommé, mixing well to pick up any crusty particles on the bottom of the pan. Return the meat, add the garlic, and cook over low heat, covered, for another 5 to 10 minutes, or until the meat is tender. Blend the cornstarch with the cold water and add along with the soy sauce. Cook over low heat, stirring with a wire whisk, until the sauce is thickened and smooth. Taste for seasonings and correct. Serve at once with hot rice.

Serves 4 or 5

BEEF CURRY

2	pounds top round or boneless sirloin, sliced a scant ½ inch thick	1	clove garlic, minced
½	cup flour	2	teaspoons curry powder
½	teaspoon salt Freshly ground pepper	½	teaspoon dry mustard
3	tablespoons oil	½	pound mushrooms, sliced
2	medium-sized onions, thinly sliced	½	cup seedless raisins
1	cup consommé	1	large apple, peeled and cut into chunks
1	cup water	½	cup water chestnuts, sliced

Trim the meat and cut into 1-inch squares. On a square of waxed paper, combine the flour, salt, and pepper. Dredge the meat pieces in the seasoned flour. In a large, heavy kettle or Dutch oven, heat the oil and brown the meat well on all sides. Do just one layer of meat at a time and remove the browned pieces with a slotted spoon and set aside. When all the meat is browned, cook the onions in the pot until golden, then remove and set aside. Pour off any fat that remains in the pot. Put the consommé and water in the pot and stir well to loosen any crusty particles at the bottom. Add the garlic, curry powder, mustard, meat, and onions and mix well. Reduce the heat, cover the pot, and cook until the meat is tender (about 40 to 50 minutes). If you are making this ahead of time, this would be a good point at which to stop, since the completion of the dish takes only about 10 minutes and the meat can be refrigerated until the dinner hour.

Add the mushrooms, raisins, apple, and water chestnuts and cook another 10 minutes. Taste for seasonings and correct. Serve with hot cooked rice and a selection of accompaniments such as chutney, chopped cucumber, pickled onions, and chopped peanuts.

Serves 6 to 8

SWEET-AND-SOUR MEATBALLS

In addition to performing well as a main course, these good-tasting little meatballs can be served as an hors d'oeuvre. They also make a splendid addition to a buffet (or a fine cold nibble, except that rarely are any left).

Sauce

½ pound brown sugar
½ cup raisins
3 8-ounce cans tomato
sauce

1 1-pound-4-ounce can
pineapple chunks in
pineapple juice,
drained (reserve ½ cup
juice)

Meatballs

2½ pounds well-trimmed
round steak, ground
5 slices white bread,
crusts removed
½ cup skim milk
¼ cup bread crumbs
1 small Bermuda
onion, grated

2 cloves garlic,
crushed
2 tablespoons brown
sugar
1 teaspoon salt
Freshly ground
pepper
3 tablespoons oil

It is best to begin by making the sauce, since it has to
cook for a long time, during which you can prepare the
meatballs. In a good-sized kettle, combine the brown
sugar, raisins, tomato sauce, pineapple chunks, and ½ cup
of pineapple juice. Simmer slowly for 1 to 1½ hours, until
the sauce cooks down and thickens.

Place the meat in a large bowl. With a fork, beat the
bread and milk together until fluffy and add to the meat.
Add the bread crumbs, onion, garlic, brown sugar, salt,
and pepper and work with your hands until the meat is
smooth and light. Form into small balls about the size of a
walnut. Dip your hands into cold water from time to time
to avoid sticking as you form the balls between your
palms. Chill the meatballs in the refrigerator for half an
hour or so before cooking. In a heavy skillet, heat the oil
and brown the meatballs. Don't crowd them; you will
need room to turn them so they will be brown on all
sides.

Add the browned meatballs to the sauce and simmer,
covered, over very low heat for 1 hour.

Serves 12

SWEDISH MEATBALLS

As with the preceding recipe, these can be served as a
chafing dish hors d'oeuvre or a main course, or on occasions when you want just fork food.

1 pound lean veal, ground	1 teaspoon salt
	1 clove garlic, minced
½ pound lean round steak, ground	1 small onion, grated
	Freshly ground pepper
3 slices white bread, crusts removed	¼ teaspoon nutmeg
	1 carrot, finely grated
⅓ cup skim milk	3 tablespoons oil

Sauce

2 tablespoons flour	1 teaspoon Kitchen Bouquet
½ teaspoon salt	
Freshly ground pepper	1 teaspoon dried dill or 1 tablespoon fresh snipped dill
2 cups skim milk	

In a good-sized bowl, mix together the veal and beef. With a fork, beat the bread and milk together until fluffy and add to the meat. Add the salt, garlic, onion, pepper, nutmeg, and carrot. Beat well and work with your hands until the meat mixture is smooth and light. Form into small balls, about 1 inch. They can be made a little larger if you are using them as a main course instead of an hors d'oeuvre. Dip your hands frequently into cold water to avoid sticking as you form the balls between your palms. Chill in the refrigerator for half an hour or so before cooking.

Heat the oil in a large, heavy skillet and brown the meatballs evenly. Don't crowd them in the skillet. Remove them with a slotted spoon as they are browned and set aside.

Use the oil remaining in the skillet for the sauce. You need about 1½ tablespoons, so add a little if there doesn't seem to be enough. Scrape up whatever little crusts there are on the bottom of the pan—they will do the sauce nothing but good. Blend in the flour, salt, and pepper, stir well, and add the milk slowly, stirring with a wire whisk, until the sauce becomes thickened and smooth. Add the Kitchen Bouquet and dill and cook over low heat a minute longer. Return the meatballs to the sauce and simmer, covered, over low heat 30 minutes longer. Taste and correct the seasoning.

Serves 10 to 12 as hors d'oeuvre;
6 to 8 as main course

MEAT LOAF WITH MUSHROOM SAUCE

What is more reassuring than a meat loaf in the refrigerator over a weekend? It is splendid cold, also, with a tossed salad or a bowl of coleslaw.

1 pound lean round steak, ground
1 pound lean veal, ground
1 teaspoon salt
  Freshly ground pepper
3 slices white bread, crusts removed

½ cup skim milk
1 large onion, grated
2 tablespoons Worcestershire sauce
3 tablespoons chili sauce
1 clove garlic, minced
1 teaspoon dry mustard

Combine the meats, salt, and pepper. With a fork, mix the bread and milk until fluffy and add, then mix in the remaining ingredients. Beat well and work with your hands until the meat mixture is smooth and light. Oil a flat baking dish and pat the meat into a loaf shape. Bake for 50 minutes to an hour in a preheated 375° oven. Transfer to a warm serving platter and cover with Mushroom Sauce (below). For a different presentation, the meat may be packed in an oiled ring mold and unmolded on a baking pan before being cooked.

Mushroom Sauce

4 tablespoons oil
4 tablespoons flour
2 cups skim milk
½ teaspoon salt
1 teaspoon paprika
1 small clove garlic, crushed

1 package MBT chicken broth powder, dissolved in ½ cup hot water
½ pound mushrooms, thinly sliced

Heat 2 tablespoons of the oil in a small saucepan. Blend in the flour and stir until it bubbles. Slowly add the milk, stirring with a wire whisk until the mixture thickens and becomes smooth. Sir in the salt, paprika, garlic, and dissolved broth powder. Reduce the heat and cook a minute longer. Remove from the heat.

In a small saucepan, heat the remaining 2 tablespoons of oil and sauté the sliced mushrooms for 5 minutes. Add the mushrooms to the sauce and mix. Taste and correct the seasoning. Keep the sauce hot over just-simmering water. If it gets too thick, thin it out with a little water or consommé.

Serves 6 to 8

SWEET-AND-SOUR STUFFED CABBAGE

Recipes for stuffed cabbage are as numerous and varied as seashells in the Great Barrier Reef. People compete with each other in their claims for the excellence of their particular formulas. So please understand that it is in all humility that I concede this is positively the best, as attested to by sweet-and-sour-stuffed-cabbage experts. The fact that it was my mother's does not prejudice my opinion. If you have time, I suggest that you double the recipe and freeze the other half.

1 large head cabbage	½ cup orange juice
1 pound lean round steak, ground	1 10½-ounce can consommé
1 pound lean veal, ground	12 uncooked prunes
¾ cup cooked rice	¼ cup raisins
1 onion, grated	Salt, pepper, and paprika to taste
¾ cup bread crumbs	2 cups tomato sauce
¾ cup cold water	2 tablespoons (or more) lemon juice
1 teaspoon salt	
Freshly ground pepper	2 tablespoons brown sugar
1 medium-sized onion, cut up	Gingersnaps, crumbled (optional)
1 No. 2 can apricot halves	

Cut out the cabbage core, place the cabbage in a kettle, cover with boiling water, and cook gently, covered, for about 5 minutes, or until the leaves are flexible enough to handle. You may want to keep the water simmering in the pot since sometimes, if the cabbage is tough, the inner leaves need an additional few minutes of immersion.

While the cabbage is softening, combine the meats, rice, grated onion, bread crumbs, water, salt, and pepper and mix well. Work with your hands until the meat is spongy and light.

Cut out the tough part of the veins at the bottom of the cabbage leaves. Place a mound of the meat mixture about the size of an egg on each leaf. Roll and fasten with toothpicks. Place the cabbage rolls in a large covered kettle with the cut-up onion. Add the apricots and juice, orange juice, consommé, prunes, and raisins. Season with salt, pepper, and paprika to taste. Let come to a boil, then add just enough water to barely come within an inch of the top of the cabbage rolls. Cook slowly, uncovered, for 1 hour. Add the tomato sauce, lemon juice, and brown sugar. Taste and add more of whatever you think it needs. Simmer slowly for 2 hours, covered.

Remove the cabbage rolls from the kettle and place in a roaster pan, cover with some of the sauce, tuck the fruits among them, and bake in a 300° oven for 1 hour, until glazed and golden brown.

If the remainder of the sauce seems thin, thicken with crumbled gingersnaps. When ready to serve, remove the cabbage rolls to a large heated platter and cover with the sauce. Serve extra sauce in a gravy boat.

Serves 8 generously

BRAISED SWISS STEAK

1 3-inch-thick slice of bottom round steak (about 3 pounds)	½ teaspoon salt
	Freshly ground pepper
1 clove garlic, peeled	4 tablespoons oil
½ cup flour	2 cups sliced onions
1 teaspoon dry mustard	1 cup consommé

Trim all fat from the steak. Rub both sides of the meat with the garlic. Mix together the flour, mustard, salt, and pepper. With the edge of a saucer or a meat mallet, beat the seasoned flour into the steak until all is absorbed. In a heavy skillet, heat the oil and brown the steak well on both sides. Transfer the steak to an ovenproof casserole. Using the same skillet in which you browned the steak, cook the onions until transparent and limp. Add the consommé and mix well, scraping the bottom of the pan to loosen the browned particles. Bring to a simmer and pour the mixture over the top of the steak. Cover the casserole and bake in a slow oven (325°) for 1½ to 2 hours, or until completely tender.

Serves 6 to 8

GLAZED CORNED BEEF AND CABBAGE

The corned beef at the corner delicatessen is not on our recommended list because it is generally wreathed in fat. However, careful selection of the meat and proper cooking can provide an acceptable corned-beef-and-cabbage feast for the aficionados of this hearty fare. Select only a first-cut corned brisket of beef—the second cut contains a layer of fat that is impossible to deal with. And when you get your nice streamlined first cut into your kitchen, trim the fat top and bottom.

1 first-cut corned brisket of beef, about 4 pounds, well-trimmed	1 medium-sized head of cabbage
Boiling water	6–7 medium-sized potatoes
2 onions, sliced	6–7 large carrots

Glaze

2 tablespoons oil	3 tablespoons vinegar
5 tablespoons catsup	⅓ cup brown sugar
1 tablespoon Dijon mustard	Pinch ground cloves

Place the meat in a large kettle and fill with boiling water, enough to completely cover the meat. Add the onions. Simmer slowly, covered, until the meat is tender. Figure the cooking time from 50 minutes to 1 hour per pound. While the meat is cooking, prepare the glaze. In a small saucepan, combine the oil, catsup, mustard, vinegar, brown sugar, and cloves and bring to a boil. Reduce the heat and simmer for a minute or two. When the meat is done, remove it, reserving the liquid in the kettle, and place in a lightly oiled shallow roasting pan. Pour the glaze over the top. Bake uncovered in a preheated 350° oven for 30 to 40 minutes, or until glazed and brown.

While the meat is in the oven, cut the cabbage into 4 or 5 sections and remove the core. Peel the potatoes and cut in half. Scrape the carrots and cut in half. Cook all the vegetables in the large kettle with the corned beef stock. The potatoes will take about 20 minutes, the carrots about 15, and the cabbage about 10, so add them to the stock in that order.

To serve, carve the corned beef into thin slices, place on a warmed platter, and surround with the cabbage, potatoes, and carrots.

Serves 6 to 8

LAMB

BROILED LEG OF LAMB

This may well turn out to be your favorite method of preparing leg of lamb. The meat is butterflied; that is, removed from the bone and flattened. It is then broiled for just 30 minutes. This method of cooking has many advantages, not the least of which is the huge amount of fat that is removed while the meat is still uncooked. This is fat that would normally melt into the meat while roasting (and then into you). Also, the varying thicknesses of the meat provide portions that are rare, medium, and well done, thus suiting a variety of preferences. Then there are the ease of preparation and the opportunity for split-second timing. I don't put the meat into the oven until my guests or family are assembled, so there is no tension about kitchen damage caused by latecomers. And perhaps I should have placed this last at the top of the list—the delicious taste. Even people who don't like lamb love this.

Most butchers, including those in supermarkets, are cooperative about boning a leg of lamb, and I hope yours is too. (It looks so easy when they do it and the once I tried was a disaster.) When the butcher gets through trimming it, you will take over from where he left off.

6- 7-pound leg of lamb, boned and trimmed of all fat

Marinade

1 cup oil
4 tablespoons lemon
  juice
1 teaspoon salt
½ teaspoon freshly
  ground black pepper
2 tablespoons parsley,
  chopped

1 teaspoon oregano
½ teaspoon basil
2 bay leaves, crumbled
3 onions, thinly sliced
3 cloves garlic, sliced
  Seasoned salt

Spread the leg of lamb flat and trim every bit of fat and sinew on both sides. The piece of meat may look a bit untidy when you finish, but not to worry. It will pull itself together nicely during the cooking.

In a large, shallow enamel or glass dish, combine all the marinade ingredients except the seasoned salt and mix thoroughly. Marinate the meat in this mixture overnight, turning it a number of times. Refrigerate if the kitchen is warm, but be sure to have the meat at room temperature when you are ready to cook it.

The broiling will take only 30 minutes—never any longer. Preheat the broiler for 15 minutes. Place the meat on the broiler rack and sprinkle it lightly with seasoned salt such as Lawry's and a little of the marinade. Forget the onions; they will just turn black and add nothing aesthetically or otherwise. Place the broiler rack about 4 to 5 inches below the heat and broil for 15 minutes.

Turn the meat with kitchen tongs, and again use a little of the marinade and a light sprinkle of seasoned salt. Broil for an additional 10 or 12 minutes. A slight cut in the thickest part of the meat will show if it has reached the proper shade of pink or needs an additional 2 or 3 minutes under the heat.

When done, remove immediately and slice against the grain in ¼-inch slices. Arrange on a warmed platter garnished with watercress. As an extra bonus, I often garnish the platter with canned pear halves that have been stained a pleasant shade of green by marinating in crème de menthe for a few hours.

Serves 8

LAMB CURRY

2 pounds lamb from
leg, well trimmed and
cut into 1-inch cubes
1 teaspoon salt
Freshly ground pepper
2 tablespoons oil
(more if needed)
1 cup chicken broth
2 cups water
1 celery stalk with
leaves
1 bay leaf
3 medium-sized onions,
chopped
2 large stalks celery,
sliced crosswise into
½-inch slices

4 tablespoons flour
½ teaspoon powdered
ginger
2 teaspoons curry
powder
¼ cup white raisins
1 red apple, skin left on,
cut into small chunks
2 tablespoons lemon
juice
4 cups hot cooked rice
½ pound mushrooms,
sliced and sautéed in
oil
Minced parsley

Sprinkle the lamb with the salt and pepper. In a large, heavy skillet or a Dutch oven, heat 2 tablespoons of oil and brown the meat, one layer at a time, turning to brown on all sides. Transfer to a large saucepan. Add the chicken broth, water, celery stalk, and bay leaf and simmer over low heat for 50 minutes, or until the meat is almost tender. Skim the broth as needed. Strain the stock and if you have more than 2½ cups, boil rapidly to reduce it to that amount.

While the meat is simmering, add the onions and sliced celery to the skillet in which you browned the meat and cook until the onions are limp and golden. Add more oil if needed. Sprinkle with the flour and stir until the flour turns light brown. Add the ginger and the curry powder to taste—curry powders vary in strength as do preferences, so you will have to decide how much (it's better to be gentle; you can add more later). Slowly stir in the 2½ cups of stock. Stir with a wire whisk until the sauce becomes thickened and smooth. Add the meat, raisins, apple, and lemon juice. Taste for seasoning and correct. Simmer for 25 minutes longer or until the meat is completely tender.

Pack the rice in an oiled ring mold and unmold on a warm platter. Fill the center of the ring with the mushrooms, sprinkle with the parsley, and surround the rice ring with the lamb curry. Serve with chutney.

Serves 4 or 5

SWEDISH LAMB IN DILL SAUCE

Do try to use fresh dill when you make this. The dried dill will do in a pinch, but not as well as the fresh.

3 pounds lamb from leg, well trimmed and cut into 3-inch cubes (also extra lamb bones, if possible)
4 cups (or more) of water
1 teaspoon salt
2 carrots, scraped and sliced
1 stalk celery with leaves
1 bay leaf
10 peppercorns, bruised
1 clove garlic, crushed

3 sprigs fresh dill or 1 teaspoon dried dill
12 small white onions, left whole and peeled
3 tablespoons oil
3 tablespoons flour
2 tablespoons white vinegar
½ teaspoon sugar
Freshly ground pepper
3 tablespoons snipped fresh dill or 2 teaspoons dried dill

In a large kettle or a Dutch oven place the lamb (and bones) with the water—enough to cover the meat. Add the salt, carrots, celery, bay leaf, peppercorns, garlic, and dill sprigs (or dried dill). Cover partly, bring to a boil, reduce the heat, and simmer until the lamb is tender (1 hour or more). Skim the surface as needed. After cooking ½ hour, add the onions. When the meat is done—the best way to determine this is simply by tasting it—remove the meat and onions from the pot with a slotted spoon and set aside. Strain the stock through a double thickness of cheesecloth, return it to the kettle, and boil over moderately high heat until it is reduced to about 3 cups. It is desirable to refrigerate this stock for a few hours and remove the fat before finishing the preparation.

Heat the oil in a large skillet or saucepan. Blend in the flour and stir in the skimmed broth, mixing with a wire whisk until the sauce is thickened and smooth. Add the vinegar, sugar, pepper, and snipped fresh dill (or dried dill) and cook over low heat for 5 minutes longer. Taste for seasoning and correct.

Add the meat and onions to the sauce and heat thoroughly. Serve with boiled rice or broad noodles.

Serves 6 or more

LAMB AND EGGPLANT

1 teaspoon salt
2 medium-sized eggplants, peeled and cut into 1-inch cubes
2 tablespoons oil (or more)
2 medium-sized onions, thinly sliced
2 pounds lamb from leg, well trimmed and cut into 1-inch cubes

1 cup chicken broth
1 1-pound can whole tomatoes, well drained
½ cup dry white wine
    Salt and freshly ground pepper
1 clove garlic, peeled and left whole
1 tablespoon flour
2 tablespoons water
    Chopped parsley

Sprinkle the salt over the eggplant and set aside while you prepare the sauce and meat. In a heavy skillet, heat the 2 tablespoons of oil and cook the onions over moderate heat until they are transparent and ever so lightly browned (about 10 to 12 minutes). With a slotted spoon remove them and place them in a Dutch oven or a casserole. Add oil to the skillet if you need it, increase the heat, and quickly brown the lamb. Don't overcrowd—do just one layer at a time, turning it to brown evenly. Add the meat to the onions in the casserole. Pour off any fat remaining in the skillet. Add the chicken broth, stirring well to dissolve the crusty particles at the bottom of the pan. Add the tomatoes and bring to a boil. Remove from the heat and add the wine and salt and pepper to taste. Pour the mixture over the meat in the casserole and bring to a boil. Reduce the heat, cover, and simmer for 45 minutes.

After the eggplant has rested for the 45 minutes, drain well and add to the lamb with the garlic on a toothpick, so you won't lose it. Cook over low heat for 30 to 40 minutes longer, or until the lamb is tender. Before serving, remove the garlic and thicken the sauce by dissolving the flour in the water and stirring it in. Taste again for seasoning. Sprinkle the top with the parsley and serve in a casserole.

Serves 5 or 6

SHASHLIK

Skewered lamb is an easy company dish, for it can be readied well in advance and takes a minimum of fussing at the last minute.

3 pounds lamb from leg	1 teaspoon oregano
1 medium-sized onion, grated	2 tablespoons chopped parsley
3 tablespoons lemon juice	⅔ cup oil
1 clove garlic, minced	8 large white mushroom caps
1 teaspoon salt	3 firm tomatoes
Freshly ground pepper	

Trim all fat and gristle from the meat and cut into 1½-inch cubes. In a large glass bowl combine the onion, lemon juice, garlic, salt, pepper, oregano, parsley, and oil. Mix well and add the meat. Marinate for a few hours, or preferably overnight. If the kitchen isn't too warm, marinate at room temperature, but for an overnight procedure you will want to refrigerate it. Turn the meat from time to time.

When you are ready to cook, wash and dry the mushroom caps and quarter the tomatoes. Preheat the broiler 10 to 15 minutes so it will be very hot. Place the meat on skewers with pieces of tomato and a mushroom on each. Place the skewers on a heated broiling pan and pour some of the marinade over them with an extra dash of seasoned salt. Broil 3 to 4 inches from the heat and turn once to brown the meat on both sides. The meat will cook in 12 to 15 minutes—don't overcook it. Serve with pilaf or kasha.

Serves 6 to 8

PORK

By its very nature, pork may not seem an ideal choice for a diet pattern concerned with lowering fat intake, but here too the rule of careful selection and moderation in size of portions prevails. Thorough trimming and proper cooking can give pork status enjoyed by beef or lamb in our weekly meal planning. Obviously, spareribs and fatty chops have no place in our kitchens, but there are some cuts of pork that in small portions can safely add variety to our daily bread.

CANADIAN BACON IN WINE SAUCE

1	pound Canadian bacon, sliced	Pinch of dried thyme
1½	tablespoons oil	Pinch of dried basil
1½	tablespoons flour	2 tablespoons dry sherry
1	10½-ounce can consommé	

Heat a heavy skillet and cook the Canadian bacon for about 5 minutes, turning it often. The fat, when done, is a light golden brown, different in color from the lean meat, which is a reddish brown. Remove the fat portions and discard.

For the sauce, heat the oil in a small saucepan. Blend in the flour and cook slowly until brown. Add the consommé and stir with a wire whisk until thickened and smooth. Add the thyme and basil and simmer for 15 minutes over low heat. Strain through a fine wire strainer and add the sherry. Pour over the bacon.

Serves 3 or 4

HAM SLICE WITH PINEAPPLE

1	center slice of lean, smoked ham ½ inch thick (about 1 pound) Oil	2 teaspoons brown sugar
2	slices drained canned pineapple	¼ teaspoon cinnamon
		⅓ cup pineapple juice

Lightly oil the bottom of a heavy skillet that has a cover and place over low heat. Thoroughly trim all fat from the ham, then increase the heat under the pan and sear the meat on both sides. Remove the ham and wipe the pan with a paper towel. Replace the ham in the pan with just enough oil to keep it from sticking. Cover the meat with the pineapple, sprinkle with the brown sugar and cinnamon, and add the pineapple juice. Cover the pan and simmer for 10 minutes. It should be nearly done in this time, but different varieties of ham require different cooking times, so you must be the judge. For the last 3 or 4 minutes, uncover and baste with the juice a few times.

Serves 2 or 3

HAM SLICE WITH ORANGES

In this fruit-and-ham preparation the ham slice is baked. An accompanying macaroni casserole and a tossed salad of crisp greens provide a satisfying dinner.

1 large lean ham slice, about 2 inches thick	1 large navel orange, peel left on, sliced
Orange juice	1½ tablespoons sugar
	½ teaspoon cinnamon

Trim the fat from the ham. Lightly oil an ovenproof dish just big enough for the ham slice. Barely cover the meat with orange juice. Place in a preheated 350° oven for about 45 minutes and baste it with the orange juice from time to time. Just before it is done, cover with the orange slices and sprinkle with a mixture of the sugar and cinnamon. Place under the broiler about 3 inches from the heat unit to caramelize the sugar.

Serves 4

BROILED HAM SLICE WITH PEACHES

One more preparation for a lean slice of ready-to-eat ham. This time it is broiled.

1 slice ready-to-eat lean ham, 1½–2 inches thick	4 canned peach halves

Glaze

¼ cup honey   2 tablespoons lemon juice

Trim all fat from the ready-to-cook (or tenderized) ham. Broil about 4 inches from the heat until thoroughly cooked and lightly browned. Remove the broiler pan, turn the slice, and place the fruit on the uncooked side. With a pastry brush dipped in a mixture of the honey and lemon juice, paint the ham and fruit lightly. Return to the broiler and place 5 or 6 inches from the heat, since the fruit will burn if it is too close to the unit. Broil slowly and brush with the glaze several times. When nicely browned and heated through, transfer to a warmed platter. Garnish with parsley or watercress.

Serves 4

PORK WITH ALMONDS

1   pound lean pork
2   egg whites,
     unbeaten
2   tablespoons flour
1   teaspoon salt
3   tablespoons oil
1   teaspoon powdered
     ginger
1¼ cups chicken broth
1   cup diced carrots

½   cup green pepper,
     diced
1   8-ounce can water
     chestnuts, drained
     and sliced
2   tablespoons
     cornstarch
2   tablespoons dry
     sherry
½   cup slivered almonds
     Oil

Trim all fat from the pork and cut the pork into 1-inch cubes. Mix together the egg whites, flour, and ½ teaspoon of the salt. Coat the meat with the mixture. In a large, heavy skillet, heat the oil and ½ teaspoon of the salt. Add the meat and brown well on all sides. Pour off any excess fat in the pan. Add the ginger and 1 cup of the chicken broth and stir to pick up any crusty particles in the bottom of the pan. Cover and simmer over low heat for 15 minutes. Add the carrot and green pepper and cook 5 minutes longer. Add the water chestnuts. In a small bowl combine the cornstarch, sherry, and ¼ cup of the chicken broth. Add to the skillet, stirring with a wire whisk until the sauce is thickened and smooth. This may be made in advance and reheated briefly at serving time.

To brown the slivered almonds, heat a little oil in a small skillet, add the almonds, and shake the pan over medium heat so that they brown evenly. When ready to serve, transfer the meat to a heated platter and sprinkle with the almonds.

Serves 4

BRAISED PORK CHOPS

4 lean loin pork chops, 1 inch thick
½ teaspoon salt
2 tablespoons oil (more if needed)
1 large onion, thinly sliced
½ pound mushrooms, thinly sliced
2 tablespoons soy sauce
4 tablespoons dry sherry

2 tablespoons lemon juice
½ teaspoon powdered ginger
1 clove garlic, crushed
1 8-ounce can water chestnuts, drained and sliced
4 slices lemon
Minced parsley

Select the leanest chops you can find and trim all visible fat. Sprinkle the chops with the salt. In a heavy skillet with a heatproof handle (or a heatproof casserole) heat the oil and brown the chops well on both sides over medium heat. Remove the chops, add a bit more oil if needed, and cook the onion and mushrooms until the onions are limp. Push them to one side, return the chops to the skillet, and cover them with the onion mixture. In a small bowl, combine the soy sauce, sherry, lemon juice, ginger, and garlic and mix thoroughly. Pour this over the chops. Cover and place in a preheated 350° oven for 30 minutes. Sprinkle the water chestnuts over the chops and top each chop with a slice of lemon. Cover and bake 20 minutes longer. Transfer to a warmed platter and sprinkle the chops with the parsley. Mashed butternut squash and steamed new potatoes go well with this.

Serves 4

LISA'S BAKED PORK CHOPS

When my Swiss friend first gave me this recipe, it seemed to me it contained an inordinately large quantity of apples and onions. She was firm and unyielding, however. "Two apples and two onions per chop," she insisted. And she was quite right. The apples and onions blend together into a flavorful mélange—not a gravy but a kind of thick puree which, besides tasting good, acts as a fine meat extender and transforms a thin, skimpy chop into an adequate portion.

4 lean loin pork chops (about 1 pound)
8 apples, peeled, cored, and sliced
8 onions, thinly sliced
Salt

Trim all fat from the chops. Lightly oil an ovenproof dish that has a tightly fitting cover—preferably a dish that can be used for serving. Place a layer of the apples and onions on the bottom of the dish and arrange the chops over it. Sprinkle the chops lightly with salt. Spread the remaining apples and onions over the top of the meat. Cover the baking dish and place in a preheated 325° oven. Bake ignored for 3 hours (not a typographical error; 3 hours is correct).

Serves 4

PORK STIR-FRY

This dish is cooked very quickly over relatively high heat. All ingredients should be prepared beforehand.

1 pound very thinly sliced pork from loin
2 medium-sized onions, thinly sliced
1½ stalks celery
1½ tablespoons oil
2 cloves garlic, minced
¼ cup chicken broth
2 tablespoons dry vermouth
½ teaspoon salt
Freshly ground pepper
1 teaspoon arrowroot or cornstarch
1½ tablespoons soy sauce
2 tablespoons chopped chives
Boiled rice

It is essential that the meat slices be as thin as possible. Trim the meat thoroughly, removing all fat and gristle. Cut the meat into julienne strips. Slice the onions very thinly and cut the celery into thin half-moon slices.

In a heavy skillet, heat the oil and add the onions and celery. Cook for 2 minutes. Add the garlic and meat strips. Cook over high heat until the meat loses its raw look (about 3 minutes). Add the chicken broth and vermouth and boil for 1 minute.

Add the salt and pepper. Dissolve the arrowroot or cornstarch in a small amount of cold water. Add the soy sauce and arrowroot or cornstarch mixture and cook until the sauce thickens and becomes shiny. Remove from the heat, transfer to a warmed serving bowl, sprinkle with the chives, and serve at once with hot boiled rice.

Serves 4

PORK FILLETS IN MUSHROOM SAUCE

Certainly the most desirable cut of pork for our purposes is a lean loin of pork that has been boned and trimmed of all fat. With the bone removed from the meat, it is possible to do a fairly complete job of fat removal.

1	4- 5-pound lean loin of pork	½	pound mushrooms, sliced
¼	cup flour	1	clove garlic, minced
¼	teaspoon dried rosemary, crushed	2	tablespoons flour
½	teaspoon salt	1	cup evaporated skimmed milk
	Freshly ground pepper	½	teaspoon Bovril
3	tablespoons oil	2	tablespoons lemon juice
1	onion, sliced	2	tablespoons chopped parsley

Have your butcher remove bones from the loin of pork. This will leave you a strip of solid meat from which your butcher and then you will trim the fat bordering it. Cut the meat into slices 1 inch thick. Combine the flour with the rosemary, salt, and pepper and dredge the meat slices lightly in the seasoned flour. Heat 2 tablespoons of the oil in a heavy skillet and brown the fillets slowly on both sides. Over very low heat, let the meat simmer, covered, while you prepare the sauce.

In a separate pan, sauté the onion and mushrooms in the remaining tablespoon of oil until the onion slices are just wilted. Add the garlic and cook a minute or two longer. Sprinkle the 2 tablespoons of flour over the mushroom mixture and stir until the flour is absorbed. Slowly add the evaporated skimmed milk, stirring with a wire whisk until the sauce is thickened and smooth. Stir in the Bovril and the lemon juice. Taste and correct the seasoning. Pour the sauce over the fillets and simmer over very low heat a few minutes longer. Transfer to a warmed platter and sprinkle with the parsley. I suggest leaf spinach and fried apple rings with this.

Serves 6

JUDY'S PORK ROAST

Since this glazed, shiny pork roast is as nice to look at as it is delicious to eat, we generally carve it at the table.

1 4- 5-pound lean loin of pork
½ teaspoon salt

Freshly ground pepper
¼ teaspoon rosemary, crushed

Glaze

⅓–½ cup soy sauce
½ cup catsup
¼ cup honey

2 large cloves garlic, crushed

Have your butcher bone a loin of pork and trim all fat. Roll the roast and tie it securely. Place the meat on a rack in a shallow roasting pan and sprinkle with the salt, pepper, and rosemary. Place in a preheated 350° oven and roast for 1½ hours.

While the roast is in the oven, prepare the glaze. In a small bowl, mix together the soy sauce, catsup, honey, and garlic. (If you are using a domestic soy sauce, the half cup is safe, but some of the imported ones are much saltier and you might want to use less.) After the roast has been in the oven for 1½ hours, pour off all fat and spread the glaze over the top of the meat. Return to the oven for another hour, or until the meat is tender when tested with a fork. Baste often with the glaze. The honey will turn darker as it bakes, so if it appears to scorch or get too brown, cover it lightly with aluminum foil. Transfer the roast to a heated platter and garnish with watercress and preserved kumquats or spiced red apples.

Serves 6

VEAL

I wish the veal we get these days were whiter, more delicate, and less expensive. Every once in a while, however—not often enough to spoil us—my butcher produces a piece of veal that recalls for me the beautiful milky white stuff my mother served when I was a little girl, which, as my grandchildren remind me, was a very long time ago. I also have a recollection of my mother's Thursday afternoon Sewing Circle saying harsh things about a member who hedged on her chicken salad by adding veal. Wouldn't those girls be surprised if they were to learn that chicken breasts and lean pork loin are now called "poor man's veal"?

But enough of nostalgia. Veal is a highly desirable meat for those of us concerned with cholesterol. One of the best cuts of meat for low-fat dieters is the veal scallop, or *scaloppine* as its Italian originators call it. Born out of the stringencies of the limited meat supply in Italy, these tender little slices are a shining example of a necessity being turned into a virtue. The *scaloppine* are ideally cut from the leg, trimmed of all fat, and pounded thin. One pound will serve three or four adults most adequately, which compensates somewhat for the inflated cost. This is but further proof of how our debt to the Italians extends beyond their producing Michelangelo, Leonardo, pasta, and Gucci bags.

The shoulder, rump, and leg (but don't shop for a leg of veal during times when the budget is tight) make fine roasts. The bone on the first two mentioned can be removed and the fat trimmed. Don't bother with the breast—it is too fat and impossible to trim thoroughly. For stew, I generally buy a rump or shoulder and cut it up myself. That way, I'm sure it will be manicured to a fare-thee-well. Unless your butcher is your good and true friend, use great caution when buying chopped veal. If you have any doubts, it might be safer to buy a rump, shoulder, or some other lean cut, trim it yourself, and put it through your own food grinder. Then you can be sure that there won't be any fat or trimmings in your chopped meat.

A word of warning about buying those prepackaged breaded veal patties one finds in frozen food departments: don't.

ROAST OF VEAL

The rump, shoulder, boneless loin, and a portion of the leg are all suitable for roasting. (I'm not going to mention the eye of the rib—beluga caviar is less expensive, I think.) The rump or shoulder is generally an easily available cut, and the roast is easier to carve if the bone is removed. But be sure to collect the bone from the butcher—it makes wonderful minestrone soup. Since there is a good deal of waste on a veal roast, get a large one. By the time the bone is removed and the fat trimmed, it won't be *that* big.

1 4- 5-pound rump or shoulder of veal, bone removed	2 tablespoons oil
	1 large onion, chopped
	1 large carrot, grated
1 teaspoon salt	1 stalk celery, grated

Sauce

½ cup dry white wine	½ teaspoon salt
¼ teaspoon garlic powder	Freshly ground pepper
½ teaspoon dried basil	½ teaspoon sugar

Trim every vestige of fat and sinew from the veal. Sprinkle with the salt. Preheat the oven to 350°. Pour the oil into a roasting pan and heat on top of the stove. Sear the meat in the hot oil, turning frequently to brown all over. Spread the onion, carrot, and celery over the top of the meat, cover the roasting pan, and place in the oven.

After 15 minutes, reduce the heat to 300° and roast for 2 hours, or until the meat is tender. When done, remove the meat from the roasting pan and set aside to cool. Place the gravy in a bowl and refrigerate.

Half an hour before you are ready to serve, remove what fat there is (there won't be much) from the gravy. Rub the gravy and vegetables through a strainer or whir in a blender. Place the gravy in a large skillet. Add the sauce ingredients. Mix well, taste, and correct the seasoning. If the gravy is too thick, thin it with water or consommé or a splash of wine. Keep the sauce warm over low heat. Slice the veal in thin slices and place in the hot gravy. Warm through and serve.

Serves 6 to 8

STUFFED SHOULDER OF VEAL

1 4- 5-pound shoulder of veal, bone removed (reserve bones)
1 teaspoon salt
Freshly ground pepper
3 tablespoons oil
1 onion, chopped
1 stalk celery with leaves, finely chopped
1 clove garlic, crushed
2 tablespoons minced parsley

2 cups soft bread cubes or crumbs
1 egg white, unbeaten
¾ cup chicken broth
1 stalk celery
1 onion, thinly sliced
1 bay leaf
3 sprigs parsley
1 tablespoon oil
4–5 carrots, scraped and cut in halves
2 tablespoons tomato paste
½ cup dry white wine

Trim all fat and sinew from the shoulder of veal. Spread out flat, skin side down, and sprinkle lightly with ½ teaspoon of the salt and a few grinds of pepper.

In a large, heavy skillet, heat the oil and cook the chopped onion, celery with leaves, and garlic until the onion is limp. Add the minced parsley and bread cubes or crumbs and cook for a minute. Remove from the heat and toss with the egg white, 3 tablespoons of chicken broth, and remaining salt and pepper. Mix well and spread this mixture over the veal. Roll the veal from the wide edge and tie securely with string.

Lightly oil a roasting pan and make a layer of the celery stalk, onion slices, bay leaf, and parsley sprigs at the bottom. Place the veal roast, seam side down, on top of the vegetables. Lightly salt and pepper the roast if desired and dribble a tablespoon of oil over the meat. Arrange the bones and carrots around the roast.

Place in a preheated 425° oven for 20 minutes, or until the top of the roast is the least bit brown. Mix together the tomato paste, remaining chicken broth, and wine and pour over the veal. Reduce the heat to 350° and cook for about 2 hours longer, or until the meat is tender. After the first half hour of cooking, turn seam side up, bake 30 minutes, then turn seam side down for the balance of the cooking time. Baste frequently during the entire cooking period. Add more broth or wine if the sauce seems to be drying out. If the roast gets too brown, cover it with aluminum foil.

When done, remove the strings, slice in ¼-inch slices, and transfer to a warmed serving platter. Strain the sauce, pour it over the veal, and garnish with the carrots.

Serves 8 to 10

SCALOPPINE IN WINE

Ten minutes of preparation are all that are needed for this noteworthy main course.

1 pound veal scaloppine	½ bay leaf, crumbled
¼ cup flour	Pinch dried sage
½ teaspoon salt	½ cup dry white wine or dry sherry or Marsala
Freshly ground pepper	1 tablespoon chopped parsley
3 tablespoons oil	

Unless your butcher has already done this, place the slices of meat between two pieces of waxed paper and pound them until they are properly flattened out. Like fashion mannequins, they can't be too thin.

Combine the flour, salt, and pepper on a square of waxed paper. Lightly dredge the meat slices in the seasoned flour. Heat the oil in a heavy skillet and brown the meat slices over moderately high heat. If they are thin enough, they will need only 3 or 4 minutes on each side. Transfer them to an ovenproof dish and keep warm in a 250° oven while you prepare the sauce.

Pour off most of the fat remaining in the skillet. Add the bay leaf, sage, and wine. Swish this around, gathering up the brown particles on the bottom of the pan. Simmer for just a minute and pour the sauce over the meat slices. Sprinkle with the parsley and serve with lemon wedges.

Serves 3 or 4

VEAL PICCATA

Piquant lemon-flavored scaloppine.

1½ pounds veal scallopine, cut into 12 pieces	3 tablespoons lemon juice
⅓ cup flour	¼ cup dry white wine
½ teaspoon salt Freshly ground pepper	2 tablespoons fresh parsley, finely chopped
3 tablespoons oil	12 thin slices lemon
1 clove garlic (optional)	Chopped parsley

Place the meat slices between 2 pieces of waxed paper and pound very thin. On a square of waxed paper, combine the flour, salt, and pepper. Dredge the meat lightly in the seasoned flour. In a large, heavy skillet, heat the oil with the garlic clove (if desired), brown the garlic, then remove it and discard. Brown the veal pieces 3 or 4 minutes on each side over moderately high heat. Pour off the excess oil. Reduce the heat and add the lemon juice, wine, and 2 tablespoons of parsley. Scrape the bottom of the pan to gather up the crusty particles. Simmer covered over very low heat for another 7 or 8 minutes. Remove to a heated platter and garnish each scallop with a slice of lemon and chopped parsley.

Serves 6

VEAL BIRDS

6 large scaloppine, pounded thin (about 1½ pounds)	Salt and pepper
	2 tablespoons oil

¼ cup finely chopped onion
¼ cup finely chopped mushrooms
1 10-ounce package frozen chopped spinach, thawed
Dash of Tabasco
¼ teaspoon dried basil
½ teaspoon salt
1 tablespoon grated Parmesan cheese
½ teaspoon grated lemon rind
2 tablespoons oil
1 tablespoon flour
1 cup chicken broth
1 tablespoon lemon juice

Place the pounded slices of scaloppine on a flat surface and sprinkle lightly with salt and pepper.

In a medium-sized skillet, heat 2 tablespoons of oil and cook the onions and mushrooms until the onions are limp. Add the spinach, Tabasco, basil, salt, cheese, and lemon rind. Cover and simmer for 5 minutes.

Divide the spinach stuffing among the 6 portions. Spread each slice with stuffing and roll like a jelly roll. Secure with toothpicks or string.

Heat 2 tablespoons of oil in a skillet and brown the veal birds on all sides. Transfer the veal to a casserole. Add the flour to the remaining fat in the skillet, mix well, and cook for a minute or two. Add the chicken broth slowly and stir well, picking up all the crusty particles at the bottom of the pan. Add the lemon juice and bring to a boil. Taste for seasonings and correct. Pour the sauce over the meat and bake, covered, in a preheated 350° oven for 40 minutes.

Serves 6

VEAL WITH ARTICHOKE HEARTS

1½ pounds scaloppine
½ cup flour
½ teaspoon salt
Freshly ground pepper
1 teaspoon sweet paprika
½ cup cornflake crumbs
½ cup skim milk
1 10-ounce package frozen artichoke hearts
2 large fresh tomatoes
3 tablespoons oil
¼ cup chicken broth

Cut the scaloppine into portion-sized pieces and pound. On a square of waxed paper, combine the flour, salt, pepper, and paprika. Place a mound of cornflake crumbs on another square of waxed paper. Dredge the meat in the seasoned flour, then dip lightly in the milk and coat with the cornflake crumbs. Refrigerate for 1 hour to give the coating time to adhere well.

Cook the artichoke hearts according to the directions on the package. Drain and set aside. Peel the tomatoes by plunging them in boiling water for a minute. The skins can then be easily slipped off. Cut the tomatoes into eighths.

Heat the oil in a large, heavy skillet. Add the breaded scaloppine and cook until golden (about 5 minutes on each side). When done, transfer to a shallow ovenproof baking dish.

To the same skillet, add the artichoke hearts and tomatoes and cook about 5 minutes, or until they are heated through. Keep tossing them so they do not scorch. Pour off any excess fat in the skillet and discard. Add the chicken broth to the skillet to dissolve the brown particles clinging to the bottom of the pan and stir. Pour the pan gravy, artichoke hearts, and tomatoes over the scaloppine, cover the baking dish tightly with aluminum foil, and place in a preheated 350° oven for 20 to 30 minutes.

Serves 6

SWISS VEAL

1½	pounds veal cutlet (from leg) ¼ inch thick	½	cup skim milk
3	tablespoons oil	2	tablespoons flour
1	cup dry white wine	2	tablespoons cold water
½	teaspoon salt	1	tablespoon lemon juice
	Freshly ground pepper	½	teaspoon dried basil
		2	tablespoons parsley, chopped

Trim the veal slice well and cut into strips about ¼ inch wide. In a large, heavy skillet heat the oil and brown the veal strips on both sides. Don't crowd them—you may not be able to cook all of them at one time. Add more oil if needed. Remove the meat from the pan when done and pour off any fat remaining in the skillet. Add the wine and stir to dissolve any crusty particles at the bottom of the pan.

Return the meat to the skillet and simmer uncovered for 10 minutes. Season with the salt and pepper and add the milk. Simmer over very low heat another 5 minutes. Dissolve the flour in the water and add to the sauce, stirring with a wire whisk until the sauce is thickened and smooth. Add the lemon juice. Add the basil and heat another minute or so. Taste and correct the seasonings. Remove to a heated serving platter and sprinkle with the parsley. Serve with cooked rice or broad noodles.

Serves 5 or 6

VEAL ANNIE

Annie is our daughter. Like most people today who combine a full-time job with running a household (and being run by a couple of teenagers along the way), she has no time to indulge in wasted motions and elaborate preparations. She calls this dish "Veal Mishmash," we call it Veal Annie, and everyone calls it delicious.

1½	pounds veal scaloppine	½	pound mushrooms, sliced
2	tablespoons oil	½	teaspoon salt
2	cups peeled Italian canned tomatoes, drained		Freshly ground pepper
1	large green pepper, cut in ½-inch strips	¼	teaspoon oregano
		¼	teaspoon basil
1	large onion, thinly sliced	1½	tablespoons flour

Trim the scaloppine and pound thin between two pieces of waxed paper. Cut the veal into portions about 6 inches square. Heat the oil in a large, heavy skillet and brown the meat well on both sides, then add all the remaining ingredients except the flour. Sprinkle the flour over all and cook uncovered for 20 minutes, stirring frequently. Taste for seasoning and correct.

Serves 5 or 6

BRAISED VEAL CHOPS

4 large lean veal
chops (preferably
loin)
½ teaspoon salt
Freshly ground
pepper
⅓ cup flour
5–6 tablespoons oil
1 onion, finely
chopped
½ cup chicken broth
¼ cup dry sherry

2 cups tiny potatoes or
potato balls, cooked
or canned
Paprika
½ pound mushrooms,
sliced and sautéed in
oil
2 tablespoons lemon
juice
2 tablespoons chopped
parsley
¼ teaspoon dried tarragon

Trim the chops of all fat, season with the salt and pepper, and dredge in the flour. In a large, heavy skillet, heat 3 tablespoons of the oil and cook the chops for 10 minutes on each side or until nicely browned. Remove the chops to an oiled shallow ovenproof baking dish and place in a 350° oven for 45 minutes. Keep covered until the last 10 minutes of cooking.

Add a little oil to the pan in which the chops were cooked (if needed) and cook the onion until it is golden in color. Add the chicken broth and sherry and stir well to dissolve the particles on the bottom of the pan. As soon as the sauce is ready, pour it over the chops in the oven.

In the same skillet, heat 2 tablespoons of oil. Sprinkle the potatoes or potato balls with paprika and brown.

For the last 10 minutes of cooking, spread a layer of the mushrooms sprinkled with the lemon juice over the chops. Surround the chops with a border of browned potatoes. Sprinkle the parsley and tarragon over all and bake uncovered.

Serves 4

VEALBURGERS

Instead of hamburgers . . .

1 pound lean ground
veal

½ teaspoon salt
Freshly ground pepper

¼ teaspoon thyme	3 slices bread, crusts
1 tablespoon oil	removed
2 tablespoons finely	½ cup skim milk
chopped green pepper	1 egg white, unbeaten
1 tablespoon pimiento,	Cornflake crumbs
finely chopped	Oil for frying

Place the veal in a bowl and mix with the salt, pepper, and thyme. In a small skillet, heat the tablespoon of oil and cook the green pepper and pimiento for 5 minutes, or until the green pepper becomes tender. Add to the meat. Soak the bread in the milk and beat until fluffy. Add the bread and egg white to the meat mixture and work the meat with your hands until it is light and spongy. Form into 4 patties and roll them in cornflake crumbs. In a large, heavy skillet, heat enough oil to cover the bottom and cook the vealburgers until they are nicely browned on each side (about 5 minutes). Place in a 350° oven 15 minutes longer.

Serves 3 or 4

ABOUT PREPARING VEAL STEWS

You may find it to your advantage to prepare the veal for stews yourself. Often butchers are too busy to give the time necessary to remove gristle and fat, and it is not too demanding a chore for the cook. The shoulder and rump are the most suitable cuts. The breast is too fat and bony. The leg is ideal, of course, but this choice cut can be saved for special dishes such as scaloppine and an occasional roast.

When the veal is cooked in liquid, as for stews, it gives off quantities of scum. However, first blanching the veal greatly reduces the amount of scum and makes the constant skimming unnecessary. To blanch the veal, cover it in cold water, bring it slowly to a boil, and simmer for a minute or two. Remove the meat, drain it in a large colander, then wash it under cold water. Scour out the pot, return the meat to the pot, and proceed with the recipe. This procedure does not damage the flavor of the meat, and it is guaranteed to improve the cook's disposition, eliminating as it does the need for endless skimming.

RAGOUT OF VEAL

This is a polyunsaturated version of blanquette of veal. It has a hearty, satisfying taste that I think will not leave you longing for the heavy cream and egg yolk sauce of the blanquette.

3	pounds of veal rump or shoulder, well-trimmed and cut into 2-inch cubes	2 or 3	celery tops
		1	bay leaf
			Salt
		18	small white onions, peeled and left whole
3	cups chicken broth	1	pound mushrooms
2½	cups water	2	tablespoons oil
2	carrots, scraped and thickly sliced	1	tablespoon lemon juice
1	onion, quartered	2½	tablespoons flour
½	teaspoon thyme	2	tablespoons water
2	cloves garlic, left whole	⅔	cup skim milk
1	leek	2	tablespoons minced parsley

Blanch the veal cubes according to the directions in the preceding recipe. Place the meat in a heavy Dutch oven and cover with 2½ cups of the chicken broth and the 2½ cups of water. Add more water or broth if the meat is not completely covered. Add the carrots, onion quarters, thyme, garlic, leek, celery tops, and bay leaf. Taste for salt—the amount you need will depend on the saltiness of the broth. Bring to a boil slowly and skim any scum that appears on the surface. Simmer very slowly, partly covered, until the meat is tender but still firm (from 1 to 1½ hours).

While the meat is cooking, prepare the small whole onions and mushrooms. Cut a cross at the stem end of each onion to keep it from popping and slice the mushrooms. In a large skillet, heat the oil with the remaining ½ cup of chicken broth. Add the onions, cover the pan tightly, and cook until they are tender but still firm. Consider them done when they can be pierced easily with the point of a knife. Remove the onions with a slotted spoon and put them aside. Add the mushrooms and lemon juice to the pan and cook over medium high heat for 5 minutes. Drain them and add to the onions. Reserve whatever juices are left in the pan and add to the cooking veal.

When the veal is tender, remove the pieces to a large bowl. Use kitchen tongs for this procedure; you don't want any of the celery tops or leek or whatever clinging to the meat. Strain the veal stock through a wire strainer into a 3-quart saucepan and press down on the vegetables with the back of a spoon to extract all the juices. Boil the strained stock over high heat to reduce it to about 2 cups.

Mix together the flour with the 2 tablespoons of water and add to the veal stock, stirring with a wire whisk until the sauce is smooth and thickened. Reduce the heat and cook for 5 minutes. Skim the surface from time to time to remove scum. Add the milk and heat. Taste for seasoning and correct.

Return the meat, onions, and mushrooms to the sauce and gently mix them together. Heat thoroughly. Transfer to a serving casserole and sprinkle with the parsley. Serve with fluffy boiled rice or steamed new potatoes.

Serves 6

CURRIED VEAL

3 pounds lean veal (from rump or shoulder), trimmed
½ cup flour
1 teaspoon salt
White pepper
4 tablespoons oil
4 large onions, chopped
1 tablespoon (or more) curry powder
2 cloves garlic, crushed
1 10½-ounce can consommé
⅓ cup nonfat milk solids
1 tablespoon brown sugar
1 teaspoon white sugar
1 thinly sliced lemon with rind
¼ cup seedless raisins
4 thin slices ginger root, minced, or ½ teaspoon powdered ginger
3 large apples, pared and coarsely chopped

Cut the veal into 1½-inch cubes, trimming away the sinew and fat. On a square of waxed paper, combine the flour, salt, and pepper. Coat the meat lightly in the seasoned flour.

In a large, heavy kettle such as a Dutch oven, heat 2 tablespoons of the oil and cook the onions about 10 minutes, or until they are limp but not brown. Remove them from the pan with a slotted spoon and set aside. Heat the remaining 2 tablespoons of oil and sear the meat well over medium high heat. Don't crowd the meat or you won't be able to brown it evenly. Do the meat a single layer at a time so that each piece will have its turn at the bottom of the pan. When all the meat is browned, sprinkle the curry powder over it and mix thoroughly. Curry powders vary in intensity so I hope you know your preferred strength. Add the garlic, consommé, and nonfat milk solids and stir until well blended. Return the onions to the kettle. Add the sugars, lemon, raisins, and ginger. Cover and cook over low heat until the meat is tender (about 50 minutes). About halfway through the cooking process, add the apples. If the sauce seems too thick, you can add another ½ cup or so of consommé or water. Taste and correct the seasoning. Serve in a ring of boiled rice on a hot platter or in a chafing dish.

If you plan this for a buffet dinner—it's a splendid dish for a buffet—surround your chafing dish with small bowls containing as many of the following condiments as you can manage: chutney (a must), chopped hard-cooked egg white, slivered toasted almonds, chopped cucumber, chopped sweet white onion, radishes, raisins soaked in sherry, kumquats, chopped sweet pickles, tomato chunks, and sliced green pepper.

Serves 8

VEAL AND MUSHROOMS IN CAPER SAUCE

2	pounds lean veal (from rump or shoulder), trimmed	½	teaspoon salt Freshly ground pepper
2	tablespoons oil	⅓	cup white wine
½	pound mushrooms, sliced	2½	tablespoons capers, chopped
2	tablespoons flour	2	tablespoons parsley, chopped
1	cup chicken broth		
3	tablespoons skim milk		

Cut the veal into 1½-inch cubes, trimming away all fat and gristle. Heat the oil in a heavy kettle such as a Dutch oven and sear the veal lightly over medium high heat. Add the mushrooms and cook an additional 3 minutes, stirring a few times. Sprinkle the flour over the meat and mushrooms and blend thoroughly. Reduce the heat, add the chicken broth, milk, salt, and pepper and mix well. Cover the pan and simmer for about 50 minutes, or until the meat is tender. Add the wine and capers and heat 5 minutes longer. Taste and correct the seasonings. Transfer to a serving dish or a casserole and sprinkle with the parsley. Serve with hot cooked rice or noodles.

Serves 4 or 5

VEAL AND PEPPERS

2½–3	pounds lean veal (from rump or shoulder), trimmed	4	large peppers (green and red, if you can get them)
3	tablespoons oil	1	large onion
2	tablespoons flour	3	tablespoons oil
½	teaspoon salt Freshly ground pepper	⅔	cup chicken broth (half of the liquid may be Marsala wine)
1	1-pound can tomatoes		

Cut the veal into 1½-inch cubes, trimming away all fat and gristle. Heat 3 tablespoons of oil in a heavy kettle such as a Dutch oven and brown the veal over medium high heat. Do just one layer of meat at a time so that all the cubes will be evenly browned, turning them frequently. Sprinkle the flour, salt, and pepper over the meat and mix well. Add the tomatoes and bring to a boil. Reduce the heat, cover the pot, and simmer slowly for 30 minutes.

While the meat is cooking, wash, core, and seed the peppers and cut them into strips ¼ inch wide and 1½ inches long. Peel and thinly slice the onion. Heat 3 tablespoons of oil in a large skillet and cook the peppers and onion over low heat for 10 minutes, or until the onion slices are limp. Stir often so the vegetables don't scorch.

Add the cooked vegetables to the veal. Add the broth (with the wine, if you wish). Taste and correct the seasoning. Cover and simmer gently for another 15 minutes, or until the meat is tender. Serve with noodles or rice.

Serves 6

VEAL WITH RIPE OLIVES

2 pounds lean veal (from rump or shoulder), trimmed
½ cup flour
½ teaspoon salt
Freshly ground pepper
3 tablespoons oil
1 clove garlic, crushed
1 small onion, sliced
½ teaspoon dried rosemary, crushed
½ cup dry white wine
1 tablespoon tomato paste
1 cup (approximately) chicken broth
12 pitted black olives, sliced
Chopped parsley

Cut the veal into 1½-inch cubes, trimming away all fat and gristle. On a square of waxed paper, combine the flour, salt, and pepper and coat the veal in the seasoned flour.

In a large, heavy skillet, heat the oil and brown the meat cubes, turning often until all the surfaces have been in contact with the bottom of the pan. Add the garlic and onion and cook 3 minutes longer. Transfer the meat to a baking dish or a casserole. Add the rosemary, wine, tomato paste, and enough broth to cover the meat. Mix well. Taste for seasoning and correct. Cover the casserole securely and bake in a 325° oven for 1 hour. Add the olives and bake 30 minutes longer. Sprinkle the top with the parsley.

Serves 4 or 5

VEAL STEW WITH TOMATOES

2 pounds lean veal (from rump or shoulder), trimmed
4 tablespoons oil
2 cloves garlic, peeled
1 tablespoon parsley, chopped
1 bay leaf
½ teaspoon marjoram
½ teaspoon salt

Freshly ground pepper
1 cup dry white wine
1 teaspoon Bovril
1 1-pound can tomatoes
Chicken broth

Cut the veal into 2-inch cubes, trimming away all fat and gristle. In a large, heavy kettle, heat the oil and brown the garlic slowly. Remove the garlic and brown the meat well on all sides, turning frequently. Add the parsley, bay leaf, marjoram, salt, and pepper. Pour off the excess oil. Add the wine and cook over low heat until it evaporates. Add the Bovril, tomatoes, and enough chicken broth to cover the meat. Cover the pan and simmer over low heat until the meat is tender (about 1 to 1¼ hours). If the sauce is cooking down, add more chicken broth. Taste for seasoning and correct.

Serves 4 or 5

VEAL STEW WITH LIMA BEANS

A tossed green salad and a simple fruit dessert turn this hearty meal-in-one-dish into a satisfying family dinner.

1½ pounds lean veal (from rump or shoulder), trimmed
½ cup flour
½ teaspoon salt
   Freshly ground pepper
4 tablespoons oil
1 cup hot water
1 cup dry red wine
1 cup large dried lima beans
1 bay leaf
2 carrots, diced
½ cup diced celery
1 teaspoon Worcestershire sauce
¼ teaspoon salt
1 8-ounce can tomato sauce

Cut the veal into 1½-inch cubes, trimming away all fat and gristle. On a square of waxed paper, combine the flour, salt, and pepper and dredge the veal lightly in the seasoned flour. Heat the oil in a large, heavy skillet or pan that has a tightly fitting cover. Brown the veal well on all sides, turning frequently. When the meat is browned, pour off any excess oil. Add the water, wine, lima beans, and bay leaf, cover the skillet, and cook slowly for 1 hour. Add the carrots, celery, Worcestershire sauce, salt, and tomato sauce and cook for ½ hour longer, or until the beans and veal are tender. Taste for seasoning and correct.

Serves 4

8
Poultry

In his book *A Concise Encyclopaedia of Gastronomy*, André L. Simon, the distinguished French food expert, makes the observation that "chicken may be eaten constantly without becoming nauseating." An understatement, to be sure. If Monsieur Simon had been tuned into our wavelength, he might also have added that chicken may be eaten constantly without damage to the diner's cholesterol level.

Happily for seekers after a low-cholesterol diet, young chickens are plentiful and relatively inexpensive. They lend themselves to such a variety of preparation that they can provide a different eating experience no matter how frequently they are used. They can be broiled, baked, poached, fried, stewed, or barbecued; cooked in a brown sauce, a white sauce, a red sauce, or no sauce; they can be served hot, cold, gleaming with glaze, or highlighted in aspic—the possibilities are endless.

Let us concentrate on broilers and fryers in preference to large roasting chickens, fat hens, or capons, for obvious reasons. But even these young things harbor clumps of fat under the skin. The fat at the neck and cavity opening you know about. Cutting the chickens into serving pieces or quarters rather than splitting them in half gives you additional opportunity to do some ruthless lopping of the yellow stuff. I am always surprised at the amount of trimmings that come off a small broiler, but it is a comfort to have it resting on the kitchen countertop instead of in the finished cooked product that we serve. Whenever possible, I skin the chickens completely. The skin is not missed and the sauce that accompanies the chicken assures a succulent dish.

Since the white meat of poultry is more unsaturated than the dark, chicken breasts are ideally suited for our purpose. They are now generally available, skinned and boned, in supermarkets that sell poultry parts, unlike the time when you could get them only at specialty shops. I like to keep a supply of them in my freezer as insurance against hurricanes, blizzards, and unexpected company. Trim the membranes and visible fat before you freeze them so they can be ready on short notice.

Young turkeys may be served frequently, with the white meat earmarked for the prudent dieter. Let the children have the legs and second joints. Their arteries can take it better than ours. This might be an appropriate moment for a word of caution about the self-basting frozen turkeys now featured in many markets. The particular virtue of these birds, or so the advertisements tell us, lies in a process in which the innards of the animal are injected or infused or somehow treated with a vegetable oil, thereby ensuring juicy meat. However, coconut oil is generally used, or a combination of hydrogenated soybean and coconut oils, thereby negating the unsaturated qualities of the bird. Frozen whole turkey breasts are subject to the same treatment, so make sure when you shop for a frozen turkey or turkey breast that you do not buy the self-basting species.

It should be noted that most wild game—pheasant, quail, rabbit, and venison, among others—is low in saturated fat. This is caused by a diet of plants and berries instead of the artificially processed grains on which domestic stock is nourished.

Serve young poultry and serve it often. The recipes on the pages that follow will act as a guide for the many lovely gastronomic languages it speaks in addition to our own—French, Spanish, Italian, Indian, Hungarian, Russian, and Chinese.

OVEN-FRIED CHICKEN

Nothing could be simpler than the preparation for this crisp golden chicken. And if you do what I do, and bake the chicken pieces on a cookie sheet covered with aluminum foil, you won't even have a pot to wash.

2 1½-pound broilers,
   quartered
6 tablespoons oil
1 teaspoon salt
   Freshly ground pepper
½ teaspoon ground ginger

1 clove garlic, minced
   (optional)
1 teaspoon sweet
   paprika
   Cornflake crumbs

Wash and dry the chicken pieces thoroughly. Trim them carefully of all loose tabs of skin and visible fat. Season the oil with the salt, pepper, ginger, garlic (if desired), and paprika. Place a small mound of cornflake crumbs on a square of waxed paper.

With a pastry brush, apply the seasoned oil to both sides of the chicken pieces and roll them in the cornflake crumbs. Place the chicken on the cookie sheet and bake in a preheated 350° oven for 1½ hours.

Serves 4

LOW-CALORIE BROILED CHICKEN

This calorie-reduced but good-tasting preparation is more in the nature of a reward than a penance for sins of overindulgence.

2 1½-pound broilers,
   split
½ teaspoon salt
   Freshly ground pepper

1 teaspoon sweet
   paprika
½ cup (or more) orange
   juice

Wash and dry the chicken halves. Trim them well, ferreting out every bit of fat you can find. Preheat the broiler. Line a broiling pan with aluminum foil. Season the chickens with a sprinkling of salt, pepper, and paprika. Arrange on the broiling pan bone side up and place the pan 4 to 6 inches from the heat. Pour a little of the orange juice over the chickens and broil for 20 minutes. Turn with kitchen tongs, dribble more orange juice, and broil about 30 minutes longer, until golden brown. Baste a few times with the rest of the orange juice, or add some if needed.

Serves 4

CHICKEN ADELE

This fruited, tangy chicken dish may very well be known by some other name, but it was at Adele's house that we first had it and so it became forevermore Chicken Adele. The duck sauce was easily available in my supermarket in the Chinese foods section. It has nothing whatever to do with ducks except perhaps to improve them when cooked. It's simply a pureed fruit mélange that adds an interesting flavor to the chicken.

2 2½-pound broilers, quartered	1 cup duck sauce
2 tablespoons oil	½ cup chili sauce
½ teaspoon salt	1 medium-sized onion, thinly sliced
Freshly ground black pepper	1 1-pound can sliced peaches, drained
1 teaspoon sweet paprika	1 1-pound can pitted black cherries, drained

Wash and dry the chicken pieces well and trim all loose tabs of skin and visible fat. Preheat the broiler. Place the chickens on a broiling pan, skin side up. Dribble the oil over them, salt and pepper lightly, dust with the paprika, and broil about 4 inches from the heat until the skin is nicely brown. This may take about 20 minutes. Do not turn the chicken.

In a small bowl mix together the duck sauce, chili sauce, and onion. Transfer the chicken to a lightly oiled shallow baking pan—an ovenproof serving dish that can be brought to the table would be fine. Pour the sauce over the chicken and bake, uncovered, in a 325° oven for 1½ hours. After the first hour, remove the chicken from the oven, distribute the peaches and cherries among the chicken pieces, and return to the oven for the last half hour.

Serves 6

CHICKEN CACCIATORE

This is one dish that seems never to have gone out of style in Italian restaurants—and for good reason. But it is not hard to duplicate the best effort of a fine chef in your own kitchen.

2 2- 2½-pound broilers,
quartered
Salt and pepper
½ cup flour
4 tablespoons oil
1 medium-sized onion,
finely chopped
1 pound mushrooms,
sliced
2 cloves garlic, minced
1 teaspoon dried basil

2 tablespoons parsley,
chopped
1 2-pound-4-ounce can
Italian plum tomatoes,
drained
1 6-ounce can tomato
paste
1 teaspoon salt
Freshly ground pepper
½ teaspoon sugar
⅔ cup dry white wine or
½ cup dry Marsala

Wash and dry the broilers and remove the skin. Trim all visible fat. Sprinkle the chickens lightly with salt and pepper. Place a mound of flour on a large sheet of waxed paper and dredge the chickens in the flour, shaking off the excess. Heat the oil in a heavy skillet and brown the chickens well on both sides. Remove to an ovenproof casserole.

In the same skillet, cook the onion and mushrooms until the onion is limp and golden. Add the garlic, basil, parsley, tomatoes, tomato paste, salt, pepper, and sugar. Simmer over medium heat for 20 minutes, covered. Stir a few times. Reduce the heat, add the wine, and heat through. Taste for seasoning and correct. Pour this sauce over the chicken and bake, covered, in a preheated 350° oven 1 hour, or until the chicken is completely tender.

Serves 6

CHICKEN A L'INDIENNE

L'Indienne refers to dishes in which curry is used as an incidental seasoning and not as a main flavoring—such as in this preparation.

2 2- 2½-pound broilers,
cut in quarters
1 tablespoon oil
1 teaspoon salt
Freshly ground pepper
½ teaspoon garlic powder

2 teaspoons curry
powder
1 teaspoon sweet
paprika
2 oranges
2 tablespoons dry white
wine

Wash and dry the chickens well and trim off all fat and loose skin. Arrange the chickens in a lightly oiled baking pan and sprinkle them with the oil, salt, pepper, garlic powder, curry powder, and paprika. Grate the rind of the two oranges and sprinkle it over the chickens. Squeeze the orange juice and pour over the chicken along with the wine. Cover the pan securely with aluminum foil and bake in a 325° oven for one hour, basting a few times. If the pan seems to be getting dry, add a little wine. After an hour, remove the foil and bake uncovered 30 more minutes, or until the chickens are completely tender and nicely browned. Serve with Rice and Noodle Pilaf (page 250).

Serves 6 to 8

COQ AU VIN

Coq au Vin is the French version of what we might translate into Brown Chicken Fricassee with Red Wine. But in any language it makes for delicious eating that offers as a bonus the added flavor it gets from being cooked ahead of time and reheated.

1 3- 3½-pound fryer cut into serving pieces	¼ teaspoon thyme
5 tablespoons (or more) oil	1 clove garlic, minced
1 teaspoon salt	1 bay leaf
Freshly ground pepper	12 small white onions
¼ cup brandy	2 tablespoons water
2 cups dry red wine	½ pound mushrooms, sliced
1 cup consommé	
2 teaspoons tomato paste	2 tablespoons flour
	2 tablespoons chopped parsley

Rinse the chicken pieces and dry thoroughly (they won't brown if damp). Trim all fat and loose skin. In a heavy kettle or Dutch oven heat 3 tablespoons of the oil and brown the chicken well on all sides. Sprinkle with the salt and pepper, cover the pot, and cook over low heat for 10 minutes. Warm the brandy, pour it over the chicken, then set aflame and let the flame burn out. Add the wine, consommé, tomato paste, thyme, garlic, and bay leaf. Cover and simmer over low heat for 30 minutes.

While the chicken is stewing, peel the onions and cut a small cross at the bottom to prevent the centers from popping out during cooking. Brown the onions in 1 tablespoon of the oil in a medium-sized skillet. You won't be able to brown them evenly all around but turn them often and do the best you can. Add the water, cover the pan tightly, and braise over moderate heat for 20 minutes. Shake the pan from time to time. Remove the onions from the skillet and set aside. Add a dollop of oil if the pan is dry and sauté the mushrooms for 3 minutes, stirring frequently.

Remove the chicken to the ovenproof casserole you plan to use for serving. Boil the remaining liquid over high heat until it is reduced to 2 cups. Remove the bay leaf. Combine the flour with the remaining tablespoon of oil and add to the liquid bit by bit, stirring with a wire whisk until the sauce is thickened and smooth. Pour the sauce over the chicken. Add the onions and mushrooms. Bring the sauce to a simmer, cover the casserole, and cook over low heat for 15 minutes longer. Sprinkle with the parsley and serve.

The sauce is too delicious to waste, so you might accompany the dish with small peeled steamed new potatoes that can soak up every drop of the lovely stuff.

Serves 4

BUTTERMILK CHICKEN WITH ROSEMARY

2 2- 2½-pound fryers cut
   into serving pieces
¾ cup skim buttermilk
1 cup dry bread crumbs
½ teaspoon salt
   Freshly ground pepper

1 tablespoon Parmesan
   cheese
½ teaspoon sweet paprika
¼ teaspoon dry mustard
1 teaspoon dried
   rosemary, crushed

Remove the skin from the chickens and trim all visible fat. Wash and dry well. Place in a single layer in a lightly oiled shallow casserole or baking dish and pour the buttermilk over the chicken pieces. Cover and refrigerate for a few hours.

Mix the bread crumbs with the remaining ingredients. Coat the chicken pieces well with the crumb mixture and return to the casserole. Cover and bake in a preheated 350° oven for 1¼ to 1½ hours, or until the chicken is tender and golden. Uncover for the last 30 minutes of baking. Remove the cover from time to time and baste with the pan juices. If the sauce seems to be drying out, add a little water or chicken broth.

Serves 5 or 6

CHICKEN WITH BING CHERRIES

3   1½-pound broilers, split
1   cup flour
1   teaspoon salt
    Freshly ground pepper
½   teaspoon sweet paprika
¼   teaspoon ground ginger
4   tablespoons oil (more if needed)
1½ cups chicken broth (more if needed)

2   medium-sized onions, finely chopped
2   tablespoons cornstarch
1   No. 2½ can pitted Bing cherries, drained (reserve the juice)
½   cup dry sherry
    Salt and pepper to taste

Wash and dry the broilers and trim all fat. Dredge them in the flour seasoned with the salt, pepper, paprika, and ginger. In a heavy skillet, heat 4 tablespoons of oil and add the chicken, turning to brown both sides. Add more oil if needed. Place the browned halves in a baking pan with ½ cup of the chicken broth and 1 chopped onion. Cover the pan and bake in a preheated 350° oven for 40 minutes, basting frequently. Remove the cover and continue baking 30 minutes longer. Add more broth if needed.

While the chicken is going about its business in the oven, you can prepare the sauce. Using the same pan in which you browned the chicken, brown the remaining onion. Add more oil if needed. In a small bowl blend the cornstarch with the cherry juice. Add to the browned onion with 1 cup of chicken broth and boil, stirring with a wire whisk, until the sauce is thickened. It will look more elegant if you strain it through a wire strainer at this point to remove the onion bits. Return the strained sauce to the skillet, add the cherries and sherry, and taste to see if you want additional salt and pepper. Heat through.

Transfer the chicken to a warm serving platter and pour part of the sauce and cherries over it. Pass the remaining sauce in a gravy boat. Steamed new potatoes or fluffy rice are suitable accompaniments.

Serves 6

CHICKEN WITH APRICOTS

Chicken bathed in a delicious golden brown gravy sparked with spices and fruit.

1 2½- 3-pound broiler, cut into serving pieces	1½ cups orange juice
Sweet paprika	¼ teaspoon Tabasco
½ teaspoon salt	¼ cup sliced or chopped almonds
3 tablespoons oil	¼ cup white raisins
2 tablespoons flour	1 1-pound-1-ounce can apricot halves, drained
¼ teaspoon cinnamon	
¼ teaspoon salt	
⅛ teaspoon ground cloves	

Trim excess skin and all traces of fat from the chicken and sprinkle the chicken lightly with paprika and ½ teaspoon of salt. In a large, heavy skillet with a cover, heat the oil and brown the chicken well. Remove from the pan and set aside.

Discard all but about 1 tablespoon of drippings in the pan. Add the flour, cinnamon, ¼ teaspoon of salt, and cloves and stir. Slowly add the orange juice and stir well to pick up the crusty brown particles at the bottom of the pan. Add the Tabasco and stir with a wire whisk until the sauce comes to a boil and becomes thickened and smooth.

Return the chicken to the skillet and add the almonds and raisins. Cover the skillet and simmer over low heat until the chicken is tender (about 55 minutes). Watch the sauce and if you see it cooking down and becoming too thick, add a little water or orange juice. Taste for seasonings and correct. Add the apricots for the last 5 minutes of cooking so they will be heated through.

To serve, place the chicken on a warmed platter and spoon some of the sauce and all the fruit over it. Pass extra sauce in a gravy boat. Serve with fluffy hot rice.

Serves 3 or 4

GINGER CHICKEN

2 1½-pound fryers, split	⅓ cup chicken broth
4 tablespoons oil	(more if needed)
Salt and pepper	¾ cup ginger marmalade

Trim the chicken halves of all loose skin and visible fat. Wash and pat dry. In a large skillet, warm the oil over medium heat and brown the chickens slowly on both sides. Season them lightly with salt and pepper and place in a shallow roasting pan.

Discard any fat remaining in the skillet and add the chicken broth. Stir to dissolve any crusty particles remaining in the skillet and add the marmalade. Stir over low heat until it is completely melted and blended with the broth. Pour the sauce over the chicken and bake uncovered in a 350° oven for 1 hour, or until the chicken is tender and brown and shiny with glaze. If the sauce seems to be drying out, add more chicken broth. Transfer to a warmed serving platter and cover the chickens with the gravy remaining in the pan.

Serves 4

CHICKEN PAPRIKA

2 2½-pound broilers, cut into serving pieces	1 medium-sized green pepper
5 tablespoons oil	1 cup chicken broth
2 large onions, coarsely chopped	2 tablespoons tomato paste
2 tablespoons sweet paprika	1 package MBT chicken broth powder
1 teaspoon salt	Pinch of sugar
1 large tomato	1 cup plain low-fat yogurt

Wash and dry the chicken thoroughly. Remove the skin and trim every bit of fat. In a large kettle or a Dutch oven, heat the oil and sear the chicken lightly on both sides. There probably won't be room in the pan to do all the pieces at once, so brown as many as you can at a time. Set the chicken aside. In the same skillet, heat the onions until limp and golden (about 10 minutes). Add the paprika and salt and mix well. Return the chicken to the kettle, reduce the heat, and simmer, covered, for 10 minutes.

While the chicken is simmering, peel the tomato by plunging into boiling water for a minute. Slip off the skin and cut the tomato into chunks. Slice the green pepper in long, thin strips. Add to the kettle the tomato, green pepper, chicken broth, tomato paste, chicken broth powder, and sugar. Cover and cook over very low heat for 50 minutes, or until the chicken is tender. Add the yogurt and mix well. Taste for seasoning and correct.

Serve with broad cooked noodles. You might use the green ones, just for color contrast.

Serves 6

CHICKEN MARSALA

2 1½-pound broilers, quartered	1 cup (or more) dry Marsala wine
½ cup flour	1 4-ounce can sliced mushrooms, drained
½ teaspoon salt	1 medium-sized sweet onion, thinly sliced
Freshly ground pepper	
3 tablespoons oil	

Carefully trim all loose skin and bits of fat from the chicken. On a square of waxed paper, mix the flour with the salt and pepper and dredge the chickens in the flour mixture.

Heat the oil in a large, heavy skillet and cook the chicken pieces over medium heat, turning them until nicely brown on both sides. Add the wine, cover, and cook slowly for 30 minutes. If the liquid in the pan seems to be drying out, add more wine. Scatter the mushrooms and onion slices over the chicken and cook another 20 or 25 minutes, or until the chicken is completely tender.

Remove to a warm platter and pour the sauce over the chicken.

Serves 4

CHICKEN VERONIQUE

"Veronique" announces the presence of grapes. This same sauce—minus the powdered ginger—can transform a poached fillet of sole into Sole Veronique.

2 2½-pound frying chickens, quartered
1 teaspoon salt
   Freshly ground pepper
4 tablespoons oil
4 shallots, finely chopped
¼ pound mushrooms, sliced
1 clove garlic, minced
⅔ cup chicken broth
½ cup dry white wine
½ teaspoon powdered ginger
1 tablespoon lemon juice
½ teaspoon sugar
1 cup seedless grapes, fresh or canned
2 tablespoons flour
2 tablespoons water

Wash the chicken and dry well. Trim all extra tabs of skin and fat. Sprinkle the chicken lightly with the salt and pepper. In a heavy skillet, heat the oil and lightly brown the chicken on both sides, turning the pieces with kitchen tongs. Remove the chicken. Cook the shallots, mushrooms, and garlic about 5 minutes over moderate heat or until the shallots become limp. Stir in the broth, wine, ginger, lemon juice, and sugar and bring to a good boil. Reduce the heat and return the chicken to the skillet. Cover and cook over low heat until the chicken is tender (about 45 minutes), stirring the sauce and basting occasionally. Add the grapes and cook another 5 minutes. Remove the chicken to a serving platter and keep warm. Make a paste of the flour and water and add to the sauce, stirring with a wire whisk until the sauce is thickened and smooth. Taste for seasoning. Pour the sauce over the chicken and serve.

Serves 6

CHICKEN AND ZUCCHINI

This chicken-cum-vegetable dish can be made early in the day and reheated.

2 2½-pound broilers, quartered
1 tablespoon oil
1 teaspoon salt
    Freshly ground pepper
2 tablespoons oil
2 medium-sized onions, coarsely chopped
1 clove garlic, minced
2 medium-sized zucchini, sliced ⅜ inch thick

½ pound mushrooms, sliced
1½ tablespoons flour
1 14½-ounce can sliced baby tomatoes, drained
1 cup dry white wine
2 tablespoons tomato paste
    Salt and pepper
    Pinch of sugar
2 tablespoons minced parsley

Wash and dry the chickens well. Remove all loose tabs of skin and strips of fat. Dribble 1 tablespoon of oil over the chicken and season with the teaspoon of salt and the pepper. Place in a baking pan in a 350° oven and bake for 40 minutes.

While the chicken is baking, heat 2 tablespoons of oil in a large, heavy skillet. Add the onions and cook until they become limp (about 10 minutes). Add the garlic, zucchini, and mushrooms and cook over low heat, stirring, 5 minutes longer. Sprinkle the flour over the vegetables and stir. Add the tomatoes, wine, and tomato paste. Mix and blend the ingredients well and simmer over medium heat for an additional 10 minutes. Taste for seasoning and add salt and pepper as needed and a pinch of sugar.

Remove the chicken from the oven, place it in the skillet, and cover it well with the sauce and vegetables. If the sauce seems to be too thick, add some of the juice from the chicken. Cover the pan and simmer over very low heat for an additional 20 to 25 minutes, or until the chicken is completely tender. Sprinkle with the parsley.

Serves 6

PAPRIKA RICE AND CHICKEN

A Hungarian version of Spanish *arroz con pollo.*

2   2½-pound frying chickens, cut into serving pieces
4   tablespoons oil
8 to 10   scallions, chopped
2   green peppers, finely chopped
2   cloves garlic, minced
3   tomatoes, peeled and coarsely chopped, or equivalent canned tomatoes, well drained
1   teaspoon salt
2   tablespoons sweet paprika
3   cups chicken broth
1   cup dry white wine
2   cups long grain rice
½   cup chopped parsley

Wash and dry the chickens well. Remove the skin and trim the fat carefully. In a large, heavy skillet or Dutch oven with a tight lid, heat the oil and brown the chicken pieces well on all sides, turning them with kitchen tongs. Remove the chicken when browned and set aside.

In the same skillet, sauté the scallions, peppers, and garlic until soft (about 10 minutes). Pour off any excess oil that remains in the skillet. Add the tomatoes, salt, and paprika and stir. Add the broth and wine and stir well, getting at all the crusty particles at the bottom of the pan.

Return the chicken to the skillet and simmer, covered, for 30 minutes. Add the rice, mix through, cover, and cook over very low heat until the rice is soft and the liquid is absorbed (about 25 or 30 minutes). Add the parsley and fluff through with a fork.

Serves 6 to 8

BRUNSWICK STEW

Soup, chicken, and vegetables are all here in one zippy, delicious dish that had its origin below Mason and Dixon's Line. However, I have taken a few liberties with it, for I have always found it difficult to deal with a large piece of something that needs to be cut with a knife and fork when it is surrounded by liquid that can be handled only with a spoon. I never know what to do with all the cutlery that isn't working. Consequently, for this Brunswick stew I take the chicken off the bones after it is cooked and return it in substantial enough strips not to be overlooked, thereby simplifying the whole business. It makes a lovely family dinner.

1	2½- 3-pound fryer, quartered	
1	teaspoon salt	
1	tablespoon sweet paprika	
4	tablespoons oil	
2	medium-sized onions, sliced	
1	green pepper, diced	
3	cups water	
2	cups canned tomatoes, undrained	
2	tablespoons chopped parsley	

1	package MBT chicken broth powder
¼	teaspoon Tabasco
1	tablespoon Worcestershire sauce
¼	cup cider vinegar
2	cups whole kernel corn
1	10-ounce package frozen baby lima beans, thawed
3	tablespoons flour
3	tablespoons water

Wash the chicken pieces, remove the skin, and trim the fat. Sprinkle the chicken with the salt and paprika. In a large, heavy kettle such as a Dutch oven, heat the oil and sear the chicken on both sides. Push the chicken to one side, or remove it if there isn't room in the kettle. Cook the onions and green pepper until the onions are limp and transparent. Return the chicken to the pot and add the 3 cups of water, tomatoes, parsley, chicken broth powder, Tabasco, Worcestershire sauce, and vinegar and bring to a boil. Cover, lower the heat, and simmer for 40 minutes. Add the corn and lima beans and cook 20 minutes longer. Remove the chicken pieces and let cool. Mix the flour and 3 tablespoons of water to a smooth paste and slowly blend into the sauce. Taste for seasonings—you might like another dash of Tabasco or vinegar. Remove the chicken from the bones and cut into large strips. Leave the wings as they are. Return the chicken to the pot and continue to cook over low heat for 10 minutes, stirring. If you have a soup tureen for the stew, by all means use it. Serve the stew in large soup bowls.

Serves 4 to 6

CHICKEN MANDARIN

An interesting sweet-and-sour chicken dish for fork-food occasions.

1 2½- 3-pound fryer
3–4 cups cold water
1 celery stalk with leaves
1 onion, quartered
1 carrot, scraped and quartered
8 peppercorns
½ teaspoon salt
Pepper
1 1-pound-4-ounce can pineapple chunks in juice
2 tablespoons oil
½ pound mushrooms

2 green peppers, cut into strips
1 cup chicken broth
2 tablespoons cornstarch
1 tablespoon soy sauce
3 tablespoons vinegar
3 tablespoons sugar
Freshly ground pepper
1½–2 cups chow mein noodles

Rinse the chicken well and remove all fat. Place in a kettle with the water, celery, onion, carrot, peppercorns, salt, and pepper. Bring to a boil slowly, cover, reduce the heat to a simmer, and cook for 45 to 50 minutes, or until the chicken is tender. Skim the broth as needed. Remove the chicken when done and boil the broth to reduce. Strain the broth and set aside 1 cup. The rest can be reserved for future use. When the chicken is cooled, remove from the bones and cut into bite-sized strips.

Drain the pineapple and reserve the juice. You should have about ⅔ cup of juice. Heat the oil in a large, heavy skillet and cook the pineapple for 3 minutes, stirring a few times. Add the mushrooms and cook 3 minutes longer. Add ⅓ cup of pineapple juice and the green pepper. Cover and simmer 10 minutes over low heat. Add the chicken broth, a solution of the cornstarch mixed with the remaining ⅓ cup pineapple juice, soy sauce, vinegar, and sugar and stir with a wire whisk until the sauce is thickened and smooth. Fold in the cut-up chicken and a few grinds of pepper and heat through. Taste for seasoning and correct. Serve over the heated crisp chow mein noodles. Hot fluffy cooked rice can go along with this.

Serves 6 to 8

CORNISH HENS WITH WILD RICE STUFFING

Buy the little ones that weigh a pound. Larger hens are too big for a single portion, and splitting them robs them of some of their style—half of it, anyway.

4 1-pound Cornish hens
1 teaspoon salt
   Freshly ground pepper
   Sprinkling of garlic
   powder (optional)

3 tablespoons oil
1 6-ounce can frozen
   orange juice
   concentrate, thawed
½ cup dry sherry

Wild Rice Stuffing

½ cup wild rice
4 tablespoons oil
1 onion, finely chopped
8 medium-sized
   mushrooms, chopped
1 teaspoon salt
   Freshly ground pepper

2 tablespoons snipped
   fresh dill or 1 teaspoon
   dried dill
¼ teaspoon thyme
1 slice bread without
   crusts, crumbled

Wash the hens, pat them dry, and trim away whatever little tabs of fat you can find. Sprinkle the cavities with the salt, pepper, and garlic powder (if desired).

Cook the wild rice according to the package directions. Wild rice usually takes about 40 minutes to become soft.

For the stuffing, heat the oil in a heavy skillet and cook the onion for 10 minutes, or until it becomes slightly golden. Add the mushrooms and cook 3 minutes longer. Add the salt, pepper, dill, and thyme and heat for another few minutes. Combine the mixture with the rice and bread. Taste for seasoning.

Stuff the hens with the wild rice mixture and skewer closed. Tie the wings to the body with string and tie the legs together. Brush the hens with the 3 tablespoons of oil and sprinkle lightly with salt and pepper.

Place the hens breast side up in a roasting pan. Pour the orange juice concentrate over the hens, cover the pan tightly with aluminum foil, and place in a 325° oven for 40 minutes. Take a look from time to time; if there doesn't seem to be enough gravy, add a little water or chicken broth. Continue baking, uncovered, for another 30 to 35 minutes. Turn the hens once to give the undersides a chance to brown. Baste often. The last 15 minutes, add the sherry to the gravy and continue to baste. The hens should be brown, glazed, and very tender. Transfer to a warmed platter and pour the gravy over the hens.

Serves 4

BAKED CORNISH HENS

Cornish hens are somewhat bland, I think, and this simple mustard-crumb coating adds flavor and interest.

3 1½-pound Cornish hens, split	¼ teaspoon thyme Freshly ground pepper
4 tablespoons oil	Dijon mustard
1 teaspoon Worcestershire sauce	Cornflake crumbs

Wash and dry the Cornish hens well. Trim away the extra tabs of skin and all visible fat. In a small bowl, mix together 3 tablespoons of the oil, the Worcestershire sauce, thyme, and pepper. With a pastry brush, brush the oil mixture over both sides of the hens, coating well.

With the same brush, smear the little creatures thoroughly with mustard, coating both sides. (Use Dijon or a Dijon-type mustard; the bland mustard won't be tangy enough.) Place a mound of cornflake crumbs on a square of waxed paper and press both sides of the hens into the crumbs, giving them a substantial crumb coating. Arrange the hens on a lightly oiled baking pan, dribble a little oil over them, and bake uncovered in a 350° oven for 50 minutes, or until they are tender and browned.

Serves 6

TO COOK CHICKEN BREASTS

Besides the innumerable ways there are to prepare chicken breasts—a few of which appear on the following pages—the large solid pieces of cooked white meat are ever so useful for dishes such as Chicken Breasts in Aspic (page 298) or Hot Chicken Salad (page 267), or for times when you need a small amount of white meat chicken, as in Cannelloni (page 271). Boned and skinned breasts (in our local markets they are called "chicken cutlets") should not be boiled or stewed, for they give off a lot of scum in this process. The ideal cooking method, and simple it is, is to poach them in the oven in broth.

3 whole chicken breasts,
    boned and skinned

Sprinkle of salt and
    pepper
1 cup chicken broth

Preheat the oven to 400°. Wash the chicken breasts, pat them dry, and cut in two. Peel off the membranes and cut away all strips of fat. Season lightly with salt and pepper and place in a baking pan that holds them snugly. Add the chicken broth and cover the pan tightly with aluminum foil. Place in a 400° oven for 30 minutes, at which time they will be completely cooked through, soft, juicy, and ready to use, hot or cold.

CHICKEN BREASTS IN SHERRY CREAM SAUCE

2 whole chicken breasts,
    skinned and boned
2 tablespoons brandy
4 tablespoons oil
¼ pound mushrooms,
    sliced
2 tablespoons flour

1½ cups skim milk or
    evaporated skimmed
    milk
½ teaspoon salt
    Freshly ground
    pepper
    Pinch nutmeg
⅓ cup dry sherry
2 tablespoons grated
    Parmesan cheese

Cut the chicken breasts in two. Rub them with the brandy. In a heavy skillet, heat 3 tablespoons of the oil, brown the breasts on both sides, then remove them from the skillet and set aside. If the skillet is dry, add the remaining tablespoon of oil. Add the mushrooms and cook for 5 minutes. Sprinkle with the flour and stir in the milk, mixing with a wire whisk until the sauce is thickened and smooth. Undiluted evaporated skimmed milk makes a slightly richer sauce. Season with the salt, pepper, and nutmeg. Add the sherry and taste and correct seasoning.

Place the browned chicken breasts in a shallow baking dish, pour the sauce over them, and cover the baking dish with aluminum foil. Bake in a 350° oven for 40 minutes. Remove the foil, sprinkle the chickens with the cheese, and bake uncovered for 10 minutes longer. If the cheese hasn't browned, place the pan under the broiler for a couple of minutes just before serving.

Serves 4

CHICKEN BREASTS, CHINOIS

This is a good choice for the occasions when you know that you are going to arrive home a breath ahead of your family. If you have all the ingredients prepared in advance, the cooking time from start to finish is only about 10 minutes.

2 whole raw chicken breasts, skinned and boned	1 6-ounce package frozen Chinese pea pods
½ cup celery	3 tablespoons oil
1 1-pound can bean sprouts, drained	1 cup chicken broth
8 water chestnuts	2 teaspoons soy sauce
	2 tablespoons cornstarch
	2 tablespoons dry sherry

Wash and trim the chicken breasts and cut into ¾-inch cubes. Cut the celery crosswise into ¼-inch slices. Rinse the drained bean sprouts well in cold water. Soaking them in cold water for a few hours will make them crisper. Slice the water chestnuts. These foods can all be prepared in advance, placed in covered containers or wrapped in plastic, and refrigerated until cooking time.

Prepare the pea pods at the last minute, in order to

keep them as crisp as possible. They need only be covered with boiling salted water and heated until the ice melts. Longer cooking will make them lose their crispness.

In a large, heavy skillet, heat the oil. Add the chicken and stir for 2 or 3 minutes, or until it loses its raw look. Add the celery, bean sprouts, and chicken broth, cover, and cook for 2 minutes. Add the pea pods and water chestnuts and cook for a minute or so. In a small bowl, combine the soy sauce, cornstarch, and sherry. Add to the skillet and stir until the sauce thickens. Taste for seasonings and correct. You may need a bit of salt, depending upon the degree of saltiness of the soy sauce. Serve at once with plain boiled rice.

Serves 3 or 4

CHICKEN BREASTS IN WINE AND TOMATO SAUCE

3 whole chicken breasts, boned and skinned
½ cup flour
½ teaspoon salt
Freshly ground pepper
4 tablespoons oil
1 medium-sized onion, finely chopped

¼ pound mushrooms, sliced
1 cup tomato juice
½ cup chicken broth
¼ cup sherry
2 tablespoons chopped parsley

Cut the chicken breasts in half and wash and pat dry. Trim all fat. Place the flour on a square of waxed paper and combine with the salt and pepper. Dredge the chicken in the seasoned flour. In a large, heavy skillet, heat the oil. Brown the chicken breasts and set aside. To the same skillet, add the onion and sauté until golden, stirring often. Add the mushrooms and cook another 2 or 3 minutes. Add the tomato juice and chicken broth and bring to a good boil, mixing well to pick up the crusty particles at the bottom of the pan. Add the sherry and mix. Taste for seasonings and correct. Reduce the heat, return the chicken to the skillet, and simmer for 45 minutes, or until the chicken is tender. Transfer to a warmed platter and sprinkle the parsley over the chicken.

Serves 6

CHICKEN WITH ALMONDS

3	whole chicken breasts, boned and skinned	1½ tablespoons flour
		1 cup chicken broth
		1 cup dry white wine
4	tablespoons oil	½ teaspoon salt
2	tablespoons brandy	Freshly ground pepper
6	scallions, finely chopped	½ teaspoon dried tarragon
		Oil
1	teaspoon tomato paste	½ cup slivered blanched almonds

Cut the chicken breasts in half and wash and pat dry. Trim away all fat. In a large, heavy skillet, heat the oil and brown the chicken. Sprinkle the chicken with the brandy, heat for another minute, and remove from the skillet. In the same skillet, heat the scallions until they become soft. Pour off any fat that remains in the skillet. Stir in the tomato paste and flour and slowly add the chicken broth and wine, stirring to pick up any crusty particles at the bottom of the pan. Add the salt and pepper and stir until the mixture comes to a boil.

Reduce the heat and return the chicken to the sauce. Add the tarragon. Taste for seasoning and correct. Cover the pan and simmer over low heat for 45 minutes, or until the chicken is tender.

While the chicken is simmering, heat a small amount of oil in a medium-sized skillet and brown the almonds over low heat. Watch them carefully, for they begin to brown quickly. Keep shaking the pan so that the nuts will be evenly colored. Drain them on brown paper.

Serve the breasts on a bed of fluffy rice, pour the sauce over all, and sprinkle with the almonds.

Serves 6

GLAZED CHICKEN BREASTS

3 whole boned and
skinned chicken
breasts, split

2 tablespoons oil
½ teaspoon salt
Freshly ground pepper

Sauce

1 10-ounce glass currant
jelly
¾ cup water
1 teaspoon ground
allspice

1 tablespoon
Worcestershire sauce
2 tablespoons lemon
juice
1 tablespoon cornstarch
1 tablespoon cold water

Wash the chicken breasts and pat dry. Trim them carefully. With a pastry brush brush them lightly with the oil and sprinkle with the salt and pepper. Arrange in an oiled baking dish.

To make the sauce, combine the jelly, water, allspice, Worcestershire sauce, and lemon juice in a small saucepan over low heat. Stir until the jelly is melted and heated through. Make a paste of the cornstarch and water and add to the jelly mixture. Cook slowly, stirring constantly, until the sauce thickens and comes to a boil.

Heat the oven to 450°. Pour the sauce over the chicken breasts and bake uncovered for 15 minutes. Reduce the heat to 350° and continue baking for another 35 to 40 minutes, or until the chicken is tender. Baste frequently with the sauce. If the sauce cooks down and gets too thick, thin it out with a little water or chicken broth.

Serves 6

CHICKEN ORIENTALE

This is a handsome addition to a party buffet table. You might also consider it even without the provocation of a party or a buffet—perhaps some leftover chicken or turkey breasts. It can be prepared in the morning and heated at dinnertime. A casserole of Curried Baked Fruit (page 238) is an ideal accompaniment.

3 whole chicken breasts, boned and skinned	1 5-ounce can bamboo shoots
1 cup sliced celery	4 tablespoons oil
1 6-ounce package frozen Chinese pea pods	6 tablespoons flour
	2½ cups chicken broth
½ pound mushrooms, sliced	1 tablespoon (or more) soy sauce
	Dash of Tabasco
2 tablespoons oil	Freshly ground pepper
1 5-ounce can water chestnuts	1 cup chow mein noodles

Poach the chicken breasts according to the directions on page 166. Reserve the liquid and add chicken broth to make 2½ cups. When the chicken is cool, cut into largish flat slices.

Now for the Chicken Orientale. Prepare the vegetables first. Cook the celery in salted water for about 10 minutes—it should be crisp and underdone. Cover the pea pods in boiling salted water only until they are thawed and the ice is melted. Sauté the mushrooms in the 2 tablespoons of oil for 3 minutes. Slice the water chestnuts and drain the bamboo shoots.

In a large pot, heat the 4 tablespoons of oil and blend in the flour, stirring until bubbly. Add the chicken broth slowly, stirring constantly with a wire whisk until the sauce thickens and becomes smooth. Stir in the soy sauce, Tabasco, and pepper. Mix in the chicken, celery, pea pods, mushrooms, water chestnuts, and bamboo shoots. Taste for seasonings. You may want a bit more soy sauce, Tabasco, or perhaps a dash of salt. Transfer to an oiled 2½-quart casserole, cover with a layer of chow mein noodles, and bake in a 350° oven for 20 minutes, or until hot and bubbly. Serve with a bowl of hot, fluffy rice.

Serves 6

CHICKEN DIVAN

Another variation of a delicious all-in-one-dish meal that can be prepared in advance and refrigerated.

4	whole chicken breasts, boned and skinned	1	cup skim milk or evaporated skimmed milk
1	bunch broccoli or 2 10-ounce packages frozen broccoli spears		Salt and pepper
		¼	cup dry sherry
½	teaspoon salt	2	tablespoons grated Parmesan cheese
4	tablespoons oil	4	cups Rice and Noodle Pilaf (page 250)
5	tablespoons flour		
2	cups chicken broth	2	tablespoons chopped parsley

Split the chicken breasts. Trim and poach them according to the directions on page 166. Reserve the liquid and add to the chicken broth.

If you are using fresh broccoli, divide into flowerets, leaving about 1½ inches of stem. Cook or steam in boiling water seasoned with the ½ teaspoon of salt for 5 to 8 minutes. Don't overcook; the broccoli will have more time in the oven and you don't want to end up with a limp, droopy vegetable. Drain the broccoli and set it aside.

In a medium-sized saucepan, heat the oil, add the flour, and stir until it bubbles. Add the broth and milk slowly, stirring with a wire whisk until the sauce is thickened and smooth. Season to taste with salt and pepper and add the sherry.

Oil a large, shallow ovenproof serving dish that can be brought to the table. Place a layer of broccoli in a ring around the dish, leaving a space in the center to be filled later with Rice and Noodle Pilaf. Cover the broccoli with half the sauce. Place the chicken breasts on top of the broccoli and pour the remainder of the sauce over the chicken. Cover tightly with aluminum foil and bake in a 350° oven for 40 minutes. Remove the foil, sprinkle with the cheese, and bake uncovered 10 minutes longer. If the top isn't sufficiently browned, run the pan under the broiler for a few minutes.

Just before serving, fill the center with the pilaf. Sprinkle the parsley over the chicken.

Serves 6 to 8

CHICKEN, ARTICHOKE, AND MUSHROOM CASSEROLE

4 whole chicken
breasts, boned and
skinned
1 teaspoon salt
Freshly ground pepper
1 teaspoon sweet
paprika
6 tablespoons oil
1 pound mushrooms,
sliced
1 clove garlic, minced

2 tablespoons flour
1 cup chicken broth
¼ cup dry sherry
½ teaspoon rosemary,
crushed
1 14-ounce can
artichoke hearts (water-
packed)
2 tablespoons lemon
juice

Wash and dry the chicken breasts and cut in two. Trim all fat. Season with the salt, pepper, and paprika. In a large, heavy skillet, heat the oil. Over high heat, brown the chicken breasts well on both sides. Transfer to a large, shallow casserole that can be brought to the table. Reduce the heat to medium and cook the mushrooms and garlic for 5 minutes, stirring. Pour off any excess oil that remains in the skillet. Sprinkle the flour over the mushrooms, mix well, and add the broth, stirring to pick up any crusty particles that remain on the pan bottom. Add the sherry and rosemary. Cook over low heat for 5 minutes, stirring with a wire whisk, until the sauce is thickened and smooth. Taste and correct the seasonings. Arrange the artichoke hearts among the pieces of chicken and sprinkle all with the lemon juice. Pour the sauce over the chicken in the casserole, cover, and bake in a 350° oven for 40 minutes.

Serves 6 to 8

CHICKEN PAUPIETTES

This is my adaptation of Chicken Kiev. Chicken Kiev, as you know, consists of pounded chicken breasts that envelope a finger of cold herbed butter, which behaves on occasion like a geyser when cut into. But since geysers of butter are now far removed from our areas of interest or participation, we can still achieve a fine dish with breast of chicken that encases a palate-pleasing stuffing guaranteed not to shoot into the eye of the person cutting into it. It's a good party dish, too, because it can be prepared the day before—always a comfort on the day of the party.

3	large whole chicken breasts, boned and skinned	2	egg whites, whipped to a froth
	Salt and pepper	1	cup cornflake crumbs
¼	cup flour		Oil for frying

Mushroom Stuffing

½	pound fresh mushrooms	1	teaspoon lemon juice
1	small onion	½	teaspoon salt
2	tablespoons oil		Freshly ground pepper
2	tablespoons dry white wine	¼	cup cornflake crumbs
¼	teaspoon dried rosemary, crushed	1	tablespoon minced parsley

Cut the chicken breasts in two and trim all fat. Place the breasts between two pieces of waxed paper and pound with a wooden mallet. Make them as thin as you can, but be careful not to split the flesh. Remove from the paper and set aside.

Chop the mushrooms extremely fine. The food grinder is not recommended here, for it will reduce them to a paste, which is not what you want. Set the mushrooms aside and chop the onion finely. In a medium-sized skillet, heat the oil and cook the onion over medium heat until limp and transparent. Increase the heat, add the mushrooms, and continue to cook, stirring, until the liquid given out by the mushrooms is completely absorbed. Reduce the heat, add the wine, rosemary, lemon juice, salt, pepper, and cornflake crumbs and cook for another minute or two. Remove from the fire and cool. Stir in the parsley. Shape into six finger-shaped pieces about 2½ inches long.

Lightly salt and pepper the chicken breasts. Place a finger of stuffing in the center of each breast, fold over the sides, and roll. Fasten with a toothpick.

For your assembly line, you will need two squares of waxed paper, one with a mound of flour and the other with a small amount of cornflake crumbs. Don't spread too many crumbs at a time. They become damp from the paupiettes, and it's better to keep adding dry crumbs as you use them. Dust each roll lightly in the flour, next in the egg white, and then roll in the crumbs. Refrigerate for an hour or more so that the crumbs will harden and stick. If you are planning to cook them the following day, cover with aluminum foil and store in the refrigerator.

Let the chicken breasts come to room temperature before you start to cook them. Pour an inch of oil into a heavy skillet and heat. Fry them for 5 minutes, turning with kitchen tongs until golden brown all around. Place in a shallow baking pan and cover tightly with aluminum foil. Bake in a 350° oven for 30 minutes.

Serves 6

GARBANZO CHICKEN

Garbanzos—or *cece, gram,* or chick-pea depending on which language you are speaking—is a flavorful and versatile legume that gives a good account of itself in this preparation. This is an easy recipe to double for those occasions when the guest list is a large one.

4 whole chicken breasts, boned and skinned	1 teaspoon salt Freshly ground pepper
Salt and pepper	1 teaspoon oregano
Paprika	1 teaspoon basil
½ cup oil	½ teaspoon thyme
⅓ cup red wine vinegar	½ teaspoon rosemary
⅓ cup finely chopped celery	1 1-pound-4-ounce can chick-peas, drained
¼ cup diced red onion	1 ¼-inch-thick slice of lean baked Virginia ham (about ¼ pound)
1 clove garlic, crushed	

Split the chicken breasts in half. Trim the fat and membrane. Sprinkle the breasts lightly with salt, pepper, and paprika and place in a baking pan.

In a medium-sized bowl, blend together the oil and vinegar. Add all the remaining ingredients except the chick-peas and ham. Mix well, then add the chick-peas. Cut the ham into ¼-inch cubes and add. Pour this mixture over the chicken breasts and marinate overnight in the refrigerator. Turn the chicken a few times so that the seasoned dressing is well distributed among all the chicken pieces. Have the chicken at room temperature when you are ready to cook it. Bake uncovered in a preheated 350° oven for 45 to 50 minutes, basting a few times. Transfer to a heated platter and cover the chicken well with the chick-pea and ham sauce.

Serves 8

9
Fish

It is difficult for me to introduce the chapter on fish cookery without lapsing into a low-key panegyric about the important role the creatures that live in the sea play in a dietary concerned with good nutrition and cholesterol. Aside from the pleasures of superb eating, fish offers an unsurpassed quality of protein and as good a source of minerals as meat. The fattest fish, for the most part, contains less fat than the leanest meat, and fish fats are a relatively rich source of polyunsaturated fatty acids. Consider also that fish contains only about half the number of calories found in an equal weight of beef, pork, or lamb, thus permitting larger portions for the calorie watcher.

In our household we have made lunch synonymous with fish. This makes meal planning easier on the planner, eliminating as it does the need for a major decision. For this generally light noontime meal, your grocery store can be as useful as your fish market, and is probably more accessible. The tins of sardines, tuna, salmon, herring, and the like that line the grocer's shelves are just a can opener away from your table and lend themselves to a wide variety of serving methods.

There is scarcely a luncheon or dinner course—a fish dessert eludes me, so I'll skip that one—for which fish cannot provide a solution. Starting with kippers for breakfast and continuing through luncheon, tea or cocktail time, and dinner, you can find in the endless variety of fish, either fresh, frozen, smoked, pickled, canned, or salted, the basic materials for some memorable snacks and meals.

I believe that many households that are "fish resistant,"

for want of a better description, suffer only from underexposure to interesting and varied fish cookery. Their reluctance or lack of interest often results from uninspired or improper treatment of the finny things. It is a myth that only experts can prepare fish properly, since anyone who can read, is willing to make an effort, and can tell time can become an expert.

The last is important because fish must never be overcooked and does not improve with a wait between preparation and serving. It becomes dry and loses flavor. If you think your dinner might have to be delayed, time your preparations accordingly. Broiling or poaching fish generally requires very little time, and your family will hold up better after a 10- or 15-minute delay than the fish will. One of the secrets of the excellence of the seafood specialty restaurants is their practice of cooking-to-order.

If you should happen to live on the banks of a well-stocked river or stream, ignore the recipes. All you need is a frying pan, some polyunsaturated oil, and seasonings. The rest of us will do well to experiment with different kinds of fish and different methods of preparation.

Since it would be exceedingly difficult to consistently plan meals rich in protein and low in saturated fat without the frequent appearance of the fish family, please forgive me my poor joke about our need for a fish-ician in the successful management of our cholestrol-watching regime.

GENERAL DIRECTIONS FOR COOKING FISH

Fish are sometimes classified as fat or lean. The white-fleshed fish such as halibut, scrod or cod, and sole are lean; fish with colored flesh such as salmon and mackerel are fat. But the fat in all cases is highly unsaturated, which is what this volume is all about. The lean fish may require a bit more oil in their preparation than the fat ones.

A timing rule that generally works is to measure the fish at its thickest point and figure 10 minutes of cooking time per inch, whatever method you are using. A fillet ½ inch thick will need about 5 minutes; a 1½-inch fish steak will take a total of about 15 minutes for both sides, etc. Double the time for frozen fish. When the fish flakes easily at the touch of a fork, it is done.

TO BAKE FISH

Baking is probably the simplest of all procedures and is particularly useful when dealing with a large fish. The fish can be baked in an ovenproof dish that may then be brought to the table, thus saving the sometimes difficult job of transferring a large fish to the serving platter.

Place fish steaks, fillets, or whole fish into a generously oiled baking dish that has been heated in advance in the oven. Brush the fish lightly with a pastry brush dipped in a browning agent such as Kitchen Bouquet or Brown-Quick, dribble a bit of oil over the top, season with salt and pepper, and place in a preheated 400° oven until the fish flakes easily.

TO BROIL FISH

The broiling process is the same for all fish. Only the time varies and this depends, of course, upon the thickness of the fish. Fish steaks such as halibut, salmon, and swordfish should be turned to cook on both sides. Thinner fish such as fillets or split whole fish such as trout, mackerel, or red snapper need not be turned.

Preheat the broiler for 15 minutes. I always cover the broiler pan with two sheets of aluminum foil. There is no special mystique to this—the bottom sheet protects the broiler pan and makes the cleaning up easier, so it is a selfish act of self-preservation. The top sheet can be tucked up around the fish to make a shallow cuff, providing an enclosure which holds the juices that accrue while the fish is broiling.

After the broiler has heated, pour a little oil over the broiler pan foil and let it heat up for a minute. Turn both sides of the fish into the warmed oil and arrange on the foil. Because fish always looks more appetizing if it has a rich brown look, I always paint it lightly with a pastry brush dipped in a browning agent such as Kitchen Bouquet or Brown-Quick. Sprinkle the fish with salt and pepper and a squirt of lemon juice or white wine. Place the broiler pan about 4 inches below the heat unit. Baste during the broiling process.

For fish that must be turned, cook 5 minutes on one side, turn it carefully with a broad spatula, repeat the seasonings as above beginning with the Kitchen Bouquet, and broil for an additional 7 to 10 minutes, or whatever time is needed for it to flake easily. When done, remove the fish gently (fillets break easily), and place on a warmed serving platter. Pour over the fish any liquid that has formed. Garnish with chopped parsley or sprigs of watercress and serve at once. Serve with lemon or lime wedges and tartar sauce, if desired.

TO POACH OR BOIL FISH

The traditional method of boiling or poaching is to cover fish with a court bouillon and simmer gently, covered, until the fish flakes easily. A court bouillon, in spite of its rather imposing name, is simply a seasoned liquid in which meat, fish, and various vegetables are poached. It can be anything from plain salted water seasoned with lemon juice to the following:

Court Bouillon for Fish

Fish bones and/or fish heads (optional)
½ cup chopped onion
1 clove garlic, crushed
¾ cup dry white wine
2 quarts of water
1 teaspoon salt
10 peppercorns, crushed
1 stalk celery with leaves
3 sprigs parsley
½ bay leaf
Pinch of thyme

Combine all of the above and bring to a boil. Reduce the heat and simmer, uncovered, for 15 minutes. Strain through a fine sieve or a double layer of cheesecloth.

Place the fish in a kettle large enough to allow it to be removed easily. Cover it with the court bouillon and simmer, gently, covered until it flakes easily.

Another easy way to poach small fish is to bring to a boiling point a mixture of dry white wine and lightly salted water in any proportion you wish. You may substitute lemon juice for the wine if you like. Place the fish in the hot liquid in an ovenproof dish, cover with waxed paper, and place in a 350° oven for about 5 minutes, or until the fish flakes easily. The bland poached fish does nicely with a flavorful sauce, such as Marinara Sauce (page 333) or Mustard Sauce (page 286).

TO PAN-FRY FISH

Thin fillets or small whole fish may be fried. Coat the fish by dipping it in milk and then into cornflake crumbs or cornmeal or flour. Sprinkle with salt, pepper, and paprika. Cover the bottom of the skillet with oil, heat, and fry the fish until it is light brown. Turn and brown the other side.

TO STEAM FISH

In this procedure, the fish is cooked over the liquid instead of in it. If you don't have a fish steamer, it is simple to improvise one. You will need a fairly deep kettle with a tight cover. Place a heatproof pyrex bowl or a couple of custard cups on the bottom to support the plate or rack on which you will place the fish. This plate or rack should be well above the level of the liquid you put into the kettle. Pour water into the kettle, arrange the fish on a plate or rack, and bring the water to a boil. Cover the pot and let steam for 5 minutes. Turn off the heat and let stand another 5 minutes. Remove the fish to a serving platter and season with salt and pepper.

QUICK FISH BAKE

This can be done with practically any kind of fish fillets or steaks, fresh or frozen.

4 tablespoons tomato juice	½ teaspoon sweet paprika
4 tablespoons oil	Garlic powder
2 pounds fish fillets or steaks	2 tablespoons lemon juice
2 large onions, thinly sliced	1 thinly sliced lemon with peel
½ teaspoon salt	2 tablespoons minced parsley

In a baking pan large enough to hold all the fish in a single layer, mix the tomato juice and oil. Dip each piece of fish into the mixture to dampen it thoroughly and push the fish to one side of the pan to make room for a layer of onion slices. Place the fish over the onion slices and sprinkle with the salt, paprika, garlic powder, and lemon juice. Top with the lemon slices. Place in a preheated 400° oven and bake for 30 minutes, uncovered. If the fish steaks are thick, they may need to cook longer (between 45 minutes and an hour). Cover with aluminum foil for the first 30 minutes and finish baking uncovered. To serve, sprinkle the fish with the parsley.

Serves 4

OVEN-FRIED FISH

This is another fast and easy preparation for fresh or frozen fish fillets—sole, haddock, perch, or turbot.

2   pounds fish fillets
½ teaspoon salt
    Freshly ground pepper
½ cup oil

1   cup cornflake crumbs
    Lemon wedges
    Tartar sauce

Salt and pepper the fish fillets. Dip in the oil. Place a mound of cornflake crumbs on a square of waxed paper and coat the fillets with the crumbs. Arrange in a single layer on a lightly oiled shallow baking pan. Bake in a preheated 350° oven for 30 minutes, or until the fish tests done. Serve with lemon wedges and tartar sauce.

Serves 4

FISH FILLETS IN BOUILLABAISSE SAUCE

Since bouillabaisse, the classic among fish stews, cannot be properly made without an assortment of fish and crustaceans, we borrowed just its essence for this splendid baked fish dish. The robust, burnished gold-colored sauce is a rich blend of the herbs and spices—saffron and fennel among them—always present in the distinctive Mediterranean fish stew.

3 pounds firm-fleshed fillets—cod, haddock, halibut, etc.

Bouillabaisse Sauce

2	ripe tomatoes	1	teaspoon oregano
3	tablespoons oil	6	⅛-inch strips orange
2	large onions, finely		peel
	chopped		Pinch of saffron
1	leek, finely chopped	1	teaspoon salt
3	cloves garlic, minced		Freshly ground pepper
1½	cups white wine	2	teaspoons fennel seeds,
1	cup chicken broth		crushed
1	cup clam broth	2	tablespoons flour
	Tabasco to taste	2	tablespoons water
1	bay leaf	2	tablespoons chopped
½	teaspoon thyme		parsley
1	teaspoon basil		Lemon wedges

Wash the fish and set it aside while you prepare the sauce. Peel the tomatoes by plunging them into boiling water for a minute and slipping off the skins. Chop them coarsely. Heat the oil in a large, heavy skillet and cook the onions and leek, stirring from time to time until the onions are limp and transparent, but not browned. Add the tomatoes and garlic, cover, and simmer over low heat for about 15 minutes, or until the tomatoes are softened.

Put the mixture through a food mill. If you use a blender, blend for just half a minute or so and stop before it becomes liquefied, for the sauce should have a little texture. Return the puree to the skillet, stir in the wine, and bring to a simmer. Add the chicken and clam broths, Tabasco, bay leaf, thyme, basil, oregano, orange peel strips (skin only—no white), a good pinch of saffron, salt, pepper, and fennel seeds. (To crush the fennel seeds, place them in a small plastic bag and go over them with a rolling pin. A bottle will do if you don't have a rolling pin.) Boil the sauce for 35 to 40 minutes to reduce it. Make a paste of the flour and water. Reduce the heat and add, stirring until the sauce is smooth and thickened. Taste and correct the seasoning. Remove the bay leaf. This sauce may be made well in advance, so that the final assembling is a simple matter.

Lightly salt and pepper the fish fillets. Pour half the sauce into a large, shallow baking dish that can be used for serving. Arrange the fish fillets in the sauce and cover with the remaining sauce. (If you find that you have more sauce than you need, do refrigerate the excess. It keeps very well and you can use it later.) Bring the sauce in the baking dish to boil on top of the stove and transfer the baking dish to a 375° oven for 12 to 15 minutes, depending upon the thickness of the fish. The fish is done when it flakes easily with a fork. Sprinkle the fish with the parsley. Serve with lemon wedges.

Thick slices of boiled potatoes, sliced crossways, and some hot crusty French bread to sop up the delicious sauce are fine accompaniments.

Serves 6

ROLLED FILLETS OF SOLE

Just one of these fish "turbans" on a bed of rice makes a splendid appetizer course for a company dinner.

4	large fillets of sole	2	tablespoons white wine
1	cut lemon		Lemon wedges
½	teaspoon salt	2	cups hot cooked rice
	Freshly ground pepper		Sweet paprika
2	teaspoons oil		Parsley

Sauce

2	tablespoons oil	½	teaspoon salt
3	tablespoons flour	⅓	cup dry sherry
¾	cup skim milk		

Wash the fish and pat dry. Split the fillets in half lengthwise and rub each side with the lemon. Place the fillets with the snowy white side down, the side that was skinned toward you. Sprinkle with ½ teaspoon salt and pepper. Roll up firmly. The fish will stick to itself and will probably not need a toothpick or skewer to hold it. Stand the eight rolled fillets in a lightly oiled shallow glass or enamel baking dish or pie plate. Dribble a bit of oil over the fish and pour the white wine around the fish rolls. Bake uncovered in a preheated 350° oven for 30 minutes, basting a few times.

While the fish is baking, prepare the sauce. In a small saucepan, heat the oil, add the flour, and cook over medium heat, stirring, until bubbly. Reduce the heat and slowly add the milk and the ½ teaspoon of salt, stirring with a wire whisk until the sauce is thickened and smooth. Remove from the heat, add the sherry, and 2 or 3 tablespoons of liquid from the fish. Taste for seasoning and correct.

Arrange the fish rolls on a bed of hot cooked rice. Pour the sauce over the rolls and sprinkle lightly with the paprika. Garnish with a sprig of parsley in the center of each rolled fillet. Serve with lemon wedges.

Serves 4

Variation: To turn these into *paupiettes* of sole, roll each fillet around a finger of fresh salmon and proceed as above.

BROILED FILLET OF SOLE WITH BANANAS

Many restaurants in the little fishing village of Cascais, Portugal—one of our favorite vacation spots—feature this dish. I don't know whether or not it is authentic Portuguese fare, but all credit to whatever nation first had the inspiration to mingle the soft sweetness of the banana with the delicate blandness of the fish.

2 pounds lemon sole, gray sole, or flounder fillets
   Kitchen Bouquet
½ teaspoon salt
   Freshly ground pepper

2 or 3 bananas, peeled and split lengthwise
   Oil
2 tablespoons lemon juice

Preheat the broiler. Wash and dry the fish fillets and arrange them on a broiler pan. With a pastry brush dipped in Kitchen Bouquet, lightly paint the fillets, then sprinkle them with the salt and pepper. Place a banana half on each piece of fish and dribble a bit of oil and the lemon juice over all. Place under the broiler, about 4 inches from the heat. Broil for 7 or 8 minutes, or until the fish flakes easily. With a broad spatula, carefully remove the fillets to a warmed serving platter. Garnish with lemon wedges and serve at once.

Serves 4

POACHED SOLE À LA NORMANDE

6 fillets of sole or other thin white fish
1 cup water
1 cup dry white wine
2 large onions, cut into eighths
2 tablespoons oil

2 tablespoons flour
3 tablespoons parsley, finely chopped
½ teaspoon salt
Freshly ground pepper
6 scallions, finely chopped

Wash the fillets. In a glass or enamel baking dish that can be brought to the table, place the water, wine, and onions. Bring to a simmer on top of the stove. Arrange the fish fillets in the liquid, cover with waxed paper, and place in a preheated 350° oven for 5 minutes, or until the fish flakes easily when tested with a fork. Drain off the cooking stock, strain, and measure 1 cup. Keep the fish warm in a 250° oven while you prepare the sauce. In a small saucepan, blend the oil and flour, add the cup of stock, parsley, salt, and pepper, and stir with a wire whisk until smooth and thickened. Taste for seasoning. Pour the sauce over the fillets and sprinkle the chopped scallions on top.

Serves 6

FILLET OF SOLE AND ARTICHOKES

The versatile fillets take on a slightly different shape in this meal-in-one.

2 pounds fillet of sole
3 large old potatoes
5 tablespoons oil
¼ cup flour
1 teaspoon salt

Freshly ground black pepper
1 teaspoon sweet paprika
½ cup skim milk

1	14-ounce can artichoke hearts (water-packed)	2	tablespoons finely chopped parsley
1	tablespoon lemon juice		

Wash and dry the fish fillets. Cut them into strips 5 or 6 inches long and about 1 inch wide. Peel the potatoes, wash and dry them well, and cut into thin strips about the same size as the fish strips.

In a large, heavy skillet, heat the oil and cook the potato strips about 20 minutes, or until they are golden brown. Turn them often so that they brown evenly. Remove them with a slotted spoon and drain on absorbent paper. Keep warm in a 250° oven.

On a square of waxed paper, combine the flour, salt, pepper, and paprika and mix thoroughly. Dip the fish strips in the milk, then in the seasoned flour. Coat lightly and shake off the excess. Brown the fish on both sides in the same skillet in which you cooked the potatoes, turning the strips carefully so as not to break the pieces. Add a bit of oil if necessary. When the fish is cooked, add the drained artichokes to the skillet and heat through. Sprinkle with the lemon juice. Arrange the fish and artichokes on a heated platter, surround with fried potatoes, and sprinkle the fish with the parsley.

Serves 4

FISH FILLETS IN WINE SAUCE

2	tablespoons oil	2	pounds any thin fish fillet (sole, flounder, scrod, etc.)
3	tablespoons chopped parsley		
3	tablespoons onion or shallot, finely chopped	½	cup dry white wine
1	teaspoon salt	2	tablespoons cornflake crumbs
	Freshly ground pepper		Watercress
			Lemon wedges

Coat the bottom of a large, shallow glass or enamel ovenproof baking dish with 1 tablespoon of the oil. Spread half the parsley and onion or shallot over the bottom of the dish and sprinkle lightly with half of the salt and pepper. Arrange the fish fillets over the mixture and cover with the remainder of the parsley, onion or shallot, and oil. Sprinkle with the remainder of the salt and pepper. Pour the wine over the fish and sprinkle with the cornflake crumbs. Bake 30 minutes in a preheated 350° oven.

Just before serving, place under the broiler for a few minutes to brown. Garnish with sprigs of watercress and lemon wedges.

Serves 4

FILLET OF SOLE AMANDINE

2 pounds fish fillets
¼ cup flour
1 teaspoon salt
1 teaspoon paprika
  Freshly ground pepper
4 tablespoons oil

½ cup blanched slivered almonds
3 tablespoons lemon juice
1 tablespoon chopped parsley
  Lemon wedges.

Wash and dry the fillets. On a square of waxed paper, mix the flour, salt, paprika, and pepper. Dredge the fish lightly in the seasoned flour. Heat the oil in a large, heavy skillet and fry the fish over medium heat until lightly browned on both sides. Remove the fish to a platter and keep warm in the oven while you lightly brown the almonds in the same pan. Sprinkle them with the lemon juice and pour the pan juices and almonds over the fish. Garnish with the parsley and lemon wedges. Serve at once.

Serves 4

FILLET OF SOLE, ANCHOVY

Anchovies bring a piquancy and distinctive flavor to many dishes, not the least of which is fish. This can be made with any thin fish fillet.

2 pounds fish fillets
1 2-ounce can anchovy
   fillets
5 tablespoons oil

1 tablespoon chopped
  parsley
Lemon wedges

Wash and dry the fillets. Mash the anchovies into a paste and mix well with the oil and parsley. In a large, heavy skillet, place this mixture over low heat for 3 or 4 minutes. Increase the heat, add the fillets, and cook until golden brown on both sides. Remove the fish to a warm platter and pour the anchovy mixture over it. Garnish with lemon wedges.

Serves 4

FISH FILLETS IN MUSTARD SAUCE

2   pounds fish fillets
    (sole, flounder, cod)
3   tablespoons oil
1½ cups tomato juice
1   clove garlic, crushed
2   tablespoons finely
    chopped onion
1   tablespoon finely
    chopped parsley

2   tablespoons prepared
    mustard (Dijon-type)
½   teaspoon salt
    Freshly ground pepper
2   tablespoons
    cornstarch
2   tablespoons water
¼   cup bread crumbs
    browned in 2
    tablespoons oil

Wash and dry the fillets. In a medium-sized saucepan, combine the oil, tomato juice, garlic, onion, parsley, mustard, salt, and pepper and slowly heat to the boiling point. Make a paste of the cornstarch and water and add to the sauce, stirring with a wire whisk until the sauce is smooth and thickened.

Lightly oil a shallow baking dish that can be used for serving and arrange the fillets in a single layer. Spoon the sauce over the fish. Brown the bread crumbs in a small skillet and scatter them over the sauce. Bake in a preheated 350° oven for 30 minutes, or until the fish flakes easily.

Serves 4

FISH FLORENTINE

Here the versatile fillet is served in a good-tasting green sauce. Halibut or any fillet, such as cod, haddock, sole, or flounder, is suitable.

2 pounds fish fillets
1 cup water
¼ cup white wine
¼ cup lemon juice
½ teaspoon salt
Freshly ground pepper
3 tablespoons oil
3 tablespoons flour
1 cup skim milk
1 tablespoon Worcestershire sauce
1 10-ounce package frozen chopped spinach, cooked and drained
4 scallions, finely chopped
Salt and pepper
Cornflake crumbs

Wash the fillets and place them in a shallow heatproof glass or enamel casserole or baking dish. Add the water, wine, lemon juice, ½ teaspoon of salt, and pepper and bring to a boil on top of the stove, covered. Reduce the heat and simmer, covered, for 5 minutes. Drain the fish stock into a small saucepan and boil over medium-high heat until the sauce is reduced to two thirds of its original quantity. Set this stock aside. In the same saucepan, heat 2 tablespoons of the oil with the flour. Stir until it bubbles. Slowly add the milk and stir with a wire whisk until the sauce is smooth and thickened. Add the fish stock, Worcestershire sauce, spinach, scallions, salt, and pepper and simmer for 2 or 3 minutes. Taste and correct the seasoning. Remove from the heat.

Season the fish lightly with salt and pepper. Cover the fish with the spinach sauce and sprinkle with the crumbs. Dribble the remaining tablespoon of oil over all. Bake in a 400° oven for 8 to 10 minutes, or until the top is golden brown. Serve immediately.

Serves 4

BAKED STUFFED FISH

The choice of fish to bake can be a matter between you and your fish man. Striped bass, red snapper, large mackerel, haddock (if he happens to have one), or bluefish all take kindly to this method of preparation. The head and tail should be removed and the fish scaled and cleaned. Having the center bone removed and leaving the fish held together on one side by the skin makes the serving less complicated.

1 6- 7-pound fish, cleaned and boned

½ teaspoon salt
Freshly ground pepper

2 tablespoons oil

1 small onion, finely chopped

1 clove garlic, minced

¼ cup celery, finely chopped

1 cup cooked rice or 1½ cups fine fresh bread crumbs

2 tablespoons chopped parsley

1 tablespoon Worcestershire sauce

¼ cup toasted slivered almonds
Salt and pepper

1 tablespoon flour seasoned with salt and pepper

1 cup dry white wine

Season the fish on the inside with the salt and pepper. Place in a large, lightly oiled glass or enamel baking dish that can be used for serving.

In a good-sized skillet, heat the oil and cook the onion until it is limp. Add the garlic and cook 2 or 3 minutes longer. Remove from the heat. Add the celery, rice (or bread crumbs), parsley, Worcestershire sauce, and almonds. Toss lightly and add salt and pepper to taste. Stuff the fish with this mixture and close by securing with toothpicks or by sewing.

Rub the seasoned flour over the top of the fish and cut three diagonal gashes in the skin at equal intervals. This will help the fish to keep its shape while it bakes. Pour the wine around the fish. Place in a preheated 400° oven and bake uncovered for 15 minutes. Reduce the heat to 375° and bake 35 minutes longer, or until the fish flakes easily. Baste a few times with the pan juices.

Serves 6

BAKED FISH, SPANISH STYLE

Any thick white fish such as halibut or substantial haddock fillet may be used.

4 tablespoons oil
½ teaspoon Tabasco
2 large onions, thinly
 sliced
2 tablespoons pimiento,
 diced
3 tablespoons green
 pepper, finely chopped
2 pounds fish, 1 to 1½
 inches thick
1 teaspoon salt

Freshly ground pepper
4 thick slices tomato
3 tablespoons chopped
 chives or scallions
½ pound mushrooms,
 thinly sliced
½ cup dry white wine
1 teaspoon
 Worcestershire sauce
½ cup bread crumbs

In a large, shallow ovenproof glass or enamel baking dish that can be used for serving, combine 2 tablespoons of the oil with the Tabasco and spread over the bottom of the baking dish. Cover with a layer of the onions, pimiento, and green pepper.

Wash the fish and wipe it dry. Cut it into four portions, season with the salt and pepper, and place on the layer of onions. Cover each piece of fish with a slice of tomato sprinkled with the chives or scallions. Scatter the mushrooms over all. Add the wine.

Heat the remaining 2 tablespoons of oil in a small skillet, add the Worcestershire sauce, and brown the bread crumbs. Sprinkle them over the top of the fish. Bake uncovered in a preheated 350° oven for 35 to 40 minutes, or until the fish flakes easily. Serve at once.

Serves 4

BAKED FISH CHINOIS

A slightly unusual flavor distinguishes this fish preparation. It is suitable for halibut, salmon, haddock, or cod fillets.

2 pounds fish steaks
 or fillets
2 or 3 tablespoons soy
 sauce
½ cup dry sherry

2 tablespoons lemon
 juice
1 clove garlic, crushed
2 tablespoons oil
2 tablespoons cornflake
 crumbs

Wash the fish and pat dry. In a large, shallow ovenproof baking dish (glass or enamel), mix together the soy sauce, sherry, lemon juice, garlic, and oil. (Some soy sauces are saltier than others, so you will have to be your own judge as to the amount you use.) Place the fish in the sauce and allow to marinate for an hour. Turn it a few times.

Sprinkle the cornflake crumbs over the fish and bake in a preheated 350° oven for 30 minutes, or until the fish flakes easily. A thicker fish may require 5 or 10 minutes longer.

Serves 4

Note: This fish may also be broiled. After it has marinated, transfer to a preheated broiler and broil according to the directions on page 179. Sprinkle with the cornflake crumbs 5 minutes before completion.

BAKED FISH FILLETS WITH NOODLES

Fresh or frozen fish fillets may be used for this casserole-type dish.

½	pound broad noodles	½–¾	cup dry sherry
4	tablespoons oil	2	pounds fish fillets
2	tablespoons flour		(sole, flounder,
1	teaspoon salt		perch, or turbot)
	Freshly ground		Salt and pepper
	pepper	3	tablespoons
1½	cups skim milk		cornflake crumbs
1	cup mushrooms,		Chopped parsley
	sliced		

Cook the noodles according to the package directions. Do not overcook. Rinse and drain well, then toss lightly with 1 tablespoon of the oil. Lightly oil a large shallow baking dish and spread the cooked noodles evenly on the bottom.

In a saucepan, heat 2 tablespoons of the oil. Blend in the flour, teaspoon of salt, and pepper and stir. Over medium heat, add the milk, stirring with a wire whisk until the sauce becomes thick and smooth. Reduce the heat and cook a minute longer. In a small skillet, heat the remaining tablespoon of oil, and cook the mushrooms for 2 or 3 minutes. Mix the mushrooms into the sauce. Pour the sauce over the noodles.

Heat the sherry in a large skillet. While it simmers, add the fish fillets. Poach over medium heat only until they lose their raw look. With a slotted spoon, carefully remove them and arrange on the bed of noodles. Pour the wine left in the pan over the fish. Sprinkle lightly with salt and pepper, the cornflake crumbs, and the parsley. Bake in a preheated 350° oven for 10 minutes.

Serves 4

BROILED SALMON

Salmon has few peers among fish for the variety of textures and flavors it can assume. It is canned, pickled, and smoked, served hot, cold, unadorned or embellished with a fine sauce, and makes splendid fare at breakfast, lunch, supper, dinner, or any snack time. So much for the glories of that intrepid sea creature. We have here a number of different methods of preparation, beginning with simply broiling it, which I think is one of the nicest things to do with a fine slice of good fresh salmon.

3 pounds salmon or individual salmon steaks	Kitchen Bouquet Juice of a lemon Salt
3 tablespoons oil	Freshly ground pepper

Wash and dry the salmon. Preheat the broiler. Pour the oil into a flat shallow baking pan and heat in the oven 5 minutes. Remove the baking pan from the oven and give each side of the salmon a bath in the heated oil. Brush the fish lightly with a pastry brush dipped in Kitchen Bouquet. Dribble the lemon juice over the fish and sprinkle with salt and pepper. Place under the broiler about 4 inches from the heat and broil for 5 minutes. Turn the fish, repeat the above procedures, and broil 8 to 10 minutes longer, or until the fish flakes easily. Transfer to a heated platter, garnish with lemon wedges and parsley sprigs or watercress, and serve at once.

Serves 6

POACHED SALMON STEAKS

This may be served hot or cold. If the latter, poach the fish at least 4 hours before you plan to serve it, so that it will be well chilled. Portion-sized slices of halibut may also be used.

4 salmon steaks, about ½ inch thick (about 2 pounds)	½ cup lemon juice or white wine
4 cups water	1 medium-sized onion, sliced
1 tablespoon salt	6 peppercorns

Rinse the fish and set aside. Place the remaining ingredients in a 12-inch skillet. Bring the liquid to a rolling boil, reduce the heat, and simmer for 10 minutes. Add the fish and bring again to a boil. Reduce the heat to low, cover the skillet, and simmer for 5 to 7 minutes, or until the fish flakes easily when tested with a fork.

Use a pancake turner—a slotted one, if possible—to remove the fish steaks from the water. Drain each steak carefully while it rests on the pancake turner. Transfer to a warmed platter and serve with Easy Hollandaise Sauce (page 332).

If you are serving the fish steaks chilled, place them on a lightly oiled cookie sheet after they are drained. Refrigerate until well chilled. To serve, place each fish portion on lettuce or romaine. Pass Green Mayonnaise (page 330) or Cucumber Sauce (page 79) separately. Garnish the portions with lemon wedges, cherry tomatoes, artichoke hearts, or cold asparagus.

Serves 4

WHOLE BAKED SALMON

There are few things more impressive on a buffet table than a whole cooked salmon, pink and resplendent, resting on a bed of greens. However, many people find handling a large whole fish a perilous undertaking, requiring equipment perhaps not readily available in many of today's streamlined (a euphemism for closet-sized) kitchens. But baking a fish all neatly done up in a foil package that includes a sauce bath gives a splendid result—a moist and juicy fish.

1½	cups dry white wine or equal parts lemon juice and water	¼	cup celery leaves
		3	sprigs parsley
		¼	lemon, sliced with peel
¼	teaspoon each dried tarragon, thyme leaves, and basil	1	8- 10-pound salmon, left whole
		1	teaspoon salt

In a small saucepan, combine all the ingredients except the salmon and salt. Simmer over low heat for 30 minutes, but do not boil.

Wash the cleaned salmon and pat dry. You can leave the head on or not, as you wish. (I have a thing about fish heads with that lifeless eye gazing at me reproachfully, but that's my problem and should have no influence on you.)

Preheat the oven to 375°. In a baking pan large enough to hold the salmon, arrange a length of aluminum foil and place the salmon in the center. Pull up the sides of the foil and pour the hot liquid over the fish. Sprinkle the fish with the salt. Make a secure package of the foil, completely enclosing the fish, and crimp the edges of the foil tightly closed. Bake in the oven for about 1½ hours, or until the fish flakes easily when tested with a fork.

Remove the fish from the foil carefully and place on a long platter. When it is cool enough to handle, lift off the top skin. It isn't necessary to turn the fish in order to remove the skin on the underside, since that side is not exposed.

Garnish the salmon with parsley sprigs, pimiento strips, hard-boiled white of egg, sliced black olives, etc., artfully arranged. Serve with a bowl of Mayonnaise (page 329) or Cucumber Sauce (page 79).

Serves 12

Note: A 4- or 5-pound center cut of salmon may be prepared the same way. Reduce the amount of the court bouillon by a third and figure the cooking time between 15 and 20 minutes per pound, depending upon the thickness of the fish.

SALMON IN DILL SAUCE

4 salmon steaks
(2 pounds)
1 cup dry white wine
1 stalk celery with
leaves, finely chopped
Sprig of parsley
Bay leaf

½ teaspoon salt
Freshly ground pepper
2 tablespoons oil
6 shallots, finely chopped
1 tablespoon chopped
chives
1 tablespoon snipped dill

Wash the salmon steaks, then cut in half and reserve the skin and bones. In a medium-sized skillet, combine the wine, celery, parsley, bay leaf, salt, pepper, and fish skin and bones. Bring to a boil, cover, reduce the heat, and simmer for 20 minutes. Strain the fish stock into a large skillet, add the fish, and simmer, covered, for 5 minutes or until the fish flakes easily. Remove the fish pieces to a platter and keep warm in a 250° oven.

While the stock is simmering, heat the oil in a small skillet and sauté the shallots and chives until the shallots are golden. Add the dill and mix.

Boil the wine liquid in which the fish cooked until it is reduced to ½ cup. Add the shallot-dill mixture and blend well. Pour the sauce over the fish. Serve with lemon wedges.

Serves 4

SALMON PATTIES

A one-pound can of salmon provides a most adequate and delicious dinner for four people in the following recipe.

1 1-pound can salmon,
well drained, bones
and skin removed
2 tablespoons oil
2 tablespoons flour
¼ cup chicken broth
¼ cup skim milk
1 tablespoon grated
onion

1 tablespoon finely
chopped parsley
4 tablespoons cornflake
crumbs
2 tablespoons lemon juice
Cornflake crumbs for
coating (about ½ cup)
Oil for frying

Mash the drained, picked-over salmon. In a heavy saucepan, heat the oil. Blend in the flour and stir until it bubbles. Slowly add the chicken broth and milk, stirring with a wire whisk until the sauce is thickened and smooth. Cook 1 minute, remove from the heat, and add the salmon, onion, and parsley. Stir in the 4 tablespoons of cornflake crumbs and the lemon juice and mix thoroughly. Taste for seasoning. If the chicken broth is flavored enough, you won't need any additional seasonings.

Shape into eight patties. On a square of waxed paper, spread out the ½ cup of cornflake crumbs and roll the patties in the crumbs. If you can chill the patties in the refrigerator at this point for 15 or 20 minutes, the crumbs will adhere better, although on occasions when I didn't have time for this, I thought that the patties looked respectable on completion.

To cook the patties, heat about ⅛ inch of oil in a medium-sized skillet and fry for 2 or 3 minutes on each side, or until brown. Serve with lemon wedges.

Serves 4

Variation: Chicken patties may be made the same way, substituting 2 cups of firmly packed, finely chopped, cooked chicken in place of the salmon.

SAUTÉED SEA SQUABS

Whoever it was who first thought up renaming the highly unattractive puffer, better known as blowfish, deserves a vote of thanks. Considerably more appealing under the popular name of sea squab, it offers delicate flavor and texture that even people who are not fish fanciers find enjoyable. Skinless and with only a single center bone, it is an easy fish to eat. Sea squabs are not always uniform in size, but on an average they run about eight to a pound. Three are an adequate serving.

12 sea squabs (about 1½ pounds)	½ cup flour
Lemon juice	4 tablespoons oil
1 teaspoon salt	Lemon wedges
Freshly ground pepper	Tartar sauce

Wash and dry the fish thoroughly. Sprinkle with lemon juice, the salt, and a few grinds of pepper. Place the flour on a square of waxed paper and roll the fish lightly in it.

In a large, heavy skillet, heat the oil and cook the fish. Don't try to crowd too many into the pan at a time, as they break easily and you need room to turn them. Cook about 5 minutes on one side, turn, and cook 3 minutes on the other. Add more oil if the pan seems to be drying out. As they are done, place them in a 250° oven on a heatproof platter that can be brought to the table. Ten minutes or so in the oven won't do the cooked fish any harm, but a longer delay is not a good idea. Serve with lemon wedges and a bowl of tartar sauce.

Serves 4

SMELTS SAUTÉ

1½ pounds smelts	½ cup flour
1 teaspoon salt	4 anchovy fillets,
Freshly ground	mashed
pepper	1 tablespoon cornflake
3 tablespoons	crumbs
lemon juice	1 tablespoon chopped
¼ cup skim milk	parsley
4 or 5 tablespoons oil	Pinch of sugar

Wash the smelts, and do whatever you want to about the heads and tails but snip off the little fins. Season the fish with the salt, pepper, and 2 tablespoons of the lemon juice. Let them marinate for 10 or 15 minutes and reserve for the sauce whatever liquid is left. Combine the milk with 1 tablespoon of the oil and stir well. Dip the fish into this mixture. On a square of waxed paper, place a mound of flour and dredge the smelts. Heat 3 tablespoons of the oil in a large, heavy skillet. Fry the smelts until they are brown and crisp (about 5 minutes on each side), adding extra oil if needed. Don't crowd the fish—you may have to do them in batches. Place them on absorbent paper to drain and keep warm on a serving platter in a 250° oven while you prepare the sauce.

In the same skillet place the reserved liquid, remaining tablespoon of lemon juice, anchovy fillets, cornflake crumbs, parsley, and sugar. Cook over low heat for 2 minutes, stirring constantly, then pour over the fish.

Serves 4

CODFISH PORTUGUESE

This is a well-known traditional Portuguese dish. Its official name is Bacalhau a Gomes de Sá—generally known as Bacalhau—which, by a curious coincidence, means "codfish," in, as you might guess, Portuguese. We've eaten Bacalhau in some excellent Brazilian restaurants both in Brazil and locally, and found none better than this.

1	pound dried codfish	¼	cup black olives,
3	unpeeled potatoes		chopped finely
½	cup oil	½	teaspoon dill seed
2	large onions, sliced	⅓	cup dry white wine
1	clove garlic, crushed		Freshly ground pepper
			Chopped parsley

Soak the codfish in cold water overnight or even longer. Change the water a few times; the fish is salty. After soaking, discard the water, drain the fish, and place in a medium-sized saucepan. Cover the fish with cold water, bring to a boil, and boil for 20 minutes, or until the fish flakes easily. Remove the fish and set aside to cool. Reserve the liquid and boil the potatoes in it until tender. Flake the fish when it is cool enough to handle and remove the skin and bones, if there are any. When the potatoes are done, peel and slice them.

In a large skillet, heat the oil and cook the onions for 8 to 10 minutes, until they are limp but not brown. Add the codfish, potatoes, garlic, olives, dill seed, and wine and season with pepper. Cook for about 5 minutes, tossing lightly the whole time. Transfer the mixture to a well-oiled 1½-quart casserole and bake in a preheated 400° oven for 15 minutes. Garnish with chopped parsley. Serve hot.

Serves 4

POACHED FINNAN HADDIE

If you are not yet familiar with this fish, do make its acquaintance. Its origin is haddock that has been smoked, and, in the tradition of its source, it contains only the tiniest amount of fat. The fish has a salty tang that serves it well either as an appetizer, or as a main dish served with a delicate white sauce sparked with sherry. One pound serves four adequately as a first course, two as a main course.

To poach the fish, pour 1 inch of skim milk into a shallow skillet with a tight-fitting lid. When warm, add the fish cut into serving-size pieces. Simmer slowly, covered, for about 20 minutes, when it should flake easily. If not, 5 minutes more should do the trick. Remove from the liquid, sprinkle with chopped parsley, and serve warm.

CREAMED FINNAN HADDIE

1 pound finnan haddie	Freshly ground pepper
1½ tablespoons oil	1 tablespoon (or more),
1 tablespoon flour	sherry
1 cup skim milk (using what was left from poaching)	Chopped parsley

Poach the finnan haddie according to the directions in the preceding recipe. Remove the fish to a platter and keep warm in a 250° oven. In a small saucepan, heat the oil, add the flour, and blend over medium heat until it bubbles. Add the milk, reduce the heat, and stir with a wire whisk until thickened and smooth. Add a dash of pepper and sherry to taste. Pour over the fish, sprinkle with the parsley, and serve hot.

Serves 2

BROILED SWORDFISH STEAK

Swordfish has a hearty, almost meaty quality that assures it a welcome even among people whose favorite thing is not fish. Broiling it in this herbed sauce adds interesting flavor.

2 pounds swordfish	1 tablespoon soy sauce
steaks	¼ teaspoon dried tarragon
¼ cup oil	¼ teaspoon sweet basil
3 tablespoons chopped	½ teaspoon salt
scallions	Freshly ground pepper
3 tablespoons chopped	Juice and rind of 1
parsley	lemon
¼ teaspoon sweet paprika	

Wash and dry the swordfish steaks and place them in a lightly oiled shallow baking dish. In a small skillet, heat the oil and cook the scallions until golden. Add the remaining ingredients and simmer 2 minutes longer until thoroughly blended. Spread the sauce over both sides of the fish and marinate for at least an hour.

Preheat the broiler to very hot and place the fish steaks about 4 or 5 inches below the heat. Broil 7 to 10 minutes on each side, depending upon the thickness of the fish. Test for doneness. Serve with lemon wedges.

Serves 4

BAKED SWORDFISH STEAK VALENCIENNE

2 pounds swordfish	1 large tomato, peeled
steaks	and chopped
½ teaspoon salt	1 bay leaf
Freshly ground pepper	2 tablespoons tomato
4 tablespoons oil	paste
1 large onion, finely	¼ cup dry white wine or
chopped	clam broth
¼ cup chopped parsley	½ cup chicken broth
½ teaspoon dried thyme	Lemon slices with peel
1 clove garlic, minced	

Wash and dry the swordfish steaks and sprinkle them with the salt and pepper. Pour 2 tablespoons of the oil into a shallow glass or enamel ovenproof baking dish and arrange the fish in the dish.

In a saucepan heat the remaining oil and cook the onion, parsley, and thyme until the onion becomes limp. Add the garlic, tomato, and bay leaf and cook until the tomato is soft and the sauce is well blended. Add the tomato paste, wine or clam broth, and chicken broth and simmer 5 minutes longer. Taste for seasoning and add salt if needed. Pour the sauce over the fish, cover with thinly sliced lemon, and bake 30 minutes in a preheated 350° oven. Baste with the sauce from time to time.

Serves 4

FISH STEW

1	pound halibut	1	small carrot, thinly sliced
2	pounds filleted striped bass, pike, or other white fish, cut into 2-inch-wide strips	3	tablespoons oil
		3	cups canned tomatoes with liquid
3	cups cold water	2	stalks celery, diced
1	stalk celery with leaves	3	potatoes, peeled and cut into ¼-inch cubes
2	cloves garlic	½	cup dry sherry
2	large onions, finely chopped	1	tablespoon Worcestershire sauce
1½	teaspoons salt		Juice of 1 lemon
1	bay leaf	3	tablespoons chopped parsley
6	peppercorns, bruised		

Cut the halibut into 2-inch squares, reserving the skin and bones. Have your fish man fillet the bass or whichever fish he decides you should use for the stew and give you the bones, skin, and heads. Place all the fish trimmings in a saucepan with the water. Add the celery stalk, 1 of the garlic cloves, 1 of the onions, ½ teaspoon of the salt, bay leaf, peppercorns, and carrot. Bring to a boil, cover, and simmer for 30 minutes. Strain the fish stock and reserve.

In a large, heavy kettle, heat the oil and sauté the remaining onion until it is limp and transparent, but not browned. Crush the remaining garlic clove and add it along with the tomatoes, fish stock, remaining teaspoon of salt, diced celery, and potatoes. Bring to a boil, cover, and cook slowly for 30 minutes, or until the potatoes are tender. Add the sherry, Worcestershire sauce, lemon juice, and cut-up fish. Cook gently for about 10 minutes, or until the fish is tender. Taste for seasoning and correct. Sprinkle with the parsley and serve in large soup bowls.

Serves 6

FISH MOUSSE WITH SHRIMP SAUCE

This airy, delicate mousse can be served as an appetizer course or the main event for lunch or dinner.

1½ pounds ground uncooked haddock or cod
3 egg whites, unbeaten
1¼ cups undiluted evaporated skimmed milk

1 teaspoon salt
1 tablespoon Worcestershire sauce
1 tablespoon onion juice
½ teaspoon dry mustard
¼ cup cornflake crumbs

Shrimp Sauce

4 tablespoons oil
4 tablespoons flour
1 cup chicken broth
½ cup skim milk

¼ cup dry white wine or vermouth
¼ pound cooked shrimps, cut into small pieces

Preheat the oven to 350°. Place the fish in a good-sized bowl and add the egg whites slowly, a little at a time, beating well with each addition. Slowly add the milk, beating well. Beat in the salt, Worcestershire sauce, onion juice, and mustard and continue to beat until it is light and fluffy.

Oil a 6-cup ring mold and dust it with the cornflake crumbs. Pack the mold with the fish mixture, distributing it evenly. Cover the top with waxed paper. Place the mold in a large baking pan with about an inch of hot water at the bottom. Bake until set (about 25 to 30 minutes). When done, remove from the oven and let stand for 5 minutes. Loosen the mousse with a spatula and invert the mold on a round serving platter.

While the mousse is baking, you can prepare the sauce. In a medium-sized skillet, heat the oil and blend in the flour, but do not let it brown. After it bubbles, slowly add the chicken broth and stir with a wire whisk until the sauce comes to a boil. Gradually add the milk and wine, continuing to stir until the sauce is thickened and smooth. Taste for seasoning and correct. Simmer for a minute or so over low heat. Just before serving, add the shrimp and heat through. Pour the sauce over the mousse.

Serves 6 to 8

COLD TROUT PIQUANT

The rainbow trout that weigh under a pound each make convenient individual servings and are splendid fried or broiled. They are at their best, of course, when they are fresh; since it is not always possible to obtain them, however, the frozen or chilled ones are also most acceptable. The cold poached trout with a zingy sauce that follows is an easily prepared and delicious dish for a hot weather dinner.

6	rainbow trout	1	tablespoon vinegar
	Hot water	1	bay leaf
½	teaspoon salt	1	stalk celery with leaves

Sauce Piquant

½	cup tomato sauce	1	teaspoon grated lemon
¼	cup mayonnaise		rind
¼	cup lemon juice		Salt and pepper
			Tabasco

Rinse the trout and place in a deep skillet or pan. Cover with hot water. Add the salt, vinegar, bay leaf, and celery. Bring to a boil, reduce the heat, cover, and simmer for 6 minutes. (Frozen fish will need double the time.) Test for doneness and remove the fish from the liquid. Refrigerate for at least two hours.

In a small bowl, combine the tomato sauce, mayonnaise, lemon juice and rind, salt and pepper to taste, and a few squirts of Tabasco. Mix well. Serve the chilled fish with a bowl of the sauce.

Serves 6

SWEET-AND-SOUR FISH

This is an old family recipe, and it has continued to be a favorite. A variety of fishes may be used—trout or pike, or salmon, halibut, haddock fillets, etc. Salmon steaks are especially recommended. If you use fish steaks, cut them in half lengthwise. A whole fish is cut into 3-inch-thick slices through the bone and all.

2 pounds fish—pike, salmon, halibut, etc.

Poaching Liquid

1½	cups water	3	whole cloves
2	stalks celery	½	lemon with rind, thinly sliced
1	carrot, sliced crosswise	2	tablespoons sugar
1	tablespoon oil	½	cup vinegar
1	onion, thinly sliced	10	whole peppercorns

Thickening

10 gingersnaps
   Vinegar (about ½ cup)
¾ cup brown sugar
¼ cup raisins

¼ cup dry sherry
¼ cup blanched slivered almonds

Wash the fish and cut into large portion-size pieces.

In a deep skillet, place the ingredients for the poaching liquid. Bring to a boil, reduce the heat, and simmer for 20 minutes. Add the fish and poach gently about 10 minutes, or until the fish tests done. Remove the fish to a serving platter.

Discard the celery and cloves from the poaching liquid. In a small bowl, crumble the gingersnaps and cover with enough vinegar to dissolve them. Add to the simmering liquid along with the brown sugar, raisins, and sherry. Increase the heat and boil 4 or 5 minutes, or until the sauce is thickened and reduced by one third. Taste for seasoning. I do not generally add salt, but you decide for yourself. Just before removing from the heat, add the almonds. Pour the sauce over the fish. Serve warm or cold.

Serves 4

10
Vegetables

I don't suppose there is anyone in this hemisphere who doesn't know that vegetables are nutritious and good for one. But lots of people don't eat things because they are good for them—they eat them because they are good. So let's concentrate on that area. The honors for palate-pleasing vegetables must be divided equally between a crisp, fresh product to begin with and the method of preparation. A tired, limp thing won't improve with cooking, no matter what you do with it. Always start with the best and freshest product your market has to offer. The younger the vegetable, the less time it needs for cooking and the better the flavor. If you are fortunate enough to have access to farm-fresh produce, use the simplest cooking methods and seasonings. The natural flavors and textures of fine fresh vegetables require little enhancement. However, and comforting it can be, even the frozen vegetables are of high quality these days and can be most satisfactory.

Don't overlook the yellow and leafy green vegetables, in addition to all the others. Nature has been thoughtful in providing us with a color index for our nutritional needs. By mixing a rich palette of colors and contrasts with the vegetables we serve—green, yellow, red, white, orange, etc.—we not only provide visual pleasures at meals, but fulfill our varied mineral and vitamin requirements at the same time.

A good deal of the vitamin content of vegetables is water soluble, so it is to our advantage to cook the vegetables in as little water and for as short a time as possible. One of my favorite bits of kitchen equipment is a steamer I use for vegetables. It consists of a round pot, a shallow insert pan with holes around the rim, and a very heavy lid. There is also available in the stores a metal basket on legs that is adjustable in size, fits nicely into almost any pot, and performs most satisfactorily as a steamer.

If you have been serving a limited vegetable repertoire, try some unfamiliar ones. Experiment with new vegetables and different methods of preparation. I always suspect that somewhere in the past of most people who shrug their shoulders at vegetables lies a mess of soggy green peas and tired, limp string beans. Properly cooked and seasoned vegetables, imaginatively combined and served, can be as taste-satisfying as an elegant paté, and pay better dividends.

VEGETABLES AMANDINE

The "amandine," or "almondine," refers simply to the addition of slivered toasted almonds to a vegetable or fish dish. They add texture and flavor to what might otherwise be a workaday preparation.

For a vegetable or fish serving for four, from ⅓ to ½ cup of almonds is enough. Blanch the almonds by covering with boiling water for 3 or 4 minutes, after which you should be able to slip off the skins with no difficulty. While still warm, sliver the almonds by cutting them in two lengthwise. Heat 2 tablespoons of oil in a skillet and cook the almonds in the hot oil for a couple of minutes, or until they turn a deep golden color, turning them a few times so they brown evenly.

Cauliflowerets, broccoli, string beans, or asparagus do nicely with toasted almonds. Cook or steam the vegetables as usual, being careful (as always) not to overcook, season them with salt and pepper, and scatter the toasted almonds over them.

VEGETABLES POLONAISE

To prepare vegetables "Polonaise," brown about ½ cup of fine bread crumbs in 2 tablespoons of heated oil, add 1 teaspoon of chopped parsley, and mix well. Sprinkle over cooked vegetables in the serving dish. This will be sufficient for a serving for four.

Asparagus, cauliflower, and broccoli are favorites for this garniture.

ASPARAGUS

Besides the robins, a pleasant harbinger of spring is the first appearance in the markets of fresh green asparagus. But too often asparagus comes to the table with head bowed, limp and overcooked. This need not be so, because asparagus is really among the simplest of vegetables to prepare.

2 pounds asparagus	1½ cups water
½ teaspoon salt	

When buying asparagus, look for fresh green stalks with tight buds at the end. Try to select stalks of the same thickness so that they all need the same cooking time.

Wash the asparagus well in a couple of changes of cold water if it seems at all sandy. Cut or break off the tough white ends. Peel the lower part of the asparagus stalks. A potato peeler with a swivel blade does a perfect job.

Asparagus can be steamed upright in a steamer with a removable tray, but I find that the simplest method is to cook it in a large flat skillet with a cover. You will need about ¾ cup of water per pound of asparagus.

Bring the salted water to a boil in a skillet, add the trimmed asparagus, bring the water to a second boil, cover the pot, and simmer for about 10 minutes. Test the tips. They should be crisp but not soft. If they need a bit more cooking, replace the cover but don't let the cooking go on too long. Remove the asparagus from the skillet, place on a serving platter, and cover with browned bread crumbs or Easy Hollandaise Sauce (page 332); or serve cold, bathed in French Dressing (page 326) or Mustard Mayonnaise (page 330).

Serves 4

BEETS IN ORANGE SAUCE

Either diced or julienne canned beets may be used.

1 1-pound can beets, drained
2 tablespoons oil
2 tablespoons light brown sugar
1½ tablespoons flour
1 cup orange juice
Thin strips of peel from 1 orange
½ teaspoon salt

Drain the beets and discard the juice. Heat the oil in a medium-sized skillet, add the sugar and flour, and stir until bubbly. Add the orange juice and peel. (If you have the little knife-gadget that cuts thin strips of peel from oranges and lemons, do use it; if not, use a sharp vegetable knife and cut the peel only—not the white stuff.) Stir with a wire whisk until the sauce is smooth and thickened. Add the salt and beets and heat through.

Serves 3 or 4

BROCCOLI SAUTÉ

1 bunch broccoli (about 1½ pounds)
3 tablespoons oil
1 clove garlic, minced
4 scallions, green parts and all, thinly sliced
½ teaspoon salt
Freshly ground pepper
½ teaspoon sugar

Wash and drain the broccoli. Separate into flowerets, retaining an inch or so of stem. Trim the stringy outside of the rest of the stems and cut them into 1-inch pieces. Parboil the stems and flowerets in boiling salted water, covered, for 5 minutes. Rinse in cold water to stop cooking and drain well.

Heat the oil in a large, heavy skillet over medium high heat, add the garlic and scallions, stir, and add the broccoli flowerets and stems. Stir well to coat them with oil. Add the salt, pepper, and sugar and mix well. Cover the pan, reduce the heat, and cook 5 minutes longer, or until the broccoli is tender-crisp. Serve at once.

Serves 6

BAKED BROCCOLI AND ONIONS

2 10-ounce packages
  frozen broccoli spears
18 small white onions
3 tablespoons oil
4 tablespoons flour
1 cup skim milk
½ cup chicken broth

½ cup dry white wine
½ teaspoon salt
  Freshly ground pepper
2 tablespoons grated
  low-fat cheddar cheese
⅓ cup slivered, browned
  almonds (page 208)

Cook the broccoli according to the package directions, but undercook a little. Drain and place in an oiled shallow baking dish. Peel the onions, cut a cross at the stem end to prevent the onions from popping, and parboil in salted water for 10 minutes. The vegetables will finish cooking in the oven, so don't overdo them. Drain the onions and arrange over the broccoli.

In a small saucepan heat the oil and stir in the flour over low heat. Cook until the mixture bubbles, but don't let it brown. Increase the heat to medium and add the milk and chicken broth slowly, mixing with a wire whisk until the sauce becomes thick and smooth. Lower the heat and cook for another minute. Remove from the heat and add the wine, salt, and pepper. Taste for seasoning. Pour the sauce over the broccoli and sprinkle with the cheese. Sprinkle the top with the almonds. Bake 30 minutes in a 375° oven.

Serves 6 to 8

BRUSSELS SPROUTS WITH CHESTNUT SAUCE

2 pounds Brussels
  sprouts or 2 10-ounce
  packages frozen
  sprouts
1½ tablespoons oil
1 tablespoon flour
1 cup chicken broth

½ teaspoon salt
  Pinch white pepper
¼ teaspoon dried basil
1 cup cooked chestnuts,
  peeled and sliced
  (page 218)

If using fresh Brussels sprouts, trim off the outer leaves and wash the sprouts. Cook or steam in a small amount of salted water until just done (10 or 12 minutes). Don't overcook. The frozen ones should be cooked according to the package directions, but the same rule about not overcooking applies here also. Drain.

For the sauce, heat the oil in a heavy skillet over low heat. Add the flour, stirring until it bubbles. Stir in the chicken broth, using a wire whisk, and continue stirring until the sauce is thickened and smooth. Stir in the salt, pepper, and basil. Taste and correct the seasoning.

Add the chestnuts to the sauce. Place the Brussels sprouts in a warm serving bowl and pour the chestnut sauce over them.

Serves 5 or 6

CABBAGE WITH CARAWAY SEEDS

1 medium-sized head of cabbage	½ teaspoon salt Freshly ground pepper
3 tablespoons oil	1 teaspoon sugar
1 onion, sliced	2 tablespoons caraway
½ cup water (or dry white wine)	seeds

Cut out the cabbage core and cut the cabbage into thick slices. Wash and drain.

In a large, heavy saucepan with a cover, heat the oil and cook the onion until limp. Add the water (or wine), cabbage, salt, pepper, and sugar. Cover and cook over low heat until the cabbage is tender (20 to 30 minutes). If the cabbage seems to be in danger of scorching, add a little water or wine. The liquid should be absorbed when the cabbage is done. Sprinkle with the caraway seeds and mix through. Remove to a warm bowl to serve.

Serves 4

SWEET-AND-SOUR RED CABBAGE

A traditional accompaniment for pot roast.

1 medium-sized red cabbage (about 4 cups, shredded)	2 tablespoons oil
	½ teaspoon salt
	Freshly ground pepper
½ cup cider vinegar	1 large tart apple,
2 tablespoons brown sugar	peeled, cored, and cut into cubes

Remove the core from the head of red cabbage and slice the cabbage medium fine. Wash the cabbage and lightly drain, leaving whatever liquid adheres to it. Place it in a large, heavy saucepan with a cover. Add the vinegar, brown sugar, oil, salt, and pepper and cook over low heat for 10 minutes. Add the apple, cover, and continue cooking another 15 to 20 minutes, or until the cabbage is tender. Taste and correct the seasoning—it may need more sugar or a squirt of lemon juice, or both.

Serves 4 or 5

CABBAGE AND NOODLES

Decisions such as whether to pigeonhole this Hungarian dish (properly known as "Kraut Fleckerl") as a vegetable or a starch can try men's souls. Women's too.

1 8-ounce package broad noodles	½ teaspoon salt
	Freshly ground pepper
1 small head cabbage	2 tablespoons caraway seeds
4 tablespoons oil	
1 large onion, chopped	

Cook the noodles according to the directions on the package. Rinse with cold water to stop the cooking and drain.

Shred the cabbage in slices about the same width as the noodles. Heat the oil in a large, heavy skillet and lightly brown the cabbage and onion, turning often. When browned, cover the skillet and cook 5 minutes longer. Add the noodles, salt, pepper, and caraway seeds. Mix well and heat through. Serve hot.

Serves 4

BAKED CARROTS

5 medium-sized carrots,
  scraped and coarsely
  grated (about 3 cups)
2 tablespoons oil
1 small onion, chopped
½ teaspoon salt
  Freshly ground pepper

1 No. 2 can tomatoes
  (2½ cups), drained
  (reserve the liquid)
1 teaspoon sugar
¼ cup dry bread crumbs
1 tablespoon chopped
  parsley

Lightly oil a 1½-quart casserole and place the carrots in it. In a small skillet heat the oil and lightly brown the onion. Add to the casserole with the salt, pepper, tomato pulp, and sugar and mix well. Add ½ cup of the liquid from the tomato. Taste and correct the seasoning. Cover the casserole and bake in a 350° oven for about 45 minutes, or until the carrots are tender. If the casserole seems to be drying out, add more tomato liquid. Mix together the bread crumbs and parsley and sprinkle over the casserole for the last 5 or 10 minutes of cooking.

Serves 4

HONEYED CARROTS

3 tablespoons oil
3 tablespoons orange
  juice
1 tablespoon lemon
  juice
½ teaspoon salt

¼ teaspoon powdered
  ginger
4 tablespoons honey
4 cups carrots, scraped
  and cut into julienne
  strips (about 8 carrots)

In a large, heavy skillet with a cover, combine the oil, orange and lemon juice, salt, ginger, and honey. Mix well. Add the carrot strips and cook, covered, over low heat for 25 minutes, or until they are tender. Keep your eye on them while they are cooking and stir frequently so they won't scorch and will take on an even glaze.

Serves 6

Note: The tiny canned Belgian carrots may also be used. Prepare the sauce as above, add the drained carrots, and cook, uncovered, until they are heated through and glazed. A 1-pound can serves 4.

CARROTS VICHY

I had read that sometimes Vichy water was used in the preparation of Carrots Vichy. I tried it, but whatever changes there were from the bubbles were too subtle for me to perceive, so don't bother.

6 medium-sized carrots, scraped and sliced	1 tablespoon sugar
	½ teaspoon salt
¾ cup boiling water	1 teaspoon lemon juice
2 tablespoons oil	Chopped parsley

Place all the ingredients except the parsley in a saucepan. Cook over high heat until the water reaches a lively boil. Lower the heat, cover the pan tightly, and simmer until the water is nearly evaporated. At this point the carrots should be tender. Shake the pan so that the carrots are covered with the syrupy liquid and are glazed. Transfer them to a warmed serving bowl and sprinkle with chopped parsley.

Serves 4 to 6

GLAZED CARROTS

6 medium-sized carrots, scraped and sliced	2 tablespoons light brown sugar
2 tablespoons oil	2 tablespoons lemon juice
	Chopped chives

Boil or steam the carrots until barely tender. Drain. In a large skillet, cook the oil, sugar, and lemon juice over low heat until bubbles form. Add the carrots and cook until the liquid evaporates. Turn the slices often, so they will be evenly glazed. Sprinkle with the chives.

Serves 4 to 6

CARROT AND ONION PUREE

This light, delicate vegetable is a good choice to balance a hearty main course.

5 large carrots, scraped and grated
3 large onions, finely chopped
6 tablespoons uncooked rice
3 cups water
1 package MBT chicken broth powder
½ teaspoon salt
1 teaspoon sugar (if desired)

You may also chop the carrots, but I find it easier and quicker to shred them, using the coarse grater. Combine them with all the other ingredients except the sugar. Cook, covered, for 30 to 35 minutes, or until the rice and vegetables are tender and the water absorbed. Rub the mixture through the medium blade of a food mill—not a blender, which will destroy all texture. Return the puree to the skillet and keep warm. Taste and correct the seasoning. Add the sugar if needed. Some carrots require little or no additional sweetening.

Serves 6

CAULIFLOWER WITH ANCHOVY SAUCE

1 small head of cauliflower
1 cup water
½ teaspoon salt
6 tablespoons oil
1 large clove garlic
4 anchovy fillets, chopped
2½ tablespoons bread crumbs
Freshly ground pepper

Wash the cauliflower and separate it into small flowerets. Cook or steam in boiling, salted water over medium heat until tender. This generally takes about 12 to 15 minutes. Don't overcook.

In a small skillet, heat the oil and brown the garlic clove. Discard the garlic. Add the anchovies to the oil and stir until they are reduced to a paste. Add the bread crumbs and cook another 2 minutes.

Place the cauliflower in a warmed serving dish, sprinkle lightly with the pepper, and cover with the anchovy sauce. Toss lightly and serve hot.

Serves 4

CAULIFLOWER SAUTÉ

1 small head of cauliflower
4 tablespoons oil
2 tablespoons lemon juice
  Large lettuce leaves, washed

4 scallions, tops and all, chopped
1 clove garlic, minced
½ teaspoon salt
  Freshly ground pepper

Wash the cauliflower and separate into small flowerets. Heat 1 tablespoon of the oil in a large, heavy skillet with a cover. Add the cauliflower, sprinkle it with the lemon juice, and spread several dripping-wet lettuce leaves on top. Cover the pan and cook over low heat for about 10 minutes, or until the cauliflower is just tender. Remove the cauliflower and set aside. Discard the lettuce leaves.

In the same skillet, heat the remaining oil and sauté the scallions until lightly browned. Add the garlic and cook a minute longer. Return the cauliflower to the skillet, sprinkle with the salt and pepper, and toss well in the oil so that each floweret is coated. Cook for another 5 minutes, stirring often. Serve at once.

Serves 4

BRAISED CELERY

Cooked celery has never been as popular as it ought to be. It has a distinctive, delicate flavor that never overpowers anything it accompanies, and it really deserves wider use than being hacked up in small cubes for salads. Braised celery can be served with almost any meat or fish and is a splendid choice for even a formal dinner.

3 bunches celery
3 tablespoons oil
2 onions, chopped
1 carrot, coarsely grated

1½ cups consommé
1 small clove garlic, minced
½ teaspoon salt
  Freshly ground pepper

Remove the tough outer celery stalks. Trim the roots, but leave enough of the root to hold the stalk together. Slice off the tops and leaves, leaving the celery heart about 6 inches long. Split the hearts in two lengthwise. Each half is a portion. Save the celery you have cut off for soups, stews, and such.

At this point it is a good idea to soak the celery hearts in cold water heavily laced with salt for 20 minutes. This will draw out any sand or sediment lurking in the stalks. After soaking, rinse the celery well and parboil it in salted boiling water for 5 minutes. Remove and drain.

In a large, heavy skillet, heat the oil and cook the onions and carrot until the vegetables are brown. Remove them with a slotted spoon and set aside. Brown the celery in the skillet on both sides. Return the onion and carrot, add the consommé, garlic, salt, and pepper, and cook over low heat, covered, until the celery is soft. This may take upwards of 30 minutes, depending upon the celery. Baste and turn a few times during cooking. Test for doneness by piercing the celery center with a sharp-pointed knife. While most vegetables are best when they are crisp, crunchy, and underdone, not so with braised celery, which should be tender and soft. To serve, spoon the liquid and vegetables over the celery.

Serves 6

CHESTNUTS

Of all the nut family, chestnuts are at the bottom of the ladder in terms of calories and fat. One of the few remaining provincial delights in New York is the hot chestnut vendors who stand on street corners in the fall and winter, their carts emitting shrill whistles and the warm fragrance of chestnuts roasting. To avoid the questionable taste of eating hot chestnuts in the street, you can roast them at home.

Cut gashes on the flat side of each chestnut in the shape of the letter X. Place on a baking sheet, dribble a tablespoon of oil over them, and bake in a 350° oven for 45 to 50 minutes, or until the skins peel off easily and the chestnuts are cooked through.

To prepare chestnuts for use in cooking, cut the X-shaped gashes described above. Cover the chestnuts with boiling water and boil briskly in a covered saucepan for 25 to 30 minutes. Hold them under cold running water while you peel off the shells. If the shells do not come off easily, boil them a bit longer.

FRIED CUCUMBERS

These crisp, browned cucumber strips make a most delicious hot vegetable that goes particularly well with fish.

2 large cucumbers	1 teaspoon dried dillweed
½ cup flour	2 tablespoons water
½ teaspoon salt	1 egg white, whipped
Freshly ground pepper	until frothy
Cornflake crumbs	Oil for frying

Pare the cucumbers and quarter them lengthwise. If they are thick, you might cut them in half lengthwise and then cut each half into three strips. Cut the strips in half crosswise. Trim away all the seedy portion, leaving just the firm part.

Mix the flour with the salt and pepper and mound on a square of waxed paper. On another square of waxed paper, arrange a mound of cornflake crumbs mixed with the dillweed. Add the water to the frothy egg white and mix lightly. Dip the cucumber strips into the seasoned flour, then into the egg white, and roll in the cornflake mixture.

In a large, heavy skillet, heat a thin layer of oil and add the cucumber strips. Don't try to get more in the skillet at a time than will fit in a single layer or you won't be able to brown them evenly. Cook over low heat for about 20 minutes, turning them to brown evenly. When all are browned, cover the pan and place over low heat for an additional 5 minutes. The cucumber should be cooked through, but crisp-tender. The lemon wedges that accompany the fish will do nicely for these also.

Serves 4

BAKED CUCUMBERS

4 large cucumbers
2 tablespoons vinegar
1 teaspoon salt
3 tablespoons oil
2 shallots, finely chopped
1 tablespoon fresh dill,
snipped, or ½ teaspoon
dried dill

2 tablespoons chives,
chopped
Freshly ground pepper
1 tablespoon lemon juice
Chopped parsley

Pare the cucumbers and cut them lengthwise into quarters. Trim away the seed portion, leaving only the firm part. Cut the quarters into strips about 2 inches long and ½ inch wide. Place in a bowl with the vinegar and salt. Marinate for 30 minutes. Drain and dry well.

Place the cucumbers in an ovenproof dish and sprinkle with the oil, shallots, dill, chives, and pepper. Bake in a preheated 375° oven, uncovered, 40 to 45 minutes. Turn the cucumber slices a few times during baking. Sprinkle lightly with salt, pepper, the lemon juice, and parsley and transfer to a warmed bowl.

Serves 6 to 8

EGGPLANT AND ZUCCHINI CASSEROLE

A vegetable mélange that may be prepared in advance and baked at dinnertime.

1 large eggplant, peeled
and cut into 1-inch
slices
3 tablespoons oil
3 large onions, thinly
sliced
3 zucchini, sliced ½
inch thick
½ pound mushrooms,
sliced
2 cloves garlic, minced
1 1-pound can tomatoes,
drained

1 bay leaf
½ teaspoon oregano
½ teaspoon basil
1 green pepper, seeded
and cut into thin strips
1 teaspoon salt
Freshly ground pepper
1 teaspoon sugar
½ cup (or more) cornflake
crumbs
1 tablespoon Parmesan
cheese

Cover the eggplant with boiling water and simmer gently for 10 minutes. Drain well.

In a large skillet, heat the oil and cook the onions until limp and transparent. Add the zucchini and cook, covered, for 10 minutes. Add the mushrooms and garlic and cook uncovered for 3 or 4 minutes, stirring a few times. Add the tomatoes (if they are whole, cut them into small pieces). Mix in the bay leaf, oregano, basil, green pepper, salt, pepper, and sugar. Simmer 10 minutes longer. Taste for seasoning—you may want a bit more sugar, salt, or whatever you think it needs. If the vegetable mixture contains a lot of liquid, strain it or use a slotted spoon when transferring it to the casserole.

Oil a 2-quart casserole and place a layer of eggplant on the bottom. Cover with part of the vegetable mixture, sprinkle with some of the cornflake crumbs, and continue with alternate layers of eggplant, vegetable mixture, and cornflake crumbs until all are used, ending with the vegetable mixture and crumbs. Sprinkle with the cheese. Bake uncovered in a 350° oven for 1 hour.

Serves 8

BRAISED ENDIVE

Belgian endive is another vegetable many people are apt to overlook, saving it only for salads. My only quarrel with it is that most really do come from Belgium, and, being imported, are considerably more expensive than local produce. A few are grown in this country, but not in sufficient quantity to make a difference when the greengrocer tots up his bill. But in spite of that, it's a lovely vegetable and particularly nice braised.

8 whole endives	1 tablespoon lemon
Salted water	juice
Juice of 1 lemon	½-1 cup boiling chicken
2 tablespoons oil	broth
	Chopped parsley

Trim any outside discolored leaves from each bunch and slice away some of the root, leaving enough to hold the leaves together.

Endive sometimes has a slightly bitterish quality and unless you are particularly fond of this taste—some people are—it's a good idea to blanch the endives before you braise them. Use an enamel pot to prevent them from darkening. Boil about 2 quarts of water with 1 tablespoon of salt and the juice of a lemon (about 3 tablespoons). Place the endive in the boiling water and simmer gently for 10 minutes.

Remove the endives with kitchen tongs, drain, and place them side by side in an oiled baking dish. Sprinkle lightly with salt, dribble the oil and lemon juice over them, and add ½ cup of the chicken broth. The broth should come about halfway up the layer of endive. Add more if needed. Cover the endives with a piece of oiled waxed paper and place in a 325° oven for about an hour. They should be tender and lightly browned when done.

To serve, place on a warmed platter, reduce the liquid remaining in the baking dish over high heat if there are more than 2 tablespoons, and pour the liquid over the endives. Sprinkle with the parsley.

Serves 4

BROILED MUSHROOMS

Interestingly prepared mushrooms can serve as a second vegetable and, at the same time, as a hearty and edible garnish for the meat or poultry course. Broiled Mushrooms or the following Stuffed Mushrooms make an impressive addition to a menu.

12 large mushroom caps	3 tablespoons oil
½ cup cornflake crumbs	½ teaspoon salt
	Freshly ground pepper
1 tablespoon chopped parsley	1 clove garlic, minced

Remove the stems from the mushroom caps and save for another use. Rinse the mushroom caps and wipe dry. Mix together the cornflake crumbs and parsley and place on a square of waxed paper. In a small bowl, combine the oil, salt, pepper, and garlic.

Brush the mushroom caps with the garlic oil and roll in the seasoned crumbs. Place on a foil-covered broiler pan about 2 inches from the heat and broil 5 minutes on each side. If they seem a little dry, dribble a bit of oil on them when you turn them.

Serves 4

STUFFED MUSHROOMS

12	large mushrooms	2	slices bread, soaked in water and squeezed dry
2	tablespoons oil		
1	small onion, finely chopped	1	teaspoon mayonnaise
1	clove garlic, crushed	2	tablespoons cornflake crumbs
4	anchovy fillets, chopped		
1	tablespoon parsley, chopped	1½	tablespoons oil
	Freshly ground pepper	½	cup consommé or stock

Wash the mushrooms and wipe them dry. Remove the stems, trim off the ends, and chop the stems. Heat the 2 tablespoons of oil in a skillet and cook the mushroom stems and onion for 5 minutes. Add the garlic, anchovies, parsley, and pepper and cook another 5 minutes over medium high heat. Remove from the heat and mix in the soaked bread. Add the mayonnaise and blend well. Oil a shallow baking dish and arrange the mushrooms in it, stem side up. Fill the caps with the stuffing, mounding it nicely. Sprinkle with the cornflake crumbs and dribble a little of the 1½ tablespoons of oil over each mushroom. Pour the consommé on the bottom of the pan. Bake for 20 minutes in a preheated 375° oven. Serve hot.

Serves 4

BRAISED WHITE ONIONS

The succulent, small white onions rate more than the seasonal rush given them at Thanksgiving time, followed by oblivion for the rest of the year. They are truly a delicious vegetable and deserve more frequent appearances in most meal planning.

16–20 small white onions	2 teaspoons sugar
Boiling salted water	½ teaspoon salt
3 tablespoons oil	Freshly ground pepper

Peel the onions and cut a small cross at the bottom of each to prevent the center from popping out during cooking. Parboil them in boiling salted water (or steam them for 10 minutes) and drain well. They should be underdone at this point. Heat the oil in a heavy skillet, add the onions, sprinkle with the sugar, salt, and pepper, and cook over low heat, covered, until they are tender, browned, and caramelized from the sugar. Shake the pan frequently during cooking to turn the onions. They won't really brown evenly, so don't try.

Serves 4 or 5

CREAMED ONIONS

2 pounds small white onions	½ teaspoon salt
	Pinch cayenne pepper
3 tablespoons oil	½ teaspoon dried thyme
2 tablespoons flour	¼ cup bread crumbs
2 cups skim milk	

Peel the onions and cut a small cross at the bottom. Cook in boiling salted water (or steam) until just done (about 15 minutes). Drain and transfer to an oiled baking dish or casserole that can be used for serving.

In the same skillet, heat 2 tablespoons of the oil, blend in the flour, and stir over medium heat until it bubbles (don't let it brown). Reduce the heat and slowly add the milk, stirring with a wire whisk until the sauce becomes thickened and smooth. Add the salt, cayenne pepper, and thyme and cook 1 minute longer. Add the sauce to the onions in the casserole and mix well.

In a small skillet, heat the remaining tablespoon of oil and brown the bread crumbs. Sprinkle the crumbs over the onions. Heat the casserole, uncovered, in a 350° oven for 20 minutes, or until heated through.

Serves 4 or 5

GLAZED PARSNIPS

The parsnip is another stepchild among vegetables. Purely a case of being misunderstood, since most people like them once they have eaten them. We have won quite a few friends for them at our house, which proves something, I think.

1 pound parsnips	3 tablespoons light brown
½ teaspoon salt	sugar
5 tablespoons orange	1 tablespoon grated
juice	lemon rind
	1 tablespoon oil

Scrub the parsnips and place in a pan. Cover with boiling salted water and cook between 20 to 40 minutes, or until soft. The time varies, depending upon the age and size, but don't overcook. When done, rinse in cold water and drain. Peel off the skins and slice each parsnip lengthwise into 3 or 4 slices.

Place the slices in a lightly oiled, shallow baking dish and sprinkle the salt over them. Mix together the orange juice, brown sugar, lemon rind, and oil and pour over the parsnips. Bake in a 350° oven for 25 minutes.

Serves 3 or 4

JUDY'S GREEN PEAS

I don't suppose that canned green peas have ever been the stuff of which a gourmet's dreams are made, but Judy makes them taste great.

1 1-pound-1-ounce	1 small onion, finely
can tiny French	chopped
peas	1 stalk celery, finely
2 or 3 lettuce leaves,	chopped
shredded	2 teaspoons cornstarch
	Chopped parsley

Drain the peas and place the liquid in a small saucepan. Reserve a tablespoon or so of the liquid. Add the lettuce, onion, and celery and simmer over low heat for 10 minutes. Make a paste of the cornstarch and reserved liquid and add. Continue to cook, stirring with a wire whisk until the sauce becomes thickened and smooth. Add the peas and heat through. This generally needs no additional seasoning. Place in a warmed bowl, sprinkle with the parsley, and serve at once.

Serves 4

PEAS AND ONIONS IN MUSTARD SAUCE

2	pounds small white onions	⅛	teaspoon white pepper
1	10-ounce package frozen green peas	1½	tablespoons white vinegar
4	tablespoons oil	1½	tablespoons lemon juice
4	tablespoons flour	½	teaspoon dry mustard
1½	cups skim milk		Pinch saffron
½	teaspoon salt		

Peel and trim the onions and cut small cross gashes in the root end. Cook them in boiling, salted water (or steam them) until just done (about 15 minutes). Drain. Cook the peas according to the package directions, being careful not to overcook. Drain them.

In a medium-sized saucepan, heat the oil. Over low heat, blend in the flour until it bubbles, but don't let it brown. Increase the heat a bit and slowly add the milk, stirring with a wire whisk. Add the salt, pepper, and vinegar and continue to stir until the sauce becomes thickened and smooth. Reduce the heat. In a small bowl, mix together the lemon juice, mustard, and saffron and add to the sauce. Heat for 2 minutes, until well blended. Add the peas and onions to the sauce and heat only until warmed through. Transfer the vegetables to a warmed serving bowl.

Serves 6

RATATOUILLE

There are as many versions of the recipe for *ratatouille,* the French vegetable stew, as there are kitchens and cooks. The basic ingredients—eggplant, zucchini, tomatoes, *et al.*—remain the same, but the proportions and cooking methods vary greatly. One classic method is to sauté the vegetables separately so that each retains its own individuality when they finally meet in the stew pot. And very good it is. Another method—here detailed—is a simple and uncomplicated approach to a lovely blend of textures and flavors. It seems to me that ingredients used in cooking are in a way comparable to musical notes. All composers use the same notes, but by putting them together in a variety of combinations, they create their own style of melodic, ear-pleasing sounds. So it is with cooks and their larders, although it is the palate and the eye they seek to please.

But back to the *ratatouille*. It is a hearty, flavorful preparation that goes well with roasted or broiled beef, lamb, chicken, or fish. It is good hot or cold and may also serve as a cold appetizer course.

1 large eggplant	¼ cup oil
4 small zucchini	2 cloves garlic, crushed
2 large tomatoes	1 teaspoon salt
2 peppers (1 red, 1 green,	Freshly ground pepper
if possible)	½ teaspoon dried basil
2 medium-sized onions	

Peel the eggplant, cut into slices about ⅜ inch thick, and cut the slices into quarters. Wash the zucchini, trim off the ends, and slice the zucchini the same thickness as the eggplant. Peel the tomatoes by plunging them into boiling water for a minute and slipping off the skins. Cut the tomatoes into sections, discarding the seeds. Wash and core the peppers and cut into thin strips. Peel the onions and cut them into thin slices.

In a large, heavy kettle, heat the oil and cook the onions until limp. Add the pepper strips and zucchini and cook another few minutes. Add the eggplant, tomatoes, garlic, salt, pepper, and basil. Cover the kettle and simmer slowly for about an hour, or until the vegetables are thoroughly cooked. With a wooden spoon, move them from time to time to prevent them from scorching or sticking. Remove the cover during the last 15 minutes of cooking to reduce the liquid. Taste for seasoning and correct.

Serves 6

HOT SAUERKRAUT

1½ pounds sauerkraut
    Veal marrowbone
2   tablespoons oil
½ green pepper, diced
1   large onion, finely
    chopped

2   teaspoons flour
½ cup tomato puree
½ teaspoon salt
    Freshly ground pepper
1   teaspoon sugar

Cook the sauerkraut with the bone for 1 hour over low heat, covered. In a large, heavy skillet, heat the oil and cook the green pepper and onion until the onion is lightly browned. Transfer the sauerkraut to the skillet, stir in the flour, and mix well. Add the tomato puree, salt, pepper, and sugar and cook for another minute or two until heated through. Taste and correct the seasoning.

Serves 4 or 5

STRING BEANS, ROMAN STYLE

1 pound fresh string
  beans or 1 10-ounce
  package frozen green
  beans, French style

2 tablespoons oil
1 clove garlic, minced
¾ teaspoon oregano
1 cup tomato sauce

If you are using fresh beans, wash and drain them and slice lengthwise, French style. Steam or boil in a little boiling, salted water until tender but crisp—do not over-cook. Cook frozen string beans according to the package directions until just done. Drain.

In a medium-sized skillet, heat the oil and cook the garlic and oregano until the garlic turns golden. Add the tomato sauce and simmer for 5 minutes. Pour the sauce over the beans and mix well. Transfer to a heated bowl.

Serves 4

GENE YOUNG'S STRING BEANS

In case you are wondering who Gene Young is, she's the delightful young lady assigned by the publisher of this book as editor. At our first meeting we talked about, as you might expect, recipes. Gene asked if I ever stir-fried string beans. I hadn't, but since she told me about these I do—often. They are underdone, crisp, and crunchy—purely delicious.

1 pound fresh string beans	1 tablespoon dry sherry
1 tablespoon oil	1 tablespoon soy sauce
	1 teaspoon sugar

Wash the beans and break off the ends. Cut into 1½-inch-long pieces. Heat the oil in a skillet and cook the beans for 5 minutes, stirring them constantly. That, as you may know, is the process known as stir-frying. In a small bowl, combine the sherry, soy sauce, and sugar. Pour over the beans and mix well. Cover the skillet and cook another 5 minutes. Serve at once.

Serves 4

SPINACH, CHINESE STYLE

To continue the saga begun in the preceding recipe, after we finished the string beans, Gene asked "What about spinach? Have you stir-fried that?" I hadn't, but I did. And now I do.

1 pound fresh spinach	½ teaspoon salt
2 tablespoons oil	½ teaspoon sugar
1 clove garlic (on a toothpick for easy removal)	

Pick over the spinach, discarding any tired leaves and tough stems. Wash and drain thoroughly. In a large skillet, heat the oil and add the garlic clove. Add the spinach and stir until all the leaves are coated with the oil. If the amount of spinach seems a bit much for the skillet, have faith. It will collapse shortly. Discard the garlic.

Add the salt and sugar and stir again. Cook for 2 minutes and serve at once.

Serves 3

SPINACH AND MUSHROOM CASSEROLE

This preparation is puffy and light enough to have people mistake it for a soufflé. Half the recipe makes a splendid main luncheon dish for two.

2 10½-ounce packages frozen chopped spinach	Freshly ground pepper
3 tablespoons oil	½ cup cornflake crumbs
1 clove garlic, minced	⅔ cup mayonnaise
1 pound mushrooms, finely chopped	1 tablespoon Parmesan cheese
3 tablespoons lemon juice	Cornflake crumbs for topping
½ teaspoon salt	

Cook the spinach only until thawed. Overcooking will darken the color, and it should be as bright green as possible. Strain, pressing out every bit of water, and set aside.

Heat the oil in a large skillet and heat the garlic until it turns golden. Add the mushrooms, sprinkle with the lemon juice, salt, and pepper, and cook over medium heat for 3 or 4 minutes. Remove from the heat before the mushrooms begin to give off liquid. If liquid has formed, you have the choice of continuing to cook until it evaporates or straining the mushrooms and saving the liquid for your next stew, soup, or gravy. Add to the mushrooms the spinach, ½ cup of cornflake crumbs, and mayonnaise and mix well. Taste for seasoning. Place the mixture in a shallow oiled casserole (I use an 8 by 10 inch *au gratin* dish). Sprinkle with the cheese and cornflake crumbs and heat in a 350° oven for about 15 minutes, or until heated through.

Serves 6 to 8

BAKED ACORN SQUASH

2 tablespoons sesame seeds	½ teaspoon salt
2 acorn squashes	Paprika
2 tablespoons oil	2 tablespoons cornflake crumbs

To brown the sesame seeds, place them on an ungreased baking sheet in a 350° oven for 12 to 15 minutes.

Cut the squashes in half crosswise (parallel to the stem end). You might need to trim a thin slice from the top and bottom so that they will sit firmly on the platter and not topple. Remove the seeds and stringy pulp from the cavities, brush them with 1 tablespoon of the oil, and sprinkle them lightly with the salt and paprika. Cover the bottom of a flat baking dish with about ½ inch of water and place the squashes cut side down in the pan. Bake in a 375° oven for 30 minutes. Take a look at them once in a while to make sure the water has not evaporated, and add a bit more boiling water if necessary. Remove them from the oven and turn the cut side up. Brush with the remainder of the oil and sprinkle with the sesame seeds and cornflake crumbs. Bake another 10 minutes or so, until done.

Serves 4

Variations: Omit the sesame seeds and sprinkle with brown sugar.

Omit the sesame seeds and fill the squash cavities with cooked green peas or a combination of green peas and sliced mushrooms.

ORANGE STUFFED ACORN SQUASH

3 medium-sized acorn squashes
2 tablespoons brown sugar
½ teaspoon salt
2 tablespoons oil
¼ cup orange juice
1 teaspoon grated orange rind

Cut the squashes in half and remove the seeds and stringy parts from the cavities. Place cut side down in a baking pan with about ½ inch of water. Bake at 350° for about 40 minutes, or until the pulp is completely tender. Take a look at the pan from time to time; you may need to add a little water if it has evaporated.

When soft and cool enough to handle, scoop out the pulp and place in a bowl. Combine the pulp with the remaining ingredients and mash well. Fill the shells with the mashed pulp. You will probably find that there is just enough to fill 5 shells. Otherwise, they will be somewhat skimpy. Don't be concerned if the shells are a bit limp; they will still provide a serviceable container for the delicious filling. If you have prepared them in advance of dinner, warm them in a 350° oven for 10 to 15 minutes, or until heated through. Run them under the broiler for a few minutes to brown the tops.

Serves 5

MASHED BUTTERNUT SQUASH

If you are unfamiliar with this flavorful vegetable, I think you will be glad to know about it. In taste it is a cross between Hubbard squash and sweet potato, combining the best virtues of both.

2 pounds butternut squash	½ teaspoon salt
1 tablespoon oil	1 teaspoon brown sugar

You may peel the squash either before or after it is cooked. Cut it into chunks, remove the seeds and fibers in the lower half of the squash, and boil or steam it in a small amount of boiling salted water until tender (this generally takes about 20 minutes). Drain very well. You might even return the cooked, drained pieces to the pan and shake them over low heat for a minute or so to get rid of all the moisture. Extra moisture will not improve the finished product, which should be dry and fluffy like mashed potatoes. Mash with a potato ricer. Add the oil, salt, and sugar and mix well. Taste for seasoning. Serve hot.

Serves 4

DILLED SUMMER SQUASH

The small yellow crookneck squash can be a pleasant addition to your vegetable repertoire.

1½–2	pounds young summer squash	1	tablespoon oil
			Freshly ground pepper
½	teaspoon crushed dillseed	1	tablespoon lemon juice

If the squashes are tender, you do not need to peel them. Wash them well, trim the stem end, and slice crosswise into ⅜-inch-thick slices. Boil or steam, covered, in a small amount of salted water with the dillseed until crisp-tender (about 15 minutes). Drain well. Toss with the oil, pepper, and lemon juice.

Serves 4

BAKED SLICED SUMMER SQUASH

3	young summer squashes, unpeeled	2	tablespoons fresh dill, snipped, or 1 teaspoon dried dill
½	teaspoon salt		
	Freshly ground pepper	2	tablespoons oil
		1½	tablespoons Parmesan cheese

Try to get squashes about the same size so that the slices will be uniform. Wash them well, trim off the ends, and cut lengthwise into slices ¼ inch thick. Each squash should yield four or five slices. Arrange on a lightly oiled cookie sheet. Sprinkle with the salt, pepper, and dill. Dribble the oil over the slices and sprinkle with the cheese. Place in a 350° oven and bake for 15 to 20 minutes, or until tender. Run under the broiler for a minute or two to brown the tops.

Serves 4

Variation: Oregano may be substituted for dill.

FRIED TOMATOES

Either green or red tomatoes will do for this, as long as they are very firm.

4 firm tomatoes
¼ cup flour
1 tablespoon cornmeal
½ teaspoon salt
  Freshly ground pepper

½ teaspoon dried basil
¼ teaspoon oregano
⅓ cup oil
1 teaspoon sugar

Wash the tomatoes and cut them into thick slices. Mix together the flour, cornmeal, salt, pepper, basil, and oregano. Dredge the slices lightly in the flour mixture. Heat the oil in a heavy skillet and brown the tomato slices on both sides. Don't crowd them—cook just one layer at a time and keep the finished ones warm on top of the stove or in the oven while you complete the rest. The slices should cook in 8 to 10 minutes. Sprinkle lightly with the sugar when done.

Serves 4 or 5

BAKED STUFFED TOMATOES

6 large firm tomatoes
3 tablespoons oil
⅓ cup chopped green
  pepper
½ cup onion, finely
  chopped
½ cup fresh bread crumbs

1 12-ounce can corn
  niblets, drained
½ teaspoon salt
  Freshly ground pepper
  Sprinkling of seasoned
  salt
  Cornflake crumbs
  Chopped parsley

Slice the tops off the tomatoes, scoop out the pulp, and reserve, making the tomatoes firm shells. Turn them upside down so that the rest of the juice will drain out.

Heat the oil in a medium-sized saucepan. Add the green pepper and onion and cook until the onion becomes limp and golden. Add ½ cup of the drained tomato pulp, the bread crumbs, corn niblets, salt, and pepper and toss together. Remove from the heat. Sprinkle the inside of the tomatoes lightly with seasoned salt and fill with the corn mixture. Sprinkle the tops with cornflake crumbs. Place the tomatoes in a well-oiled baking dish and bake in a 375° oven for 20 to 25 minutes, or until the tomatoes are just cooked through. Sprinkle the tops with the parsley.

Serves 6

BAKED TOMATO HALVES

4 large ripe tomatoes
½ teaspoon salt
   Freshly ground pepper
½ cup cornflake crumbs
1 clove garlic, minced

1 tablespoon minced
   parsley
1 teaspoon dried sweet
   basil
2 tablespoons oil
1 teaspoon lemon juice

Wash the tomatoes and cut in half. Arrange in an oiled baking dish. Sprinkle lightly with the salt and pepper. Combine the cornflake crumbs, garlic, parsley, and basil and spread over the tops of the tomatoes. Dribble the oil and lemon juice over the tomatoes. Bake in a preheated 375° oven for 10 to 15 minutes, or until the tomatoes are barely tender but completely heated through.

Serves 4 to 6

Variation: These tomato halves may also be grilled. Arrange the seasoned halves on a broiler rack 5 inches from the heat. As they approach completion, raise the broiler rack so the crumbs brown nicely, but don't let them burn.

ZUCCHINI SAUTÉ

Zucchini is an outstanding member of the squash family—good-tasting, easily prepared, generally available, low in calories, and adaptable to many methods of preparation. It doesn't even need to be peeled. Occasionally one finds in the markets the very small ones that are common on the other side of the Atlantic, where they are known as *courgettes*. These are delicious simply steamed whole, sliced, and seasoned with salt and pepper and a bit of oil or polyunsaturated margarine. Failing that delicacy, we can do nice things with the more usual garden-variety zucchini.

4 medium-sized
   zucchini
2 tablespoons oil
2 large onions, sliced
½ teaspoon salt
   Freshly ground pepper

½ teaspoon dried sweet
   basil
½ teaspoon oregano
   Dash of garlic powder
   (optional)
1 tablespoon chopped
   parsley

Wash the zucchini. Trim the stem end and bottom slice. Cut the zucchini crosswise into slices ½ inch thick. In a large skillet, heat the oil and cook the onions until limp but not brown. Add the zucchini, increase the heat, and cook for 5 minutes. Add the remaining ingredients. Lower the heat, cover, and cook 15 or 20 minutes longer, or until tender but not mushy.

Serves 4 or 5

Variations: Cook a green and a red pepper, cut into ½-inch strips, along with the onion.

Add two fresh tomatoes, peeled and cut in eighths, to the zucchini for the last 15 minutes of cooking.

ZUCCHINI AND RICE CASSEROLE

This is another of those serviceable and tasteful vegetable-cum-starch combination dishes that can simplify dinner-hour chores enormously for the cook, for it can be prepared in advance and baked when needed.

5 large zucchini (about 2½ pounds)	2 cloves garlic, crushed
2 teaspoons salt	½ teaspoon dried sweet basil
½ cup (about) skim milk	3 tablespoons flour
½ cup brown or white rice	2 tablespoons Parmesan cheese
2 tablespoons oil	Freshly ground pepper
2 large onions, finely chopped	Cornflake crumbs

Wash the zucchini and trim the ends. Grate coarsely and place in a colander. Add the salt and mix well. Place the colander in a large bowl and let the zucchini stand for 10 minutes, then place the zucchini in a linen towel and squeeze the liquid into a bowl. There should be about 1½ cups. Add enough skim milk to make 2 cups of liquid. Set aside.

Boil the rice until it is almost, but not completely, done. It will finish cooking later. Drain and set aside.

In a large skillet, heat the oil and cook the onions until light brown, stirring them frequently. Add the zucchini, garlic, and basil and stir over low heat until the zucchini is moderately cooked (about 5 or 6 minutes). Mix in the flour and cook a couple of minutes longer. Stir in the 2 cups of liquid and simmer over moderate heat, stirring until thickened. Remove from the heat and add the rice, cheese, and pepper. Taste to see if it needs any other seasoning. Transfer to an oiled 6- or 8-cup ovenproof casserole. Dust the top lightly with cornflake crumbs. At this point the casserole can be held for baking later.

Heat the casserole on top of the stove until it begins to simmer. Transfer to a preheated 375° oven and bake for 40 to 50 minutes, or until the zucchini mixture becomes set.

Serves 6 to 8

COLD ZUCCHINI PIQUANT

My mother had a theory that no matter how hot the day, and how cool and light the main course, something catastrophic would happen to our insides without one steaming dish, which we were obliged to eat. (It was generally string beans, if memory serves me right.) After I was emancipated by my personal physician, I determined never to inflict like hardships on my children. Which brings us to Cold Zucchini Piquant—lovely when the thermometer climbs.

Oil
6 large zucchini
2 cloves garlic, minced
2 teaspoons dried sweet basil
2 tablespoons chopped parsley
½ teaspoon salt
Freshly ground pepper
¾ cup wine vinegar
Watercress

Fill the skillet with oil to the depth of 1 inch. Place over low heat for 5 or 6 minutes, or until a cube of bread turns golden in 30 seconds. Wash the zucchini well and discard the end slices. Cut into ½-inch slices and fry quickly in the hot oil until light brown. Remove with a slotted spoon and drain on absorbent paper. In a glass or earthenware (not metal) bowl, place a layer of zucchini, sprinkle with the garlic, basil, parsley, salt, and pepper, and repeat until all the zucchini are used.

In a small saucepan, bring the vinegar to a lively, rolling boil and boil for 1 minute. Pour immediately over the zucchini. Allow this to marinate overnight in the refrigerator. Drain and serve, garnished with watercress. The zucchini will keep in this marinade for 2 weeks.

Serves 8

CURRIED BAKED FRUIT

Based on the rule that classifies tomatoes (generically a fruit) as a vegetable (because they are served with the main course and not as a dessert), I include here this delicious fruit casserole. For the occasions when your main dish is a chicken or veal concoction cooked with vegetables, and you feel that another vegetable would be redundant, this baked fruit is perfect.

1 large can pear halves
1 large can peach halves
   or apricots, or both
1 large can pineapple
   chunks
¾ cup dark brown sugar

2 teaspoons curry
   powder
3 tablespoons
   polyunsaturated
   margarine (soft)

Drain the fruits thoroughly in a colander for an hour or so. Excess liquid remaining on the fruits will make the sauce soupy and thin. You might even blot them a bit before using them. Even after all this, the fruits will give out a lot of juice, so you need not worry about dryness. Discard the drained juice, or, if you wish, save it for another purpose.

Mix together the brown sugar and curry powder. Oil a 2-quart casserole. Arrange a layer of fruit in the bottom, sprinkle with part of the brown sugar mixture, dot with some of the margarine, and continue until all the fruits are used. Bake in a 350° oven, covered, for 50 minutes to 1 hour, or until the sauce is bubbly. Remove the cover for the last 10 minutes. Serve the fruit hot with the main course.

Serves 8

MINTED APPLE SLICES

These go well with lamb.

4 medium-sized tart apples
½ cup (about) oil

1 8-ounce jar mint jelly or mint-flavored apple jelly

Peel and core the apples and cut them into thick slices. Coat them with the oil. Heat a heavy skillet and add the apple slices in a single layer. Brown on both sides. As each batch browns, drain on absorbent paper. When all the apples are done, add the jelly and stir until it melts. Return the apples to the skillet, cover them, and simmer over low heat, stirring occasionally, for about 10 minutes, or until they are tender, plump, and green. Don't overcook; they should not be mushy. May be served warm or at room temperature.

Serves 5 or 6

11

Potatoes, Starches, and Legumes

Few foods are as maligned as the potato, which has been made the patsy for all the additional calories heaped on it in the form of butter, cream, and cheese.

Actually, a medium-sized potato, about two and a half inches in diameter, contains approximately 100 calories, the same amount as an apple, an orange, half a large grapefruit, or one slice of buttered toast. The starch content is fairly high, from 12 to 20 percent, but on the other hand, it is chock full of essential nutrients and vitamins.

The number of calories with which the potato ends up depends not only on its embellishment but also on how it is cooked. For instance, three ounces of French fried potatoes contain about 345 calories; the same amount raw and pan-fried, 240 calories; the same amount plain boiled, 71 calories.

The smallest loss of vitamin C in potatoes occurs when they are cooked in their skins for as short a time and in as little water as possible, in a tightly lidded pot. They should not be soaked in water or allowed to stand in their own steam. So much for the tuber, which has kept entire nations alive in times of disaster.

The use of dried beans and peas should not be overlooked in a dietary where meats are limited. They are an excellent source of protein, next best to that found in animal products. They lend themselves to a variety of delicious dishes that may serve as a main course.

The other starches—rice, wild rice, noodles, barley, groats, and bulgur, imaginatively prepared—can bring a considerable amount of glamour, along with substance, to any meal.

BAKED POTATOES

Allow one potato per serving, preferably an Idaho. Scrub the potatoes well with a vegetable brush, for the skin is well worth eating—flavorful and vitaminful (if there is such a word). Rub with oil to keep the skin soft. Prick the potato with a knife or skewer. I must confess I became careless about this, and once a potato actually exploded in my oven, which then proceeded to look like Pompeii after Vesuvius let loose.

In a 400° oven, the potatoes will take 1 to 1¼ hours to bake. A potato skewer plunged through the middle of the potato will reduce the time, however. To test for doneness, with a potholder squeeze the potato to see if it is soft. When you remove the potatoes from the oven, squeeze them again to make them fluffy. Cut a cross in the middle of each potato with a sharp-pointed knife to let the steam escape and avoid the potato's becoming soggy. Top each potato with a blob of plain low-fat yogurt and sprinkle with chopped chives or parsley.

STUFFED BAKED POTATOES

These may be prepared early in the day and refrigerated until time to heat them in the oven.

6 baked potatoes	1 tablespoon chopped
1 teaspoon salt	chives
Freshly ground pepper	1 egg white, stiffly beaten
2 tablespoons oil	Paprika
3 tablespoons (or more) warmed skim milk	Chopped parsley

Bake the potatoes as directed above. When done, cut a large oval slice off the top. Scoop out the insides and mash. Add the salt, pepper, oil, and milk and beat until light and fluffy. Add the chives and fold in the egg white.

Refill the potato shells with this mixture. Dust the tops lightly with paprika. Place the potatoes in a 350° oven for about 20 to 25 minutes, or until the tops are browned and the potatoes are heated through. Sprinkle with parsley.

Serves 6

PAN-CRISPED POTATOES

These are crunchy and crusty outside and mealy inside, a perfect state for a potato.

4–6 medium-sized potatoes	½ teaspoon salt
Oil for frying	Freshly ground pepper
	Paprika

Scrub the potatoes and place in a saucepan with as little boiling salted water as possible. Cover the pan and boil (or steam) until tender (between 25 and 40 minutes). When done, drain and cool. Remove the skins and slice lengthwise into eighths.

Cover the bottom of a large, heavy skillet with ⅛ inch of oil and heat. Add the potato slices. Sprinkle with the salt, pepper, and paprika. Cook over medium heat for 15 or 20 minutes, shaking the pan frequently and turning the potatoes with a spatula so they will get brown and crusty all around. Serve hot.

Serves 4 to 6

BROILED FRENCH FRIED POTATOES

Crisp golden potato sticks achieved without a bath in deep fat.

4 medium-sized potatoes	1 teaspoon paprika
¼ cup oil	Salt

Preheat the broiler for 5 minutes.

Wash and pare the potatoes. Cut lengthwise into strips ¼ inch to a scant ½ inch thick. Dry well. Pour the oil into a cookie tin and mix with the paprika. Add the potato strips and stir well to coat them with oil. Place the pan about 3 inches from the heat. Broil 10 to 15 minutes, stirring the potato sticks often, until they are golden brown on all sides. Remove to absorbent paper to drain. Sprinkle lightly with salt and serve immediately.

Serves 4

ESCALLOPED POTATOES

6 medium-sized potatoes, peeled and thinly sliced
1 large onion, grated
½ teaspoon salt
Freshly ground pepper
1 tablespoon chopped chives
½ cup grated low-fat American cheese
1½ cups (about) skim milk
3 tablespoons oil
Bread crumbs
Paprika

In an oiled 1½-quart casserole, place a layer of the potatoes and sprinkle with the onion, salt, pepper, chives, and cheese. Repeat until all the potatoes are used. There should be about 3 layers. Finish with a layer of potatoes with grated onion and cheese on top.

In a small saucepan heat the milk and oil. Pour over the potatoes so that it comes just to the top layer but does not cover the top. Sprinkle with bread crumbs and dust with paprika. Bake in a 350° oven for about 1¼ hours, or until the potatoes are tender and the top well browned.

Serves 6

PARSLEYED NEW POTATOES

The small new potatoes, like lovely small children, are at their best when dressed simply. When the tiny red-skinned potatoes are available, I steam them, scrubbed and unpeeled, which is how we eat them. Delicious. The small ones are done in about 25 minutes. Here is another way to prepare them.

2 pounds small new potatoes
2 tablespoons oil
1 teaspoon salt
Freshly ground pepper
3 tablespoons chopped parsley

Peel the potatoes and place in a saucepan with as little boiling salted water as possible. Boil, covered—or better still, steam them. Depending upon size, they may take anywhere from 20 to 35 minutes, but watch them carefully and don't overcook. When done, drain them and transfer to a warmed skillet. Shake the pan over low heat until the potatoes are dry. Add the remaining ingredients. Continue to toss until the potatoes are coated with oil and parsley. Serve hot.

Serves 6

NEW POTATOES AND PEAS

12–16 small new potatoes	½ teaspoon salt
3 tablespoons oil	⅛ teaspoon freshly
4 tablespoons flour	ground pepper
2 cups potato water	½ teaspoon dried basil
and skim milk	1 cup cooked fresh or
	frozen peas

Wash and peel the potatoes. Place in a saucepan with as little boiling salted water as possible, cover, bring to a boil, and cook until the potatoes are tender (about 20 minutes or more). Drain and reserve the liquid to use in the cream sauce. Keep the potatoes warm.

In a small skillet, heat the oil and blend in the flour. Cook until bubbly, but don't let the flour brown. Measure the potato liquid and add skim milk if it is less than 2 cups. Slowly add 1 cup of the liquid to the oil and flour, stirring with a wire whisk. Stir in the second cup of liquid slowly and continue to cook, stirring, until the sauce becomes thickened and smooth. Add the remaining ingredients and heat through for another minute or two. Place the potatoes in a warmed bowl and pour the sauce over, mixing well.

Serves 6

COTTAGE CHEESE POTATO CASSEROLE

6 medium-sized potatoes	1 tablespoon chopped
2 cups low-fat cottage	parsley
cheese	1 teaspoon salt
2 tablespoons oil	Freshly ground pepper
2 tablespoons flour	

1 tablespoon chopped fresh dill or ½ teaspoon dried dill	½ cup fine bread crumbs browned in 2 tablespoons oil
1 small onion, grated	1 tablespoon grated Parmesan cheese
⅓ cup skim milk	

Scrub the potatoes and place them in as little boiling salted water as possible. Cover the pan and cook them until soft (25 to 40 minutes). Drain. When cool, peel and slice thin.

Beat the cottage cheese with a rotary beater until it is fairly smooth. You may leave a few lumps. Add the oil and mix well.

Combine the flour, parsley, salt, pepper, and dill. Oil a 1½-quart casserole and arrange a layer of the potatoes in the bottom. Cover with a layer of the cottage cheese and sprinkle it with the seasoned flour and a little of the onion. Repeat until all the ingredients are used, ending with a layer of potatoes. Warm the milk, pour it over all, and sprinkle the bread crumbs on top. Place in a pre-heated 350° oven and bake for 25 minutes. Remove from the oven, sprinkle with the cheese, and return to the oven for 5 minutes, or until the cheese browns.

Serves 6

POTATO PUDDING

4 or 5	large potatoes	1½	tablespoons flour
1	cup boiling water	1	teaspoon salt
2	tablespoons oil		Freshly ground
½	medium onion, grated		pepper
2	egg whites, beaten until frothy		

Preheat the oven to 400°.

Peel the potatoes and grate them with a medium-fine grater into a good-sized bowl (you really will have to grate them—a blender doesn't do the same kind of job). Add the water and mix. Strain through a wire strainer, discarding the liquid that drains off. (If some of the vitamins drain off with it, that's the price you pay for potato pudding.)

Pour 1 tablespoon of the oil into an 8-inch square baking dish and place in a hot oven.

Add to the potato the second tablespoon of oil along with the remaining ingredients, and mix well. Pour into the baking dish and bake for 1 to 1½ hours, or until the pudding is crisp and brown on top.

Serves 4 or 5

GLAZED SWEET POTATOES

4 medium-sized sweet
  potatoes
2 tablespoons oil
2 tablespoons dark brown
  sugar

1 1-pound can apricot
  halves, drained
½ cup apricot syrup

Cook the sweet potatoes in a small amount of boiling salted water until tender (about 30 minutes). Peel them, cut them in two lengthwise, and place the halves, cut side up, in an oiled baking dish. Dribble the oil over them and sprinkle the brown sugar on top. Distribute the apricot halves among the sweet potatoes and pour the apricot syrup over all. Bake for about 25 minutes in a 400° oven, basting a few times with the syrup, until the potatoes are glazed and browned.

Serves 4 to 6

PRUNE AND SWEET POTATO CASSEROLE

4 medium-sized sweet
  potatoes
1½ cups cooked prunes,
  pitted (unsweetened)
½ cup brown sugar

½ cup prune juice
3 tablespoons lemon
  juice
2 tablespoons oil

Cook the sweet potatoes in a small amount of boiling salted water until tender (about 30 minutes). Peel and cut them lengthwise in slices about ⅜ inch thick. Place alternate layers of the sweet potatoes and prunes in an oiled 1½-quart casserole, sprinkling each layer with some of the brown sugar. Combine the prune juice with the lemon juice and add to the casserole. Dribble the oil over all. Bake, uncovered, in a 350° oven for 40 to 45 minutes. Baste a few times with the syrup in the casserole.

Serves 4 to 6

SWEET POTATO AND CARROT RING

We have here a vegetable-starch combination that does nicely with holiday turkey or chicken. It may be baked in a casserole or a ring form. My choice is the latter.

6 or 7 large carrots (1¼ to 1½ pounds)
3 sweet potatoes (1¼ to 1½ pounds)
2 egg whites, unbeaten

1 cup dried bread crumbs
1¼ cups skim milk
½ teaspoon salt
Few grinds of pepper
2 tablespoons brown sugar

Scrape the carrots, rinse, and slice into ⅛-inch slices. Cook, covered, in salted water until tender (about 20 to 25 minutes), then drain and mash. Don't overcook them—the carrots should be firm enough so that, after you mash them, there will still be a few firm morsels left to add variety of texture to the finished product.

Peel, wash, and cut the sweet potatoes into chunks. Cook in salted water until soft (about 20 minutes). Drain well and mash.

In a large bowl, combine the sweet potatoes and carrots. Add the remaining ingredients and mix well. Pack into an oiled 4-cup ring mold and place the mold in a baking pan with an inch or so of hot water in the bottom. Bake, uncovered, in a preheated 350° oven for 1 hour.

Remove the mold from the baking pan and loosen the pudding around the edges with a spatula. Invert the mold on a round platter and slip off. Fill the center of the ring with cooked, crisp string beans or cooked cauliflowerets sprinkled with chopped parsley for color contrast. Serve hot.

Serves 8 to 10

POPPY-SEED NOODLE CASSEROLE

2 10½-ounce cans beef
consommé
Equal amount of water
12 ounces fine noodles
2 tablespoons oil

2½ tablespoons poppy
seeds
½ cup blanched slivered
almonds
1 tablespoon oil

In a large saucepan, bring the consommé and an equal quantity of water to a boil and drop in the noodles. Cover and simmer until all the liquid is absorbed (this should take 8 to 10 minutes). When the noodles are done, add the 2 tablespoons of oil and the poppy seeds and toss well. Transfer the noodles to an oiled 2-quart ovenproof casserole.

Brown the almonds by putting them in a small skillet with the 1 tablespoon of oil and placing them over low heat. Shake the pan often to turn the nuts. Watch them carefully, for they brown quickly and should be golden and not scorched.

Sprinkle the almonds over the top of the noodles and keep the casserole warm in a 250° oven until ready to serve.

Serves 10 to 12

PINEAPPLE CREAM NOODLE PUDDING

½ pound medium or
broad noodles
2 tablespoons oil
2 cups low-fat cottage
cheese
1 tablespoon lemon
juice

1 cup canned crushed
pineapple, drained
(reserve the juice)
⅓ cup brown sugar
Cornflake crumbs

Cook the noodles for 8 minutes according to the package directions. Do not overcook. Drain well. Place in a good-sized bowl, add the oil, and toss well.

Beat 1 cup of the cottage cheese with an electric or rotary beater until it is creamy smooth. Add the lemon juice and enough drained pineapple juice (about 2 tablespoons or more) to make it the consistency of thick cream. Stir in the pineapple and brown sugar. Fold in the remaining cup of cottage cheese, lumps and all. Add this mixture to the noodles and toss lightly to distribute the pineapple-cheese mixture evenly.

Oil a 9 by 13 inch baking dish. Spread the noodle mixture in the dish, sprinkle cornflake crumbs on top, and bake in a 350° oven for 1 hour, or until the top is nicely browned. Serve hot.

Serves 8

Variation: This can do nicely for dessert with ½ cup of raisins and ½ cup of chopped nuts added to the ingredients. Increase the brown sugar to ½ cup. Combine the cornflake topping with ¼ cup of brown sugar and ½ teaspoon of cinnamon.

BAKED RICE

The following is an effortless way to produce a perfect rice dish.

3   tablespoons oil
1   small onion, chopped
½   cup chopped mush-
      rooms
1   cup uncooked rice

2½   cups boiling chicken
        broth
        Salt and pepper (if
        desired)

Over low heat, warm the oil in a 1½-quart ovenproof casserole and cook the onion until it becomes limp and transparent. Add the mushrooms and cook 2 minutes longer. Add the rice and stir with a wooden spoon until it becomes opaque. Add the chicken broth and taste to see if any additional salt and pepper are needed. Cover the casserole tightly and place in a preheated 350° oven for 1 hour. The liquid should be absorbed and the rice tender. If not, continue baking for another 10 minutes or so.

Serves 4 or 5

Variation: Chopped water chestnuts may be used in place of the mushrooms.

RICE AND NOODLE PILAF

The crisp brown noodles in this pilaf provide a pleasant contrast in texture to the tender, fluffy, individual-grained rice. For a perfect result in cooking rice, always use twice as much liquid as rice.

4	tablespoons oil	3 cups hot chicken broth
½	cup fine noodles,	or consommé (or water)
	uncooked	Salt to taste
1½	cups long grain rice	

Heat the oil in a large kettle, crunch the noodles in your hand to break them up, and sauté in the warm oil until lightly browned. Add the dry rice and stir with a wooden spoon until the rice becomes opaque. Add the chicken broth, consommé, or water. The amount of salt needed varies depending upon the seasoning in the broth, so you will have to use your judgment. Bring to a boil and reduce the heat. Place over the top of the kettle a linen towel folded large enough to cover the top but not so large as to hang dangerously near the heat. Place the kettle lid over the towel and simmer the rice slowly over very low heat for 35 minutes. As the rice cooks, the steam is absorbed by the towel and the rice grains become separate and distinct, as rice should be.

The rice can be cooked in the morning and reheated hours later with a perfect result. Just leave the rice untouched, unlooked at, and covered with the towel and lid. When you are ready to reheat it, add 2 tablespoons of water, fluff the rice, and reheat slowly over very low heat, covered with the towel and pot lid.

Serves 6

Variations: Add 1 cup of canned, drained chick-peas to the sautéed rice. Mix and add the broth.

Sprinkle ½ cup of browned slivered almonds over the rice when served. Omit the noodles in cooking.

FRIED CHINESE RICE

Small amounts of leftover cooked chicken or meat can be put to good use in this dish. However, if you wish to serve it without the meat, prepare as in the following recipe, but use half the amount of broth.

3 tablespoons oil
1 onion, finely chopped
2 stalks celery, finely chopped
½ pound mushrooms, sliced
2 cups cooked chicken or meat, cut into small dice

1 teaspoon cornstarch
1 cup chicken broth
1 tablespoon (or more) soy sauce, according to taste
4 cups cooked rice
Salt and pepper to taste

In a large, heavy skillet, heat the oil and sauté the onion, celery, and mushrooms for 5 minutes. Add the chicken or meat and brown lightly. In a small bowl, mix the cornstarch and chicken broth and blend until smooth. Add the soy sauce and mix through. Add the cornstarch mixture to the meat and vegetables and cook for a few minutes to reduce the liquid. Add the cold rice (it must be cold), break up any lumps, and stir constantly until the ingredients are well distributed and all the rice has had its turn at the bottom of the pan. Reduce the heat and let it steam through gently, but stay with it and turn it frequently. Taste for seasoning and correct. Serve at once.

Serves 6

WILD RICE CASSEROLE

This is a truly splendid company dish, offering a variety of textures and the combination of wild rice and white rice. It also has the added advantage that it can be prepared well ahead of time and reheated at the dinner hour.

½ cup wild rice
7 cups of lightly salted water or stock
½ cup white rice
4 tablespoons oil
1 medium-sized onion, finely chopped
2 stalks celery, finely chopped

½ pound mushrooms, wiped clean and sliced
1 8-ounce can water chestnuts, drained and sliced
1 tablespoon soy sauce
½ cup slivered almonds, browned in 1 tablespoon oil

Wash the wild rice in cold water, changing the water several times until it is completely clear. Soak it in cold water to cover for a few hours. In a large kettle, bring the water or stock, lightly salted, to a boil. Cook the wild rice for 20 minutes, add the white rice, and continue to cook for another 15 or 20 minutes, or until tender. Drain.

In a medium-sized skillet, heat the oil and cook the onions until they are limp and transparent but not brown. Add the celery and mushrooms and cook for an additional 5 minutes. Don't overcook the celery, for it should be crisp-tender. To the drained rice add the onion, celery, mushrooms, water chestnuts, and soy sauce and mix thoroughly. Taste for seasoning and correct. You may want to add a bit of salt or a little more soy sauce. Transfer to a lightly oiled casserole. Bake uncovered in a preheated 350° oven until heated through. This generally takes about 30 minutes.

While the rice is in the oven, brown the almonds in the tablespoon of hot oil in a small skillet. Shake them from time to time so they will brown evenly. Watch them carefully, for they turn color quickly. Just before serving, sprinkle the browned almonds over the top of the rice.

Serves 6

BAKED BEANS

Baked beans are among the few classic American dishes that have never lost their popularity or gone out of style. And for good reason. With a minimum of accompaniments—perhaps some cold meat loaf and a green salad—a substantial group of people can be handsomely fed.

1 quart (4 cups) navy beans (pea beans)	5 tablespoons molasses
	1 tablespoon sugar
1 tablespoon salt	½ cup catsup
1½ teaspoons dry mustard	1 cup boiling water

Wash the beans, cover them with cold water, and soak overnight. In the morning, drain and cover them with fresh cold water. Bring to a boil and cook slowly, covered, for not more than ½ hour. Skim the froth from time to time. To test for doneness, take a few beans on the tip of a spoon and blow on them. If they are done, the skins will pop. If not, on with the cooking, but watch carefully that you don't overcook. Mushy baked beans are a bore. Drain well when done and place in a lightly oiled casserole or bean pot.

In a small bowl, mix together the remaining ingredients. Pour over the beans. Add more boiling water if needed to cover the beans entirely. Cover the pot and bake in a 350° oven for 1 hour. Uncover the pot and bake another hour until browned on top. If the beans seem to be drying out, add a bit more boiling water.

Serves 10 to 12

BARLEY PILAF

Barley is an interesting grain that makes all too infrequent appearances. Give it some thought other than as an addendum to soup.

3 tablespoons oil	2 cups chicken broth
1 small onion, chopped	½ teaspoon Bovril
¼ pound mushrooms, sliced	½ teaspoon salt
1 cup pearl barley, uncooked	Freshly ground pepper

In a heavy skillet, heat the oil and add the onion, mushrooms, and barley. Cook slowly over medium heat, turning often until the onion is limp and the barley is golden brown.

While this is cooking, bring the chicken broth to the boiling point. Dissolve the Bovril in the broth and stir slowly into the barley mixture. Add the salt and pepper and correct the seasoning. Transfer to a lightly oiled casserole, cover, and bake for 1 hour in a 350° oven. If the liquid seems to be drying out, add more boiling water or chicken broth.

Serves 4 or 5

SCALLOPED PEA BEANS AND TOMATOES

1½ cups navy beans (pea
    beans)
1   medium-sized onion,
    sliced
1   teaspoon salt
    Freshly ground
    pepper
2   tablespoons oil
3   tablespoons flour

1¼ cups skim milk
1   cup canned
    tomatoes, drained
½   cup bread crumbs
    browned in 2
    tablespoons oil
1   tablespoon minced
    parsley

In a good-sized kettle, soak the beans in cold water to cover for 3 or 4 hours. Add the onion, salt, and pepper, cover, and bring slowly to a boil. Reduce the heat and simmer slowly until the beans are tender (about 50 minutes to an hour). Drain, reserving ¼ cup of the liquid.

In another saucepan, heat the oil and blend in the flour. Add the milk slowly, stirring with a wire whisk until the sauce becomes thickened and smooth.

Combine the beans with the ¼ cup of liquid and the tomato pulp. Stir in the cream sauce and mix well. Taste and correct the seasoning. Turn into an oiled 1½-quart baking dish. Cover with the bread crumbs and sprinkle the parsley over the top. Bake in a 375° oven for 30 minutes.

Serves 6

CORN PUFFS

These delicate little corn fritters do very well as an accompaniment for almost any meat, fish, or poultry course. Cooking them on a griddle instead of the usual deep-fat method is a saving in the calorie department.

3   egg whites
1   12-ounce can corn
    niblets, drained
¼   cup flour
1   teaspoon baking
    powder

1 teaspoon salt
1 teaspoon sugar
   Dash of nutmeg
1 tablespoon oil

Heat the griddle. It is ready when a drop of water bounces off.

Beat the egg whites stiffly. In a bowl, combine the remaining ingredients and fold in the egg whites.

Lightly oil the griddle with the oil and drop the batter by tablespoonsful onto the hot griddle. Flatten with the back of a spoon. When brown on one side, turn and brown the other. Keep warm in the oven until ready to serve. Makes 16 puffs.

Serves 4

FLAGEOLETS IN TOMATO FONDUE

These dried small green beans, imported from France, are considered a perfect accompaniment for lamb, but we like them with other meats as well. They are available in markets that specialize in fancy groceries; they are not a usual supermarket item. The small pea beans (navy beans) or dried lima beans may be substituted, but they won't be quite the same.

1 cup dried flageolets	4 whole cloves
4 cups water	1 teaspoon salt
1 onion	

Tomato Fondue

2 tablespoons oil	3 cloves garlic, minced
1 small onion, chopped	1 teaspoon salt
3 tablespoons tomato sauce	Freshly ground pepper
	¼ teaspoon sugar
3 tomatoes, peeled, seeded, and chopped (about 2 cups)	¼ teaspoon dried basil
	1 tablespoon chopped parsley
1 tablespoon tomato paste	

Soak the beans overnight in cold water to cover. The next day, drain them, transfer them to a kettle, and add the 4 cups of water, the onion studded with the cloves, and the salt. Bring to a boil, cover, and simmer slowly until the beans are tender (about 1½ hours).

While the beans are cooking, prepare the fondue. In a medium-sized saucepan, heat the oil and sauté the onion until it is limp and transparent. Add all the remaining ingredients except the parsley. Cover and simmer over low heat for 30 minutes. Remove the cover and continue cooking for another 20 minutes or more, to let the sauce thicken. Stir with a wooden spoon from time to time to prevent scorching and to break up the tomato chunks. Taste for seasoning and correct.

Drain the beans and mix in just enough of the tomato sauce to bind them—the sauce must be incidental to the beans. The sauce is delicious, and you can use whatever is left for another purpose. Transfer the beans to a warmed bowl and sprinkle with the parsley.

Serves 5 or 6

BULGUR

Or *Burghul* or *Bulghour,* a cracked wheat, is a staple food of the Middle East that can add variety to a family's starch repertoire. It is a nutritious food that also contains roughage, a desirable item in the diet. Most supermarkets now stock bulgur.

2 tablespoons oil	1 cup bulgur
1 small onion, finely chopped	2 cups hot chicken broth
	Salt and pepper to taste

In a heavy saucepan, heat the oil. Add the onion and cook over low heat until it is limp and golden. Stir in the bulgur and cook for a few minutes until lightly browned. Gradually stir in the hot chicken broth and taste to see if more seasoning is needed. Cover the pot and simmer over low heat for 15 minutes. Remove from the heat and leave covered in a warm place until ready to serve.

Serves 4

BULGUR SALAD (TABBULEH)

A pleasant summer salad with a variety of possibilities for use.

1 cup bulgur
2 cups boiling water or
  chicken broth
½ cup (or more) chopped
  parsley
½ cup (or more) chopped
  scallions
½ cup fresh mint
  leaves, chopped
¼ cup lemon juice
½ cup oil
2 or 3 tomatoes, skinned
  and chopped
Salt to taste

Soak the bulgur in the hot liquid for 1 hour. Drain and discard the excess liquid. Add the parsley, scallions, and mint leaves and mix well. Toss with the lemon juice and oil. Chill for 3 or 4 hours. Just before serving, add the tomatoes and salt.

Serves 4

Variation: Any finely chopped leftover meat or poultry can be added to provide a satisfactory one-dish hot-weather lunch. Lamb has a particular affinity for bulgur.

KASHA AND MUSHROOM CASSEROLE

Kasha, or coarse buckwheat groats, is another unusual cereal or starch.

4 tablespoons oil
1½ cups kasha
1 small onion, finely
  chopped
1 teaspoon salt
  Freshly ground
  pepper
4 cups boiling chicken
  broth
1 tablespoon Kitchen
  Bouquet
½ pound sliced
  mushrooms browned
  in 2 tablespoons oil

In a heavy skillet, heat the oil and cook the kasha over moderate heat for 10 minutes, stirring constantly. Add the onion, salt, pepper, and chicken broth. Cover tightly and cook over low heat for 25 minutes, stirring from time to time. If the kasha becomes dry, add a little boiling water. Stir in the Kitchen Bouquet and mushrooms and transfer the kasha to an oiled ovenproof casserole. Cover and bake in a preheated 350° oven for 25 minutes. The kasha should be tender but moist.

Serves 6 to 8

Variation: Add to the casserole 6 ounces of cooked noodle bows. They come in two sizes—do try to get the smaller ones. Add them at the time you are transferring the kasha to the casserole for baking and distribute the noodle bows well. As a point of information, "noodle bows" translates into *varnitchkes* in Russian (I think), thereby producing a dish properly known as *Kasha Varnitchkes*. This casserole can serve as a main supper dish.

12
Brunch, Lunch, and Supper Dishes

It occurs to me that "brunch, lunch, and supper dishes" may be more a matter of semantics and household custom than a distinct category of foods, for who is to quibble if we choose to dine off chicken salad for breakfast, pot roast at noon, or breakfast waffles at dinner?

For most Americans, however, brunch and lunch connote a light meal—a salad, a sandwich, a bowl of soup. Lunch may mean something that can be assembled from pantry supplies without the necessity for last-minute marketing.

The supper dishes included here are some of the things that come to mind for the easy informality of the occasions when a one-dish meal to serve the family or to share with friends is indicated. But throughout the book you will find many other casseroles, salads, and aspics that can be prepared in advance and require a minimum of last-minute fussing.

APPLE PANCAKE

Never did two eggs lend themselves to a greater diversity of uses than in this apple pancake. It will serve 2 or 3 handsomely—6 adequately if there are other courses—and will give a good account of itself as breakfast, brunch, or supper, or as a dinner dessert.

3 large tart apples (about 1½ pounds)	¼ teaspoon cinnamon
	¼ teaspoon nutmeg
3 tablespoons oil	1 teaspoon freshly
¼ cup sugar	ground lemon rind

Pancake

2 eggs	¼ teaspoon salt
½ cup skim milk	1½ tablespoons oil
½ cup flour	

Topping

4 tablespoons sugar   1 tablespoon lemon juice

Preheat the oven to 450°.

Pare, core, and slice the apples thinly. Heat the oil in a large skillet and cook the apple slices over low heat for 5 minutes. Combine the sugar with the cinnamon, nutmeg, and lemon rind, add to the apples, and cook, covered, for about 10 minutes, or until the apples are crisp-tender. Don't let them get mushy. Remove from the heat but keep warm while you prepare the pancake.

To make the pancake, beat the eggs with a wire whisk until lemon colored. Add the milk, flour, and salt and beat until smooth. Heat the oil in a 9-inch ovenproof round shallow baking dish or a glass pie plate, pour the batter into it, and place in the oven for about 15 minutes. After the first few minutes, the pancake will begin to puff up. Prick the batter and do it again each time it puffs up. After the first 15 minutes, reduce the heat to 350° and cook about 10 minutes longer, or until the pancake becomes golden and crisp and looks done. It will form a shell.

Remove from the oven and loosen the bottom of the pancake with a spatula. Sprinkle 2 tablespoons of the topping sugar over the pancake. Place the apple mixture over half the pancake, sprinkle the apples with the lemon juice, fold like an omelet, and remove to a warmed platter. Sprinkle the top with the remaining 2 tablespoons of sugar and serve at once.

DRIED BEEF AND TOMATOES

This recipe will stretch half a pound of wafer-thin dried beef and a can of kidney beans into an adequate meal for four.

½ pound thinly sliced dried beef	3 tablespoons oil
	2 medium onions, diced

2 tablespoons flour	½ teaspoon oregano
2 cups canned tomatoes	½ teaspoon chili powder
1½ cups canned kidney beans, drained	(or more, according to taste)

If the beef is very salty, soak it in boiling water for a minute or two. Drain well and squeeze dry. Heat the oil in a heavy skillet. Shred the dried beef and cook in the oil until the edges curl. Add the onions and cook 5 minutes more, until the onions become limp and transparent. Drain off any excess oil.

Stir in the flour and blend. Add the tomatoes slowly. Cook over low heat until thick, stirring with a wooden spoon to break up the tomatoes. Add the beans, oregano, and chili powder. Taste and add more chili powder if you want it a bit spicier.

Serves 4

FRIZZLED DRIED BEEF

I always try to have a supply of jars of dried sliced beef in the pantry, and unexpected Sunday morning breakfast or brunch guests might very well be served this creamed dried beef over toast or toasted English muffins.

½ pound sliced dried beef, shredded	2 cups skim milk
2 tablespoons oil	Freshly ground pepper
3 tablespoons flour	Toast triangles
¼ teaspoon dry mustard	Chopped parsley

If the beef is salty—and it generally is—soak it in boiling water a minute or two, drain, and squeeze dry.

Heat the oil in a heavy skillet and cook the beef for about 5 minutes or until it frizzles and gets curly. Sprinkle the flour over the beef and stir constantly until the flour turns dark brown, but is not burned. Add the mustard. Add the milk, a little at a time, and stir until the mixture thickens and comes to a boil. Add pepper and taste for seasoning. If the mixture is thicker than you wish, thin it with some additional milk. Serve on toast and sprinkle with the parsley.

Serves 4

BAKED STUFFED PEPPERS

These are equally good for a family dinner or as part of your offering at a party buffet. They may be prepared in advance and baked at the time you need them.

6 to 8	large green peppers		Freshly ground pepper
2	tablespoons oil	¼	teaspoon dried thyme
1	medium-sized onion, chopped	⅓	cup walnuts, finely chopped
1	pound lean chopped beef or veal	1	tablespoon chopped parsley
1½	cups cooked rice	½	cup skim milk
½	teaspoon salt	2	cups tomato sauce
		½	teaspoon dried basil
		½	cup chicken broth

Cut a crosswise slice from the stem end of the peppers and discard. Remove the seeds. Cover the peppers with boiling water and steep for 5 minutes, then turn them upside down, drain, and set aside.

In a large, heavy kettle, heat the oil and cook the onion until golden brown. Add the meat and cook for 5 or 6 minutes, until it loses its raw look. Remove from the heat and add the rice, salt, pepper, thyme, walnuts, parsley, and milk. Blend thoroughly with a fork.

Stuff the peppers with the meat mixture. Arrange them in an oiled baking dish, close together. Combine the tomato sauce, basil, and chicken broth in a small saucepan and bring to the boiling point. Pour over and around the peppers. Cover the baking dish tightly and bake in a preheated 400° oven 40 or 50 minutes, or until the peppers are crisp-tender. Remove the cover a few times during the baking and baste the peppers with the sauce.

Serves 6 to 8

EGGPLANT STUFFED WITH GROUND LAMB, ARMENIAN STYLE

2	large eggplants	1	pound lean, well-trimmed lamb, ground
	Salt		
3	tablespoons oil		

2 medium-sized onions,
  thinly sliced
1 small green pepper,
  finely chopped
1 clove garlic, crushed
½ cup parsley, finely
  chopped
½ teaspoon salt

¼ teaspoon allspice
½ cup canned tomatoes,
  drained
1 tablespoon tomato
  paste
½ cup water
8 slices fresh tomato
  Dried basil

Wash the eggplants, cut off and discard the stem ends, and slice each eggplant lengthwise into four quarters. Sprinkle the segments with salt, set aside for 1 hour, then wipe off the salt and dry the eggplant well. With a pastry brush dipped in the oil, brush each piece of eggplant and bake in a 450° oven until light brown (about 20 minutes).

For the stuffing, heat the remainder of the oil in a large skillet and cook the meat until it loses its raw look. Add the onions and green pepper and cook about 10 minutes longer, until the vegetables are tender. Add the garlic, parsley, salt, allspice, and tomatoes and heat through. Taste for seasoning.

To stuff the eggplant segments, make an incision down the middle lengthwise from end to end, push the flesh aside, and fill with the meat mixture. Arrange in a lightly oiled baking pan. Combine the tomato paste and water and pour into the pan between the eggplant segments. Place a tomato slice over each segment, sprinkle the tomatoes with the basil, and bake in a 375° oven for 30 minutes. Serve hot.

Serves 4

BAKED EGGPLANT WITH CHOPPED MEAT

Another good-tasting meat-extending combination.

2 large eggplants
3 tablespoons oil
3 onions, coarsely
  chopped
1 small green pepper,
  chopped (optional)
1 pound lean ground beef
1 6-ounce can tomato
  paste

½ teaspoon dried oregano
½ teaspoon salt
  Freshly ground pepper
⅓ cup dry red wine
1 tablespoon Parmesan
  cheese
  Oil

Wash the eggplants and split lengthwise. Scoop out the pulp, leaving a thin shell. Cut the pulp into small cubes and set aside.

In a large, heavy pot, heat the oil. Add the onions and green pepper (if desired) and cook until the onions are limp. Add the meat, eggplant cubes, tomato paste, oregano, salt, and pepper and cook over medium heat, stirring, until the meat loses its raw look. Add the wine, stir well, and cover. Cook over low heat for 15 to 20 minutes, or until the eggplant becomes tender but not mushy. Taste for seasonings and correct. Pile the meat mixture into shells, sprinkle lightly with the cheese, and dribble a bit of oil over each. Bake in a 350° oven for 45 minutes.

Serves 4

CHILI CON CARNE

This popular dish may not be exactly right for a champagne dinner, but it has its uses for an informal family supper.

2 tablespoons oil	1½ tablespoons (or more)
1 large Spanish onion,	chili powder
chopped	½ cup catsup
1 pound lean ground	1 cup tomato sauce
round steak	½ teaspoon salt
1 1-pound-4 ounce can	Freshly ground
kidney beans, drained	pepper

Heat the oil in a large, heavy skillet and cook the onion until golden. Add the meat and brown well, stirring constantly. Add the beans, chili powder, catsup, tomato sauce, salt, and pepper. Taste for seasonings and correct. You may want more chili powder. Simmer over low heat for 30 to 40 minutes, stirring frequently.

Serves 4

PILAF WITH CHOPPED BEEF

2 tablespoons oil	1 pound lean round
1 large onion, finely	steak, ground
chopped	1 clove garlic, mashed

⅓ cup green pepper, finely chopped	1 teaspoon salt
	Freshly ground pepper
¼ cup black olives, chopped	½ teaspoon sugar
	½ cup uncooked rice
2 cups consommé	2 tablespoons chopped parsley
1 6-ounce can tomato paste	

In a large, heavy skillet with a cover, heat the oil and cook the onion until it becomes limp. Add the meat and cook over medium high heat, stirring, until the meat is browned. Add all the remaining ingredients except the rice and parsley. Bring to a boil, add the rice, reduce the heat, and simmer over low heat until the rice is tender (about 20 minutes). Stir a few times. If there is too much liquid, remove the cover and cook another 10 minutes, or until the sauce thickens. Remove to a warm serving bowl, sprinkle with the parsley, and serve hot.

Serves 4

MACARONI WITH CHOPPED BEEF

Make this only with the special low-fat American cheese.

2 cups elbow macaroni	Freshly ground pepper
3½ tablespoons oil	
2 medium-sized onions, chopped	2 teaspoons Worcestershire sauce
½ green pepper, chopped	3 tablespoons flour
	2 cups skim milk
1 pound lean ground round steak	½ pound imitation American cheese, cut into small chunks
2 canned tomatoes, drained	¼ teaspoon salt
1 teaspoon dried basil	Freshly ground pepper
1 teaspoon dried oregano	Dash of Tabasco
	Grated Parmesan cheese
½ teaspoon salt	

Cook the macaroni in boiling salted water until barely tender (8 to 10 minutes). Be careful not to overcook, since it will later be baked. Rinse in cold water and drain well. Set aside.

In a large, heavy skillet, heat 1½ tablespoons of the oil. Add the onions and green pepper and cook until the vegetables are tender and the onions limp and transparent. Add the meat and cook until it loses its raw look. Break up the tomatoes into small chunks with a wooden spoon and add along with the basil, oregano, ½ teaspoon of salt, pepper, and Worcestershire sauce. Cook for 3 or 4 minutes.

In a medium-sized saucepan, heat the remaining 2 tablespoons of oil. Add the flour and cook, stirring, until it bubbles. Slowly add the milk, stirring with a wire whisk, and continue to stir over medium heat until the sauce becomes thickened and smooth. Reduce the heat to very low, add the cheese chunks, and stir until they melt. Add the ¼ teaspoon of salt, pepper, and Tabasco and taste for seasoning.

Oil a 2½- or 3-quart casserole. If there is any excess liquid in the meat skillet, pour it into the bottom of the casserole. Add the macaroni and toss with about ⅓ of the cream sauce. Spoon the meat mixture over the macaroni and cover with the remaining cream sauce. Sprinkle with the grated cheese. Place the casserole, uncovered, in a preheated 400° oven and bake for 30 minutes, or until it is heated through and bubbly. If the top isn't brown enough, place it under the broiler for a couple of minutes.

Serves 6

STUFFED ZUCCHINI

Try to get stubby, fat zucchini without any sudden twists or curves, since they will need to be hollowed out.

A cup of finely minced chicken may be substituted for the tuna fish.

4 plump medium-sized zucchini, unpeeled
1 7-ounce can tuna fish, or 1 cup cooked chicken, minced
2 slices of bread, crusts removed, soaked in water and squeezed dry

2 tablespoons oil
1 tablespoon chopped parsley
Freshly ground pepper
1 tablespoon mayonnaise
½ teaspoon dry mustard
1 clove garlic, minced

1	8-ounce can tomato	Freshly ground pepper

1 8-ounce can tomato   Freshly ground pepper
   sauce   ½ cup chicken broth
½ teaspoon salt

Wash the zucchini, cut off the end slices, and scoop out the center with an apple corer, leaving a reasonably thick outer shell. Cut the zucchini pulp into small cubes and reserve. In a small bowl, combine the tuna fish or chicken, bread, 1 tablespoon of the oil, parsley, pepper, mayonnaise, and mustard. Mix to a smooth paste. Pack the zucchini with the mixture.

In a shallow ovenproof baking dish, heat the remaining oil over medium heat and brown the garlic. Add the tomato sauce, salt, pepper, and chicken broth and heat through. Place the stuffed zucchini in the sauce, add the cubed zucchini, and cook in a 375° oven for 40 to 50 minutes, or until the zucchini is tender. Baste from time to time.

Serves 4

HOT CHICKEN SALAD

In case you have a notion that a hot salad is an impossibility because the mayonnaise would separate or do something else equally disastrous, I urge you to try this. The variety of textures it contains adds interest to a highly satisfactory main dish for a brunch or supper. Turkey may be substituted for the chicken.

3 cups cooked chicken,   1 tablespoon grated
   cut into cubes   onion
2 teaspoons oil   ½ teaspoon salt
½ cup slivered almonds   ½ cup water chestnuts,
2 cups sliced celery   thinly sliced
1 cup mayonnaise   ¼ cup grated low-fat
2 tablespoons lemon   American cheese
   juice   ½ cup cornflakes, lightly
                               crushed

Place the cubed chicken in a good-sized bowl.

Heat the oil in a small skillet and brown the almonds over low heat. Shake the pan frequently. The nuts brown quickly, so keep a careful watch and remove them from the heat as soon as they begin to turn color.

Combine the chicken with the celery, mayonnaise, lemon juice, onion, salt, water chestnuts, and almonds and toss thoroughly. Transfer to a lightly oiled shallow casserole or baking dish that can be used for serving. Sprinkle the top with the cheese and cornflakes. Bake in a 350° oven for 20 to 30 minutes, or until heated through.

Serves 4 or 5

CHICKEN CHOW MEIN

Even if this version of a Chinese dish is thoroughly Americanized, bearing no resemblance to the dish of the same name in China, it's a general favorite and provides an answer to what to do with some leftover chicken or turkey.

2 cups cooked chicken or turkey	1 1-pound can bean sprouts, rinsed in cold water and drained
2 tablespoons oil	½ cup bamboo shoots, drained
2 large onions, thinly sliced	2 tablespoons cornstarch
4 large celery stalks, split, cut diagonally in 1-inch lengths	1 tablespoon (or more) soy sauce
½ cup mushrooms, sliced	Freshly ground pepper
2 cups chicken broth	Cooked rice
½ cup water chestnuts	Chow mein noodles

Cut the chicken or turkey into large bite-sized pieces and set aside. In a large skillet, heat the oil and cook the onions until slightly soft. Add the celery, mushrooms, and 1½ cups of the chicken broth. Cook over low heat for 10 minutes, stirring a few times.

Add the water chestnuts, bean sprouts, and bamboo shoots. In a small bowl, combine the remaining ½ cup of chicken broth with the cornstarch and soy sauce and stir until smooth. Add this to the skillet along with the chicken or turkey. Add the pepper and mix well. Simmer for 10 minutes, stirring, until the mixture becomes thickened and smooth. Taste for seasoning—you may want to add some additional soy sauce or even a squirt of Tabasco.

Serve with hot boiled rice and chow mein noodles that have been warmed in the oven. Watch the noodles carefully, for they brown very quickly.

Serves 6

MOUSSAKA (GREEK EGGPLANT AND MEAT CASSEROLE)

Moussaka is a popular native dish in Greece. It has many different versions—a confusing situation for an American recipe-hunter in Greece. The nice young lady in charge of the gift shop in our hotel came to my aid, however. Her English was imperfect and my Greek nonexistent but, with the help of sign language and friendly bilingual passersby, we evolved the formula that follows. If any ingredients were lost in the translation of Greek to English, we haven't missed them. The native dish is sometimes made with a custard topping of eggs, cheese, and milk, and just as often is not. We'll stay with the latter, for obvious reasons.

2 large eggplants
⅓ cup oil
3 large onions, finely chopped
2 pounds lean ground lamb or veal
¼ cup tomato sauce
2 tablespoons tomato paste
1 teaspoon salt
Freshly ground pepper
½ teaspoon cinnamon
¼ teaspoon nutmeg
⅓ cup dry red wine
2 cups cooked rice
2 tablespoons Parmesan cheese
Bread crumbs
Paprika

Peel the eggplants and cut them into slices about ½ inch thick. Paint the slices lightly with a pastry brush dipped in the oil and place under the broiler until they are lightly browned. Turn the slices and repeat. They will finish cooking in the oven, so they need not be cooked through. Set aside.

In a large, heavy skillet, heat the remaining oil and cook the onions until they are brown. Add the meat and cook, stirring, for about 10 minutes, or until it has lost its raw look. Mix the tomato sauce with the tomato paste and add, along with the salt, pepper, cinnamon, nutmeg, and wine. Mix well and simmer over low heat, stirring often, until all the liquid is absorbed.

Oil a 3-quart casserole. Place a layer of the rice on the bottom. Cover with a third of the meat mixture. Cover with a layer of eggplant and continue with layers of rice, meat, and eggplant until all are used, ending with a layer of meat. Sprinkle with the cheese and bread crumbs and dust lightly with paprika. Bake in a preheated 375° oven for 40 minutes. This can be made well in advance and reheated.

Serves 8 to 10

VITELLO TONNATO
(COLD VEAL IN TUNA SAUCE)

This is a popular Italian antipasto that can also serve for a cold supper or as a buffet dish.

3–4	pounds boneless veal roast, fat removed	2	stalks celery, coarsely chopped
10	anchovy fillets, drained	4	sprigs parsley
½–¾	cup oil	½	teaspoon salt
1	large onion, sliced		Freshly ground pepper
2	whole cloves	1	cup dry white wine
1	bay leaf	1	7-ounce can tuna fish
1	clove garlic, crushed	3	tablespoons capers, drained
2	carrots, sliced	3	tablespoons lemon juice
			Chopped parsley
			Lemon slices

Have the butcher tie the roast into an evenly shaped roll. The leg is the choice cut, but a boned shoulder or rump may also be used. Cut 2 anchovies into small pieces, pierce the roast here and there with a sharp-pointed knife, and insert pieces of the anchovies into the openings.

Heat 2 tablespoons of the oil in a heavy kettle or Dutch oven and brown the meat evenly all around. Add the onion slices, cloves, bay leaf, garlic, carrots, celery, parsley, salt, pepper, and wine. Bring to a boil slowly, cover the kettle, reduce the heat, and simmer gently until the meat is tender (about 2 hours). Remove the meat from the kettle, cool, and refrigerate.

Continue to simmer the ingredients in the kettle until the sauce is reduced to 2 cups. This may take 30 to 40 minutes. Pour into a bowl, cool, and refrigerate. Skim the fat when chilled. If the roast was very lean, chances are that there won't be much fat, but we must be ever watchful.

Puree the skimmed gravy and vegetables. A blender is perfect for this. Add to the blender the tuna fish, remaining anchovies, 1 tablespoon of the capers, and lemon juice. Blend in at low speed the remainder of the oil to make a creamy mixture. The sauce should be the consistency of heavy cream. If it is too thick, thin it out with additional lemon juice.

Slice the cold meat thinly, place in a large shallow glass or pottery (not metal) dish, and spoon the sauce over it. Marinate for a few hours or overnight. Serve cold, sprinkled with the remaining capers. Garnish with the parsley and lemon slices.

Serves 6 to 8

CANNELLONI

Cannelloni are not so complicated as a first glance might suggest, since much of the preparation can be done well in advance. The crepes can be made the day before, wrapped in aluminum foil, and stored in the refrigerator. The chicken can also be cooked and chopped, so that the final assembling is simple. The results are well worth the effort. These make a fine appetizer course or a brunch or supper dish.

Crepes

2	eggs	1 cup flour
½	teaspoon salt	1 tablespoon brandy
1½	tablespoons oil	(optional)
1¼	cups skim milk	

Beat the eggs well with a rotary beater. Beat in the salt, oil, and milk. Add the flour and beat until the batter is completely smooth. Let rest for at least 30 minutes. The batter should be the consistency of heavy cream. If it is thicker than that, thin it out with more milk or perhaps a couple of splashes of brandy.

Lightly oil a 6-inch skillet and heat until a drop of water bounces off. Pour as little batter as is needed to thinly cover the bottom and tilt the skillet quickly to distribute evenly. When lightly brown, turn the crepe and brown the other side.

I find it a time-saver when preparing the crepes to use a second 7- or 8-inch skillet, heated and lightly oiled. At the time you turn a crepe, transfer it to the second skillet. Thus while the second side is browning in the larger skillet, you can proceed with the next crepe in the smaller one. Place the crepes on a towel and repeat the process until all the batter is used. This should yield 16 to 18 crepes. Stack the crepes when cool. It should not be necessary to re-oil the pan, but do it if the crepes stick.

Sauce

4	tablespoons oil	½	teaspoon salt
4	tablespoons flour		White pepper
2½	cups skim milk, warmed	⅛	teaspoon nutmeg

Filling

2	tablespoons oil	2	cups cooked chicken, chopped
3	tablespoons minced onion	¼	teaspoon oregano
3	tablespoons celery, finely chopped	½	teaspoon basil
2	tablespoons carrot, coarsely grated		Freshly ground pepper
1	10-ounce package frozen chopped spinach, cooked and drained	¾	cup dry white wine
		1	tablespoon Parmesan cheese

Start with the sauce. In a medium-sized saucepan, heat the oil, add the flour, and stir over medium heat until bubbly. Reduce the heat, slowly add 2 cups of the milk, and stir constantly with a wire whisk until the sauce becomes thickened and smooth. Stir in the salt, pepper, and nutmeg. Remove from the heat, cover with a piece of waxed paper to prevent a skin from forming, and set aside.

For the filling, heat the oil in a good-sized skillet and cook the onion, celery, and carrot for 5 minutes, stirring a few times. The vegetables should be crisp and underdone, thereby providing interesting texture to the finished dish. Add the spinach, chicken, oregano, basil, pepper, and white wine. Mix well and simmer until the wine is reduced. Add ½ cup of the sauce to the mixture and mix well. Thin out the rest of the cream sauce with the remaining ½ cup of milk.

To assemble the cannelloni, place a generous finger of filling along the center of each crepe and roll, cigar fashion. Place seam side down in an oiled shallow baking dish and continue until all the crepes are filled. Pour a generous dollop of sauce over each crepe and sprinkle with some of the cheese. Heat in a 450° oven for 10 minutes, or until the tops are nicely browned. Serve 2 cannelloni per portion.

Serves 8 or 9

SALMON CASSEROLE

A pound of flaked, cooked fish fillets may be substituted for the salmon.

6 ounces elbow macaroni
1 1-pound can salmon
1 cup (or more) skim milk
2 tablespoons oil
2 tablespoons flour
1 teaspoon salt
Freshly ground pepper
½ teaspoon dry mustard

2 tablespoons Worcestershire sauce
2 tablespoons lemon juice
¼ cup pitted black olives, sliced
½ teaspoon dried dill
½ cup bread crumbs, browned in 2 tablespoons oil

Cook the macaroni according to the package directions. Drain and set aside.

Drain the salmon, reserving the juice. Add enough milk to the juice to make 1½ cups of liquid. Carefully pick over the salmon and remove the skin and bones. In a medium-sized saucepan, heat the oil. Blend with the flour over low heat. Add the salt, pepper, mustard, and Worcestershire sauce. Continue to stir with a wire whisk and add the milk and salmon juice mixture. Cook until thickened and smooth. Add the lemon juice and cook a minute longer. Add the macaroni, olives, dill, and flaked salmon. Taste for seasoning and correct.

Transfer to a 1½-quart oiled casserole and sprinkle with the bread crumbs. Bake in a preheated 375° oven for 30 minutes.

Serves 4

QUICK FISH STEW

With the ingredients for this good-tasting fish stew stashed in your freezer and larder, you will need only about half an hour or so to produce the finished product. Accompanied by hot bread or some biscuits and a tossed salad, it provides a fine program for a lunch or supper.

2 tablespoons oil
1 large onion, chopped
½ green pepper, diced
1 1-pound-12-ounce can tomatoes in tomato puree
1 10¾-ounce can chicken broth
1 10½-ounce can minced clams, drained (reserve the juice)

1 1-pound package frozen cod or perch fillets, partially thawed
1 7-ounce can shrimps, drained
⅓ cup pasta (elbow macaroni or small shells)
½ teaspoon salt
Freshly ground pepper
Sprinkle of garlic powder (optional)
⅓ cup dry sherry

In a medium-sized pot heat the oil and cook the onion and green pepper until soft, but not brown. Add the tomatoes and puree, chicken broth, and reserved clam juice. Cook over low heat for 15 minutes, stirring from time to time and breaking up the tomatoes with a wooden spoon.

Cut the fish fillets into 1-inch squares and add to the soup. Rinse the shrimps in cold water and add. (A friend told me of her belief that canned shrimps were invented by someone who hates shrimps. Maybe so, but they do just fine in this.) Add the clams, pasta, salt, pepper, and, if desired, garlic powder. Simmer, covered, for 10 minutes, then add the sherry and heat thoroughly. Taste for seasonings and correct.

Serves 6

TUNA CASSEROLE WITH TOASTED ALMOND SAUCE

2 7-ounce cans tuna fish
2 10-ounce packages frozen asparagus tips
3 tablespoons oil
½ cup chopped almonds
4 tablespoons flour
½ teaspoon salt

Freshly ground pepper
Pinch of nutmeg
2 cups skim milk
2 tablespoons dry sherry
Paprika

Drain the tuna and break into large chunks. Cook the asparagus according to the package directions and drain well.

Arrange the asparagus in a well-oiled baking dish that can be used for serving (an 8-inch square glass baking dish will do nicely). Cover the asparagus with the tuna chunks. In a skillet, heat the oil and brown the almonds lightly. Blend in the flour, salt, pepper, and nutmeg and cook until the flour bubbles. Slowly add the milk and cook until thickened and smooth, stirring constantly with a wire whisk. Remove from the heat and stir in the sherry. Pour the sauce over the tuna and asparagus. Sprinkle with paprika. Bake in a preheated 350° oven for 25 or 30 minutes.

Serves 5 or 6

TUNA FISH SPAGHETTI SAUCE

1 7-ounce can tuna fish
1 tablespoon oil

1 clove garlic, mashed
1 tablespoon chopped parsley

Pinch of salt   4   tablespoons tomato
Freshly ground pepper   paste
1 2-pound-4-ounce can   ½   teaspoon dried oregano
Italian plum tomatoes   ½   teaspoon dried basil
                                       Pinch of sugar

Drain and flake the tuna fish. In a large, heavy skillet, heat the oil and cook the tuna fish, garlic, and parsley over very low heat for 10 minutes, or until the tuna is lightly browned. Add the salt, pepper, tomatoes, and tomato paste and simmer for 1 hour, uncovered. With a wooden spoon stir frequently to break up the tomatoes. Add the oregano, basil, and sugar and cook another 5 minutes. This makes sufficient sauce for a pound of spaghetti or other pastas.

Serves 4 to 6

BAKED MACARONI

This can be made with elbow macaroni or one of the more unusual pastas, such as the thick stuff that comes in short twisted pieces and looks like a spring.

½ pound macaroni   2   cups skim milk
4 tablespoons oil   1½ cups low-fat cottage
½ cup onions, chopped   cheese
2 tablespoons celery,   2   tablespoons fresh
   finely chopped   chopped chives (or 1
1 clove garlic   teaspoon dried chives)
3 tablespoons flour   ¼   teaspoon paprika
½ teaspoon salt   ½   cup bread crumbs,
   Freshly ground   browned in 2
   pepper   tablespoons oil
½ teaspoon dried   1   tablespoon Parmesan
   oregano   cheese

Cook the macaroni in boiling salted water until just tender—do not overcook. Transfer to a colander and rinse with cold water to stop the cooking.

In a heavy saucepan, heat the oil and cook the onions, celery, and garlic for 10 minutes, or until the onions are limp and transparent. Discard the garlic. Blend in the flour, salt, pepper, and oregano. Slowly add the milk, stirring constantly with a wire whisk until the sauce is thickened and smooth. Simmer another minute over low heat. Taste and correct the seasoning.

Add to the cottage cheese the chives and paprika and mix well. Oil a 2-quart or 8 by 8 inch baking dish. Put a layer of sauce on the bottom, cover with half the macaroni, the cottage cheese, and the other half of the macaroni, and top with the remainder of the cream sauce. Sprinkle with the bread crumbs and cheese. Bake in a 350° oven for 35 to 40 minutes, or until the top is brown and the sauce bubbly.

Serves 3 or 4

SPAGHETTI WITH GREEN SAUCE

2 tablespoons oil	1 teaspoon anchovy
½ cup chicken broth	paste
1 large clove garlic,	1 teaspoon dried basil
minced	2 tablespoons chopped
1 10-ounce package	parsley
frozen chopped	2 tablespoons Parmesan
spinach	cheese
1½ cups low-fat cottage	Salt and freshly
cheese	ground pepper to taste
	1 pound spaghetti

In a medium-sized saucepan, combine the oil, chicken broth, and garlic and bring to a boil. Add the spinach and cook, covered, until thawed (about 5 minutes). Stir a few times.

Place the cottage cheese in a bowl (or a blender) and beat until fairly smooth. A few small lumps won't do any damage. Add the anchovy paste and mix well. Add the basil, parsley, and cheese and blend. Combine the cottage cheese mixture with the spinach and mix well. Taste to see if you want any additional salt and pepper. Keep the spinach and cheese sauce warm over very low heat.

Cook the spaghetti according to the package directions. Rinse and drain. When ready to serve, place the cooked spaghetti in a deep bowl and pour the spinach sauce over it.

Serves 4 to 6

SANDWICHES

FISHBURGERS

A practical solution for a lunch menu manufactured from the cup of leftover fish from last night's dinner.

1 tablespoon oil	½ teaspoon salt
1½ tablespoons green pepper, finely chopped	¼ teaspoon dry mustard
	1 teaspoon Worcestershire sauce
1 tablespoon onion, finely chopped	1 cup cooked fish, flaked
2 teaspoons flour	4 hamburger rolls
½ cup skim milk	

In a medium-sized saucepan, heat the oil and cook the green pepper and onion until the onion becomes limp and transparent. Sprinkle the flour over all and blend in the milk, stirring constantly with a wire whisk until the sauce becomes thickened and smooth. Add the salt, mustard, and Worcestershire sauce and mix well over low heat. Add the fish and heat. Toast the split hamburger rolls lightly (or warm them in the oven) and divide the fish mixture among the 4 rolls, spreading it on the bottom half. Cover with the top half and serve hot.

Serves 4

HOT VEAL SANDWICH

Every household manager knows the frustration of that little bit of leftover meat—not enough for another meal, and too much to ignore.

1 cup cooked veal, minced	Salt
	Freshly ground pepper
1 tablespoon chopped pickle	4 slices of bread
	Dijon mustard
1 tablespoon chopped onion	4 slices of tomato
	Chopped parsley
3 tablespoons mayonnaise	1 tablespoon oil
2 teaspoons Worcestershire sauce	

Combine the meat, pickle, onion, mayonnaise, and Worcestershire sauce. Add salt and freshly ground pepper to taste. Toast the bread on one side. Spread a little mustard on the untoasted surface of each slice and cover with part of the meat mixture. Top each slice with a slice of tomato, sprinkle with the parsley, and dribble a bit of the oil over the tomato. Place the slices under the broiler and broil until they are heated through and the tomato is browned.

Serves 4

SANDWICH FILLINGS

If you have been accustomed to thinking of sandwich fillings in terms of chopped egg, a ham-and-swiss, cream cheese and ——, hamburger or hot dog, or bacon and egg, here are some suggestions for acceptable replacements:

Cucumber Spread:

½ pound low-fat cottage cheese; 1 cucumber, peeled, seeded, and diced; 1 tablespoon chopped chives; salt and pepper; lemon juice; dash of cayenne; enough mayonnaise to bind the mixture together. (Serves 3 or 4)

Salmon-Onion:

1 7-ounce can salmon, drained and flaked; ⅓ cup chopped celery; 1 tablespoon chopped onion; 2 tablespoons mayonnaise; 2 teaspoons lemon juice. (Serves 3 or 4)

Chicken Salad:

1 cup finely cubed chicken; 2 tablespoons finely chopped celery; 1 teaspoon finely chopped onion; 2 teaspoons sweet pickle relish; 1 teaspoon lemon juice; pinch of salt and pepper; 3 tablespoons mayonnaise. *Serves 3*

Sardine Sandwich:

Thinly sliced rye bread; polyunsaturated margarine to spread on bread; 1 can boneless and skinless sardines in water or soybean oil, well-drained; thinly sliced onion; squirt of lemon juice; lettuce leaves. *Serves 2*

Tuna Fish Salad:

1 7-ounce can tuna fish, drained and flaked; 3 table-

spoons finely chopped celery; 2 tablespoons minced onion; 1 tablespoon minced green pepper; salt and paprika; ¼ cup mayonnaise; lettuce leaves. *Serves 3 or 4*

Tuna Fish and Cottage Cheese:

1 7-ounce can tuna fish, drained and flaked, mixed with 3 tablespoons low-fat cottage cheese, 1 tablespoon fresh basil, and 3 tablespoons mayonnaise thinned with 1 teaspoon lemon juice. *Serves 3 or 4*

Toasted Tuna Fish Salad and Low-Fat American Cheese:

Middle Eastern bread (pita) split, filled with tuna fish salad topped with a slice of low-fat American cheese spread with Dijon mustard, toasted in the oven until the cheese begins to melt.

Tuna-Cucumber:

1 7-ounce can tuna fish, ¾ cup finely chopped cucumber, 2 tablespoons finely chopped onion, and 1 teaspoon fresh basil, combined with 4 tablespoons mayonnaise; lettuce leaves. *Serves 3 or 4*

Garden Salad Sandwich:

8 ounces low-fat cottage cheese; ½ cup chopped watercress; 1 tablespoon finely chopped onion; 1 teaspoon lemon juice; pinch of salt; sliced red radishes. *Serves 3*

Peanut Butter Combinations:

(1) Creamed with a dollop of polyunsaturated margarine. (2) With tomato slices. (3) Mixed with grated carrot.

Watercress, Cucumber, and Tomato on Toast:

Peeled and thinly sliced cucumber; washed and drained watercress; thinly sliced tomato; toasted bread; mayonnaise.

Smoked Salmon:

Pumpernickel bread spread with a thin layer of farmer cheese that has been softened with a teaspoon of skim milk; thinly sliced smoked salmon; a squirt of lemon juice; thinly sliced sweet onion.

13

Once-in-a-While

The Once-in-a-While Department is reserved for foods such as shellfish and organ meats such as liver, which, while low in saturated fats, are high in cholesterol. There was a time when some of the researchers in the field of nutrition and atherosclerosis felt that exogenous cholesterol—that is, the natural cholesterol in foods—had little effect on the cholesterol in the human body, which, after all, constantly manufactures its own. They limited eggs, for example, not because of the large amount of cholesterol in them but because of the high proportion of saturated fat. This thesis has now been disproved, and we know that exogenous cholesterol can and does raise body cholesterol.

In the crustacean family, lobsters and oysters head the list in relation to the amount of cholesterol they contain. For example, ordinary fish (fishfish I call it in contrast to shellfish) has about 70 milligrams of cholesterol in a 3½-ounce portion, while the same amount of lobster contains 200 milligrams. The animal organs—kidney, heart, liver, sweetbreads, tongue, and brains—are all higher in cholesterol than the muscle of the same animal. Mind-boggling is the thought of the 1,700 milligrams of cholesterol in 2 ounces of brains. (I have sat at a restaurant table across from people lapping up huge portions of brains swimming in black butter. Just watching them certainly raised my cholesterol, and I hate to think what it did to theirs.) On the other hand, liver contains 300 milligrams of cholesterol in 3½ ounces and is highly regarded by many for its flavor and nutrient value.

One cannot make a blanket statement on how much and how often foods high in cholesterol can be eaten, but we are assured that most people who observe a diet that limits the high cholesterol foods may safely include a modest portion of shellfish or liver from time to time— liver perhaps once a month and shellfish more frequently. A portion of about 3 ounces of shellfish is within the realm of respectability in terms of size; and if the rest of the intake is low in cholesterol on the given day, the cholesterol is not likely to take any giant surge upward. We must, however, exclude the small group of people, distinct from the general population, with extremely high cholesterol (the medical term is hypercholesterolemia), who require tighter restriction of cholesterol intake. For this group, once in a while could mean something else— like Christmas or a birthday.

The recipes that follow are planned to limit the amount of the main ingredients by adding other foods that blend into a satisfying dish that will not leave the follower of a low-fat diet feeling deprived.

CLAUDIA'S CLAM CHOWDER

This is for people who like clam chowder with tomato— Manhattan, in other words. The unusual addition of cooked pasta makes it a complete meal, and we have served it as the main event of informal Sunday night suppers. Hot crusty French bread, a tossed salad, and fruit for dessert make our guests—and us—happy and replete.

24	chowder clams		Freshly
4	cups (or more) water		ground pepper
1	1-pound-13-ounce can tomatoes	2	tablespoons parsley, chopped
2	onions, sliced	5	small potatoes, peeled
4	tablespoons oil		and diced
1	teaspoon salt	½	pound elbow macaroni

Scrub the clams well with a stiff brush and rinse several times. Be sure they are tightly closed; discard any that are not. Place in a large kettle with about 1½ inches of salted water at the bottom, cover the kettle tightly, and steam for 8 to 10 minutes, only until the shells open. Do not use any clams that remain closed.

Reserve the clam broth and add enough water to make 4 cups. Place in a large pot. Cut the clams into small pieces and add. Add the tomatoes, juice and all, onions, oil, salt, pepper, parsley, and potatoes. Simmer over low heat for 30 minutes.

Meanwhile, cook the elbow macaroni according to the package directions and drain. Keep warm over boiling water. When ready to serve, ladle a small portion of macaroni into each bowl of soup.

Serves 8

COQUILLE ST. JACQUES

This unclassic version of a classic dish makes a splendid appetizer for any occasion.

1 pound bay or sea scallops
¾ cup dry white wine
6 shallots, finely chopped
2 tablespoons oil
¼ pound mushrooms, thinly sliced
3 tablespoons flour
½ cup skim milk, warmed

1 package MBT chicken broth powder
2 tablespoons lemon juice
Freshly ground black pepper
1 tablespoon Parmesan cheese
Cornflake crumbs

If you are using the large sea scallops, cut them into quarters. The bay scallops are generally small enough to be used as they are. Wash the scallops and place them in a small saucepan with the wine and shallots. Bring to a boil slowly, reduce the heat, and cook only until the scallops have lost their raw look and become opaque (8 to 10 minutes should do it). Strain and reserve the liquid.

In a good-sized skillet, heat the oil and cook the mushrooms for 3 minutes, turning frequently. Add the flour and stir until it becomes bubbly. Slowly add the milk and beat with a wire whisk until the sauce is smooth. Add the wine in which the scallops have cooked, chicken broth powder, lemon juice, and pepper and continue to beat with a whisk until the sauce is thickened and smooth.

Add the scallops and shallots and mix well. Taste and correct the seasoning. Heap the mixture into 6 oiled scallop shells or individual ramekins. Sprinkle with the cheese and cornflake crumbs. Place under the broiler for a few minutes to brown. Serve hot.

Serves 6

CLAMS ROCKEFELLER

This is scarcely the conventional preparation of Clams Rockefeller, but it is delicious nevertheless. I generally have the makings in the pantry and freezer, and on the occasions when I need to spark up a dinner for an unexpected last-minute guest this provides a lovely appetizer course. It takes no more than 5 minutes to put together and everyone always asks for the recipe, which I take as a sign of approval. The small amount of clams in each serving makes it acceptable for more frequent use than any other shellfish dish.

1 10-ounce package frozen chopped spinach	½ cup mayonnaise
	2 tablespoons lemon juice
1 10½-ounce can minced clams	1 tablespoon Parmesan cheese
⅓ cup cornflake crumbs	Additional cornflake crumbs

Cook the spinach just long enough to melt the ice crystals—it should be kept as green as possible. Drain well and squeeze out every bit of liquid. Drain the clams thoroughly, again pressing out every drop of liquid. In a small bowl combine the spinach, clams, cornflake crumbs, mayonnaise, and lemon juice and mix well. Lightly oil baking shells or ramekins and fill with the spinach and clam mixture. Sprinkle each with the cheese and cornflake crumbs. Heat in a 350° oven for 15 minutes, or until heated through. Serve hot.

Serves 5 or 6

Note: These are a good item for a cocktail party, served in small clam shells. Your fish man will probably be glad to give you a few dozen clam shells that he has denuded of contents. Scrub them well and heat them in a 350° oven for an hour or so. They will bleach out sparkling white and you can use them over and over. The above recipe will fill about 20 small shells. Serve with cocktail forks.

CRAB L'AIGLON

When you are in a festive, brandy-burning, chafing dish mood, you might give this a thought.

1 pound fresh lump crab meat	½ cup dry white wine
3 tablespoons oil	½ teaspoon dried tarragon
6 scallions, finely chopped	½ teaspoon salt
	White pepper
1 small clove garlic, crushed	2 tablespoons chopped parsley
1 small green pepper, finely chopped	¼ cup brandy
	Toast triangles

Pick over the crab meat carefully for any stray bits of shell. In a medium-sized saucepan, heat the oil. Sauté the scallions, garlic, and green pepper until the scallions are soft and golden, but not brown. Add the crab meat, wine, tarragon, salt, and pepper and heat thoroughly. This may be done in the chafing dish, or you may transfer it from the kitchen pot at this point. Add the parsley and mix. Warm the brandy, ignite it, and pour it over the crab-meat mixture. Serve on toast triangles when the flames die out.

Serves 6

CRAB CAKES WITH MUSTARD SAUCE

Make the crab cakes small and serve two per portion. They can be done well in advance and browned just before serving.

1 pound fresh lump
crab meat
2 egg whites
½ cup mayonnaise
¼ cup minced scallions
2 tablespoons finely
minced celery
1 teaspoon
Worcestershire sauce

1 tablespoon lemon
juice
2 slices white bread,
crusts removed
1 egg white
2 tablespoons water
½ cup flour
½ cup bread crumbs
½ cup oil

Pick over the crab meat to remove bits of shell. Beat the 2 egg whites to a froth and combine with the crab meat. Add the mayonnaise, scallions, celery, Worcestershire sauce, and lemon juice and mix carefully. Be gentle so that you don't break up the crab-meat lumps completely. At lump crab meat's present price, it would be a pity to destroy its character and reduce it to a mashed-potato consistency. Crumble the bread finely and add to the crab-meat mixture. Form into 16 small balls, about the size of a large walnut.

Beat the egg white to a froth and add the water. Place a mound of the flour on one square of waxed paper and a mound of the bread crumbs on another. Dip the crab cakes lightly into the flour, then the egg white, then the bread crumbs. Refrigerate until time to cook, then heat the oil in a heavy skillet and brown the cakes on all sides. Add more oil if needed. Serve with Mustard Sauce (below).

Serves 8

Mustard Sauce

2 tablespoons oil
2 tablespoons flour
1 cup skim milk
½ cup consommé or
chicken broth
2 tablespoons
prepared mustard

1½ tablespoons
Worcestershire sauce
1 teaspoon grated onion
or ½ teaspoon
dehydrated onion flakes
Freshly ground pepper

In a small saucepan, heat the oil, blend in the flour, and when it begins to bubble, slowly stir in the milk, beating with a wire whisk. Reduce the heat and mix in the consommé or chicken broth. Add the mustard, Worcestershire sauce, onion, and pepper. Cook for 2 or 3 minutes over low heat, beating with a wire whisk until the sauce is smooth and thickened. Taste for seasoning—you may want a bit more mustard or Worcestershire sauce if you like it spicier. I do not use a strong Dijon mustard for this because I would prefer that the sauce not overpower the taste of the crab meat. Keep the sauce warm until ready to serve, but do not let it boil. If the sauce gets too thick (it should be the consistency of heavy cream) thin it out with a tablespoon or so of consommé.

Yields 1½ cups

BOILED SHRIMPS

Four or five medium-sized shrimps serve as a perfectly adequate portion for an appetizer. Standard Operating Procedure is to accompany the shrimps with a cocktail sauce made of chili sauce, a bit of prepared horseradish, a dash of Worcestershire sauce, and lemon juice. A wedge of lemon accompanies the shrimp cocktail.

Shrimps, like all their crustacean relatives, must never be overcooked. They respond to this heroic treatment by getting tough—a poor return for our pains. Cooking them as described below will keep them tender and juicy.

1 cup water	3 peppercorns
1 teaspoon salt	1 pound unpeeled raw
½ bay leaf	shrimps, fresh or frozen
2 stalks celery, leaves and all, cut into 3-inch pieces	

Make a stock of the water, salt, bay leaf, celery, and peppercorns. Bring to a boil in a covered kettle and boil for 5 minutes.

Add the shrimps, cover, bring to a boil, reduce the heat, and simmer for just 3 minutes—that's all. If you are using frozen shrimps, they will need a little more time, but as soon as they turn pink, they are done. Uncover the pot and remove it from the heat. (The shrimps can remain in this stock until you are ready to use them, without toughening.) Peel and clean the shrimps.

SWEET-AND-SOUR SHRIMP

This dish with Oriental overtones presents a most delectable blend of flavors. It's a quick one to cook if you have all your ingredients lined up and prepared before you start putting it together.

1½	pounds shrimps	1	green pepper, cut into
¼	cup brown sugar		¼-inch strips
2	tablespoons	2	small onions, cut in
	cornstarch		rings
½	teaspoon salt	2	carrots, cut julienne in
¼	cup cider vinegar		2-inch lengths
1	tablespoon soy sauce	1	cup cauliflower, broken
¼	teaspoon powdered		into flowerets and
	ginger		sliced
1	1-pound-4-ounce can	3	cups hot cooked rice
	pineapple chunks in		
	pineapple juice (drain		
	and reserve the juice)		

Cook the shrimps as described in the preceding recipe. Peel and clean.

In a large pot, mix together the brown sugar, cornstarch, and salt. Add the vinegar, soy sauce, and ginger and mix well. Add the pineapple juice and cook over medium heat, beating with a wire whisk until the sauce is smooth and thickened. Add the pineapple chunks, green pepper, onions, carrots, and cauliflower and cook, covered, for 8 to 10 minutes. The vegetables should be crisp-tender. Add the shrimps and heat through. Serve immediately on a bed of the rice.

Serves 6

SCAMPI

Scampi are the Italian variety of the crustacean that we know as shrimp, generally prepared in a highly seasoned sauce. They make an excellent hot hors d'oeuvre or appetizer course that can be served in the living room. They are quickly and easily prepared, and half an hour or more in the chafing dish before they are eaten won't hurt them a bit.

30	large shrimps,	3	large cloves garlic,
	uncooked		sliced
½	cup flour	1	teaspoon oregano
1	teaspoon salt	1	teaspoon basil
	Freshly ground pepper	1	tablespoon minced
⅔	cup oil		parsley
½	teaspoon salt		

Wash the shrimps, remove the shells (leaving the tails), devein, and pat dry with paper towels. Combine the flour with the teaspoon of salt and the pepper. Dredge the shrimps lightly in the seasoned flour and shake off the excess. You don't want a heavy coating on the shrimps—too much flour will make them gloppy.

Pour the oil into a large, heavy skillet. Add the ½ teaspoon of salt, garlic, oregano, basil, and parsley and place over low heat. I am not a bit subtle about the garlic in this preparation. If the three cloves are smallish, I might very well add another, with a few dashes of garlic powder for good measure. Everyone seems to like these very garlicky, but taste the seasoned oil and decide for yourself.

When the oil is hot (3 or 4 minutes), add the shrimps, as many as will make a single layer in the skillet. If you crowd them they won't cook properly. Cook them only until they turn pink (2 to 3 minutes on each side). When done, remove with a slotted spoon, and continue until all are cooked. Place in a chafing dish or a casserole with a candle warmer and pour a little of the seasoned oil in which they were cooked over them. Use small plates and forks for serving—they are too moist for finger food.

Serves 8 to 10

SHRIMPS, GREEK STYLE

This is suitable as either an appetizer or an entrée. The mingling of the flavors of the tomatoes, wine, and feta cheese with the bland crustaceans produces a most appealing taste.

6–8	medium-sized	3	tablespoons oil
	tomatoes or 1	1	clove garlic,
	1-pound-12-ounce		minced
	can peeled tomatoes	½	cup dry white wine

2 tablespoons parsley, minced	Freshly ground pepper
½ teaspoon dried oregano	2 pounds uncooked shrimps
¼ teaspoon sugar	¼ pound feta cheese
1 teaspoon salt	

If you are using fresh tomatoes, peel them by plunging them into boiling water for half a minute or so and slipping off the skins. If using canned tomatoes, drain them and discard the liquid. Whether the tomatoes are fresh or canned, chop them into small chunks and place in a large saucepan with 1 tablespoon of the oil, the garlic, wine, 1 tablespoon of the parsley, the oregano, sugar, salt, and a few grinds of pepper. Simmer, uncovered, over low heat for 25 to 30 minutes, until the mixture becomes thickened but not reduced to a puree. The small chunks of tomato lend interest to the finished dish. Mix the sauce from time to time, using a wooden spoon, to make sure it doesn't scorch.

While the sauce is cooking, prepare the shrimps. Remove the shells and the dark vein around the outside perimeter. Rinse the shrimps and pat dry. In a large skillet, heat the remaining 2 tablespoons of oil and sauté the shrimps until they turn pink (5 or 6 minutes). Turn them during cooking.

Place the cooked shrimps in a shallow, lightly oiled baking dish large enough to hold them in a single layer. An 8 by 12 inch dish will do nicely. Cover with the tomato sauce and sprinkle with the crumbled feta cheese and the remaining tablespoon of minced parsley. Bake uncovered in a 375° oven until heated through (about 10 minutes). Hot fluffy boiled rice is a good accompaniment.

Serves 6 to 8 as appetizer;
4 to 6 as main course

CURRIED SEAFOOD

A combination of seafood in a tangy curry sauce that can serve admirably for a family or company dinner.

2 pounds raw shrimps	2½ cups skim milk
1 pound sea scallops	1 cup chicken broth
1 pound mushrooms	1 teaspoon salt
2 cloves garlic, crushed	Freshly ground pepper
½ cup oil	2 teaspoons prepared mustard
2 tablespoons lemon juice	2 tablespoons Worcestershire sauce
1 large onion, finely chopped	1 tablespoon (or more) curry powder
6 tablespoons flour	Cooked rice

Shell and devein the shrimps. Wash and drain well. Wash the scallops and cut them in two. Set the shrimps and scallops aside. Rinse and wipe the mushrooms dry, slice, add the garlic, and sauté in 2 tablespoons of the oil for 5 minutes, tossing frequently. Sprinkle with the lemon juice.

In a large skillet, heat 2 tablespoons of the oil and sauté the shrimps and scallops until the shrimps are pink and the scallops have lost their raw look and become opaque (6 to 8 minutes). Remove from the skillet with a slotted spoon and set aside. In the same skillet, cook the onion until it is limp and transparent. Add the remainder of the oil and blend in the flour, stirring constantly. Stir in the milk and chicken broth slowly, and add the salt, pepper, mustard, Worcestershire sauce, and curry powder. The amount of curry powder will vary, depending upon how strong it is and how hot a curry you like, so be gentle when you add it. Once it is in, there isn't much you can do about it. Over low heat, cook and stir until the sauce is thickened and smooth. Gently fold in the shrimps, scallops, and mushrooms. Taste for seasoning and correct. Keep warm but do not boil. Serve with hot fluffy rice and some of the following condiments:

Diced apple marinated in lemon juice	Chutney
Raisins soaked in sherry	Chopped cucumber
Chopped peanuts	Pickled watermelon rind

Serves 10

BROILED SCALLOPS

This may be made with either bay or sea scallops.

2 pounds scallops	2 cloves garlic
½ cup oil	2 tablespoons parsley
2 tablespoons scallions, finely chopped	½ teaspoon salt
½ teaspoon dried basil	Freshly ground pepper
½ teaspoon tarragon, finely crumbled	2 tablespoons cornflake crumbs
	Lemon wedges

Wash the scallops and drain well. Heat the oil in a small skillet, add all the remaining ingredients except the cornflake crumbs and lemon wedges, and cook for 3 minutes, stirring. Discard the garlic cloves, add the cornflake crumbs, and cook a minute longer. Arrange the scallops in a shallow heatproof baking dish and pour the mixture over them, mixing well so the scallops will be thoroughly covered with oil. Ideally, the scallops should marinate in the sauce for a few hours in the refrigerator.

When you are ready to cook them, preheat the broiler and place the pan on the broiling rack about 4 inches from the heat. Turn the scallops during the cooking so they will be brown on all sides. The larger sea scallops will need 10 to 12 minutes; the bay scallops, about 8. If they are not brown enough, raise the rack nearer the heat unit for a minute or two at the very end. Transfer into a warmed serving bowl or deep platter and serve at once, accompanied by lemon wedges.

Serves 4 or 5

GLAZED DUCK WITH BING CHERRY SAUCE

The meat of duck is polyunsaturated, but the fatty envelope with which nature has encased it may limit its use. However, the steaming and roasting process described here gets rid of a good deal of the fat and makes it acceptable "once in a while." But the prudent dieter in the household will do well to leave the skin on the plate. The delicious fruit sauce will compensate for any dryness in the meat.

5–6 pound duckling	1 large onion, cut into
1 teaspoon salt	eighths
Freshly ground	2 stalks celery, cut into
pepper	2-inch lengths
1 cup (or more) water	1 cup orange juice

Salt and pepper the duckling inside and out. Place on a rack in a large soup kettle with a cover. Add water to the pot to the depth of 2 inches. Add the onion and celery. Cover the pot, bring to a boil, and reduce the heat. Steam for 1½ hours.

Preheat the oven to 325°. After the duck is steamed, remove from the kettle and drain thoroughly. Cut the duck into quarters with poultry shears and snip the loose skin and whatever fat is visible. Place the trimmed pieces of duck on a rack in a baking pan and roast uncovered for 1½ hours, or until the skin is crisp and brown. Pour off the fat two or three times while it is cooking. The last 20 minutes, add the orange juice and baste a few times.

Remove the duck to a warmed serving platter and cover with Bing Cherry Sauce (below). Pass extra sauce in a gravy boat.

Bing Cherry Sauce

¾ cup brown sugar	1 teaspoon prepared
1 6-ounce can frozen	mustard
orange juice	1 tablespoon cornstarch
1 1-pound can pitted	¼ cup cold water
Bing cherries (reserve	¾ cup dry sherry
6 ounces cherry juice)	

Combine the brown sugar, undiluted orange juice, and cherry juice in a saucepan. Bring to a boil and simmer for a minute. Add the cherries and mustard. Dissolve the cornstarch in the water, add to the sauce, and simmer for 5 minutes, stirring constantly, until the sauce is thickened and shiny. Just before serving, add the sherry and heat through.

Serves 4

CHICKEN LIVERS AH LINN

1 pound chicken livers
3 tablespoons soy sauce
4 tablespoons oil
½ pound mushrooms, sliced
1 1-pound can pineapple tidbits, drained (reserve the juice)
½ cup blanched slivered almonds
1½ cups pineapple juice and chicken broth
2 tablespoons cornstarch
1 tablespoon sugar
¼ cup vinegar
Freshly ground pepper
1 6-ounce package frozen pea pods
Cooked rice

Trim the livers, cutting away all fat and membranes clinging to them. Cut in half and marinate in the soy sauce for 10 minutes, turning them a few times so that the livers will be well seasoned with the sauce.

Heat the oil in a large, heavy pot and add the livers. Cook for 10 minutes, turning frequently so they will brown evenly. Add the mushrooms, cover, and cook 5 minutes longer. Remove the cover, add the pineapple tidbits and almonds, and simmer over very low heat while you prepare the sauce.

Add enough chicken broth to the juice drained from the pineapple to make 1½ cups of liquid. Place in a small saucepan. In a cup, dissolve the cornstarch in a few tablespoons of the liquid and add. Mix in the sugar, vinegar, and a few grinds of pepper. Cook over low heat, stirring constantly, until the sauce becomes thickened and shiny. Pour the sauce over the chicken livers and mix.

Place the pea pods in ¼ cup of boiling salted water and heat only until all the ice particles are melted and the pea pods are thawed. Drain well and add to the chicken livers. Taste for seasoning—you may want to add a sprinkle of salt. Heat through and serve at once with hot fluffy rice.

Serves 4

CALVES' LIVER SAUTÉ

1 pound calves' liver, sliced ¼ inch thick
½ teaspoon salt
Freshly ground pepper

¼ cup flour
4 tablespoons oil
2 medium-sized onions,
thinly sliced
½ cup dry white wine

2 tablespoons tomato
puree
½ teaspoon sugar
2 tablespoons parsley,
finely chopped

Cut the calves' liver slices into 1-inch squares. Sprinkle them with the salt and pepper and lightly dredge with the flour. In a large, heavy skillet, heat the oil and add the onions. Cover and cook over low heat until they are soft and transparent, but don't let them brown. Add the pieces of liver, increase the heat, and cook, stirring frequently, until the meat is browned (about 3 or 4 minutes). When the meat is done, pour off any excess fat that remains in the skillet. Put the wine, tomato puree, and sugar in the skillet. Mix well and scrape the bottom of the pan to pick up any browned particles adhering to it. Cook an additional 2 or 3 minutes. Transfer to a warmed platter and sprinkle with the parsley.

Serves 4

SPAGHETTI WITH MEAT SAUCE AND CHICKEN LIVERS

3 tablespoons oil
2 medium-sized
onions, chopped
¾ pound lean round
steak, ground
2 cloves garlic, sliced
3½ cups tomato puree or
1 No. 2½ can Italian
tomatoes forced
through a sieve
1 6-ounce can Italian
tomato paste

1 teaspoon salt
Freshly ground pepper
1 teaspoon dried basil
1 teaspoon oregano
1 tablespoon sugar
½ pound mushrooms,
sliced
½ pound chicken livers
Salt and freshly ground
pepper
2 tablespoons oil
1 pound spaghetti

In a large, heavy skillet or Dutch oven, heat the 3 tablespoons of oil. Add the onions and cook until transparent. Add the meat and stir over medium heat until it is browned. Add the garlic, tomato puree, tomato paste, salt, pepper, basil, oregano, and sugar. Cook slowly for 1½ to 2 hours, uncovered, stirring frequently. After the first hour, add the mushrooms. If the sauce gets too thick, thin it out with a little water or some canned consommé—or, better still, a little Marsala wine. Taste before serving to correct the seasoning.

Shortly before the sauce is ready, cut the chicken livers into quarters and carefully trim all bits of fat and membrane adhering to them. Salt and pepper the livers. In a skillet, heat the 2 tablespoons of oil, add the livers, and brown them well, turning carefully to make sure all surfaces are seared. When all the livers have been browned, cover the skillet and cook for 10 minutes over low heat. Add the sautéed livers to the meat sauce.

Somewhere along the line, you will have to take care of the spaghetti. Bring a large quantity of salted water to a rolling boil in a large pot. Drop the spaghetti in and let it bend its own way into the water. Don't overcook—7 or 8 minutes should do it nicely. Taste it to make sure that it is *al dente*—"firm to the teeth," the literal Italian translation. When done, drain it well in a colander and toss with a little oil. This will keep the strands separated. If the spaghetti has to wait, keep it warm in a colander placed over simmering water. Serve the meat sauce on the spaghetti.

Serves 6

SPAGHETTI OR LINGUINE WITH CLAM SAUCE

A white clam sauce makes an interesting change from the more commonly served tomato sauce for spaghetti.

¼ cup oil
3 cloves garlic, sliced
1 teaspoon dried basil
1 tablespoon green
   pepper, finely chopped
1 15-ounce can chopped
   clams and juice or tiny
   whole clams

¼ cup chopped parsley
   Freshly ground pepper
2 cups clam juice or 1
   cup clam juice and 1
   cup dry white wine

In a heavy skillet, heat the oil. Add the garlic, basil, and green pepper and cook for 3 minutes. Add the clams and simmer another 5 minutes. Add the parsley, pepper, and clam juice (or clam juice and wine) and simmer another 30 minutes over low heat, or until the sauce cooks down a little. The clam juice is generally seasoned enough not to require additional salt, but taste it to make sure. Serve the sauce hot over spaghetti or linguine, with additional sauce in a gravy boat.

Serves 6

14
Aspics and Molds

TO UNMOLD ASPICS

Prepare the mold form by rubbing it ever so lightly with a crumpled paper towel dipped in oil. Or you might use a few spritzes of a coating product such as Pam to facilitate the unmolding process.

When unmolding an aspic, first carefully loosen the edges of the aspic from the mold with a knife or a spatula. Dip the mold up to its rim into a bowl of warm water quickly, for about 10 seconds. Lift the mold from the water, shake it to loosen the aspic, place the serving plate on top of it, and, holding the mold and plate firmly, turn the whole thing over. The mold should slip off easily, leaving the aspic just where it belongs. Or invert the mold on the serving plate and cover it with a cloth wrung out in very hot water, repeating a few times.

CHICKEN BREASTS IN ASPIC

The impressive appearance and delicious flavor of this aspic are—happily for the cook—out of proportion to the small amount of effort involved in assembling it. It does splendidly for a buffet, a hot-weather lunch, or an informal Sunday night supper. It is my simplified version of an elaborate concoction and, as you can see from the list of ingredients, it abounds with shortcuts.

| 3 | whole chicken breasts | 2 | 10½-ounce cans Campbell's consommé |

1½	tablespoons gelatin	1	15-ounce can (or jar)
4	slices thin, lean		small white onions
	Danish ham	1	15-ounce can tiny
1	tablespoon dried		Belgian carrots
	oregano		Salad greens and
			assorted vegetables
			for garnish

Cut the chicken breasts in two, giving you six halves. Cook according to the directions on page 166. Let cool.

Empty the consommé (please note we use Campbell's consommé that has gelatin added) into a saucepan and sprinkle the gelatin over the top to soften. Heat until the gelatin is completely dissolved.

Lightly oil a deep round 2-quart bowl (the conventional 2-quart Pyrex casserole dish is perfect). Line the sides of the bowl with the ham slices, overlapping them. Pour about ½ inch of consommé in the bottom of the bowl and chill in the refrigerator until set. If you like, you can place in the thin layer of aspic a few slices of raw carrot cut into fancy shapes with perhaps a few sprigs of parsley garlanded around them, or an arrangement of thinly sliced olives and pimiento. When unmolded, this topping will give the aspic additional style.

While the layer of aspic is firming, add the oregano to the remaining consommé and heat for a minute. Heating intensifies the flavor of dried herbs. Drain the onions and carrots. Slice the chicken breasts into large, flat slices.

When the layer of aspic is firm—and this doesn't take long—you are ready to assemble the dish. Alternate layers of chicken with layers of onions and carrots until all the ingredients are used. Pour the consommé over all and chill until set (3 to 4 hours). Unmold on a large round platter and surround with salad greens, cold asparagus, cherry tomatoes, and/or artichoke hearts.

A cold rice salad goes well with this.

Serves 5 or 6

FISH LOAF ASPIC

This is as appetizing to look at as it is delicious to eat. It makes a perfect luncheon or supper entrée and can also serve as an appetizer course for a special dinner.

3–3½ pounds red snapper or 2 pounds fillet of flounder or
haddock

Fish Stock

Fish bones and head   3 cups water
1 onion, quartered   1 cup chicken broth
3 celery stalks and leaves   1 cup dry white wine
2 carrots, scraped and   1 teaspoon salt
  thinly sliced   Freshly ground pepper

Aspic

2 tablespoons   2 tablespoons lemon
  unflavored gelatin   juice
½ cup cold water   1 small onion, grated
  Pimiento strips   ½ teaspoon salt
1 tablespoon capers   Freshly ground pepper
1 cup celery, finely   2 tablespoons
  chopped   mayonnaise
2 tablespoons minced
  parsley

If you are using the red snapper, have your fish man
fillet it for you and give you the head and bones for the
stock. If you are using the fillets of fish, substitute an 8-
ounce bottle of clam juice for one of the cups of water in
the stock.

In a large kettle, boil together the stock ingredients for
20 minutes. Add the fish, reduce the heat, and simmer
slowly for another 15 minutes, until the fish is done but
not falling apart. Remove the fish from the kettle. When
cool enough to handle, skin and flake, searching carefully
for all bones. Strain the stock and reserve the carrots. If
you have more than 3½ cups of stock, reduce it to that
amount by boiling briskly.

To make the aspic, soften the gelatin in the cold water.
Heat in the hot fish stock until dissolved. Lightly oil a loaf
pan and arrange on the bottom of the pan the sliced carrots, pimiento strips, and capers. Cover with a thin
layer of the fish stock-gelatin mixture and refrigerate
until set. Cool the remainder of the gelatin mixture in the
refrigerator for half an hour or so.

Mix together the remaining aspic ingredients and add
to the gelatin mixture. Add the fish and mix well. Pour
into the loaf pan and chill until firm.

Unmold on a platter on a bed of romaine or chicory and garnish with cold asparagus or artichoke hearts that have been marinated in French dressing. This can be served with a variety of sauces: Cucumber Sauce (page 79) or Russian Dressing (page 330) or the following sauce:

Dill Yogurt Sauce

1 cup mayonnaise	1 teaspoon onion juice
½ cup plain low-fat yogurt	1 tablespoon snipped fresh dill or ½ teaspoon dried dill
3 tablespoons lemon juice	

Blend all the ingredients together and chill.

Serves 6 to 8 as main course;
10 to 12 as appetizer

TUNA SALAD MOLD

When is a tuna fish salad not a tuna fish salad? When it is served as a refreshing aspic, thus taking on a slightly different dimension.

1 tablespoon unflavored gelatin	1 tablespoon lemon juice
¼ cup cold water	2 7-ounce cans tuna fish, drained and flaked
1 cup boiling water	
¾ cup mayonnaise	⅔ cup chopped celery
2 teaspoons Dijon mustard	1 teaspoon onion, finely chopped

Sprinkle the gelatin over the cold water to soften. Add to the boiling water and stir over low heat until dissolved. Cool, then mix in the mayonnaise, mustard, and lemon juice. Blend well. Add the tuna fish, celery, and onion and mix thoroughly. Pour into a lightly oiled ring mold or a round-bottomed bowl. Chill until firm. Unmold on a round platter lined with romaine or other salad greens. Lettuce cups filled with cold mixed vegetables laced with French dressing provide an interesting garnish and accompaniment.

Serves 4 or 5

COTTAGE CHEESE TOMATO ASPIC

This opaque, rosy aspic has quite enough character to stand on its own but still makes a fine foil for accompanying salads or vegetables.

2 cups low-fat cottage cheese	2 envelopes unflavored gelatin
1 cup chili sauce	½ cup cold water
	¼ cup mayonnaise

Beat the cottage cheese until it is smooth and free from lumps and becomes the consistency of sour cream. Force the chili sauce through a sieve. Combine the creamy cheese and smooth chili sauce. (If you are using a blender, blend the cheese and chili sauce together.)

Sprinkle the gelatin over the water. When it is softened, place over low heat and stir until dissolved. When cooled, add to the cheese mixture. Stir in the mayonnaise and blend thoroughly.

Pour into a lightly oiled 4-cup ring mold and refrigerate until firm. Unmold on a platter lined with greens. You might want to place a small bowl of mayonnaise in the center of the ring.

Serves 6

TOMATO ASPIC

A good-tasting basic tomato aspic that blends well with all flavors and won't steal the spotlight from important, highly seasoned salads or other dishes.

2 tablespoons gelatin	1 tablespoon onion juice
½ cup water	
2 cups tomato juice	1 tablespoon lemon juice
⅔ cup water	
⅔ cup tomato sauce	½ teaspoon salt
2 teaspoons Worcestershire sauce	

Sprinkle the gelatin over the ½ cup of water. In a medium-sized saucepan, combine the tomato juice, ⅔ cup of water, and tomato sauce and heat to the boiling point.

Add the softened gelatin and stir over very low heat until the gelatin is completely dissolved. Cool the mixture and add the remaining ingredients. Pour into a lightly oiled 4-cup ring mold or individual molds. Refrigerate until firm (3 or 4 hours).

Serves 5 or 6

JELLIED BEET SALAD

This hearty jellied salad mold is one of our old reliables for buffet suppers, doubled or even tripled. I do it in a ring form and fill the center with either cold mixed vegetables tossed with French dressing or artichoke hearts vinaigrette.

1 1-pound can julienne beets	2 teaspoons grated onion
1 cup beet juice	1 tablespoon (or more) prepared horseradish
1 3-ounce package raspberry gelatin	½ cup coarsely shredded carrot
⅔ cup orange juice	
2 tablespoons vinegar	½ cup finely diced celery
1 teaspoon salt	Watercress

Drain the juice from the beets. Heat the beet juice to the boiling point and remove from the heat. Dissolve the raspberry gelatin in the hot liquid and add the orange juice, vinegar, salt, onion, and horseradish. If the horseradish is mild, you may need more than 1 tablespoon, but you will have to decide. The taste should be a bit on the sharp side. Cool the gelatin mixture and refrigerate until thick and syrupy, then add to it the beets, carrot, and celery. Turn into a lightly oiled ring mold and chill until firm. Unmold on a round platter and garnish with watercress.

Serves 6 to 8

CRANBERRY RELISH MOLD

This has been a family standby at Thanksgiving, Christmas, New Year's—whatever the occasion that calls for a 22-pound turkey or a covey of fowl to feed our ever-loving and ever-growing family.

2 tablespoons
  unflavored gelatin
½ cup cold water
2 cups apple juice
2 cups (½ pound) raw
  cranberries
1 orange

1 medium-sized
  apple
¾ cup sugar
¾ cup walnut meats,
  coarsely broken
Preserved kumquats
Watercress

Sprinkle the gelatin over the water and allow to soften. Heat 1 cup of the apple juice to the boiling point, add the softened gelatin, and stir until completely dissolved. Add the remaining cup of apple juice and refrigerate until thick and syrupy.

Wash the cranberries and drain well. Slice the orange, skin and all, and remove all seeds. Peel and core the apple. With the medium knife of a food grinder, grind together the cranberries, orange, and apple. Add the sugar, stir well, and chill. When the gelatin has become syrupy, fold in the chilled fruit mixture. Add the nuts and turn into a lightly oiled 6-cup ring mold. Refrigerate until firm. Unmold and garnish with preserved kumquats and sprigs of watercress.

Serves 6 to 8

WHOLE CRANBERRY SAUCE

2 cups sugar
2 cups water
1 pound (4 cups) fresh
  cranberries, washed and
  picked over

2 teaspoons grated orange
  rind

In a medium-sized skillet, dissolve the sugar in the water. Boil for about 5 minutes until a thick syrup forms. Add the cranberries and simmer gently, uncovered and without stirring, for another 5 minutes. Add the orange rind. Pour the mixture into a large lightly oiled mold and chill until firm. Unmold to serve.

Yields 1 quart

PINEAPPLE SALAD MOLD

A chicken or seafood salad menu will get a fine boost from this fruited mold.

1 3-ounce package lime
  gelatin
1 cup boiling water
1 20-ounce can crushed
  pineapple
1 cup low-fat cottage
  cheese, beaten until
  smooth

½ cup celery, finely diced
1 tablespoon pimiento,
  chopped
½ cup walnuts, coarsely
  chopped
Salad greens

Stir the gelatin in the boiling water until dissolved. Chill until thick and syrupy, then add the undrained pineapple, cottage cheese, celery, pimiento, and walnuts. Pour into a mold or an 8-inch square cake pan, lightly oiled. Chill until firm. Unmold and serve on crisp salad greens.

Serves 4 to 6

HORSERADISH RING

This ring filled with seafood makes an impressive first course.

1 3-ounce package lime
  gelatin
1 cup boiling water
½ cup cold water
1 cup low-fat cottage
  cheese

1 medium-sized
  cucumber
4 red radishes
2 tablespoons (or more)
  prepared horseradish

Dissolve the gelatin in the boiling water, then add the cold water. Chill in the refrigerator until thickened and syrupy.

Beat the cottage cheese until smooth and creamy. Peel the cucumber and slice very thin. Wash the radishes, leaving the red skin, and slice thin.

When the gelatin has reached the consistency of unbeaten egg white, add the cottage cheese, cucumber, radishes, and horseradish. Mix well. Taste to see if more horseradish is needed. The horseradish flavor should not be so subtle that no one knows it is there—so use your judgment. The bottled horseradishes come in different strengths, so it's impossible to be specific. You may have a mild one and will need double or more the quantity here called for. Lightly oil a 6-cup mold, pour the gelatin mixture into it, and refrigerate until firm.

Unmold on a round platter. Fill the center with fish or seafood of your choice seasoned with either Russian Dressing (page 330) or Garlic Mayonnaise (page 328).

Serves 4 to 6

WINE CHERRY MOLD

A happy thought with either hot or cold poultry.

2 3-ounce packages black
   cherry gelatin
2 cups boiling water
1 large can (No. 2 or 2½)
   pitted Bing cherries,
   drained

1 cup cherry juice
½ cup port wine
1 large navel orange,
   peeled and diced
Watercress
Preserved kumquats

Dissolve the gelatin in the boiling water. Drain the cherries and measure the juice. If there is less than a cup of juice, add water to make up the difference and add to the gelatin. Add the wine. Lightly oil a 6-cup mold and pour the gelatin mixture into it. Cool and refrigerate until it becomes thick and syrupy, then add the cherries and orange, distributing them evenly. Chill until firm.

Unmold on a round platter and garnish with watercress and kumquats.

Serves 6 to 8

AMBROSIA RELISH

This is an excellent relish with meat and poultry. It puzzles as much as it pleases, for no one seems to be able to identify its main ingredient.

4 cups julienne beets (2
   1-pound cans)
1 orange, thinly sliced
1 lemon (juice and rind)
3 cups sugar

¼ cup crystallized ginger,
   cut into small pieces
¼ cup blanched slivered
   almonds, coarsely cut

Drain the beets and discard the juice. Soak them overnight in cold water. The following day, drain them thoroughly and place in a large, heavy saucepan.

Cut the orange slices into small pieces, leaving the skin on. Add to the beets along with the juice and grated rind of a lemon. Add the sugar and crystallized ginger. Cook over low heat for about 1¼ hours, until the syrup cooks down and the julienne strips (you really can't call them beets at this point because they bear no resemblance to their origin) are glazed and a lovely, deep amber color. Add the almonds to the mixture and heat through for a minute. When cool, place in a covered jar and refrigerate. It will keep for weeks if no one eats it—an unlikely prospect.

Yields about 1 quart

FROSTED GRAPES

These make a dainty fruit garnish for cold poultry, molded salads, or meats.

Small clusters of seedless grapes	Superfine granulated sugar
1 egg white, slightly beaten	Canned peach halves, drained

Dip the grape clusters into the egg white. When they are nearly dry, sprinkle with the sugar and set in the center of the peach halves.

BAKED ORANGES

These go wonderfully with a chicken dish. And covered with a meringue piped through a pastry tube, and then browned in the oven, they will also do for dessert.

6 large navel oranges	Sugar to taste
1 1-pound-4-ounce can crushed pineapple	¼ cup sherry
Juice of 1 lemon	½ cup walnuts, finely ground

Cut a thick slice off the top of each orange at the stem end. Scoop out the pulp from all the orange, including the cut-off slice, and place in a large saucepan with the entire contents of the can of pineapple. Add the lemon juice and sugar to taste and cook until it becomes the consistency of a thin marmalade. This may take a couple of hours over low heat, but just let it alone, except for stirring it every once in a while.

While it is cooking, scallop the orange shells. I do this with my small embroidery scissors. Two little snips that come together in the middle make a sawtooth edge, and very nice they look. It's the kind of idiot work that is welcome on a day you are fussing for guests—it gives you a chance to sit down.

When the orange-pineapple stuff is thick and syrupy enough, add the sherry, mix, and refill the shells. Sprinkle with the nuts. Bake in a 350° oven for 20 minutes. Do not refrigerate. Serve at room temperature. Garnish the main course platter with the oranges.

Serves 6

15
Salads

Few things can add as much interest to a meal at such small effort, while returning as much in important nutritional value, as a good salad. And *good* doesn't have to mean exotic. It can be a mélange of everyday ingredients, carefully put together and mixed with loving care in a tasteful dressing. It can be an appetizer course; a refreshing fruit, chicken, fish, legume, or vegetable salad to serve as a main course; or mixed greens that have been washed, dried, crisped, broken to size, and lightly tossed in a zippy dressing.

Salads are a valuable ally in a cholesterol-watching program. Homemade salad dressings offer an excellent means of including additional quantities of polyunsaturated oils in our diets. A delicious mayonnaise, a tart French dressing, or a creamy garlic mayonnaise (see recipes) are easily prepared. Also, the very nature of most salad ingredients means that no overzealous cook has had time to boil out any of the vitamins contained in them. Too, salads offer bulk and variety for the calorie-counters.

It's a good idea to use leftover vegetables such as peas, carrots, string beans, and broccoli in a cold salad, since a second heating further destroys their vitamin content. Laced with a tangy dressing and a bit of chopped onion, they will do fine, but please don't throw them into a bowl of mixed greens. They will lose their identity in the hodgepodge and dilute the crispness of the other ingredients.

Let the mixed salad *really* be mixed. The popular iceberg, or Simpson, lettuce is as dependable as a pair of old shoes, but, like old shoes, it can be improved upon. Vary it with other greens such as romaine, chicory, escarole, Belgian endive, and Boston or Bibb lettuce, and don't neglect some dark green tender young spinach leaves and shredded raw red cabbage. Bibb lettuce is a delicious green, but expensive and not always available. Fresh Boston lettuce has much the same quality and is easier to come by.

Greens should be washed and thoroughly drained as soon as you get them home. A flexible wire basket is excellent for this. Drain the moisture out of the greens and store them in the refrigerator in plastic bags. You can prepare them an hour or two in advance of dinner and keep them chilled in the salad bowl. The dressing can wait until the last minute, or you run the risk of a soggy salad, perish forbid.

Whatever the role of the salad—to begin the meal, as the mainstay, or just some mixed greens to add zest and variety to the meal—give it the benefit of your best. This means the best in quality and freshness of the ingredients you buy and the best of your talent in making it as attractive as you can.

FRUITED CHICKEN SALAD

3 whole chicken breasts, cooked, or 3 cups white meat chicken cut into bite-sized pieces
1 cup celery, chopped
1 8-ounce can white grapes, drained

1 cup pineapple chunks, drained
⅓ cup slivered almonds, browned in 1 teaspoon oil
¾ cup mayonnaise
1 tablespoon lemon juice

If you are starting with uncooked chicken breasts, poach them according to the directions on page 166. When cool, cut them into bite-sized cubes.

In a large bowl, combine the chicken with the remaining ingredients and toss gently until thoroughly mixed. Refrigerate until ready to serve. Serve in a bowl or on a platter lined with salad greens.

Serves 5 or 6

Variation: Curry fanciers may add to the mayonnaise (before tossing) from a teaspoon to a tablespoon of curry powder, depending on the strength of the curry and taste preference.

FRUIT SALAD AND COTTAGE CHEESE PLATE

This is just one version of a cottage cheese and fruit arrangement that we use when the fruits are in season. You may add or subtract as you wish.

1 honeydew melon
Curly endive or chicory
1½ cups low-fat cottage cheese
1 small cantaloupe
2 bananas, cut in quarters
1 large red apple, unpeeled, cored, and sliced
2 tablespoons lemon juice

1 pint strawberries
1½ cups seedless grapes
2 navel oranges, peeled and cut into sections
Small can pineapple chunks in pineapple juice (reserve the juice)
Fresh blueberries (if available)

Slice the honeydew melon crosswise to make four rings. Peel the rings, remove the center seeds, and place the rings on a bed of curly endive or chicory on your prettiest luncheon-size plates. Place a mound of the cottage cheese in the center of each ring.

Scoop tiny melon balls from the remaining honeydew and from the cantaloupe. Sprinkle the bananas and apple slices with the lemon juice to keep them from discoloring. If the strawberries are large and lovely, do not remove the hulls.

Surround the slice of honeydew on each plate with a clump of melon balls, a mound of strawberries, grapes, orange sections, apple crescents, banana quarters, pineapple chunks, etc. A few fresh blueberries sprinkled over all will add a nice color contrast. Chill well and serve cold with Fruit Salad Dressing (page 327) or the following:

Cottage Cheese Fruit Dressing

½ cup low-fat cottage
cheese
¼ cup mayonnaise

1 teaspoon lemon juice
½ cup pineapple juice
from pineapple chunks

Beat or blend the cottage cheese until smooth and creamy. Blend in the remaining ingredients and mix well.

Serves 4

HALIBUT SALAD

1½ pounds fresh halibut
2 cups cold water
5 whole allspice
1 teaspoon salt
1 large onion, quartered
1 tablespoon vinegar
¼ teaspoon sugar
⅓ cup celery, finely
chopped
¼ cup green pepper,
finely chopped

¼–½ cup mayonnaise
Pinch of curry
powder (optional)
1 tablespoon
chopped dill or ½
teaspoon dried dill
Tomato wedges,
green pepper rings,
sliced cucumber for
garnish

Wash the halibut. In a medium-sized skillet, combine the water, allspice, salt, onion, vinegar, and sugar. Bring to a boil and simmer for 5 minutes. Add the halibut, reduce the heat to a simmer, and cook, covered, for 20 to 25 minutes, or until the fish flakes easily. Remove from the heat and leave the fish in the stock until it is cold. The spice in the stock gives the fish a nice flavor, so give it plenty of time to permeate. When we are planning this salad for dinner, I like to cook the fish in the morning and refrigerate it in the stock all day until time to assemble the salad.

When cold, flake the halibut. Add the celery, green pepper, enough mayonnaise to moisten (either with or without the curry powder), and the dill. Toss lightly and serve on a bed of lettuce. Garnish with the tomatoes, green pepper, and cucumber.

Serves 4

CHEF'S SALAD

4 cups assorted
salad greens, broken
into bite-sized
pieces
3 tomatoes, cut into
wedges
1 green pepper, cut
into rings
4 or 5 sliced radishes
1 carrot, coarsely
grated
1 tablespoon finely
minced onion

Freshly ground
pepper
1 tablespoon fresh dill,
snipped
½ cup (or more) French
dressing
1 whole cooked chicken
breast, cut into
julienne strips
4 slices low-fat
American cheese, cut
into strips
Watercress

In a large bowl, combine the chilled salad greens, tomatoes, green pepper, radishes, carrot, onion, pepper, and dill. Toss with sufficient French dressing to coat the greens thoroughly. Arrange the chicken and cheese strips over the top. Garnish with watercress.

Serves 4

Variation: Russian dressing may be substituted for the French dressing.

SALADE NIÇOISE

This is another recipe of which there are any number of variations. We have eaten so-called authentic versions of Salade Niçoise in various places in France, and all of them turned out to be different. In each place another ingredient ranging from tuna fish and salad greens to boiled potatoes was omitted. However, included always were tomatoes, olives, green pepper, and anchovies.

Some purists take issue with the presence of boiled potatoes. As you can see, the latitude for preparation of a Niçoise is great.

1 pound string beans
3 medium-sized potatoes
3 ripe tomatoes
2 green peppers
1 large red onion
½ cup pitted black olives
1 2-ounce can anchovy fillets

2 7-ounce cans tuna fish
2 cups coarsely shredded lettuce
Crisp salad greens, lettuce or romaine
⅓ cup minced fresh parsley

Dressing

3 tablespoons wine vinegar
⅔ cup oil
1 clove garlic, minced
1 teaspoon salt

2 teaspoons Dijon mustard
½ teaspoon dried sweet basil

Break the string beans into 1½-inch lengths and cook in boiling water until tender-crisp. Drain and run under cold water to stop the cooking. (There are those who maintain that the string beans should be raw, but I think they are better slightly cooked.) Boil the potatoes, then skin and slice. Peel the tomatoes by plunging them into boiling water for half a minute and slipping off the skins, then cut them into wedges. Core the green peppers and cut them into thin rings. Slice the onion thinly. Cut the olives into eighths. Rinse the anchovies in cold water and drain. Drain the tuna fish well and break into large flakes.

Mix the dressing ingredients in a small bowl and beat with a fork until well blended.

To assemble, place the shredded lettuce on the bottom of a large bowl and line the bowl with leaves of lettuce or romaine. Arrange in pie-shaped mounds over the bed of greens the green beans, potatoes, tomato wedges, and green pepper. Scatter the onion, olives, anchovies, and tuna fish over the top. Garnish with the parsley.

Serve well chilled as an hors d'oeuvre or a main dish. Toss with dressing at the table just before serving.

Serves 6 to 8 as appetizer;
4 to 6 as main course

SALMON SALAD

1 1-pound can salmon
1 tablespoon lemon
   juice
1 cup celery, finely
   chopped
¼ cup diced green
   pepper

1 tablespoon minced
   onion
½ teaspoon salt
   Freshly ground pepper
⅓ cup mayonnaise
   Capers

Drain the salmon and remove the skin and bones. Flake and sprinkle with the lemon juice. Reserve a few large choice flakes for garnish. Add to the rest of the salmon the celery, green pepper, onion, salt, and pepper and gently blend in the mayonnaise. Serve in lettuce cups, or scoop out tomatoes and fill them with the salad. Top each portion with a dollop of mayonnaise, a few salmon flakes, and a sprinkling of capers.

Serves 4

SPINACH AND MUSHROOM SALAD

Spinach now seems to have assumed its rightful place among popular salad greens. This is a delicious salad that can do even as a main course for a summertime lunch.

1 pound fresh young
   spinach
½ pound firm white
   mushrooms

6 scallions, chopped
   Sliced red onion rings
1 cup Garlic Croutons
   (page 316)

Dressing

½ cup mayonnaise
2 teaspoons Dijon
   mustard
4 tablespoons lemon
   juice
⅓ cup oil

1 tablespoon tarragon
   vinegar
   Pinch of sugar
½ teaspoon salt
   Freshly ground pepper

Strip the spinach leaves from the stems, wash under running cold water, and drain well in a wire basket. Pat the leaves dry; any excess moisture on salad greens dilutes the dressing and prevents the oil from coating the leaves.

Wipe the mushrooms clean. Break off the stems and save them for your next stew or soup. Slice the caps about ¼ inch thick.

Combine the dressing ingredients and beat with a wire whisk until well blended and smooth.

Tear the spinach leaves into large bite-sized pieces and toss in a salad bowl with the mushrooms and scallions. Arrange the onion rings and croutons over the salad. At the table, or just before serving, pour the dressing over the salad and toss lightly.

Garlic Croutons: Remove the crusts from 3 slices of white bread and cut the bread into ¼-inch cubes. Heat 2½ tablespoons of oil in a skillet and cook 1 large clove of crushed garlic, stirring for a minute, without browning. Add the bread cubes and toss frequently until golden brown. Drain on absorbent paper.

Serves 3 as main course;
4 to 6 as side dish

MIXED VEGETABLE SALAD

1 medium-sized bunch romaine lettuce	½ cup mayonnaise
1 14-ounce can artichoke hearts (water-packed)	2 tablespoons tomato sauce
2 cups raw cauliflower flowerets	1½ tablespoons lemon juice
1 cup celery	2 tablespoons fresh snipped dill
1 medium-sized red onion	½ teaspoon salt
1 large carrot	Freshly ground pepper
5 radishes	1 green pepper, cut into thin rings
½ cup French dressing	

Separate the romaine, wash and dry the leaves, and place in a plastic bag or crisper in the refrigerator. Drain the artichokes and cut in half if they are large. Thinly slice the cauliflowerets, celery, onion, carrot, and radishes. Place all these vegetables in a bowl, add the French dressing, mix well, and marinate for a few hours in the refrigerator.

Blend together the mayonnaise, tomato sauce, lemon juice, dill, salt, and pepper and chill.

When ready to serve, drain the marinated vegetables thoroughly and toss with the mayonnaise mixture. Transfer to a salad bowl lined with the romaine. Garnish with the green pepper rings.

Serves 6

TOSSED GREEN SALAD

1	small head Boston lettuce	8	small artichoke hearts (optional)
	Small bunch romaine	3	tablespoons red wine vinegar
2	clusters Belgian endive	1	teaspoon salt
2	cups (about) fresh spinach	1	clove garlic, minced
2	cups (about) chicory or escarole	¼	Freshly ground pepper teaspoon dry mustard
½	cup oil	2	tablespoons sesame
6	anchovy fillets, diced		seeds, browned in 1 teaspoon oil

You will need a large salad bowl to give the tosser enough room for the tossing. Wash all the salad greens and dry them well. Break them into generous bite-sized pieces. Toss with the ½ cup of oil, adding it gradually and stopping when all the leaves glisten. Add the anchovies and the artichoke hearts (if desired). In a separate bowl combine the vinegar with the salt, garlic, pepper, and mustard and mix well. Add to the salad and toss again. Sprinkle with the sesame seeds.

Serves 8

CAESAR SALAD

You will never miss the whole coddled egg present in the traditional Caesar salad. The blender-made creamy dressing is pleasant and full-bodied, one that you may like well enough to use on a variety of other salads.

1 head romaine lettuce	1 2-ounce can anchovy
1 small head Boston lettuce	fillets
	1 cup Garlic Croutons (page 316)

Dressing

¾ cup oil	1 teaspoon sugar
3 tablespoons wine vinegar	½ teaspoon salt
	Freshly ground pepper
1 clove garlic, minced	1 tablespoon Parmesan cheese
½ teaspoon Worcestershire sauce	

Wash, crisp, and dry the lettuce. Tear it into bite-sized pieces and place in a salad bowl. Rinse the anchovy fillets in cold water and cut in thirds. In an electric blender, blend for 1 minute all the dressing ingredients. Add the anchovies to the greens and toss with the dressing, adding it gradually and using just enough to coat the greens. Sprinkle the croutons over the salad.

Serves 6

ARMENIAN STRING BEAN SALAD

I never knew why Ellie's string bean salad tasted better than anybody else's until one day I happened to see her make it. It's what is done with the onion, I think, that gives it the special texture and taste.

1 pound string beans	¼ cup snipped fresh dill
1 large onion	¼ cup oil
1 tablespoon salt	2 tablespoons vinegar
2 tomatoes, diced	½ teaspoon salt
½ cup finely minced fresh parsley	

Cut the string beans into 1½-inch lengths. Cook in boiling salted water, covered, until crisp-tender—do not overcook. Rinse in cold water to stop the cooking. Drain and set aside.

Slice the onion into thin rings and place in a shallow bowl. Add the tablespoon of salt. With the heel of your hand crush the onion until it becomes limp and the juices run out. Rinse the onion rings in cold water to wash out the salt. Drain well.

Return the onion to the bowl and add the tomatoes, beans, parsley, and dill. Toss lightly with the oil. Add the vinegar and ½ teaspoon of salt and toss again. Chill until ready to serve.

Serves 4 to 6

MIXED BEAN SALAD

Legumes provide an excellent source of protein. Interestingly prepared, they can serve as a main course for a lunch or a light supper. This salad is also a fine addition to a buffet.

1 1-pound can green beans	½ cup green pepper, diced
1 1-pound can waxed beans	1 red onion cut into thin rings
1 1-pound can red kidney beans	½–⅔ cup oil
	⅓ cup cider vinegar
1 1-pound can chick-peas	¼ cup sugar
	Salad greens

Drain all the beans and the chick-peas thoroughly and combine in a bowl. Add the green pepper and onion rings. Use as much oil as you need to coat the beans, adding it gradually and tossing lightly. Combine the vinegar and sugar and add to the beans, tossing gently. Taste for seasoning. Marinate overnight in the refrigerator. Serve in a bowl lined with salad greens.

Serves 12 or more

PICKLED BEETS

6 or 8 fresh-cooked beets or 1 1-pound can sliced beets	2 tablespoons water
	⅓ cup sugar
6 tablespoons vinegar	2 tablespoons honey

If you are starting with fresh beets, leave them whole, with the root ends and about 2 inches of the tops attached. Cook in boiling water to cover until tender (25 to 35 minutes). Remove the beets from the water and slip off the skins. Slice the beets ¼ inch thick and place in a bowl.

Combine the vinegar, water, sugar, and honey in a saucepan and bring to a boil. Simmer until the sugar is dissolved. Pour the hot mixture over the beets. When cool, cover the bowl and refrigerate at least 24 hours before using.

Serves 4 to 6

PICKLED BEET AND ENDIVE SALAD

2 clusters Belgian endive
2 cups sliced pickled beets
¼ cup beet liquid
1 sweet onion, sliced in thin rings
¼ cup French dressing
Watercress
1 tablespoon chopped parsley

Slice the Belgian endive clusters crosswise into rings ¼ inch thick. Combine with the pickled beets, beet liquid, onion, and French dressing and marinate for an hour or so. To serve, drain the vegetables and arrange on individual salad plates. Garnish with sprigs of watercress and sprinkle the parsley over the beets.

Serves 4 to 6

COLESLAW

3 cups shredded cabbage
3 tablespoons oil
⅓ cup warm (not hot) vinegar
1 teaspoon salt
Freshly ground pepper
2 tablespoons sugar
1 tablespoon finely chopped onion
1 tablespoon chopped pimiento
1 teaspoon celery seeds
½ teaspoon Dijon mustard, mixed with 2 tablespoons mayonnaise
Green pepper rings
Cherry tomatoes

Prepare the cabbage by cutting a small head into quarters, removing the core, and shredding very fine with a sharp knife. Discard any coarse pieces. Place the cabbage in a large bowl and toss with the oil and vinegar. Add all the remaining ingredients except the green pepper and cherry tomatoes. Mix well. Cover the bowl and chill in the refrigerator. Garnish with the green pepper and cherry tomatoes.

Serves 4

CUCUMBER SALAD

Cucumbers are never crisper or more refreshing than in this salad.

2 large cucumbers	Few grinds of black
½ cup white vinegar	pepper
2 tablespoons water	2 tablespoons chopped
¼ cup sugar	parsley
½ teaspoon salt	

Do not peel the cucumbers unless they are heavily waxed, a frequent situation with cucumbers sold in supermarkets in large urban areas. However, even with the waxed varieties, when you scrape the skins leave tiny strips of the dark green peel here and there for eye appeal. And whether you use the cucumbers peeled or unpeeled, score them with the tines of a fork to fancy them up before slicing them very thin.

In a deep bowl, combine the remaining ingredients and mix well. Add the cucumber slices and cover them with a plate and a weight. (The cans that are taking up space in your refrigerator make fine weights.) Refrigerate about 3 hours. Drain the cucumbers to serve. The marinade can be saved and used again.

Serves 4

Variations: Add a thinly sliced onion to the above recipe.

Sprinkle the insides of scooped-out tomatoes with salt

and pepper and fill with cucumber salad bathed in plain low-fat yogurt.

LIMA BEAN SALAD

This and some cold asparagus provide a pleasant diversion for a hot-weather lunch.

2 cups fresh or frozen lima beans
2 tablespoons chopped parsley
1 clove garlic, minced
1 large sweet onion
4 tablespoons oil

1 tablespoon cider vinegar
½ teaspoon salt
Freshly ground pepper
Paprika
Cherry tomatoes

Cook the lima beans in a small amount of boiling salted water until tender but not mushy. Rinse with cold water to stop the cooking and drain well. Place in a bowl with the parsley and garlic. Add about half the onion, finely chopped, and toss lightly. (Slice the remainder of the onion very thin to use as a garnish.) Add the oil slowly, tossing gently, until the beans are well coated. Add the vinegar by half-teaspoons, tossing lightly, until well blended. Mix in the salt and pepper. Taste and correct the seasoning. Chill in the refrigerator at least 1 hour. Serve on a bed of lettuce, sprinkle lightly with paprika, and garnish with the onion rings and cherry tomatoes.

Serves 3 or 4

LENTIL SALAD

Lentils are another fine food often overlooked in our meal planning. Lentils have made great strides since the time when they had to be cooked for the better part of a day before they became soft enough to eat. Now the quick-cooking variety needs only half an hour or so of cooking. This salad can also be served warm as the starch at dinner.

1 cup lentils
Onion stuck with
cloves
½ bay leaf
4 cups water
1 teaspoon salt
3 tablespoons oil
1½ tablespoons red wine
vinegar

½ cup red onion,
chopped
¼ cup pimiento,
chopped
2 tablespoons minced
parsley
Freshly ground
pepper

In a medium-sized pot, place the lentils, onion, bay leaf, water, and salt and simmer covered from 30 to 40 minutes, or until tender. Don't let the lentils get mushy. Drain well and discard the onion and bay leaf.

Transfer the lentils to a bowl and, while still warm, toss with the oil, coating well, then add the vinegar slowly. Add the red onion, pimiento, parsley, and pepper and toss well. Taste and correct the seasoning.

Serves 6

GERMAN POTATO SALAD

This is a particularly fine salad for party days when the refrigerator is crammed full, because it does not need to be refrigerated. More than that, it mustn't be.

3 pounds small potatoes
½ cup (or more) oil
½ cup (or more) vinegar
1 onion, chopped fine
1 teaspoon salt
Freshly ground pepper

¼ teaspoon paprika
¼ cup chopped parsley
Parsley sprigs or
watercress, green
pepper rings, and
pimiento strips

The essential in this preparation is warm vinegar on warm potatoes. Having established that keynote, scrub the potatoes, place in as little boiling salted water as possible, cover the pot, and cook until done. Drain at once. While the potatoes are still warm, peel and slice them. Add enough oil, tossing lightly, to coat the potatoes and make them shiny. Heat the vinegar to the boiling point and add slowly, using as much as you need to moisten the mixture. Add the onion, salt, pepper, paprika, and parsley.

Toss well and taste for seasoning. You may want to add a bit more salt or perhaps just a pinch of sugar. Arrange in a mound on a platter and garnish with parsley sprigs or watercress, green pepper rings, and pimiento strips. Serve at room temperature.

Serves 8

RICE SALAD

1 cup uncooked rice
¼ cup oil
2 tablespoons wine vinegar
¼ cup pimiento, finely chopped
1 8-ounce can water chestnuts, thinly sliced
¼ cup scallions, finely chopped

½ green pepper, finely chopped
1 tablespoon mayonnaise
½ teaspoon curry powder (optional)
Salt
Freshly ground black pepper

Cook the rice according to the package directions. To the warm rice add the oil and toss lightly. Add the vinegar and toss again. Add the pimiento, water chestnuts, scallions, and green pepper and toss lightly. Combine the mayonnaise and curry powder and add to the rice. Add salt and pepper according to preference. The curry powder may also be increased. People are rarely ambivalent about the way they feel toward curry, so I put in just a soupçon—not enough to incur the displeasure of those not enthusiastic about it, but just enough to add flavor interest.

TOMATO SALAD

Basil has a natural affinity for tomatoes, and a combination of ripe, juicy tomatoes and fresh basil can be a Lucullan treat.

3 large ripe tomatoes   ⅓ cup cider vinegar

4 tablespoons oil	2 tablespoons fresh
1 medium-sized onion,	basil, chopped, or ½
chopped	teaspoon dried basil
½ teaspoon salt	Watercress
Freshly ground pepper	

Slice the tomatoes about ⅓ inch thick. In a medium-sized bowl, combine the remaining ingredients and beat well with a fork or a wire whisk. Add the tomato slices, cover with the dressing, and marinate in the refrigerator for an hour or so. Arrange the drained slices on a platter garnished with watercress.

Serves 3

WALDORF SALAD

I am told that any dish with the name Waldorf was created by the famous Oscar of the Waldorf. Perhaps he did originate this pleasant fruit-and-nut mixture, although somehow this homey, tearoomy concoction seems out of character for the legendary Oscar. Tearoomy or not, it is an extremely taste-pleasing salad that, in larger quantities, can do as a main lunch course.

Juice of ½ lemon	½ cup seedless grapes,
2 large or 3 medium-	cut in half
sized apples, peeled,	⅓–½ cup mayonnaise
cored, and diced	2 tablespoons chopped
1 cup chopped celery	fresh mint or 1
½ cup broken walnut	teaspoon dried
meats	mint leaves
⅓ cup raisins	

Squeeze the lemon juice over the apple cubes. Add the celery, nuts, raisins, and grapes and mix with enough mayonnaise to moisten. Serve well chilled on crisp greens, sprinkled with the chopped mint.

Serves 2 as main dish;
4 as side dish

16

Dressings and Sauces

In addition to the dressings and sauces in this chapter, there are a number of other dressings and sauces scattered throughout the book. You will find them listed in the index.

FRENCH DRESSING

French dressing, also known as *sauce vinaigrette,* is basically a blending of oil and vinegar in whatever proportion pleases you. A popular formula and one we like is four times as much oil as vinegar, but you can always start with a little less vinegar and increase it according to your taste. You will generally need about ½ to ⅔ cup of dressing for 8 servings. Always add the dressing gradually while tossing. In this way you will use as much as you need, so that the salad greens are coated and not inundated.

1 cup oil
2 tablespoons wine or cider vinegar
2 tablespoons lemon juice
1 teaspoon Dijon mustard
¼–½ teaspoon sugar

½ teaspoon Worcestershire sauce (optional)
1 clove garlic, minced (optional)
Salt and pepper

Measure all the ingredients into a jar. Cover tightly and shake well.

Yields 1¼ cups

HERBED FRENCH DRESSING

Raw or parboiled vegetables such as cauliflowerets, broccoli slices, button mushrooms, or asparagus tips make fine salads when marinated for 30 minutes or more in a tangy dressing such as this one. Their official name then becomes vegetables *vinaigrette*.

To 1 cup of basic French Dressing (above), add:

1 tablespoon finely chopped onion or shallots
1 tablespoon finely chopped parsley
1 teaspoon finely chopped capers

2 teaspoons finely chopped tarragon or ½ teaspoon dried tarragon, finely crumbled
1 tablespoon finely chopped sour pickle (optional)

Combine all the ingredients in a jar and blend well.

Note: Instead of the tarragon, you may substitute the same quantity of either dill or basil.

FRUIT SALAD DRESSING

⅓ cup undiluted frozen lemonade concentrate, thawed

2 tablespoons honey
⅓ cup oil
½ teaspoon celery seeds

Combine all the ingredients in a jar. Cover tightly and shake well.

Serves 8

CREAMY ANCHOVY DRESSING

1 2-ounce can flat anchovies
½ cup oil
½ cup evaporated skimmed milk
¼ cup wine vinegar

Freshly ground pepper
1 clove garlic, cut in two
¼ teaspoon sugar
2 tablespoons chopped parsley

Drain the oil from the can of anchovies and discard. Cut the anchovies into ¼-inch lengths and place in a pint screw-top jar. Add the remaining ingredients and shake vigorously until the dressing is creamy and smooth. Chill until ready to use. Remove the garlic before serving.

Yields 1¼ cups

COTTAGE CHEESE DRESSING

This is a good dressing for cucumbers that have been salted and then soaked for an hour in ice water. Add some thinly sliced white radishes.

1 cup low-fat cottage cheese	½ teaspoon salt
4 tablespoons oil	1 small clove garlic, minced
2 tablespoons lemon juice or cider vinegar	¼ teaspoon dry mustard
1 tablespoon sugar	Freshly ground pepper

Beat the cottage cheese in an electric blender or with a beater until creamy and smooth. Add the remaining ingredients and blend until smooth. Taste and correct the seasonings. Keep chilled until ready to use.

Yields 1⅓ cups

GARLIC MAYONNAISE (AIOLI)

If you don't like garlic, I can't promise this will convert you. However, if you feel about garlic as we do, you will never be without a jar of this in your refrigerator. It is wonderful on any kind of salad from mixed greens through cabbage, chicken, fish, or tomato aspics—or as a dip for vegetables or shrimps.

1 egg	1½ teaspoons black pepper
½ teaspoon minced garlic (3 or 4 cloves, depending on size)	2 teaspoons sugar
¾ tablespoon salt	1½ cups oil
1½ teaspoons dry mustard	½ cup (scant) cider vinegar

In a good-sized mixing bowl, beat the egg with an electric beater at high speed until thick and lemon colored. Add the garlic, salt, mustard, pepper, and sugar. Add the oil very slowly, trickling it in drop by drop at first, until the emulsion beats up nice and thick. Add the vinegar—also slowly—and continue beating a few minutes longer. This will probably take about 10 to 12 minutes from beginning to end, with results worth the time.

Yields 2½ cups

MAYONNAISE

I had heard so many tales about the complications of making mayonnaise—how it separated and didn't thicken and so forth—that I approached the project for the first time with considerable trepidation. I found to my delight that it couldn't be simpler. I don't chill the beater, and I don't chill the bowl as I had been warned I must. The whole business takes less than 15 minutes in my electric beater, and it comes out perfect each time—creamy, rich, smooth, and high in polyunsaturated fatty acids. In view of all this, I strongly urge you to make your own.

1	whole egg	1	teaspoon dry mustard
2	tablespoons lemon juice	¼	teaspoon paprika
1¼	teaspoons sugar	2	cups oil
1	teaspoon salt	1	tablespoon vinegar

With the electric beater at high speed, beat the egg with 1 tablespoon of the lemon juice until frothy. Add the sugar, salt, mustard, and paprika and beat well. Add 1 cup of the oil in a tiny trickle—slowly—until the mixture becomes thick. Don't try to hurry this part, but as soon as the mixture becomes thick and emulsified, you can add the oil more quickly. When the mixture is very thick, add the remaining tablespoon of lemon juice and the vinegar. Continue adding the remainder of the oil gradually until the mayonnaise is well blended, thick, and creamy.

Yields 3 cups

Variations: Mayonnaise can be a base for a great variety of different dressings, a list of which follows. The amounts of the ingredients listed below are to be added to 1 cup of mayonnaise.

Green Mayonnaise: 3 tablespoons finely chopped raw spinach, ½ tablespoon chopped parsley, 1 teaspoon chopped chives.

Dill Mayonnaise: ¼ cup fresh snipped dill, 1 teaspoon chopped chives.

Horseradish Mayonnaise: 1 tablespoon horseradish (or more, according to taste).

Mustard Mayonnaise: 1 tablespoon Dijon or Dusseldorf mustard.

Yogurt Mayonnaise: 1 cup yogurt, 1 teaspoon sugar, dry mustard to taste. (This is a suitable dressing for potato salad or coleslaw.)

RUSSIAN DRESSING

1 cup mayonnaise	1 teaspoon
⅓ cup chili sauce	Worcestershire sauce
½ teaspoon dry mustard	2 teaspoons lemon juice

Combine the mayonnaise with all the other ingredients and blend well. Keep chilled until ready to use.

Serves 8 or more

TARTAR SAUCE

Standard Operating Procedure with a simple broiled or fried fish. As long as you are making it, you might just as well make a goodly supply. In a covered jar in your refrigerator, it will keep indefinitely. The ingredients are variable, but this is our favorite.

1½ cups mayonnaise	1 teaspoon Dijon or
3 pimiento-stuffed olives, finely chopped	Dusseldorf mustard
	1½ tablespoons chopped
1 tablespoon capers, chopped	parsley
	1 teaspoon minced
2 tablespoons sour pickle, chopped	onion
	⅛ teaspoon dried tarragon

| 1 teaspoon chopped | 1 tablespoon (or more) |
| chives | lemon juice |

Combine all the ingredients and mix well. Taste for seasoning. Chill.

Yields about 1 pint

SOUR CREAM SUBSTITUTE

This can be used as a base for dips when combined with herbs and seasonings, and as a dressing for salads or cold vegetables.

1 cup low-fat cottage	¼ teaspoon salt
cheese	1 tablespoon lemon
2 tablespoons skim milk	juice

A blender will quickly convert this to the appearance and consistency of sour cream. If you do not have a blender, the same effect can be achieved with an electric beater at high speed. Either way, combine all the ingredients and beat away until it becomes smooth and creamy.

Yields about 1¼ cups

CREAM SAUCE

THIN

1 tablespoon oil	Dash of white pepper
1 tablespoon flour	1 cup skim milk
½ teaspoon salt	

MEDIUM

2 tablespoons oil	Dash of white pepper
2 tablespoons flour	1 cup skim milk
½ teaspoon salt	

THICK

3 tablespoons oil	Dash of white pepper
4 tablespoons flour	1 cup skim milk
½ teaspoon salt	

The procedure to make any one of these three sauces is the same. Heat the oil in a small saucepan. Blend with the flour thoroughly over low heat, but don't let it brown. Add the seasonings and, over medium heat, while stirring constantly, slowly stir in the milk until the mixture thickens and bubbles. Reduce the heat and cook a minute longer.

You may substitute consommé, meat or fish stock, or wine for part of the milk. If you wish to give the sauce added flavor, the milk you add may be scalded beforehand with a few thin slices of onion and a few sprigs of parsley, or a bay leaf and clove, according to your taste. Strain the milk before proceeding with the sauce.

Yields 1 cup

CURRY SAUCE

A quick sauce for leftover meat or poultry. This amount is sufficient for 4 cups of the main ingredient.

2 tablespoons oil	¼ teaspoon powdered ginger
1 medium-sized onion, chopped	½ teaspoon salt
1 tablespoon flour	1½ cups chicken broth
1 teaspoon curry powder (or more, according to taste)	½ cup tomato juice
	½ tablespoon brown sugar

In a small saucepan, heat the oil and sauté the onion until limp and transparent. Sprinkle the flour, curry powder, ginger, and salt over the onion and, over medium heat, while stirring constantly with a wire whisk, slowly stir in the chicken broth and tomato juice. Add the brown sugar and cook, stirring, until the sauce becomes thickened and smooth. Reduce the heat and simmer 2 or 3 minutes longer. Taste and correct the seasoning.

Yields 2 cups

EASY HOLLANDAISE SAUCE

This creamy, lemony sauce is most satisfactory with asparagus, broccoli, or any other vegetable you used to consider as a likely prospect for a hollandaise topping.

½ cup mayonnaise   1 tablespoon lemon juice
2 tablespoons hot water

With a wire whisk blend the mayonnaise and hot water. Over very low heat, add the lemon juice and stir with a wire whisk. Serve at once over vegetables.

Yields ⅞ cup

MARINARA SAUCE

This is a most useful and delicious sauce that can go over pasta, rice, shrimp, or fish. It freezes well, so that you might consider doubling the recipe when you prepare it and freezing half for future use.

3 tablespoons oil
6–8 scallions or 2 onions, chopped
1 1-pound-13-ounce can Italian plum tomatoes
2–3 cloves garlic, thinly sliced
1 teaspoon dried basil

1 teaspoon dried oregano
½ teaspoon salt
Freshly ground pepper
½ teaspoon sugar
1 6-ounce can tomato paste
6 ounces dry white wine

In a good-sized pot, heat the oil and sauté the scallions (or onions) until transparent and limp. Push the tomatoes through a sieve with a wooden spoon, discarding the seeds, and add to the pot. Add the garlic, basil, oregano, salt, pepper, and sugar and cook over low heat for 1 hour, partly covered. Add the tomato paste, then fill the can with the wine and add. Continue cooking for another hour, partly covered. Taste for seasoning and correct.

Yields 1 quart

17
Breads, Cakes, and Pastries

The limitation on dairy products in a low-fat dietary presents no obstacle to the vast assortment of hot breads, cakes, and desserts that can still be produced. They can be as lavish, eye-filling (and caloric, if you wish) as in the freewheeling days of uncounted egg yolks and unmeasured butter and heavy cream.

While most commercial bakeshop products, with the exception of bread and rolls, do not meet the requirements of a cholesterol-lowering diet, anything is possible in our own kitchens. With a willing spirit at the mixing bowl, no family need yearn in vain for baked goodies and confections.

MUFFINS

Muffins are one of the simplest of all hot breads to prepare. They can add variety to any meal.

2	scant cups unsifted all-purpose flour	2½	teaspoons baking powder
2½	tablespoons sugar	1	egg
½	teaspoon salt	1¼	cups skim milk
		4	tablespoons oil

Preheat the oven to 400°. Oil 12 3-inch muffin cups or 16 2½-inch muffin cups.

Mix together the flour, sugar, salt, and baking powder. Beat the egg lightly and combine with the milk and oil. Stir into the flour mixture only enough to moisten all the flour. If you overbeat muffin batter, the finished product will have pointed heads and an uneven grain. Spoon the batter into the oiled cups, filling them ⅔ full. Bake about 25 minutes, or until nicely browned. Let stand a minute or two before removing from the pan. Serve warm.

Makes 12 to 16

BUTTERMILK MUFFINS

An eggless muffin.

1½ cups unsifted all-purpose flour	½ teaspoon salt
2 tablespoons sugar	1 cup skim buttermilk
½ teaspoon baking soda	3 tablespoons oil

Preheat the oven to 400°. Oil 12 2½-inch muffin cups.

In a medium-sized bowl, mix together the flour, sugar, soda, and salt. Add the buttermilk and oil and stir only enough to moisten all the flour. Spoon the batter into the oiled cups, filling them ⅔ full. Bake about 25 minutes, or until nicely browned. Let stand for a minute or two, then remove from the pan. Serve warm.

Makes 12

BUTTERMILK MARMALADE MUFFINS

Follow the directions in the preceding recipe. Fill the muffin cups ⅓ full, place ½ teaspoon of orange marmalade on the batter in each cup, and cover with the remaining batter. The built-in dollop of marmalade makes these an excellent teatime muffin.

Makes 12

CORN BREAD OR MUFFINS

1 cup all-purpose flour	½ teaspoon salt
1 cup yellow corn meal	1 egg
3 teaspoons baking powder	1¼ cups skim milk
2 tablespoons sugar	¼ cup oil

Heat the oven to 425°. Oil 12 3-inch muffin cups or an 8 by 8 inch pan.

Sift the flour and measure 1 cup. Place in a bowl with the corn meal, baking powder, sugar, and salt and mix. In a separate bowl, beat the egg lightly and combine with the milk and oil, mixing well. Combine with the dry ingredients and mix only until the flour is completely moistened—don't overbeat. Pour into an oiled pan or into muffin cups, filling them about ⅔ full. Bake until golden brown. The corn bread will bake in about 30 minutes and the muffins in about 20.

Yields 16 corn-bread squares
or 12 muffins

BAKING POWDER BISCUITS

These taste best when they come directly from the oven to the table, so do try to bake them at the last minute.

2 cups unsifted all-purpose flour	½ teaspoon salt
	⅓ cup oil
3 teaspoons baking powder	⅔ cup skim milk

Preheat the oven to 450°. Combine the flour, baking powder, and salt in a medium-sized bowl. Mix the oil and milk together in a cup and add to the flour mixture, mixing well with a fork. The dough should be soft but not sticky. Flour your hands lightly and make a round ball of the dough. Place it on a square of waxed paper and knead a few times to make it smooth. Pat it out to ½-inch thickness. Cut the biscuits with an unfloured 2-inch (or smaller) biscuit cutter. Place the biscuits, well separated, on an ungreased cookie sheet. Bake for 12 to 15 minutes, until lightly browned. Serve immediately, piping hot.

Makes 1½ to 2 dozen

POPOVERS

2 eggs	1 cup skim milk
1 cup flour, sifted	2 tablespoons oil
½ teaspoon salt	

Beat the eggs lightly with a fork. Sift the flour and salt together and beat in. Beat in the milk, but don't overbeat. Popovers are better when not overbeaten, so stop when you have a thin, perfectly smooth batter. Add the oil.

Pour into 10 or 12 well-oiled 3-inch muffin cups, custard cups, or popover tins, filling them about ⅔ full. Place in a cold oven and set the temperature for 425°. Bake for 30 to 35 minutes, or until puffy and brown. If the popovers seem to be getting too brown after 20 minutes or so, you can reduce the temperature to 375°. When done, pierce the popovers with a sharp-pointed knife to dry them out, unless you prefer them moist inside. Remove at once from the cups.

Makes 10 to 12

SCONES

Hot from the oven, or split and toasted, and served with fruit preserves, these are a fine breakfast or lunch idea.

2 cups sifted flour	1 tablespoon oil
1½ tablespoons baking powder	1 cup skim milk
½ teaspoon salt	Granulated sugar for topping
1 tablespoon sugar	

Preheat the oven to 300°. Sift together the flour, baking powder, salt, and sugar. Add the oil and slowly stir in the milk.

Turn out on a floured board and knead lightly for half a minute—no more. Add more flour if the dough is too sticky to handle. Cut the dough in half and shape each half into a ball. Roll out one ball at a time into a round ½ inch thick. Place on a lightly oiled baking sheet and cut each round into 6 pie-shaped wedges. Sprinkle lightly with sugar. Bake 30 minutes or until a cake tester comes out dry. Serve hot.

Makes 12

HOT GARLIC BREAD

Dinner guests never ignore this hot crusty bread, as they often do rolls. It is particularly good for a buffet. We like our bread quite garlicky, but the degree of this seasoning is up to you. Season ½ cup of oil with 2 or 3 or more cloves of crushed garlic until you achieve the garlic flavor that pleases you. Mix in a pinch of salt. If you don't use all the oil, it can be kept in a covered jar in the refrigerator until the next time you need it. It will keep indefinitely.

Start with a good crusty French or Italian loaf. Cut a clove of garlic in half and rub the cut surface lightly over the outside crust. Slash the loaf into 2-inch wedges, but don't cut all the way through. Stop about ½ inch away from the bottom crust. Add 1 tablespoon of chopped parsley to the garlic oil. With a pastry brush, apply the oil to both sides of each wedge, being careful not to amputate any of them. Place the loaf in the center of a sheet of aluminum foil, close the foil tightly, crimping the edges, and heat in a 350° oven for 20 minutes until the loaf is thoroughly heated. To serve, place the loaf, foil and all, on a long bread platter. Fold the foil down to make a frill around the loaf.

DATE-ORANGE BREAD

This fruity, nutty loaf is actually less a bread than a cake. It is a substantial loaf that can substitute for the no-longer acceptable commercial pound or raisin cakes.

½ cup boiling water	¼ teaspoon baking soda
2 tablespoons oil	½ teaspoon salt
1 cup sugar	1⅓ cups chopped dates
1 egg, lightly beaten	2 tablespoons grated
⅓ cup orange juice	orange rind
2 cups sifted all-purpose flour	½ cup coarsely chopped walnuts
2 teaspoons baking powder	

Preheat the oven to 350°.

Combine the boiling water with the oil in a large mixing bowl. Add the sugar. In another bowl beat the egg lightly and stir in the orange juice. Add to the sugar mixture and mix well.

Reserve a couple of tablespoons of the flour for dredging the dates. Add to the remainder of the flour the baking powder, soda, and salt and mix through. Add the flour mixture gradually to the egg and sugar mixture, stirring only enough to blend well. Dredge the dates lightly with the reserved flour. (A simple way of chopping the dates is to cut them with kitchen scissors whose blades have been dipped in vegetable oil, which prevents the dates from sticking.) Add to the batter the dates, orange rind, and nuts, stirring just enough to distribute evenly.

Turn the batter into a lightly oiled 9 by 5 inch loaf pan. Bake 50 to 55 minutes, until the loaf is browned and has pulled away a tiny bit from the edges. Allow to cool in the pan for 10 minutes before loosening and removing.

Yields 1 loaf

CRANBERRY BREAD

This is another bread-cake loaf that can be served as dessert or can be used to round out a slim supper menu. It freezes well and is one of those recipes you might whip up at cranberry time and stash away in your freezer.

2	cups fresh cranberries	1	egg
2½	cups flour, sifted	½	cup skim milk
1	cup sugar	2	tablespoons oil
½	teaspoon salt	½	cup walnuts, coarsely chopped
2	teaspoons baking powder	¼	cup orange juice
½	teaspoon baking soda	1	tablespoon grated orange rind
1	teaspoon cinnamon		

Preheat the oven to 375°. Chop the cranberries and set aside. In a large bowl, mix together the flour, sugar, salt, baking powder, soda, and cinnamon.

In another bowl, beat the egg lightly and add the milk, oil, nuts, orange juice and rind, and cranberries. Mix well. Add the contents of this bowl to the dry ingredients and mix thoroughly. Transfer to an oiled 9 by 5 inch loaf pan. Mound the batter high along the edges of the pan and low in the center so the loaf will bake without a center hump. Bake about an hour, or until a cake tester comes out dry. Cool for 10 minutes and remove from the pan.

Yields 1 loaf

PEANUT BUTTER BREAD

This is generally a success with the peanut butter enthusiasts among our acquaintances, particularly the small ones. They think thin slices of this bread made into a sandwich with grape or currant jelly are superspecial. Do use the nonhydrogenated peanut butter.

2	cups flour, sifted	⅓	cup sugar
3⅓	teaspoons baking powder	½	cup peanut butter
½	teaspoon salt	1½	cups skim milk

Preheat the oven to 350°.

In a medium-sized bowl, mix together the flour, baking powder, salt, and sugar. Add the peanut butter and, with a fork, mix lightly but thoroughly with the dry ingredients. Add the milk and beat thoroughly. Pour into an oiled 9 by 5 inch loaf pan. Smooth the top of the batter. Bake for 1 hour, or until a cake tester comes out dry. Cool in the pan for 15 minutes and remove.

Yields 1 loaf

FRENCH BREAD

This yields two loaves of crusty French bread in the true continental style. It requires about 3 hours for three risings, but otherwise small effort.

3½	cups sifted all-purpose flour	1½	teaspoons salt
1¼	cups warm water	2	teaspoons sugar
1	package dry yeast	1	tablespoon oil
			Corn meal

Place the flour on a square of waxed paper. In a large mixing bowl, pour the warm water, sprinkle in the yeast, and stir until dissolved. Add the salt, sugar, and oil and mix. Stir in enough flour to make a soft dough (you will need between 3 and 3½ cups). Knead the dough on a lightly floured board for 10 minutes or so, until it is smooth, elastic, and satiny. Place in an oiled bowl, turning it once so that the greased side is up. Cover the bowl and let the dough rise in a warm place (80 degrees), free from drafts, until it doubles in bulk. This should take about an hour. Punch down the dough and let rise again until it doubles. This will take about 30 minutes.

Place on a floured board, cover the dough, and let rest for 10 minutes. Divide the dough in half. Roll each half into an oblong 8 by 10 inches. Beginning at the wide side, roll up the rectangle tightly toward you. Pinch the edges together to seal. With a hand on each end, roll gently back and forth to lengthen to about 16 inches. Taper the ends of the loaf.

Place the two loaves on oiled baking sheets sprinkled with cornmeal. Brush the loaves with Cornstarch Glaze (below) and allow them to rise again, uncovered, in a warm place, free from drafts, for 1½ hours. Brush again with glaze. Cut 5 or 6 diagonal slashes in each loaf ¼ inch deep.

Preheat the oven to 400°. Place the loaves in a hot oven. After 10 minutes, remove them, brush again with glaze, and return to the oven. Bake 20 to 25 minutes longer, or until done.

Cornstarch Glaze

1 teaspoon cornstarch	½ cup boiling water
1 teaspoon cold water	

Blend the cornstarch and cold water. Stir slowly into the boiling water and cook until clear, stirring constantly. Cool slightly before using.

Yields 2 loaves

ONION-CARAWAY SEED BREAD

2½	cups sifted all-purpose flour	1	tablespoon oil
1	package dry yeast	2	teaspoons caraway seeds
¼	cup warm water	½	teaspoon salt
1	cup low-fat cottage cheese	2	tablespoons sugar
4	teaspoons instant minced onion	¼	teaspoon soda
		1	egg

Place the flour on a square of waxed paper. In a small bowl soak the yeast in the warm water and stir to dissolve. Heat the cottage cheese in a small pan over low heat until it becomes lukewarm, then combine it in a large mixing bowl with the onion, oil, caraway seeds, salt, sugar, soda, egg, and yeast mixture. Mix well. Add 1 cup of the sifted flour and beat it well. Gradually stir in the remainder of the flour, using as much as you need to make a stiff dough.

Place the dough in a greased bowl, turning it once so that the greased side is up. Cover with waxed paper and then with a towel. Allow it to double in bulk in a warm place free from drafts (about 1 hour). Punch down the dough and place in a well-oiled 2-quart heatproof casserole. Cover with a towel and allow it to rise again in a warm place free from drafts until doubled in bulk (30 to 40 minutes).

Preheat the oven to 350°. Bake for 40 to 50 minutes, or until nicely browned. Remove from the casserole, invert so that the rounded side is up, cut into pie-shaped wedges, and serve hot.

Yields 8- or 9-inch round loaf

SWEDISH TEA RING

This can be formed into 2 rings or one enormous and impressive ring adequate to serve 12.

3¾ cups sifted all-purpose flour	1 teaspoon butter flavoring
1 package dry yeast	¾ cup skim milk
¼ cup lukewarm water	1 egg, lightly beaten
¼ cup sugar	3 tablespoons oil
½ teaspoon salt	

Filling

⅓ cup sugar	¼ cup raisins
1½ teaspoons cinnamon	2 teaspoons oil
¼ cup walnuts, chopped	

Vanilla Glaze

1¾ cup confectioners sugar, sifted	1½ teaspoons vanilla
	1½ tablespoons water

Topping

⅓ cup chopped candied   ½ cup chopped walnuts
cherries or other fruits

Place the flour on a square of waxed paper.

In a small bowl, combine the yeast and lukewarm water and stir to dissolve. In a large mixing bowl, combine the sugar, salt, butter flavoring, milk, egg, oil, and yeast mixture and stir. Add half the flour and mix well. Add the remaining flour gradually and mix with your hands until it forms a ball of dough. Turn onto a lightly floured board and gently pat it out to flatten. Fold the dough down toward you and with the heels and palms of your hands press down and away from you (kneading), using an even, rolling motion. Continue this until the dough feels smooth, satiny, and elastic. Place the dough in an oiled bowl and turn it once so that the oiled side is up. Cover with waxed paper and then with a towel. Place in a warm spot free from drafts until it doubles in bulk (about 1 hour). Punch down. Cover again with waxed paper and a towel and allow to rise again in a warm spot free from drafts until nearly double (45 minutes to an hour). Punch down.

Roll the dough into a 9 by 15 inch rectangle. Prepare the filling by mixing together the sugar, cinnamon, walnuts, and raisins. Brush the dough with 2 teaspoons of oil and sprinkle with the sugar mixture. Roll up tightly, beginning at the wide side. Pinch the edges of the roll together tightly to seal it. Stretch the roll to make it even. Place the sealed edge down and form into a ring on an oiled cookie sheet. Pinch the two ends together firmly to seal the ring.

For the gussied-up look we are going to give the ring, make cuts with scissors around the outside perimeter of the ring about an inch apart, cutting into the ring about halfway. Turn these slices on their sides, so that the cinnamon and sugar striations show. This creates a loopy, scalloped effect. Cover the ring with a towel and let rise in a warm place free from drafts until double in bulk (45 minutes to an hour). Bake in the center of a preheated 375° oven until golden brown (25 to 30 minutes). Frost while still a bit warm with the Vanilla Glaze and sprinkle the top with the candied fruit and the nuts.

Yields 1 large or 2 medium-sized rings

CINNAMON COFFEE CAKE

This is a beaten, not a kneaded, dough that requires three risings.

3½ cups sifted all-purpose flour	½ teaspoon salt
2 packages dry yeast	½ cup skim milk
½ cup lukewarm water	1 egg
⅓ cup sugar	6 tablespoons oil

Coating

5 tablespoons oil	1½ teaspoons cinnamon
1 teaspoon butter flavoring	½ cup walnuts, chopped
¾ cup light brown sugar	¼ cup seedless raisins

Place the flour on a square of waxed paper.

In a small bowl combine the yeast with the lukewarm water and stir to dissolve. In a large mixing bowl, combine the sugar, salt, milk, and yeast mixture and stir well. With the electric mixer at medium speed, beat an egg into this mixture and add 2 cups of the flour. Beat well and add the 6 tablespoons of oil. Add the remainder of the flour slowly. It may be necessary to beat in the last of the flour by hand, using a wooden spoon. Beat until the dough is completely smooth. Cover the bowl with waxed paper and a towel, and place in a warm spot free from drafts until it doubles in bulk (about 1 hour). Punch down with a spoon, cover with waxed paper and a towel, and let it rise again until nearly double in bulk (45 minutes to an hour). Punch down.

To make the coating, combine the 5 tablespoons of oil with the butter flavoring in a small bowl. In another bowl, combine the brown sugar and cinnamon. Have ready the walnuts and raisins.

Oil an 8- or 9-inch springform or tube pan, 4 inches high. Scoop out small balls of the dough, about the size of a walnut, dunk lightly in the oil, roll in the cinnamon and sugar, and place in a layer in the bottom of the pan, scarcely touching. (If you are using a springform, leave a space in the middle.) When the pan bottom is covered, sprinkle with half the nuts and raisins. Repeat with the remaining dough for the top layer, sprinkle with the remaining nuts and raisins, and dribble whatever oil is left over the top. Cover again with waxed paper and a towel and let rise in a warm place free from drafts until nearly doubled (45 minutes to an hour).

Bake in a preheated 350° oven for 40 to 45 minutes, or until golden brown. Take a look at the cake after 35 minutes and, if the top seems to be getting too brown, cover with a piece of aluminum foil. When done, loosen and remove from the pan at once and let the cake cool on a wire rack.

If you wish, dribble some Vanilla Glaze (page 342) over the top.

Serves 10 to 12

BUTTERSCOTCH COOKIES

1	cup light brown sugar, firmly packed	½	teaspoon baking soda
6	tablespoons oil	¼	teaspoon cream of tartar
1	egg, beaten	½	teaspoon vanilla
1¾	cups sifted flour	½	cup chopped walnuts

In a medium-sized bowl, combine the brown sugar and oil and mix until smooth. Add the egg, flour, soda, and cream of tartar and mix well until thoroughly blended. Add the vanilla and nuts. Divide the dough into four parts and, with your hands, fashion them into rolls 1 inch in diameter and about 6 inches long. Wrap them in waxed paper and refrigerate at least 1 hour.

Preheat the oven to 375°. Slice the cookies about ¼ inch thick and place 1 inch apart on an oiled cookie sheet. Flatten them so they will be thin and uniform in size. Bake for 15 minutes. For a crisper cookie, leave them in the oven an additional 4 or 5 minutes.

Yields about 5 dozen

OATMEAL FRUIT COOKIES

These freeze very well, and you might consider doubling the recipe and tucking some away.

1 cup sifted flour
½ cup plus 2 table-
    spoons sugar
½ teaspoon baking
    powder
¼ teaspoon soda
½ teaspoon cinnamon
½ teaspoon salt
1½ cups rolled oats
    (quick or regular)

½ cup raisins or currants
¼ cup candied fruit,
    finely chopped
½ cup coarsely chopped
    walnuts
½ cup oil
1 egg, lightly beaten
¼ cup skim milk

Preheat the oven to 400°.
Sift together the flour, sugar, baking powder, soda, cinnamon, and salt. Add the rolled oats, raisins or currants, candied fruit, and nuts and mix thoroughly. Add the oil, egg, and milk, in that order. Mix until completely blended. Drop by teaspoonfuls on ungreased baking sheets about 1½ inches apart. Bake 10 to 12 minutes, until the cookies are a bit brown around the edges.

Makes 3 dozen

APPLE-NUT SQUARES

1 egg, lightly beaten
¾ cup sugar
½ teaspoon vanilla
½ cup flour
1 teaspoon baking
    powder

¼ teaspoon salt
2 medium-sized tart
    apples, peeled and
    chopped
½ cup broken walnuts

Preheat the oven to 350°.
Combine the egg, sugar, and vanilla. Sift together the flour, baking powder, and salt and add to the egg mixture. Fold in the apples and walnuts. This makes a stiff batter. With a spatula spread it evenly in an oiled 8 by 8 inch baking dish. Bake for 35 minutes, or until a cake tester comes out dry. Cut into 9 squares. Serve warm.

Serves 9

OLD-FASHIONED SUGAR COOKIES

1 cup flour, sifted
1 teaspoon baking
    powder

½ teaspoon salt
1 teaspoon grated
    lemon rind

1 egg
⅓ cup oil
1 teaspoon vanilla
½ teaspoon butter
flavoring (optional)

6 tablespoons sugar
2 tablespoons finely
chopped walnuts

Preheat the oven to 400°.

In a small bowl mix together the flour, baking powder, salt, and lemon rind. In a medium-sized bowl, beat the egg well with a fork, stir in the oil and vanilla, and the butter flavoring if desired, and blend in 5 tablespoons of the sugar. Add the flour mixture to the egg mixture and blend well. Drop by teaspoonfuls 2 inches apart on ungreased cookie sheets. Flatten each cookie with the lightly oiled bottom of a glass dipped in the remaining tablespoon of sugar and continue dipping the glass in the sugar as needed. Sprinkle the cookies with the nuts, lightly pressing them into the cookies. Bake 8 to 10 minutes, until the cookies are very lightly browned. Remove at once from the cookie sheets.

Yields 30 2-inch cookies

BUTTERSCOTCH BROWNIES

1 cup dark brown sugar,
firmly packed
¼ cup oil
1 egg, unbeaten
1 teaspoon vanilla
½ cup walnuts, coarsely
chopped

⅔ cup cake flour, sifted
1 teaspoon baking
powder
½ teaspoon salt
Confectioners sugar

Preheat the oven to 350°.

Combine the brown sugar and oil with the electric mixer—it will make short shrift of the sometimes lumpy brown sugar. Add the egg and mix well. Add the vanilla and fold in the nuts. Mix together the flour, baking powder, and salt and fold into the sugar mixture, stirring only until well blended.

Spread evenly in an oiled 8 by 8 inch baking pan. Bake for 25 to 30 minutes. Cut into squares while still warm. Dust lightly with confectioners sugar when cool.

Yields 16 squares

FRUIT-NUT MERINGUES

These do nicely with a fruit or sherbet dessert at the end of a hearty meal.

2 egg whites at room temperature
⅛ teaspoon salt
⅛ teaspoon cream of tartar
¾ cup superfine sugar
½ teaspoon vanilla
1 teaspoon lemon juice

¼ cup walnuts, finely chopped
⅓ cup dates, finely chopped
3 tablespoons mixed candied fruits, finely chopped (citron, cherries, orange peel, lemon peel, etc.)

The trick with meringues, if it can be considered a trick, is to add the sugar slowly. Otherwise, the meringue will not be stiff enough and will resemble tired marshmallow. You may use an electric beater.

With this word of caution, beat the egg whites with the salt and cream of tartar until stiff but not dry. At this point the meringue will form peaks that fall to the side. Add the sugar a tablespoon or so at a time, beating well after each addition. Beat after all the sugar is used until the mixture will crease and can be cut through with a knife. Beat in the vanilla and lemon juice. Gently fold in the nuts, dates, and candied fruits and blend well to distribute.

Lightly oil and flour a large cookie sheet, tapping the pan to shake off any excess flour. Drop the meringues onto it from a teaspoon. Bake in a slow (250°) oven for 30 to 35 minutes. Let cool slightly and remove with a spatula. Cool completely before storing in airtight containers.

Yields 3 to 3½ dozen

Variation: For Chocolate Meringues, beat 2 to 3 tablespoons of dry cocoa into the meringue after the sugar has been added. Omit the fruits. Proceed as above.

PECAN KISS CAKES

2 egg whites at room temperature
⅛ teaspoon salt

⅛ teaspoon cream of tartar
1 cup brown sugar

2	tablespoons white sugar	1½	cups coarsely chopped pecans or walnuts

Preheat the oven to 350°.

Beat the egg whites with the salt and cream of tartar until soft peaks form. An electric beater can be used for the entire process. Slowly beat in the sugar, a tablespoon or so at a time, until the meringue is stiff and shiny and stands in firm peaks. Fold in the nuts, distributing them well. Lightly oil and flour a large cookie sheet, tapping the pan to shake off any excess flour. Drop the meringue by spoonfuls, leaving room between. Place in a 350° oven for 5 minutes, then reduce the heat to 300° and bake for another 20 to 25 minutes, or until the meringues are set. Let them cool slightly, then remove them with a spatula.

Yields 24 to 26

DATE CONFECTIONS

These are not really a cookie or a candy, so I call them confections, which will serve for either purpose.

½	pound pitted dates, coarsely cut	½	cup sugar
1	egg white, unbeaten	½	teaspoon grated lemon rind
1	cup pecans or walnuts, coarsely broken	½	teaspoon vanilla
			Pinch of salt

Preheat the oven to 275°.

Use kitchen scissors for cutting the dates; they are easier to use than a knife or a chopper. (Coat the blades of the scissors with vegetable oil so that the dates don't stick.) In a small bowl mix all the ingredients together. Refrigerate for 2 hours, uncovered. Line a cookie sheet with ungreased aluminum foil. Form the date mixture into tiny balls the size of cherries and place on the sheet. Bake until the nuts that peek out from the dates are delicately brown (about 25 to 30 minutes).

Yields 25 to 30

SPICE SQUARES

This has been one of our family's cakebox mainstays for years, dating from a time when eggless, butterless, milkless cakes were a novelty and long before we knew of any reason to limit these ingredients. Rich in taste and fragrant with spices, it is always successful. As an added bonus, the whole preparation takes place in one saucepan.

1 cup dark brown sugar	1 tablespoon warm water
1 cup water	2 cups sifted flour
1½ cups raisins	½ teaspoon baking powder
⅓ cup oil	½ cup walnuts, coarsely broken
1 teaspoon cinnamon	Confectioners sugar
¼ teaspoon each cloves, salt, and nutmeg	
1 teaspoon soda	

Preheat the oven to 350°.

In a saucepan, boil together for 3 minutes the brown sugar, cup of water, raisins, oil, cinnamon, cloves, salt, and nutmeg. Cool the mixture.

Dissolve the soda in the tablespoon of warm water and add to the boiled mixture. Mix together the flour and baking powder and beat into the mixture. Fold in the nuts. Spread evenly in an oiled 8 by 12 inch baking pan and bake 25 minutes, or until a cake tester comes out dry. When cool, sprinkle with confectioners sugar and cut into squares.

Yields 24 squares

GINGERBREAD RING

½ cup polyunsaturated margarine (soft)	1 teaspoon cinnamon
½ cup brown sugar	½ teaspoon ground cloves
1 egg, well beaten	1 teaspoon baking soda
1½ cups unsifted flour	⅛ teaspoon salt
1 teaspoon ground ginger	½ cup molasses
	½ cup boiling water

Preheat the oven to 375°.

In a good-sized bowl, cream the margarine with the sugar, then beat in the egg. In another bowl, combine the flour, ginger, cinnamon, cloves, soda, and salt and mix well. Combine the molasses and boiling water in a measuring cup and mix well.

Add the flour mixture alternately with the molasses mixture to the creamed sugar, beating well between additions. Transfer the batter to a lightly oiled and floured 4-cup ring mold. Bake for 30 minutes, or until the cake tests done with a cake tester.

Cool in the mold for 15 minutes and turn out on a round cake platter. The center can be filled with a whipped topping, scoops of ice milk, or Banana Fluff (page 374).

Serves 8 to 10

APPLESAUCE CAKE

A moist, fruity, nutty, spicy loaf.

1 cup seedless raisins	1 teaspoon baking soda
2 tablespoons sherry or rum	3 tablespoons warm water
1 cup applesauce	1¾ cups flour, sifted
¾ cup sugar	½ cup walnuts, coarsely chopped
¼ teaspoon salt	Confectioners sugar
⅓ cup oil	
1 teaspoon cinnamon	
½ teaspoon ground cloves	

Preheat the oven to 350°.

Moisten the raisins with the sherry or rum and set aside. In a medium-sized mixing bowl, combine the applesauce, sugar, salt, and oil and mix well. Add the cinnamon and cloves. Dissolve the soda in the warm water and mix in. Sprinkle a little of the flour over the raisins to coat them. Beat the remainder of the flour into the applesauce mixture. Add the raisins and nuts and mix thoroughly. Pour into an oiled 9 by 5 inch loaf pan and bake for 45 to 55 minutes, or until a cake tester comes out dry. When cool, remove from the pan and dust the top lightly with confectioners sugar.

Yields 1 loaf

JIFFY COFFEE CAKE

This quickly made cake is prepared and baked in the same cake pan.

1 cup flour, sifted	¼ cup oil
1½ teaspoons baking powder	⅓ cup sugar
	1 egg
¼ teaspoon salt	½ cup (about) skim milk

Topping

1 tablespoon oil	½ cup chopped walnuts
2 tablespoons sugar	2 tablespoons skim milk
½ teaspoon cinnamon	

Preheat the oven to 350°.

Sift together the flour, baking powder, and salt. Pour the ¼ cup of oil into an 8-inch round cake pan and oil the sides of the pan. Stir in the sugar with a fork and cover with the flour mixture. Break the egg into a measuring cup and add enough milk to make ¾ cup. Mix well and pour into the cake pan, stirring until all the flour is absorbed and the batter is smooth. Bake for 25 minutes.

Remove the cake from the oven, dribble the tablespoon of oil over the top of the cake, sprinkle with a mixture of the sugar, cinnamon, and nuts, and pour the 2 tablespoons of milk over the topping. Return to the oven for 5 minutes. Cut into wedges and serve warm.

Serves 8 to 10

TEA CAKE

This is a delicious and obliging cake that comes out of the oven complete with topping.

1½ tablespoons lemon juice or vinegar	1 cup brown sugar
	¾ cup oil
1 cup skim milk	1 teaspoon baking powder
2½ cups sifted flour	
½ teaspoon cinnamon	1 teaspoon baking soda
½ teaspoon nutmeg	1 egg, lightly beaten
¾ cup (scant) sugar	⅔ cup white raisins

1	cup walnuts, coarsely broken	¼	heaping teaspoon cinnamon

Preheat the oven to 375°. Oil a 9- or 10-inch tube pan.

Add the lemon juice or vinegar to the milk and set aside. In a large bowl, combine the flour, ½ teaspoon of cinnamon, nutmeg, and sugar. Mix with a fork. There will be some lumps in the mixture; remove ¼ cup of the largest ones and set aside for the topping.

To the flour mixture in the large bowl add the oil, baking powder, soda, egg, and the milk in that order, beating well between each addition. Add the raisins and nuts and mix well. Pour the batter into the pan.

Add the ¼ teaspoon cinnamon to the topping mixture, mix, and sprinkle over the batter. Bake for 50 to 55 minutes, or until a cake tester comes out dry. Cool for at least 20 minutes and remove from the pan.

Serves 10 to 12

CHOCOLATE LOAF CAKE

A quickly made, moist, not-too-sweet, and delicious chocolate cake with good texture. The only unusual ingredient is mayonnaise, which, on second thought, is not too unusual, since mayonnaise is a combination of egg yolk and oil—two standard cake ingredients.

2	cups flour, sifted	⅓	cup cocoa
1¼	cups sugar	1	cup cold water
½	teaspoon salt	1	teaspoon vanilla
1¾	teaspoons baking soda	¾	cup mayonnaise

Preheat the oven to 350°.

In a medium-sized bowl, combine the flour, sugar, salt, soda, and cocoa and mix well. Add the water and vanilla and beat until smooth. Add the mayonnaise and beat well until the batter is completely smooth and free from lumps—about 100 strokes. Oil a 9 by 5 inch loaf pan. Line the pan bottom with waxed paper and oil the waxed paper. Transfer the batter to the pan and bake for 50 minutes, or until a cake tester comes out dry. Let cool thoroughly before removing from the pan (at least 20 minutes). Invert the cake on a platter and remove the waxed paper. You may use an icing if you like, but the cake has such a rich, fudgy taste that a little powdered sugar sprinkled over the top to give it a finished look is all it needs.

Serves 8 to 10

Variation: This may also be baked in two 8-inch round layer cake pans, prepared with oiled waxed paper as above. Bake for 30 or 35 minutes. Frost with white boiled icing or any other icing you like.

APPLE CAKE

3 medium-sized apples, peeled and cut into small chunks	1 teaspoon cinnamon
	½ teaspoon salt
	½ teaspoon nutmeg
1 cup sugar	1 teaspoon baking soda
1 egg, lightly beaten	½ cup walnuts, coarsely chopped
½ cup oil	
1½ cups flour, sifted	½ cup raisins

Preheat the oven to 350°.

Place the diced apples in a bowl with the sugar. Allow to stand for 10 minutes. Add the egg and oil and blend lightly. Add the flour, cinnamon, salt, nutmeg, and soda and stir only until blended. Stir in the nuts and raisins. Transfer to an oiled 8 by 8 inch baking pan and bake for 55 minutes, or until a cake tester comes out dry. Cut into squares when cool. This may be served with Whipped Topping (page 374).

Yields 16 squares

APRICOT UPSIDE-DOWN CAKE

2 egg whites	¼ teaspoon baking soda
Pinch of salt	½ teaspoon salt
¾ cup sugar	2½ tablespoons oil
1 cup plus 2 tablespoons sifted flour	½ cup skim buttermilk
	1½ teaspoons vanilla
3 teaspoons baking powder	

Topping

2 tablespoons oil	6 maraschino cherries
2 tablespoons brown	(optional)
sugar	1 1-pound-1-ounce can
	apricot halves, drained

Preheat the oven to 350°.

Oil a 9-inch round glass cake pan and lightly flour the sides. Beat the egg whites with the pinch of salt until soft peaks form. Gradually beat in ¼ cup of the sugar and continue beating until the meringue is stiff and shiny.

Sift the remaining sugar, flour, baking powder, soda, and salt into another bowl. Add the oil, buttermilk, and vanilla and beat until smooth. Fold in the meringue and blend well.

For the topping, mix the oil and brown sugar in a cake pan and spread evenly over the bottom. Place half a maraschino cherry in the center of each apricot half (if desired) and arrange the apricots cut side down over the bottom of the pan in a pleasing design. (You may substitute pineapple slices or canned peach crescents.) Pour the batter over the fruit and bake for 35 minutes, or until it tests done. Remove from the oven and lightly run a spatula around the cake, loosening the sides. Invert the cake onto a serving platter and allow it to cool for 15 minutes. Remove the cake pan from the cake when cooled.

Serves 10

MOCHA UPSIDE-DOWN CAKE

For people suffering from chocolatomania. The symptoms? An overwhelming desire for something chocolate.

1 cup flour, sifted	3 tablespoons cocoa
⅔ cup sugar	3 tablespoons oil
⅛ teaspoon salt	½ cup skim milk
2 teaspoons baking powder	1 teaspoon vanilla

Topping

¼ cup brown sugar	1 cup cold double-
¼ cup white sugar	strength coffee
3 tablespoons cocoa	

Preheat the oven to 350°.

Mix together the flour, sugar, salt, baking powder, and cocoa. Blend in the oil, milk, and vanilla and beat until smooth. Oil a 9-inch round glass cake baking dish, 2 inches deep, and spread the batter evenly in it.

For the topping, combine the sugar and cocoa, mix well, and sprinkle evenly over the batter. Pour the coffee over the top. Bake for 40 minutes. Invert the cake, or perhaps we should call it pudding, on a serving dish. Lift off the pan and allow the sauce to drip down over the pudding. Serve warm or cold.

Serves 8

ANGEL FOOD CAKE

The angel food cake mix is the only prepared cake mix I know of at this time that is acceptable for cholesterol-concerned people. When using the mix, you can make a coffee-flavored cake by either substituting strong coffee for the water or by adding a tablespoon of instant coffee to the dry mix.

The following recipe is for those who prefer to make their own. Angel food cakes can be tricky, so follow the directions precisely.

1 cup sifted cake flour	1¼ teaspoons cream of tartar
1¼ cups superfine granulated sugar	¼ teaspoon salt
1¼ cups egg whites (about 12)	1 teaspoon vanilla
	¼ teaspoon almond extract

Have the egg whites at room temperature before you start. They won't achieve maximum volume if they are cold. Preheat the oven to 325°.

Sift the flour with ½ cup of the sugar 3 times and set aside.

In a large bowl, using either a wire whisk, a rotary beater, or an electric mixer, beat the egg whites until foamy. Add the cream of tartar and salt and beat until soft peaks form when the beater is lifted out of the meringue.

Add the remaining sugar 2 tablespoons at a time, beating about 10 seconds after each addition. Add the vanilla and almond flavoring.

Place the flour and sugar mixture in the sifter and sift about 3 tablespoons over the surface of the meringue. Do not stir or beat the flour into the meringue; this will diminish the amount of air you have just pumped into it. Instead, cut and fold the flour-sugar mixture gently into the meringue with a wide rubber spatula, cutting down through the center of the mixture, lifting a small amount, and turning it over, moving the bowl a quarter of a turn with each stroke. Cut and fold only until the flour disappears—not more than 10 strokes. Repeat this process until all the flour and sugar are added and are completely blended.

Push this batter, which will be very thick, into an ungreased 10-inch tube pan, trying not to stir it in the moving process. With a knife, carefully cut through the batter 5 or 6 times, to make sure there are no large air bubbles. Smooth the batter so it is level and even.

Bake 55 to 60 minutes. The cake is done when the top springs back when lightly touched. Don't worry if deep cracks appear in the top of the cake. That's *comme il faut* with this species of cake.

As soon as the cake is removed from the oven, invert the pan on a bottle or the neck of a funnel and let it hang until it is cold—that is, unless your baking pan is equipped with legs that raise the edges of the pan while cooling.

To remove the cake from the pan, loosen from the sides and tube with a spatula. Turn the pan over and hit the edge sharply to loosen.

Angel food cake does not freeze well. Having no fat, it becomes tough, but slices of the cake are delicious toasted.

Yields 10-inch cake

Variations:

Cocoa Angel Food Cake: Reduce the flour to ¾ cup and sift with the ½ cup of sugar as in the preceding recipe, adding ¼ cup of cocoa.

Mocha Angel Food Cake: Add to Cocoa Angel Food Cake 2 teaspoons of instant coffee and proceed as above.

CHIFFON SPICE CAKE

2   eggs, separated
    Pinch of salt
½   cup sugar
2¼ cups cake flour, sifted
1   teaspoon baking
    powder
¾   teaspoon baking soda
¾   teaspoon salt

¾   teaspoon nutmeg
½   teaspoon ground cloves
¾   teaspoon cinnamon
1   cup brown sugar,
    firmly packed
⅓   cup oil
1   cup skim buttermilk

Preheat the oven to 350°. Lightly oil and flour two 8- or 9-inch round layer cake tins.

Beat the egg whites until frothy, add the pinch of salt, and gradually beat in the sugar, a little at a time, until the meringue is very stiff and shiny. Set aside.

Sift the flour and, in a large bowl, combine it with the baking powder, soda, salt, nutmeg, cloves, cinnamon, brown sugar, oil, and ⅔ of the buttermilk. Beat for a minute with the electric beater at medium speed, or 150 strokes by hand. Scrape the sides and bottom of the bowl frequently. Add the remaining buttermilk and the egg yolks. Beat an additional minute, continuing to scrape the sides and bottom of the bowl. Carefully fold in the meringue and blend well. Divide the batter in the prepared pans. Bake 30 to 35 minutes, or until the layers test done. Cool and remove from the pans. Frost with Fluffy White Icing (page 375).

Serves 10 to 12

APRICOT CAKE

1   cup sugar
2   eggs, well beaten
1¾ cups cake flour
½   teaspoon salt

2½ teaspoons baking
    powder
½   cup skim milk
⅓   cup oil
1   teaspoon vanilla

Preheat the oven to 375°.

In a good-sized bowl, mix the sugar with the eggs and beat until light. Sift together the flour, salt, and baking powder. In a measuring cup, stir the milk and oil to a froth. Add alternately with the flour to the sugar and egg mixture, beating well after each addition. You can do this in an electric mixer if you have one. Beat in the vanilla.

Oil and lightly flour two 8- or 9-inch round cake tins. Divide the batter between them. Bake for 25 to 30 minutes, or until the cake tests done with a cake tester. Let cool for 5 minutes in the pans. Turn out and cool on racks.

Apricot Filling and Meringue

2	cups dried apricots	¼	teaspoon cream of tartar
1½	cups water		Pinch of salt
1	cup sugar		
1	teaspoon lemon rind	4	tablespoons sugar
2	egg whites	1	teaspoon lemon juice

Wash the apricots. Place in a saucepan with the water, cover, and simmer for about 30 minutes until tender. Put through a sieve or a food mill, juice and all. Add the cup of sugar and the lemon rind to the apricot puree. Cook slowly until thick, stirring frequently.

Split the cake layers in half. Reserve ⅔ of the puree for the meringue and spread the rest between the 3 bottom layers.

Beat the egg whites with the cream of tartar and salt until soft peaks form. Beat in the 4 tablespoons of sugar very slowly, a little at a time, and continue beating until the meringue becomes stiff and glossy. Fold in the remaining puree and the lemon juice. Frost the top and sides of the cake with the apricot meringue, giving it additional eye appeal with twirls and swirls.

Serves 10 to 12

Note: It is easier to split cake layers after they have stood for a few hours, so make the layers the first thing in the morning or even the day before you plan to use them.

TWO-EGG SPONGE CAKE

This airy, delicate cake can do yeoman's service for practically any occasion. Baked in two 8- or 9-inch round layers, filled with icing, custard, or fruit preserves, and generously covered with a fluffy frosting, it can be a fine party affair.

You may also bake it in a single layer in a 2-inch-deep 8 by 12 inch pan. It will yield from 24 to 28 servings and can be dressed up with fruit, a thin chocolate glaze, any of the uncooked toppings on pages 373–74, or served plain with a sprinkling of confectioners sugar. I generally freeze half for future use when I bake it in this single layer. Like most cakes and breads, it can be frozen, thawed, and refrozen and be none the worse.

2 eggs, separated	3 teaspoons baking
Pinch of salt	powder
1½ cups sugar	½ teaspoon salt
2¼ cups cake flour, sifted,	⅓ cup oil
or 2 cups all-purpose	1 cup skim milk
flour, sifted three	1 teaspoon vanilla
times	1 teaspoon grated
	lemon rind

Preheat the oven to 350°. Have the egg whites at room temperature. Beat the egg whites with the pinch of salt until frothy. Add ½ cup of the sugar, a little at a time, beating well between each addition, and continue beating until the meringue becomes stiff and shiny and stands in firm peaks.

Sift the rest of the sugar with the flour, baking powder, and salt into a large mixing bowl. Add the oil, half the milk, the vanilla, and the lemon rind and beat with the electric mixer at medium speed for 1 minute (or 150 strokes by hand). Scrape the bottom and sides of the bowl constantly. Add the rest of the milk and the egg yolks and beat a minute longer, continuing to scrape the sides of the bowl.

With a spatula, fold the stiffly beaten meringue gently into the batter. Turn the bowl a little each time you cut the meringue down through the batter, across the bottom, and up and over.

Pour the batter into two oiled and lightly floured 8- or 9-inch round layer cake pans, or an 8 by 12 inch oblong pan.

Layers will need 30 to 35 minutes for baking; the oblong pan, 40 to 45 minutes. Bake until a cake tester comes out dry, the tops are nicely browned, and the sides begin to pull away from the pan.

Remove the layers from the pan when cool. Frost with Sea Foam Frosting (page 376) or your choice of frosting.

RUM CAKE

2 eggs	1 tablespoon oil
¼ teaspoon salt	1 cup sifted cake flour
1 cup sugar	1 teaspoon baking
1 teaspoon rum	powder
flavoring	Apricot preserves
½ cup skim milk	

Preheat the oven to 350°.

Beat the eggs until thick and lemon colored. The electric mixer will be fine. Beat in the salt, sugar, and rum flavoring. In a small saucepan heat the milk and oil to the boiling point. Beat this into the egg mixture. Sift the flour and baking powder and add to the mixture, beating only until smooth—no longer.

Oil a 9-inch round cake pan 2 inches deep or a 9-inch springform. Pour the batter into the pan and bake for 35 to 40 minutes, or until the cake tests done.

While the cake is baking in the oven, make the following:

Rum Coffee Syrup

⅔ cup sugar	¼ cup (or more) rum
⅔ cup strong coffee	

Combine the sugar and coffee in a small saucepan. Stir over low heat until the sugar dissolves. Boil 5 minutes and cool. Add the rum.

When the cake is finished, remove it from the oven and allow it to cool in the pan for 10 minutes. Turn the cake layer out of the pan on a round platter and spoon the syrup slowly over the entire surface of the warm cake.

Let the cake rest overnight. It is always easier to split a cake that has had a chance to firm up a bit after leaving the oven. Split the layer equally into two parts. (I always stick a few toothpicks around the outside perimeter of the cake as a guide.) Cover the bottom half with Rum Cream Filling (next page) and replace the top.

Rum Cream Filling

1 package vanilla pudding mix	1½ teaspoons rum flavoring
1¾ cups (scant) skim milk	

Prepare the vanilla pudding according to the package directions, reducing the amount of milk to a scant 1¾ cups. Add the rum flavoring and mix. Pour into a bowl, cover with waxed paper or foil, and chill in the refrigerator. When thoroughly chilled, beat with a rotary beater until the pudding is light and fluffy.

Cover the top of cake with a thin coating of apricot preserves—just enough to glaze it. Make a border around the top of the cake with Apricot Meringue (below), run through a pastry tube.

Apricot Meringue

1 egg white	2 tablespoons sugar
¼ teaspoon cream of tartar	2 tablespoons apricot preserves
Pinch of salt	¼ teaspoon vanilla

Beat the egg white with the cream of tartar and salt until it forms soft peaks. Add the sugar slowly, a little at a time, and continue beating until the meringue becomes stiff and glossy. Fold in a little of the clear part of the apricot preserves, without the fruit, which would clog the pastry tube. Blend well and add the vanilla. Refrigerate the cake until ready to serve.

Serves 10 to 12

FRUIT TORTE

Strawberries, blueberries, or raspberries, shiny with glaze, are equally effective on this torte. It must rest at least 8 hours, so plan to make it the first thing in the morning or, better still, the day before you use it.

Torte

3 egg whites	1 cup sugar
Pinch of salt	1 teaspoon vanilla
¼ teaspoon cream of tartar	1 teaspoon baking powder

| 1 | cup graham cracker crumbs | ¾ | cup walnuts, finely chopped |

Glazed Berries

| 1 | pint berries | 2 | teaspoons cornstarch |
| 1 | cup currant jelly | 1 | tablespoon lemon juice |

Preheat the oven to 350°. Oil a 9- or 10-inch springform. Have the egg whites at room temperature. In a medium-sized bowl beat them with the salt and cream of tartar until soft peaks form. Add the sugar slowly, a couple of tablespoons at a time, beating well between each addition, until the meringue is stiff and shiny and stands in firm peaks. Beat in the vanilla and baking powder. Carefully fold in the crumbs and nuts. Pour into the springform and bake for 20 to 30 minutes, or until the top is light brown and well set. Remove from the oven and let cool. When completely cool, remove the sides from the springform. Let stand at least 8 hours before serving.

Two hours before you are ready to serve it, cover with the glazed berries and refrigerate.

To glaze the berries, melt the jelly over low heat in a small saucepan, stirring constantly. Dissolve the cornstarch in the lemon juice and add to the melted jelly. Cook 3 or 4 minutes, until the mixture thickens and becomes clear. Cool, then add the berries and mix lightly to coat them completely. Arrange over the top of the torte.

Serves 10

GLAZED CHEESECAKE

If you have been under the impression that a smooth, creamy cheesecake can be achieved only with cream cheese, lots of eggs, and cream, this recipe should be a welcome one. Made with cottage cheese and skim milk, it has a completely satisfying texture and taste. A variety of fruit toppings, described below, can be made according to your mood and the ingredients available in your pantry.

Graham Cracker Crust

| 1¼ | cups graham cracker crumbs | ¼ | cup sugar |
| | | ⅓ | cup oil |

Lightly oil a 9- or 10-inch springform and blend the crumbs, sugar, and oil together in it. Pack the mixture firmly on the bottom and sides of the pan with your fingers, bringing the crumbs to within an inch of the top of the rim. Bake in a 350° oven for 10 minutes. Let cool while you prepare the cheesecake.

Cheesecake

1½ pounds (3 cups) low-fat cottage cheese
¾ cup sugar
3 tablespoons flour
2 eggs

1 scant cup skim milk or evaporated skimmed milk, undiluted
¼ teaspoon salt
½ teaspoon vanilla
Juice and grated rind of 1 lemon

Preheat the oven to 350°.

In the large bowl of your electric mixer, beat the cottage cheese at high speed until perfectly smooth. The success of your cake depends upon the vigor of this operation. If any lumps remain in the cheese, the cake will have a grainy texture, so give the beating procedure plenty of time. Blend in the sugar and flour and continue beating until thoroughly mixed.

Add the eggs one at a time and beat well after each addition. Reduce the mixer speed to low and add the milk, salt, vanilla, and lemon juice and rind. Taste the mixture to see if it is sweet enough. (Sometimes I add a dollop of artificial sweetener.) The mixture will be quite thin. Ladle it carefully into the cooled graham cracker crust. Bake 50 minutes, or until set. Don't overbake it; it will firm as it cools. Let cool at least ½ hour before adding the glaze.

Bing Cherry Glaze

1 1-pound can pitted black Bing cherries

Cornstarch
3 tablespoons lemon juice

Drain the juice from the cherries and reserve it. Arrange the cherries over the top of the cake. Measure the cherry juice and mix with cornstarch to the proportion of 1 tablespoon of cornstarch to 1 cup of liquid. Place in a small saucepan and add the lemon juice. Cook over medium heat, stirring constantly, 2 or 3 minutes, or until the syrup thickens and becomes shiny and transparent. When cool, pour evenly over the cherries. Refrigerate the cake.

Fresh Strawberry Glaze

1 pint fresh strawberries	2 teaspoons cornstarch
½ cup sugar	1 tablespoon sugar

Wash the berries, slice them, and place in a small bowl with the ½ cup sugar. Mix lightly. Let stand about 2 hours, until the sugar draws ½ cup of juice from the berries.

Drain off the juice and place in a saucepan with the cornstarch and the tablespoon of sugar. Stir until smooth. If the juice looks too light, add a drop or two of red food coloring. Cook over medium heat until the mixture is thickened and shiny (2 or 3 minutes). Place the berries on top of the cake and spread the glaze evenly over them.

Frozen strawberries or raspberries may also be used for the glaze. Defrost the berries and follow the directions for Bing Cherry Glaze (above). Taste for sweetness; the frozen berries are usually not sweet enough, and you may have to add sugar.

Apricot Glaze

½ cup sugar	1 tablespoon lemon juice
2 tablespoons cornstarch	1⅓ cups cooked or canned apricots, drained
¼ cup undiluted frozen orange juice, thawed	

In a small saucepan, combine the sugar and cornstarch and stir in the orange and lemon juice. Put the apricots through a food mill or blender and add this puree to the pan. Cook over medium heat, stirring constantly, until it comes to a boil and becomes thick and clear (2 or 3 minutes). When cool, spread over the cheesecake.

Plain Cheesecake

Using the basic cheesecake recipe (above), increase the vanilla to 1 teaspoon and add ½ teaspoon of cinnamon.

Reserve ⅓ cup of crumbs from the crust mixture and spread over the top of the cake before baking.

Serves 10 to 12

PEACH CUSTARD TART

Preheat the oven to 375°.

Crust

1¼ cups flour
1½ teaspoons sugar
½ teaspoon salt
2½ tablespoons cold skim milk

6 tablespoons oil
½ cup walnuts, finely chopped

In a medium-sized bowl, mix together the flour, sugar, and salt. Combine the milk and oil in a measuring cup and whip with a fork until creamy. Pour over the flour mixture and mix until completely dampened. Mix in the nuts.

Lightly oil an 8- or 9-inch springform and transfer the flour mixture to the pan. With your fingers, firmly press the mixture evenly over the bottom and halfway up the sides of the pan.

Filling

1 1-pound-14-ounce can sliced peaches, drained
½ cup peach syrup
½ cup sugar
½ teaspoon cinnamon

1 egg, slightly beaten
1 cup undiluted evaporated skimmed milk

Drain the peach slices well, reserving ½ cup of syrup. Arrange them over the bottom crust in the springform. Mix together the sugar and cinnamon and sprinkle evenly over the peaches. Bake for 20 minutes.

Meanwhile, combine the reserved syrup, egg, and milk. After the 20 minutes of baking, remove the springform from the oven and pour the egg mixture over the peaches. Return to the oven and continue baking for 35 minutes longer, or until the custard is firm except in the very center. This will become firm on standing.

Cool for about 20 minutes and remove the sides of the springform. You can even off the top crust with a paring knife if it is a bit jagged or projects above the filling. Serve at room temperature.

Serves 9

PIE PASTRY

Pie crusts made with oil are tender, but they never achieve the degree of flakiness and delicacy that we get in pie dough made with conventional solid white shortenings. For this reason, I have given up two-crust pies—not an unmixed blessing, for few of us need the calories in the second crust anyway.

The following recipe yields a 9-inch pie shell. For two crusts, double all the ingredients except the salt.

1⅓ cups sifted flour	⅓ cup oil
¾ teaspoon salt	3 tablespoons cold skim milk

Mix together the flour and salt. Pour the oil and milk into a measuring cup but do not stir. Add the liquid to the flour and stir to mix. Press into a smooth ball and flatten it a little.

Put the dough between two 12-inch squares of waxed paper. Dampen the tabletop to prevent slipping. Roll out the dough to form a circle to the edges of the paper. Remove the top sheet of paper, invert the dough over a pie plate, ease into the plate, and peel off the paper. Flute the edge.

If the shell is to be baked with a filling, bake at the temperature required for the filling. For a baked shell that will be filled later, prick the entire surface of the crust and place in a hot oven preheated to 450°. Bake for 8 to 10 minutes, until the crust is golden. To prevent the crust from billowing up and losing its shape during baking, cover with waxed paper and some beans or a weight of some kind, such as an aluminum foil pie plate.

DEEP-DISH APPLE PIE

1 cup dark brown sugar	¼ teaspoon cinnamon
	¼ teaspoon salt
1 tablespoon flour	2 tablespoons lemon
¼ teaspoon nutmeg	juice

1 tablespoon grated	1 tablespoon oil
lemon rind	Pie pastry for 1 crust
3 pounds tart apples	(page 367)
(about 6 to 8), peeled,	1 tablespoon egg white,
cored, and sliced about	lightly beaten
⅜ inch thick	Sugar

Preheat the oven to 425°. Combine the brown sugar, flour, nutmeg, cinnamon, salt, and lemon juice and rind. Toss with the apples to coat them. Transfer to a lightly oiled deep baking dish or pie pan. Dribble the tablespoon of oil over the apples. Cover the apples with the crust and flute the edges. Brush with the egg white and sprinkle with sugar. Cut a few decorative slits in the top crust for the steam to escape.

Bake for 15 minutes, then reduce the heat to 375° and bake another 20 to 30 minutes, until the crust is nicely browned and the juice begins to bubble through the slits.

Serves 8

APPLE MERINGUE TART

The juxtaposition of two events such as the availability of crisp cooking apples and the occasion for an important dessert may be dealt with most satisfactorily with this fruity, refreshing tart. On second thought I suppose it isn't really a tart, since it has no bottom crust, but the tapioca gives the apples enough cohesiveness to allow it to slice nicely.

3 pounds (6 to 8) crisp	1 tablespoon sugar
tart cooking apples	4 tablespoons quick-
⅓ cup white wine	cooking tapioca
Grated rind of 1 lemon	½ cup currant jelly

Meringue

3 egg whites at room	⅛ teaspoon cream of
temperature	tartar
Pinch of salt	¾ cup sugar
	½ teaspoon vanilla

Preheat the oven to 250°.

Peel and core the apples. Cut into not-too-thin slices— about ¼ to ⅜ inch thick. Place the slices in a large saucepan with a tightly fitting cover. Add the wine, cover the pot, and cook slowly for about 10 minutes. Shake the pan frequently, holding the lid in place. Do not overcook the apples—they should be a bit tender but firm, for they will have additional time to cook in the oven. Remove the apples from the heat and add the lemon rind, sugar, and tapioca. Toss to coat the slices evenly.

Lightly oil a 10-inch glass or porcelain ovenproof pie dish that can be used for serving. Spread the apples evenly over the bottom. Dot with the jelly.

To prepare the meringue, beat the egg whites with the salt until frothy. Beat in the cream of tartar until soft peaks form. Slowly add the sugar, a little at a time, and beat until the meringue is very stiff and glossy. Beat in the vanilla.

Pile the meringue over the apple slices, making a swirl pattern with the back of a spoon. Or better still, pipe the meringue through a pastry bag, using a large star tip.

Bake for 55 to 60 minutes. Cool and serve at room temperature.

Serves 8 to 10

APRICOT VELVET PIE

This may be made with conventional piecrust, a graham cracker crust, or the following:

Meringue Crust

3 egg whites at room temperature	¾ cup sugar
¼ teaspoon cream of tartar	¾ cup finely chopped walnuts
Pinch of salt	1 teaspoon orange extract

Preheat the oven to 275°.

Beat the egg whites until foamy. Add the cream of tartar and salt and continue beating until soft peaks form. Beat in the sugar slowly, a couple of tablespoons at a time, until the meringue is thick and glossy. Fold in the nuts and orange extract. Lightly oil and flour a 10-inch pie plate. Spread the meringue evenly over the bottom and sides and bake for 50 minutes to an hour. Cool thoroughly before filling.

Filling

1	pint (2 cups) dried apricots	2	egg whites
1	cup water	2	tablespoons sugar
1	cup sugar	⅓	cup chilled apricot nectar
3	tablespoons lemon juice	⅓	cup dried skim milk
½	cup orange juice	2	tablespoons lemon juice
	Dash of cinnamon	3	tablespoons sugar
1	tablespoon unflavored gelatin		Slivered, toasted almonds or chopped walnuts
1½	cups cold water		
1	teaspoon almond extract		

In a medium-sized saucepan, place the apricots, cup of water, cup of sugar, 3 tablespoons of lemon juice, orange juice, and cinnamon. Simmer until the apricots are tender and the liquid is syrupy (20 to 30 minutes). While they are cooking, sprinkle the gelatin into the cold water to soften and heat until thoroughly dissolved, stirring constantly.

Puree the apricots (and syrup) in a blender or a food mill. Add the almond extract. Combine the puree with the gelatin mixture and chill until it becomes thick and is beginning to set. When it reaches this stage, beat well with a rotary beater.

Beat the egg whites until soft peaks form. Add the 2 tablespoons of sugar, a little at a time, beating well between each addition, until the meringue is stiff and shiny.

Pour the apricot nectar into a medium-sized bowl and add the dried milk. Whip 3 or 4 minutes, until soft peaks form. Add the 2 tablespoons of lemon juice and continue whipping 3 or 4 minutes longer, while gradually adding the 3 tablespoons of sugar. Whip until stiff peaks form.

Gently fold the meringue into the apricot mixture. Fold in the whipped milk and blend well. Pour the mixture into a baked meringue or pastry shell and sprinkle the top with the nuts. Chill until firm.

Serves 8 to 10

LIME CHIFFON PIE

1	3-ounce package lime gelatin	¾	cup boiling water
		½	cup sugar

Grated rind of 1 lemon
½ cup dried skim milk
½ cup ice water
2 tablespoons lemon juice

1 baked pastry shell
(page 367) or Graham
Cracker Crust (page 363)
2 tablespoons freshly
grated orange rind

Dissolve the gelatin in the boiling water. Add 4 table-spoons of the sugar and stir until dissolved. Add the lemon rind. Chill until syrupy (30 to 40 minutes).

Place the dried milk in a chilled mixing bowl. Add the ice water and beat 3 or 4 minutes until soft peaks form. Add the lemon juice and continue beating. Add the remaining sugar gradually, beating all the while until the mixture stands in stiff peaks. Fold this billowy white mass into the syrupy gelatin and combine thoroughly. Turn into a pastry shell (or crumb crust) and spread evenly. Sprinkle the top with grated orange rind. Chill until firm.

Serves 8

FRUIT PIE WITH COTTAGE CHEESE LATTICE

1 No. 2 can pitted sour
  red cherries (2½ cups)
1 10-ounce package
  sliced frozen
  strawberries, thawed
1 cup sugar
¼ teaspoon salt

2 tablespoons quick-
  cooking tapioca
2 tablespoons
  cornstarch
2 tablespoons lemon
  juice
1 unbaked pastry shell
  (page 367)

Cottage Cheese Garnish

10 ounces skim-milk
   cottage cheese
2 teaspoons sugar

½ teaspoon vanilla
1 teaspoon lemon juice

Preheat the oven to 425°.

Drain the cherries and strawberries. Reserve the juice. In a small saucepan, mix together the sugar, salt, tapioca, and cornstarch. Add the two fruit syrups and cook over low heat, stirring constantly, until thick and clear (this will take 7 or 8 minutes). Remove from the heat, mix in the cherries and strawberries, and add the lemon juice.

Allow to cool a little before pouring into the pie shell. Bake for 20 to 30 minutes, or until the crust is golden.

For the garnish, beat the cottage cheese until completely smooth and creamy. Add the sugar, vanilla, and lemon juice. When the pie is baked and completely cooled, decorate the top, lattice fashion, with the cottage cheese mixture forced through a pastry tube.

Serves 8

PEACH COBBLER

½ cup sugar
1 tablespoon cornstarch
1 1-pound-4-ounce can sliced peaches
1 tablespoon lemon juice
½ teaspoon cinnamon

1 cup sifted all-purpose flour
1 tablespoon sugar
½ teaspoon salt
1½ teaspoons baking powder
3 tablespoons oil
½ cup skim milk

Preheat the oven to 400°.

In a saucepan, combine the ½ cup of sugar and the cornstarch. Add the peaches and syrup and the lemon juice. Bring to a boil, stirring constantly, and boil for 1 minute. Pour into a 1½-quart casserole and sprinkle with the cinnamon. Place in the oven while you prepare the biscuit topping.

Sift together the flour, sugar, salt, and baking powder into a small mixing bowl. Add the oil and milk and stir. Drop by spoonfuls onto the hot fruit. Bake 25 to 30 minutes, or until the biscuits are golden brown. Serve warm.

Serves 6

STRAWBERRY MERINGUES

3 egg whites
Pinch salt
¼ teaspoon cream of tartar
¾ cup sugar
½ teaspoon vanilla

1 teaspoon grated lemon rind
1 cup currant jelly
2 teaspoons cornstarch
1 tablespoon lemon juice
1 pint large strawberries, hulls removed

Preheat the oven to 250°.

Beat the egg whites until foamy, add the salt and cream of tartar, and continue beating until soft peaks form. Beat in the sugar, a little at a time, until the meringue is thick and glossy and stands in firm peaks. Fold in the vanilla and lemon rind.

Lightly oil and flour a cookie sheet. Tap the pan to remove any excess flour. With two spoons, form 3-inch nests of meringue, flattening the bottoms and coaxing up the sides so there will be a place for the filling. You might use a pastry bag with a broad fluted tip to run a border of meringue around the outside rim of each nest. Bake for 1 hour, but don't allow the meringues to brown. Remove at once with a broad spatula and set aside.

In a small saucepan, melt the jelly. Dissolve the cornstarch in the lemon juice, add to the melted jelly, and cook until the jelly becomes clear and thickened. When cool, place the hulled strawberries in the jelly and coat well.

When ready to serve, fill the meringue shells with the glazed strawberries. It is well not to do this too far in advance of serving, for the shells can get a bit soggy from the glaze.

Serves 6 or 7

TOPPINGS FOR CAKES

For occasions when you want to spoon a topping over slices of plain cake, angel food cake, etc.

Strawberry Whip

1   10-ounce package frozen strawberries, thawed
¾ cup sugar

2   egg whites
1   teaspoon lemon juice
Pinch of salt

Drain half the juice from the berries and reserve. You might want to add a bit of the juice for coloring after the topping is stiffly beaten. Combine the berries, sugar, egg whites, lemon juice, and salt and beat with the electric beater until thick and fluffy.

A package of raspberries may be substituted for the strawberries.

Makes about 1 cup

Banana Fluff

2 or 3 medium-ripe bananas
½ cup sugar
1 egg white
1 teaspoon lemon juice

Pinch of salt
Few drops of yellow coloring (optional)
1 tablespoon rum (optional)

Slice the bananas and combine with the sugar, egg white, lemon juice, and salt. Beat with the electric beater until thick and fluffy. Add coloring and rum if desired.

Makes about 1 cup

Red Currant Fluff

1 cup red currant jelly (or any other tart jelly)
1 egg white

1 teaspoon lemon juice
Few drops red food coloring (optional)

With the electric mixer, whip together the jelly, egg white, and lemon juice. Add coloring if desired.

Makes about 1⅓ cups

Chocolate Glaze

2 tablespoons cocoa
2 tablespoons water
1 tablespoon oil

1 tablespoon corn syrup
1 cup confectioners sugar, sifted

In a small saucepan, combine the cocoa, water, oil, and corn syrup. Cook and stir over low heat until the mixture is smooth. Remove from the heat and gradually add the sugar, beating constantly until the glaze is smooth and creamy. This will cover an 8 by 12 inch cake.

Makes about 1 cup

WHIPPED TOPPING

This whipped topping is low in calories and completely unsaturated. It answers a need for those who think that a serving of gelatin dessert or fruit or cake looks naked without some adornment.

The addition of gelatin to the whipped topping gives it

a staying power that it did not have when we first learned that we could turn skim milk powder into a reasonable facsimile of whipped cream. It can now be made a few hours in advance and stored in the refrigerator. In fact, it must be, to give the gelatin time to firm up.

1 teaspoon gelatin
¼ cup cold skim milk
3 tablespoons boiling water
½ cup ice water

½ cup dry skim milk
3 tablespoons sugar
1 tablespoon oil
½ teaspoon vanilla
1 teaspoon lemon juice

Chill the bowl and beater in the refrigerator.

Soften the gelatin in the ¼ cup of milk. Add to the boiling water and stir until completely dissolved. Set aside to cool and thicken. It should be the consistency of unbeaten egg white.

Measure the ice water into the chilled bowl. Add the skim milk powder and beat at high speed for 3 or 4 minutes until soft peaks form. Add the sugar, still beating, then the oil, vanilla, and lemon juice. Add the gelatin mixture, while continuing to beat at high speed. The beating process should take 8 to 10 minutes in all, to incorporate as much air as possible into the topping. Refrigerate until ready to use.

You may substitute any chilled fruit juice for the ice water.

Yields 2½ to 3 cups

FLUFFY WHITE ICING

Based on my own experience, I wanted to call this Never Fail Icing, but I hesitate to tempt fate. At any rate, I have never missed with it, and it's ever so much simpler than the one that directs you to beat over boiling water. The electric beater does all the work, and you end up with a bowlful of very nice frothy stuff.

½ cup boiling water
1 cup sugar
1 egg white

1 teaspoon vanilla
¼ teaspoon cream of tartar

Combine all the ingredients in the small bowl of the beater. Beat at high speed for 10 minutes.

Yields enough for tops and sides of two 8- or 9-inch layer cakes

SEA FOAM FROSTING

2⅓	cups dark brown sugar		Pinch of salt
⅔	cup water	⅛	teaspoon cream of tartar
2	egg whites	1	teaspoon vanilla

In a saucepan combine the sugar and water. Heat slowly to dissolve the sugar before it begins to boil. Cover the pan and boil for 2 or 3 minutes. Remove the cover and bring to the soft ball stage (240°). At this temperature the syrup, when dropped from the edge of a spoon, will spin a thick thread that will then develop a very thin thread, which seems to curl back on itself and disappear.

While the syrup is cooking, beat the egg whites with the salt until stiff. Remove the syrup from the heat and pour in a thin stream over the egg whites in a good-sized bowl, beating until the frosting becomes thick enough to hold its shape. (You can do this with an electric beater.) When the ingredients are all combined, beat in the cream of tartar and vanilla. If the frosting becomes too thick, you can thin it with a teaspoon of boiling water or a bit of lemon juice. Spread the frosting at once over the cooled cake.

Yields enough for 8- or 9-inch two-layer cake

18
Desserts

FRUIT DESSERTS

A choice of desserts never seems a problem to me in the spring and summer when the fruit stores smell like flower shops and are just as tempting, spilling over with melons, berries, grapes, and other splendid fruits fragrant with natural sweetness. I truly can't think of a better way to top off a fine dinner than with a mélange of fresh fruits, attractively served and perhaps sparked with some liqueur or brandy. The lovely continental custom of serving a bowl or basket of choice fruits at the close of the meal is worthy of emulation, particularly since they not only taste wonderful but have indisputable value as a source of essential nutrients in our diet.

MACÉDOINE OF FRUITS

Whatever is fresh and available at your fruit market can go into this. Figure about 6 cups of fruit for 6 servings.

I always include fresh, sectioned oranges, which provide a juicy base, but you could also use a 10-ounce package of frozen mixed fruits, which, when thawed, will give you enough liquid.

To section an orange or a grapefruit, peel it and remove every bit of the white membrane that lines the skin. Hold the fruit in one hand over a bowl in order not to waste a drop of the juice, and with a sharp-pointed knife cut between the membranes that separate the sections. Peel out the fruit section, cut at the next membrane, and remove the section, continuing until all the segments are removed. After you have mastered the technique—it takes a bit of practice—you will find that it goes quickly and that the segments are appetizingly firm and whole.

These are some of the fruits that may go into the macédoine. Use at least four or five.

apples	oranges
bananas	peaches
fresh sweet cherries	pears
grapes (seedless or	pineapple
pitted)	raspberries
grapefruit	strawberries
melon balls	

lemon juice	6 tablespoons liqueur
sugar to taste	(kirsch, Cointreau,
	maraschino, Grand
	Marnier, etc.)

Wash, peel, core, drain, and cut the fruit into 1-inch pieces. Sprinkle with lemon juice to prevent discoloration. Sweeten according to taste with superfine granulated sugar or confectioners sugar. Add the liqueur and stir. Refrigerate at least 4 hours and stir occasionally so that all flavors will blend. To serve, transfer to a glass serving bowl and serve at the table. On occasion, I have topped the fruit with scoops of lemon ice.

BAKED RED APPLES

A state of perfection for baked apples is not achieved, ironically, by baking them. This procedure makes them brown and wrinkled. For best results, the apples should be steamed first to make them tender, then glazed under the broiler. Start with the largest and best baking apples you can find, such as firm Rome Beauties or Northern Spies.

6 fine baking apples	3 orange slices,
¾ cup sugar	unpeeled
½ teaspoon cinnamon	

3 lemon slices,	1 teaspoon red
unpeeled	cinnamon candies or a
⅔ cup water	few drops of red
	vegetable coloring
	Sprinkle of sugar

Wash and core the apples, leaving the skin intact at the very bottom. Peel them about a third of the way down.

Mix the sugar and cinnamon together and place in a layer in the bottom of a covered heavy pot deep enough to hold the apples. Layer the orange and lemon slices over the sugar. Place the apples, peeled side down, on the sugar and fruit slices. Tint the water red by heating it with the candies until they dissolve or by adding the red coloring. Pour the water over the apples. Cover the pot tightly and steam on top of the stove for 15 minutes over low heat. Remove the cover and carefully turn the apples over, then replace the cover and continue to steam until they are fork-tender. This may take from 15 to 40 minutes longer, depending on the type of apple. Watch them carefully; don't overcook. It is the necessity for judgments like this that makes cooking an art and not a science.

When the apples have reached the proper degree of doneness—soft enough to let a spoon pierce them easily, yet firm enough to maintain their shape—remove the lid from the pot, sprinkle a bit of sugar over the apples, and place under the broiler so that the tops will be glazed, crisp, and bubbly.

Serves 6

LOW-CALORIE POACHED APPLES

These rosy whole apples also make a colorful accompaniment for a pork roast or a broiled chicken.

6 firm red apples	2 cups boiling water
2 ⅜-ounce packages	
dietetic raspberry	
gelatin	

Core and peel the apples. Dissolve the gelatin in the boiling water in a pot large enough to hold all the apples.

Add the apples and simmer gently, covered. Try to prepare the apples and get them into the liquid as quickly as possible before they turn brown. Lemon juice should not be added in this case because it will dilute the rosy color. Turn the apples frequently, top to bottom, so they will cook evenly and take on a uniform blush. Simmer until they are tender enough to offer no resistance when pierced with a sharp point. (I find a knitting needle a splendid instrument for testing.) Do not overcook. It is impossible to be definite about cooking time, for it varies with different kinds of apples. A McIntosh may soften within minutes, whereas a Delicious or Rome Beauty can take from 20 to 45 minutes, so watch them carefully and remove them from their crimson bath before they get mushy. When the desired state of tenderness has been reached, remove the apples to a shallow dish and spoon some of the gelatin mixture over them. You can discard the remainder of the gelatin or let it firm up and serve small cubes of it with the apples. Serve chilled.

Serves 6

BANANAS IN YOGURT

This fine fruit is too often neglected at dessert time. From the standpoint of flavor, nutrients, flexibility, economy, and availability, bananas are outstanding. We fry them, bake them, broil them, and even flame them. And they are delicious in the following combination:

3–4 sliced ripe bananas
1 8¾-ounce can white seedless grapes, drained, or ¾ cup fresh seedless grapes
1 orange

2 tablespoons sugar
1 cup low-fat vanilla yogurt
¼ cup orange juice
Grated rind of an orange

In a large bowl, combine the bananas with the grapes. Grate the orange rind and set aside. Finish peeling the orange, removing all the white stuff and membranes. Slice the orange about ¼ inch thick and cut each slice into 4 or 6 segments. Add to the bananas with the sugar, yogurt, and orange juice. Toss lightly to mix. Refrigerate, covered, for about an hour.

Serve in individual dessert bowls, garnished with a little of the grated orange rind.

Serves 5 or 6

Variation: ½ cup of fresh large blueberries may be added when in season.

BAKED BANANAS

Heat the oven to 375°. Split bananas lengthwise, leaving them in their skins, and place in a baking dish. Sprinkle a little lemon juice and brown sugar over them and bake for 20 to 25 minutes, or until they are soft and browned. Serve 2 halves per portion.

BANANAS BAKED IN ORANGE JUICE

6 firm bananas	⅛ teaspoon cinnamon
2 tablespoons lemon juice	⅛ teaspoon nutmeg
2 tablespoons orange juice	⅓ cup brown sugar
1 orange, peeled and cut in pieces	3 tablespoons crystallized ginger, chopped (optional)

Preheat the oven to 325°. Lightly oil a shallow 9 by 11 inch baking dish. Peel the bananas, split them lengthwise, and arrange in the dish. Sprinkle the lemon juice, orange juice, and orange chunks over them. Mix the cinnamon and nutmeg with the sugar and sprinkle over the bananas. Dot with the ginger if desired. Bake 25 to 30 minutes or until the bananas are tender and browned. Baste a few times while baking.

Serves 6

MERINGUE-BAKED BANANAS

6 firm bananas	Pinch salt
2 tablespoons lemon juice	¼ teaspoon cream of tartar
3 tablespoons crystallized ginger, finely chopped	6 tablespoons sugar
3 egg whites at room temperature	1 teaspoon vanilla

Preheat the oven to 325°. Lightly oil a baking sheet. Peel the bananas and cut in half lengthwise. Arrange on the baking sheet, with the two halves side by side, cut side down, leaving space between the pairs. Sprinkle with the lemon juice and dot with the ginger.

Beat the egg whites with the salt and cream of tartar until they stand in soft peaks. Add the sugar slowly, a little at a time, beating constantly until the meringue is stiff and shiny. Beat in the vanilla. With a pastry tube or two spoons, spread the surfaces of the banana pairs with the meringue. Bake for 15 to 20 minutes, or until the meringue is light brown. Remove from the baking sheet with a broad spatula and serve warm.

Serves 6

FLAMING BANANAS

4 firm bananas	½ cup orange juice
1 tablespoon oil	¼ teaspoon cinnamon
1 tablespoon lemon	¼ teaspoon nutmeg
juice	¼ cup sherry
¼ cup brown sugar	⅓ cup rum, warmed

Preheat the oven to 350°.

Peel the bananas and roll in the oil to coat. Sprinkle with the lemon juice and place in an oiled shallow baking dish.

Combine the brown sugar, orange juice, cinnamon, nutmeg, and sherry. Heat slightly and pour over the fruit. Bake for 20 to 25 minutes, or until the bananas are tender, basting a few times with the syrup. Transfer to a chafing dish, pour the rum over them, and ignite.

Serves 4

BAKED FRUIT COMPOTE

1 large can peach halves	Juice of 2 oranges
1 large can apricot halves	2 tablespoons lemon juice
1 large can pitted Bing cherries	¼ cup orange peel, thinly sliced

¼ cup lemon peel, thinly
  sliced
4 tablespoons brown
  sugar

2 ounces kirsch
  (optional)
½ cup coarsely chopped
  walnuts

Drain all the fruits and discard the juice. In a small saucepan, combine the orange and lemon juice and peel with the sugar. Simmer over low heat for 5 minutes.

Place the drained peach and apricot halves in a glass baking dish. Cover with the warmed syrup and bake in a 325° oven for 30 minutes, stirring from time to time. Add the cherries, kirsch (if desired), and nuts for the last 10 minutes of baking. Serve hot.

Serves 6

FRESH FRUIT PLATTER

This is a convenient way to serve fruit for a buffet. The individual chunks of melons and pineapple generally find favor with guests who might hesitate to attempt a large piece of fruit.

1 large, sweet pineapple
  Strawberries
1 cantaloupe

1 honeydew melon or
  watermelon portion, or
  both
  Seedless grapes

Divide the pineapple lengthwise into four quarters, cutting right through the leaves so that each quarter will have its own plume. Trim away the core sections. With a sharp knife, separate the pineapple from the shell in one piece. Slice the pineapple into ½-inch wedges, leaving them in place on the shell. Sugar lightly if the pineapple is not sweet enough. Place an unhulled strawberry on each pineapple wedge and secure with a toothpick. Arrange the pineapple quarters on a large flat serving tray. Remove the rinds from the cantaloupe and the honeydew and/or watermelon and cut the fruit into strips or crescents. Surround the pineapple shells with mounds of grapes cut into small bunches, a section of cantaloupe strips, a section of honeydew strips, etc., until all are

used. Other small fresh fruits in season, such as cherries
and apricots, may be added.

Serves 8

Note: The pineapple shells alone do nicely as a dessert.
If the fruit is very large, you may want to cut it in sixths
rather than quarters.

CHERRIES FLAMBÉE

There may be nothing new about flaming cherries
served over vanilla ice cream—or, in our case, ice milk—
but it is a festive operation that helps sustain a party
mood.

1   17-ounce can pitted
    Bing cherries
⅓ cup cherry juice
½ cup thin orange peel
2   tablespoons sugar
	4 tablespoons orange
	    liqueur (Curaçao,
	    Grand Marnier)
	½ cup warm brandy
	1 quart vanilla ice milk

Drain the Bing cherries, reserving ⅓ cup of juice. Cut
thin shavings from orange skins (called zests) and shred
very fine. Combine with the cherry juice and sugar in a
small saucepan and simmer over very low heat for 3 or 4
minutes. Add the cherries and liqueur and heat through.
Transfer to a chafing dish. Ignite the brandy (see On
Burning Brandy, page 394) and pour the flaming fruit over
individual portions of the ice milk.

Serves 6

MELON MEDLEY

3 small cantaloupes
1 cup blueberries,
   strawberries, or
   raspberries
	1 small pineapple, cored,
	   peeled, and diced in ½-
	   inch cubes
	6 tablespoons grenadine
	2 tablespoons lime juice

Cut the cantaloupes into halves. You may need to trim
the bottoms a little so they will rest firmly on the plate.

Scoop out melon balls from the cantaloupes and even out the insides of the melons with a teaspoon to make a smooth, unruffled surface. Combine the melon balls with the berries, pineapple, grenadine, and lime juice. Taste to see if you want more sweetening and add sugar if needed. Refrigerate the fruit for a few hours. Scallop the tops of the cantaloupe shells. When ready to serve, fill the shells with the fruit.

Serves 6

BAKED DESSERT PEACHES

6 large freestone peaches, unpeeled
1 egg white at room temperature
Pinch salt
⅛ teaspoon cream of tartar

2 tablespoons sugar
½ teaspoon almond extract
3 tablespoons sliced almonds

Preheat the oven to 350°.
Wash and dry the peaches. Cut each in half and remove the pit. Scoop out a tiny bit of the peach pulp in the center to make a bigger cavity and reserve. Place the peach halves in an oiled baking dish and bake for 1 hour.
Once the peaches are in the oven, you can prepare the meringue. In a small bowl, beat the egg white with salt and cream of tartar until frothy. Slowly beat in the sugar and beat until the meringue becomes shiny and stands in stiff peaks. Beat in the almond extract and fold in the reserved diced peach pulp.
After the peaches have been in the oven 30 minutes, remove them, fill the cavities with the meringue, sprinkle with the almonds, and return to the oven for the last 30 minutes. Serve at room temperature.

Serves 6

PEACHES IN RASPBERRY SAUCE

6 large fresh peaches
1 cup water
½ cup sugar

1 1-inch vanilla bean
3 tablespoons lemon juice

Raspberry Sauce

1 10-ounce package
frozen raspberries,
thawed
1 tablespoon sugar
1 teaspoon cornstarch

2 tablespoons cold
water
3 tablespoons kirsch
(optional)
¼ cup blanched slivered
almonds

Peel the peaches carefully. In a saucepan large enough to hold all the peaches without crowding, make a syrup of the water, sugar, vanilla bean, and lemon juice. Bring to a boil, reduce the heat to a simmer, and add the peaches. Poach them in the syrup until done. This may take 15 to 20 minutes—perhaps longer if the peaches are very firm. Simmer until fork-tender but not mushy. When they are soft enough, remove from the syrup. Do not refrigerate.

To make the sauce, combine the raspberries with the sugar in a small saucepan. Mix the cornstarch with the water and add to the raspberries. Simmer for 3 minutes, or until thickened and clear. Remove from the heat and mash through a sieve or a food mill. Return to the saucepan and heat just enough to warm through. Remove from the fire, add the kirsch (if desired), and mix. Spoon the warm sauce over the peaches and sprinkle with the almonds.

Serves 6

BAKED PEARS

4 large, firm pears,
Anjou or Bosc
½ cup brown sugar
1 cup water

2 tablespoons apricot
preserves
3 tablespoons lemon juice

Preheat the oven to 325°.

Wash the pears and cut in half lengthwise. Do not peel them. You can do a tidy job of removing the core and seeds with a small melon ball scoop. In a small saucepan, boil together the sugar, water, apricot preserves, and lemon juice for 5 minutes. Arrange the pear halves cut side down in a 9 by 13 inch glass baking dish. Pour the boiling syrup over the pears and bake for 1 hour, or until they are tender, basting them with syrup from time to time. Let the pears cool in the syrup. They may be served warm or chilled. I generally discard most of the syrup. It has performed its duty in making the pears glazed and delicious and is now nothing but some expendable calories.

Serves 4 or more

POACHED PEARS WITH SHERRY CUSTARD SAUCE

6 large, firm pears (Anjou, Bartlett, or Bosc)
3 tablespoons lemon juice

1 cup sugar
2 cups water
4 strips lemon peel

Sherry Custard Sauce

½ package custard flavor or vanilla pudding
1¾ cups skim milk

¼ cup sherry
Sliced almonds

Peel the pears with a swivel-bladed vegetable peeler. Leave the stems on but remove the eye at the bottom of the core with a small knife. Trim the bottom of the pears so they will stand firmly on their bases when done. Place each pear as it is peeled in a bowl with the lemon juice and water to cover.

Combine the sugar, 2 cups of water, and lemon peel in a pot large enough to hold all the pears without crowding. Cook over low heat until the sugar dissolves. Bring to a boil and boil for 1 minute. Drain the pears and add them to the boiling syrup. Cover the pan, reduce the heat to low, and simmer the pears 25 minutes or longer, or until they can be pierced easily with a skewer or a knitting needle and offer no resistance in the center. The cooking time varies with different kinds of pears, and it is impossible to be specific about how long they will need. Use your judgment, being careful not to let them overcook and become mushy.

When the pears are done, remove them carefully and place in a flat dish. Discard the lemon peel and pour some of the syrup over the pears. Refrigerate.

For the sauce, cook the pudding with the milk according to the package directions. Transfer to a small bowl and cover the surface of the pudding with a piece of waxed paper. When cool, beat with a rotary beater if the sauce has congealed. Add the sherry and mix well. To serve, place the pears in dessert bowls, pour a little of the custard sauce over each, and sprinkle with a few thinly sliced almonds.

Serves 6

PEARS IN WINE

These pears take on a lovely tint from the wine. A day or two in the refrigerator after cooking and before serving won't hurt them a bit—will even improve them, in fact.

6 large, firm pears (Bosc, Bartlett, or Anjou)	1 2-inch piece cinnamon stick
3 tablespoons lemon juice	4 strips lemon peel
2 cups port wine	1 whole clove
1 cup water	1 tablespoon cornstarch
1 cup sugar	2 tablespoons cold water

Prepare the pears as in the preceding recipe and place in a bowl with the lemon juice and water to cover. In a pot large enough to hold the pears without crowding, combine the wine with the cup of water, sugar, cinnamon stick, lemon peel, and clove. Cook over low heat until the sugar dissolves. Bring to a boil and boil for 1 minute. Drain the pears and add them to the boiling syrup. Cover the pan, reduce the heat to low, and simmer the pears 25 minutes or longer, or until they can be pierced easily through the thickest part with a skewer or a knitting needle.

When the pears are done, remove them from the syrup with a slotted spoon and place in a deep serving dish. Remove from the syrup the cinnamon stick, lemon peel, and clove and discard. Add to the syrup a paste made from the cornstarch dissolved in the 2 tablespoons of water. Stir constantly over low heat until the sauce becomes thickened and shiny. Spoon the syrup over the pears. Refrigerate when cool.

Serves 6

PRUNE COMPOTE

A jar of these prunes in your refrigerator can serve as a breakfast fruit or dinner dessert. The coffee loses its identifying flavor and enhances the taste of the prunes, while making a rich, dark syrup.

1 pound large sweet prunes
1 cup strong coffee
2 tablespoons lemon juice

Water
1 cup canned crushed pineapple

Wash the prunes and place in a saucepan with the coffee. Add the lemon juice and enough water to cover the prunes. Cover the pan and simmer gently for 20 minutes over low heat. Add the pineapple and bring to a brisk boil. Pour at once into a heatproof bowl and cover tightly with a lid or foil. The hot syrup will continue to tenderize the prunes and make them expand. When cool, refrigerate. Serve 3 to 5 prunes (depending on the size) per portion, with the sauce generously spooned over them.

Serves 6

ORANGES ORIENTALE

6 navel oranges
1 cup sugar
¾ cup water
1 tablespoon lemon juice

2 tablespoons orange liqueur (Curaçao, Grand Marnier, etc.)

With a sharp knife, remove the outer rind from 3 of the oranges, making sure to include only the rind and not the bitter white inner pulp. Slice the rind into thin strips, julienne style. You should have a generous cupful of julienne strips.

Peel the remaining oranges and remove every bit of the white covering on all. You may have to scrape off the excess white membranes with a small knife. Carefully remove the center white core, and, ever so slightly, separate the sections at one end of each peeled orange so it will sit firmly on the plate. Place the oranges on a serving platter or dish.

In a saucepan, combine the strips of orange peel with the sugar and water. Bring to a boil, reduce the heat, and simmer slowly until the peel becomes tender and glossy (about 15 minutes).

When the syrup is thickened, and the peel tender, add the lemon juice and orange liqueur, heat quickly, and pour at once over the oranges. Chill. These may be prepared the day before you use them. Serve each orange with the sauce and a generous crown of the candied rind.

Serves 6

DESSERT STRAWBERRIES

One can never fault the choice of strawberries to top off a fine dinner. When they are at their very peak—large, perfect, juicy—I like to serve them completely unadorned, hulls intact, heaped in a crystal bowl. We pass the strawberries accompanied by a bowl of confectioners sugar. The guests ladle out their own servings of berries and sugar and do their own dipping.

STRAWBERRIES GRAND MARNIER

It was a very fancy restaurant where we had these—candlelight, carved paneling, gleaming napery. I don't remember where it was, but I do remember the strawberries. At the nearby serving table, the maitre d', with great style and flourish, anointed, splashed, and gently tossed the lovely red berries awaiting us. He made a final taste of the sauce, nodded, and proceeded to serve the berries in huge oversize brandy snifters. And even though the style and flourish are absent in my presentation of them (I do them in the kitchen with no audience and we don't own any oversize brandy snifters), they are always most enthusiastically received.

3 pints strawberries	2 tablespoons lemon juice
2 tablespoons sugar	1 tablespoon brandy
Juice of 1 orange	3 tablespoons Grand
1½ tablespoons grated	Marnier
orange rind	

Wash and hull the berries carefully, drain well, and place in a good-sized bowl. Cut up and lightly mash a couple of berries at the bottom of the bowl to add some color to the sauce. Add the sugar and mix. Add the remaining ingredients and toss gently, being careful not to bruise the berries. Taste the sauce. You may think it needs a bit more sugar or lemon juice, or an extra dollop of Grand Marnier. Chill for an hour or two. Serve in dessert bowls with the sauce.

Serves 6 to 8

Variation: When the blueberries are in season, a cup or so can be added to the strawberries. They provide interesting color contrast.

STRAWBERRIES SUPREME

1 quart strawberries	1 10-ounce package
Sugar	frozen strawberries,
2 tablespoons Cointreau	thawed
(or orange juice)	1 egg white
	6 tablespoons sugar
	1 tablespoon lemon juice

Hull and wash the strawberries, then drain well. Sugar lightly—the berries should be tart. Place in a bowl, add the Cointreau (or orange juice), and refrigerate until ready to serve.

Drain the frozen, thawed berries, reserving the juice. In a medium-sized bowl combine the egg white, sugar, lemon juice, drained strawberries, and half the juice (the other half may be kept for another use). Beat with an electric beater until fluffy. Place whole berries in individual dessert bowls, top with the whip, and serve at once.

Serves 4

APRICOT CREPES

This is an impressive party dessert. The crepes may be made the day before, which leaves the last-minute fixing a simple matter. Don't worry about refrigerating the crepes overnight. I have done it successfully many times.

Crepes

3 eggs	1 scant cup flour
½ teaspoon salt	1⅔ cup skim milk
1½ teaspoons sugar	2 tablespoons oil
2 tablespoons brandy	Apricot preserves

Apricot Sauce

1 20-ounce can apricot halves	3 tablespoons liqueur (Cointreau, Curaçao, Grand Marnier, etc.)
1 12-ounce can apricot nectar	4 tablespoons warm brandy
Grated rind of 1 orange	
3 tablespoons lemon juice	

To make the crepes, beat the eggs with an electric beater until light and add the salt, sugar, and brandy. Beating constantly, add alternately the flour, milk, and oil. The batter should be the consistency of heavy cream. If too thick, thin it with a bit of water or skim milk. Let the batter rest at room temperature for 1 hour. I suppose there is a perfectly logical reason for this, but I don't know what it is. I only know that if you don't, the crepes won't cook properly in the frying pan, so straighten out your dish closets, clean the silver, or read a book, and come back later.

To cook the crepes, lightly oil a 6-inch skillet. (Keep a small bowl of oil at hand for reoiling the skillet when necessary. You won't need much.) Place the skillet over medium heat until a drop of water sizzles and bounces off. I find a soup ladle convenient for pouring the batter. Use as little batter as will cover the bottom of the pan because the crepes should be thin and delicate. Tilt the pan quickly so that the entire bottom is covered with batter. After the first few, you will be able to judge how much batter you need for each crepe. Cook over medium heat until the underside of the crepe is delicately browned. Transfer the uncooked side to a second 7- or 8-inch skillet, heated and lightly oiled. While the second side is browning in the larger skillet, you can start cooking the next pancake in the smaller one. Transfer the finished crepes to a towel. Repeat until all the batter is used, stacking the crepes on top of each other when completely cooled. This should yield from 20 to 24 crepes. Wrap them in aluminum foil and store in the refrigerator if you are planning to use them the next day.

For the sauce, drain the apricots. Place the apricot syrup in a saucepan with the apricot nectar, orange rind, and lemon juice. Cook uncovered for 15 minutes to reduce. Just before serving, add the apricot halves and liqueur and heat through.

Spread each crepe with apricot preserves, roll into a cylinder, and place in a lightly oiled shallow pan. Don't stack them; lay them side by side. A jelly-roll pan is useful for this. Spoon some of the sauce over them to keep them moist. Cover with aluminum foil. While the main part of the meal is being eaten, put them into a 400° oven for about 10 minutes so they will be piping hot. At dessert time, transfer them to your chafing dish. Sprinkle some fine sugar over them and cover them with sauce and fruit. Pour the brandy over the crepes and ignite. When the flame burns out, serve on a warm plate, two crepes to a serving, with sauce and fruit on each.

Serves 10 to 12

CREPES NORMANDIE

24 crepes
5 medium-sized apples, peeled, cored, and thinly sliced
6 tablespoons white sugar

¾ teaspoon cinnamon
3 tablespoons brown sugar
1 tablespoon oil
½ cup warm apple brandy

Make crepes as for Apricot Crepes (preceding recipe). In a heavy saucepan, combine the apple slices, white sugar, and cinnamon. Cook over low heat until the apples wilt (about 8 to 10 minutes), stirring frequently. Cool for 15 minutes.

Place a tablespoon of the apple mixture on each crepe and roll carefully. Arrange the rolled crepes in a large, flat oiled baking pan. Moisten the brown sugar with the oil and sprinkle the mixture over the crepes. Heat in a 350° oven for 10 minutes. Transfer to a chafing dish. Pour the brandy over the top and ignite.

Serves 10 to 12

ON BURNING BRANDY

For a long time I waged a losing fight with what my family laughingly called Operation B.B. (burning the brandy). I warmed it, just as the books advise, and poured it lovingly and hopefully over the contents of the chafing dish. I lit matches until the air was thick with phosphorus fumes, and all I had to show for my trouble was an ashtray filled with burnt-out matches. Sometimes, if I was lucky, a feeble blue light would flicker for a fraction of a moment. If you turned your head, you would miss the whole show. And all that good brandy wasted! I watched enviously when the dignitaries in flossy restaurants, with a flick of the bottle, would set off a flame that practically licked the ceiling. (I have a sneaking suspicion that there is some kind of hanky-panky involved—maybe a bottle of kerosene concealed in their sleeves.) At any rate, came the dawn at long last. Now I warm the brandy in the kitchen, tote it to the dining table, and light it just before I pour it into the chafing dish. The dish comes alive with dancing flames that would make any headwaiter green with envy. When I tell people about this monumental discovery, I am inevitably greeted with a "I always knew that; why didn't you ask me?" kind of answer. For goodness sake—why didn't somebody tell me?

PUDDINGS, SOUFFLÉS, AND FROZEN DESSERTS

APPLE SNOW

2	teaspoons gelatin	3	tablespoons sugar
2	tablespoons cold water	2½	cups applesauce
⅓	cup dried skim milk	1	teaspoon grated lemon rind
⅓	cup chilled apple juice	⅛	teaspoon cinnamon
2	tablespoons lemon juice	⅛	teaspoon nutmeg

Sprinkle the gelatin over the 2 tablespoons of cold water to soften. Stir over hot water until dissolved.

In a chilled bowl whip the dried milk with the apple juice for 3 or 4 minutes, until it stands in soft peaks. Add the lemon juice and continue to beat until completely stiff. Gradually beat in the sugar.

Add the dissolved gelatin to the applesauce and mix in the lemon rind, cinnamon, and nutmeg. Fold in the whipped milk and combine thoroughly. Mound in dessert bowls or sherbet glasses and chill until set (about 2 hours).

Serves 6

APPLE CRISP

This is really the inside of an apple pie without the crusts.

4–5	large tart apples	½	cup water
1	teaspoon cinnamon	½	cup flour
½	cup white sugar	½	cup brown sugar
2	tablespoons lemon juice	3	tablespoons oil

Preheat the oven to 350°.

Core, peel, and slice the apples. Oil a 1½-quart casserole and place the apple slices in it. Combine the cinnamon and white sugar and add to the apples. Add the lemon juice and water and mix lightly. In a small mixing bowl, blend the flour, brown sugar, and oil until crumbly. Sprinkle this over the apples. Bake in a 350° oven for 50 minutes, or until it is browned and the apples are tender. Serve warm.

Serves 4 or 5

COTTAGE CHEESE AND FRUIT PUDDING

½	package vanilla pudding mix	½	teaspoon vanilla
1	cup skim milk	1	10-ounce package frozen peach slices, thawed
2	tablespoons sugar		
1½	cups low-fat cottage cheese, beaten until smooth	1	10-ounce package frozen raspberries, thawed

Prepare the pudding mix with the milk according to the directions on the package. After it is cooked, add the sugar, stir until dissolved, and cool.

With an electric beater, beat the cottage cheese until it becomes smooth and creamy, the consistency of sour cream. Blend into the cooled vanilla pudding and mix well. Add the vanilla.

Divide into individual dessert bowls. Top with the peach slices and partially drained raspberries. Chill.

Serves 6

COFFEE SPONGE

You can reduce the calories practically to the vanishing point by substituting artificial sweetener for the sugar.

1⅔ cups strong coffee	⅓ cup sugar
1 tablespoon unflavored gelatin	1 teaspoon vanilla
	⅛ teaspoon cinnamon

Place ½ cup of the coffee in a small saucepan. Sprinkle the gelatin over the coffee to soften. Add the sugar and cook over low heat, stirring until the sugar and gelatin are dissolved. Remove from the heat and add the remainder of the coffee, vanilla, and cinnamon. Refrigerate until it becomes a little thicker than the consistency of unbeaten egg white. This will take about an hour.

Beat with a rotary beater until it doubles in volume and becomes fluffy and light, then mound in dessert bowls and chill.

Serves 6

LOW-CALORIE PINEAPPLE FLUFF

1¾ cups unsweetened pineapple juice	1 teaspoon artificial sweetener
1 tablespoon unflavored gelatin	4 tablespoons sugar
	⅛ teaspoon salt

Place the pineapple juice in a small saucepan and sprinkle the gelatin over it. When softened, add the sweetener and place over low heat, stirring until the gelatin is dissolved. Add the sugar and salt and heat for another minute until the sugar dissolves.

Transfer to a bowl and chill until the mixture becomes a little thicker than the consistency of unbeaten egg white (about an hour).

Beat with a rotary beater until the mixture becomes fluffy and doubles in volume, then mound in dessert bowls and chill.

Serves 4

FRUIT WHIP

The supplies of baby food I have made it a practice to keep on hand against unexpected visits from the grandchildren—first David, then Betsy, and now Noah—serve two purposes: Keeping the small ones nourished and also making excellent quick fruit whip desserts.

2 egg whites	7¾ ounces pureed fruit
¼ teaspoon salt	(prune, apricot, peach,
3 tablespoons sugar	plum, etc.) or grated
	raw apple or
	applesauce
	1 tablespoon lemon
	juice

Beat the egg whites and salt until frothy. Add the sugar slowly, a little at a time, and beat until stiff. Fold in the pureed fruit and lemon juice and blend well. Mound in dessert bowls and chill.

Serves 4

POOR MAN'S RICE PUDDING

Very likely this rice pudding earned its name because of the paucity of its ingredients, which makes it a good choice for us.

2 tablespoons oil

½ cup uncooked rice

3 cups skim milk

¼ cup sugar

⅛ teaspoon salt

⅛ teaspoon cinnamon

⅛ teaspoon nutmeg

½ teaspoon vanilla

⅓ cup seedless raisins

Preheat the oven to 325°.

Lightly oil a 1-quart heatproof casserole. Over low heat, heat the oil in it and add the rice. Stir constantly until the rice whitens and becomes opaque. Do not let it brown.

In a small saucepan, combine the milk, sugar, salt, cinnamon, and nutmeg and cook over medium heat, just to the point where bubbles appear at the outside edges. Add to the rice in the casserole and heat through for just a minute, until the milk bubbles. Remove the casserole from the heat and mix in the vanilla and raisins. Cover the casserole (aluminum foil will do if there is no cover) and bake for 1½ hours, or until the pudding is firm and the grains of rice are soft. Serve warm or cold.

Serves 4 or 5

LEMON PUDDING

¾ cup sugar

3 tablespoons flour

Juice and grated rind of 1 lemon

Pinch of salt

1 egg, separated

1 cup skim milk

1 egg white

1 tablespoon oil

Preheat the oven to 350°. Have the eggs at room temperature.

Lightly oil a 1½-quart ovenproof casserole. Mix together in it the sugar, flour, lemon juice and rind, and salt. Beat the egg yolk, add it to the milk, and blend into the flour mixture. In another bowl, beat the two egg whites until stiff. Gently fold into the mixture in the casserole. Mix in the oil. Place the casserole in a pan of hot water and bake in a 350° oven for 45 minutes.

The sponge will rise to the top, leaving a delicate lemony sauce to spoon over each portion. Serve warm.

Serves 4

PINEAPPLE ICE BOX CAKE

This tart, light dessert provides a splendid ending to a hearty dinner. It may be made a day in advance.

Filling

1 13-ounce can evaporated skimmed milk, undiluted
1 1-pound-4-ounce can crushed pineapple
1 tablespoon unflavored gelatin

¼ cup cold water
1 cup sugar
Juice of 2 lemons (at least 6 tablespoons)
Grated rind of 1 lemon
1 3-ounce package lemon gelatin

Crust

1¼ cups graham cracker crumbs
3 tablespoons sugar

⅓ cup oil
1 teaspoon grated lemon rind

Pour the milk into an ice cube tray and place it in the freezer. Drain the pineapple and reserve ½ cup of the juice. (Use the pineapple that is packed in pineapple juice rather than syrup.) In a small bowl, sprinkle the unflavored gelatin over the cold water to soften.

In a saucepan, combine the sugar, lemon juice and rind, and reserved pineapple juice. Bring to a boil over low heat, stirring constantly to dissolve the sugar. When boiling, remove from the heat, add the lemon gelatin, and stir until dissolved. Add the softened unflavored gelatin and stir over low heat until it dissolves. Transfer to a bowl and refrigerate until thickened.

To prepare the crust, in an oiled 9- or 10-inch springform combine the graham cracker crumbs, sugar, oil, and lemon rind. Mix well and pat the crumbs evenly over the bottom and along the sides of the pan. Place in a preheated 350° oven for 10 minutes. Remove and cool.

When the milk has become a bit frozen and mushy, transfer to a bowl and beat with an electric beater until it stands in stiff peaks, like whipped cream. Gently fold the whipped milk into the thickened gelatin and add the crushed pineapple, mixing lightly. Mound the mixture in the crumb-lined springform and refrigerate until firm.

Serves 8 to 10

SNOW PUDDING

Another pleasing and refreshing hot-weather dessert.

1 tablespoon gelatin	3 egg whites at room
½ cup cold water	temperature
1 cup boiling water	¼ teaspoon cream of tartar
1 cup sugar	Pinch of salt
¼ cup lemon juice	1 teaspoon grated lemon rind

Sprinkle the gelatin over the cold water to soften. Add the boiling water, sugar, and lemon juice and stir until the gelatin and sugar are dissolved. Place in the refrigerator until it reaches the consistency of unbeaten egg white (from 1 to 1½ hours).

In a deep bowl, beat the egg whites until frothy. Add the cream of tartar and salt and continue to beat until the egg whites are glossy and stand in stiff peaks. Fold the meringue into the thickened gelatin mixture, mix in the lemon rind, and blend well. Mound into dessert bowls and chill. Serve with Apricot Sauce or Blueberry Sauce (below).

Serves 6

Apricot Sauce

⅔ cup sugar 1 tablespoon lemon juice
1½ cups apricot nectar

Combine the sugar and apricot nectar and boil for 5 minutes. Remove from the heat and stir in the lemon juice. Chill.

Yields 1½ cups sauce

Blueberry Sauce

This sauce should be made only with fresh blueberries. Neither the frozen nor the canned ones justify the effort (or the port wine). It's a good sauce for puddings or ice milk.

1 tablespoon cornstarch	3 thin lemon slices
¾ cup port wine	1½ cups blueberries,
½ cup sugar	washed and drained

In a small saucepan, combine the cornstarch and wine and stir until smooth. Add the sugar and lemon slices and bring to a boil while stirring. Reduce the heat to a simmer and continue stirring until the sauce is slightly thickened and transparent (3 to 5 minutes). Remove from the heat. When cool, discard the lemon slices and add the blueberries. Chill well.

Yields 2 cups

STRAWBERRY SOUFFLÉ

This is a pleasant and comparatively low-calorie dessert.

5 egg whites
  Pinch of salt
6 tablespoons
  confectioners sugar

1 10-ounce package
  frozen strawberries,
  thawed and drained
  (reserve the juice)

Sauce

1 teaspoon sugar
1 tablespoon Grand
  Marnier or Kirsch

The reserved
strawberry juice

Preheat the oven to 350°. Oil a one-quart soufflé dish and dust lightly with sugar.

Beat the egg whites with the salt until soft peaks form. Add the sugar, a tablespoon at a time, beating well after each addition, until the mixture stands in very firm peaks. Gently fold in the strawberry pulp, making sure it is well distributed.

Transfer the mixture to the prepared soufflé dish and mound it so that it is higher in the center than the sides. Bake for 30 minutes.

While it is baking, add the sugar and liqueur to the strawberry juice and taste for sweetness. Do not refrigerate.

After 30 minutes the soufflé should be puffy and browned on top. Remove from the oven and serve at once. Serve the sauce separately.

Serves 4 or 5

BANANA SOUFFLÉ

3 large ripe bananas,
  mashed (about 1½
  cups)
⅓ cup sugar
1 tablespoon lemon
  juice

5 egg whites at room
  temperature
Pinch of salt
½ teaspoon baking
  powder
1 tablespoon cornstarch

Preheat the oven to 375°. Oil a 1-quart soufflé dish and dust lightly with sugar.

In a good-sized bowl, mash the bananas until smooth. Combine with the sugar and lemon juice and set aside.

Beat the egg whites with the salt until stiff and glossy. Blend in the baking powder and cornstarch during the beating process and beat until stiff peaks form. Add the beaten whites to the banana pulp and, with a rubber spatula, gently cut and fold the meringue into the pulp, turning the bowl a little with each cutting motion. Pour into the prepared soufflé dish and mound the mixture higher in the center than the sides. Bake for 30 minutes, or until set. Serve at once.

Serves 4

COLD PRUNE SOUFFLÉ

12 ounces pitted dried
   prunes
1 cup water
½ cup prune juice
1 tablespoon gelatin
¼ cup dry white wine
¼ cup boiling orange
  juice

¼ teaspoon salt
⅛ teaspoon cinnamon
3 egg whites at room
  temperature
Pinch of salt
½ cup sugar

Cook the prunes in the water until tender. Reserve ½ cup of the prune juice. Chop the prunes finely and set them aside. The chopped prunes will add interesting texture which would be lost if the prunes were to be pureed in a food mill or a blender.

Soften the gelatin in the wine. Add the orange juice and stir until the gelatin is completely dissolved. Combine the gelatin with the prunes and reserved prune juice. Allow to cool and start to thicken, then beat with a wire whisk until light and foamy. Beat in the salt and cinnamon.

Beat the egg whites with the pinch of salt. When soft peaks form, beat in the sugar slowly until the meringue becomes stiff and glossy and stands in firm peaks. Fold the meringue into the prune mixture, blending well. Transfer the mixture to a lightly oiled mold and chill until set. Unmold to serve. Accompany with Lemon Sauce or Creamy Dessert Sauce (below).

Serves 4 to 6

Lemon Sauce

⅔ cup sugar
½ cup water
   Grated rind of 1 lemon
   Juice of 2 lemons
   (about 6 tablespoons)

Scant teaspoon
cornstarch, dissolved
in 1 tablespoon cold
water

Combine the sugar, water, and lemon rind and juice and boil for 7 or 8 minutes. Add the cornstarch mixture and cook another 2 or 3 minutes, stirring until smooth and shiny. Serve hot or cold.

Yields about 1 cup

Creamy Dessert Sauce

2 egg whites
1 cup confectioners
  sugar
¼ cup hot skim milk

1 teaspoon vanilla
1 tablespoon Grand
  Marnier

Beat the egg whites until they hold soft peaks. Gradually beat in the sugar until the meringue becomes stiff and glossy. Continue beating while you add the milk, vanilla, and Grand Marnier. Serve chilled.

Yields about 1 cup

SPICED NUTS

Either walnuts or pecans may be used. Both sweet and spicy, the coated nuts make a fine accompaniment for dessert and coffee.

1 egg white, unbeaten
2 tablespoons water
½ cup sugar
½ teaspoon salt
1 teaspoon cinnamon

¼ teaspoon ground cloves
¼ teaspoon nutmeg
2 cups large pecans or
  walnut halves

Preheat the oven to 300°.

In a small bowl, combine the egg white with the water and beat with a fork until frothy. Add the sugar, salt, cinnamon, cloves, and nutmeg and mix. Add the nuts to the mixture and coat well. Spread out on a very lightly oiled cookie sheet and bake for 40 to 45 minutes, turning the nuts once or twice.

Yields 2 cups

FROZEN DESSERTS

CREAMY APRICOT SHERBET

If you wish, you can further reduce the limited number of calories by substituting 1½ teaspoons of artificial sweetener for the sugar and using dietetic-pack apricots.

To dress this dessert up, serve in pretty dessert bowls and flank the scoop of sherbet with two or three large apricot halves that have been marinated in apricot liqueur.

1 tablespoon gelatin
2 cups skim milk
½ cup dried skim milk
¼ cup sugar

1 1-pound can apricots,
  drained and pureed
2 tablespoons lemon juice

In a small saucepan, soak the gelatin in ½ cup of the milk until it becomes softened. Place over low heat until the gelatin is dissolved, stirring constantly. Pour into a large mixing bowl and add the remaining liquid, dried milk, sugar, apricots, and lemon juice. With an electric beater, beat for 3 or 4 minutes, until the mixture thickens a bit. It won't get really thick, so don't try.

Place the mixture in a 5½ by 10 inch ice tray in the freezing compartment of the refrigerator and freeze until partially firm. Transfer to a bowl. If it seems quite hard, attack it with a fork and your beater and beat until smooth and creamy, but not melted. Replace in the freezer. Beat once more in 30 minutes and chill until firm.

Serves 4 to 6

CRANBERRY SHERBET

½ pound fresh whole cranberries (about 2⅓ cups)
1¼ cups cold water
1 cup plus 2 tablespoons sugar
½ envelope (1½ teaspoons) gelatin

2 tablespoons cold water
¼ cup boiling lemon juice
½ teaspoon grated lemon rind
2 egg whites at room temperature
Pinch of salt

In a covered saucepan, combine the cranberries with the 1¼ cups of cold water and cook for about 10 minutes, or until the skins pop. Force the berries and liquid through a food mill. Add the sugar to the puree and mix thoroughly. Soften the gelatin in the 2 tablespoons of water. Add the lemon juice and stir until dissolved. Add the dissolved gelatin to the cranberries. Mix well and add the lemon rind.

Pour into an ice tray, place in the freezer compartment, and freeze until mushy. Meanwhile, beat the egg whites with the salt until they are stiff and glossy and stand in firm peaks. The cranberry mixture seems to get stiff quickly, but don't worry about it if you find that it has become quite hard. Transfer it to a mixing bowl and soften it with a fork. Beat with an electric mixer until it becomes fluffy and increases in volume. Fold the egg whites into the cranberry mixture and return to the freezer. Freeze until firm.

Serves 5 or 6

MINT SHERBET

For an imposing dessert, dribble some crème de menthe over a scoop of this and serve in parfait glasses.

1   tablespoon gelatin   1½ tablespoons fresh
1½ cups cold water   mint leaves, finely
¾   cup boiling water   chopped, or 1½
1   cup sugar   tablespoons crème de
½   cup lemon juice   menthe or ½ teaspoon
2   egg whites   peppermint flavor
    Pinch of salt   Few drops green
                                     vegetable coloring
                                     (optional)

Soften the gelatin in ½ cup of the cold water. Add the boiling water and stir until dissolved. Add the sugar, remaining cup of cold water, and lemon juice and beat well with a rotary beater. Pour the mixture into an ice cube tray and place in the freezing compartment of the refrigerator.

Beat the egg whites with the salt until they become stiff and glossy and stand in firm peaks.

When the mixture is frozen around the edges, transfer to a large chilled bowl and beat vigorously until creamy and foamy. Stir in the mint or crème de menthe or peppermint flavor. Fold in the egg whites. Add coloring, if desired. Replace in the freezer and freeze until firm.

Serves 6

RASPBERRY ICE

Fresh raspberries have been practically priced out of reach of ordinary folks in the area where we live. But this smooth, fruited ice serves as a reminder of their fine taste and rosy color.

1   10½-ounce package   3 tablespoons lemon
    frozen raspberries,   juice
    thawed   1 tablespoon corn syrup
⅔ cup sugar   2 egg whites
¼ cup orange juice   Pinch of salt

Mash the raspberries well. I don't strain them because I find the texture of the unstrained berries pleasing, and most people seem to agree. Add the sugar, orange and lemon juice, and corn syrup. Mix well. Place in an ice cube tray and freeze until firm.

Beat the egg whites with the pinch of salt until they are stiff and glossy. Remove the raspberries to a chilled bowl, whip until light, and fold in the egg whites. Return to the freezing tray and replace in the freezer until firm.

Serves 6

STRAWBERRY MOUSSE

This mousse does equally well in a parfait glass or generously heaped on sliced angel food cake.

½ cup dried skim milk
½ cup chilled strawberry
   juice (from frozen
   strawberries)
2 tablespoons lemon
   juice
4 tablespoons sugar

2 10-ounce packages
   frozen sliced
   strawberries, thawed
   and drained
1 egg white
   Pinch of salt

In your electric mixer, beat the dried milk with the ½ cup of chilled strawberry juice. Beat until soft peaks form (about 3 or 4 minutes). Add the lemon juice and continue beating until firm peaks form (3 or 4 minutes longer). Slowly beat in 2 tablespoons of the sugar.

In another bowl, mash the strawberries with the remaining 2 tablespoons of sugar and mix well until smooth. Beat the egg white and salt until it stands in firm peaks. Fold together the whipped milk, strawberries, and egg white. Freeze in a tray in the freezing compartment of the refrigerator until firm (about 3 hours).

Serves 6

Menus

BREAKFAST

Sliced Orange
Buttermilk Chiffon Pancakes with Warmed Maple Syrup

Fruit Juice
Cottage Cheese Pancakes with Braised Apple Slices

Half Grapefruit
Frizzled Dried Beef on Toasted English Muffin

BRUNCH

Prune Compote
Baked Kippered Herring
Grilled Tomato   Corn Puffs

Tomato Juice
Canadian Bacon in Wine Sauce
Spinach and Mushroom Salad
Swedish Tea Ring

V-8 Juice
Clams Rockefeller
Apple Pancake

LUNCH

Watercress and Pea Soup
Salade Niçoise
Spice Squares

Chilled Cucumber Soup
Rolled Fillets of Sole
Rice   Carrots Vichy
Snow Pudding with Apricot Sauce

Tomato Aspic Ring Filled with
Cucumber Salad
Salmon Patties
Spinach and Mushroom Casserole
Cheesecake

Gazpacho
Salmon Mousse with Cucumber Sauce
Mixed Vegetable Salad
Cottage Cheese Fruit Pudding

Caponata
Fish Mousse with Shrimp Sauce
Baked Stuffed Tomato
Apricot Upside-down Cake

Cream of Tomato Soup
Hot Chicken Salad
Wild Rice Casserole
Peach Custard Tart

DINNER

Smoked Brook Trout with Horseradish Sauce
Broiled Leg of Lamb
Flageolets in Tomato Fondue
Minted Apple Slices
Angel Food Cake with Strawberry Whip

Cream of Carrot Soup
Roast Fillet of Beef Bordelaise
Baked Stuffed Potato   Caesar Salad
Macédoine of Fruits

Stuffed Mushrooms
Fish Fillets in Bouillabaisse Sauce
Armenian String Bean Salad
Strawberries Grand Marnier

Asparagus Vinaigrette
Grilled Salmon Steaks

Steamed New Potatoes   Baked Cucumber
Poached Pears in Sherry Custard Sauce

Mushrooms Trifolati
Chicken with Apricots
Broccoli Sauté
Chiffon Spice Cake

Potage Vert
Stuffed Shoulder of Veal
Pickled Beet and Endive Salad
Meringue-baked Bananas

SUPPER

Onion Pie
Fish Chowder
Hot Garlic Bread   Tossed Green Salad
Fruit Torte

Asparagus Appetizer
Chicken Orientale
Baked Curried Fruit
Ice Milk with Blueberry Sauce

Minestrone
Cannelloni
Mixed Greens with Garlic Mayonnaise
Fresh Fruit Platter   Pecan Kiss Cakes

Hearts of Palm
Codfish Portuguese
Braised Celery   Mixed Green Salad
Fluffy Lemon Ice Box Cake

Broiled Grapefruit
Chicken Breasts in Aspic
Rice Salad
Chocolate Loaf Cake

Carrot Vichysoisse
Vitello Tonnato (Cold Veal in Tuna Sauce)
Cold Bulgur Salad   Cold Zucchini Piquant
Pears in Wine

Summary
for Cholesterol Watchers

	RECOMMENDED	USE SPARINGLY	AVOID
MEATS *	BEEF: Eye, top and bottom round; flank steak; fillet; lean ground round LAMB: Leg, well trimmed PORK: Lean loin; trimmed ham steak; Canadian bacon VEAL: Scallopine; loin chops; rump or shoulder; leg; eye roast	Liver	All richly marbled beef; all visible fat; spareribs; frankfurters; sausage; bacon; luncheon meats; brains, sweetbreads, kidney, tongue, etc.
POULTRY	Young chickens, preferably skinned; turkey (white meat); Cornish hen; squabs	Duck (no skin)	Fat poultry and skin; goose
FISH AND SHELLFISH	All fish, fresh, dried, frozen, smoked; fish canned in soybean or cottonseed oil or water	Shellfish (shrimp, clams, etc.)	
EGGS	Egg whites: unlimited. Up to 3 egg yolks per week		More than 3 egg yolks a week, including those used in cooking

* Limit the meat portion to 4 to 6 ounces uncooked. Beef, lamb, and pork should be served no more than 4 times a week.

DAIRY PRODUCTS	Skim milk, dry and liquid; low-fat cottage cheese; skim milk buttermilk; canned evaporated skimmed milk; special low-fat cheeses; low-fat yogurt; farmer cheese; sapsago; ice milk	Cheeses made from partially skimmed milk	Sweet cream; sour cream; whole milk; butter; whole milk cheeses; nondairy cream substitutes (which usually contain coconut oil); chocolate milk; ice cream; whole milk yogurt
FRUITS AND VEGETABLES	All fruits; all vegetables raw or cooked in polyunsaturated fats	Olives and avocados (both high in monounsaturated fat	Vegetables prepared in sauces of unknown ingredients
FATS AND OILS	Safflower, corn, cottonseed, soybean, sunflower oils; mayonnaise and homemade salad dressings made with polyunsaturated oils; special polyunsaturated margarines	Olive oil may be used occasionally for flavor, but it is low in polyunsaturates and does not take the place of recommended oils	Ordinary margarines; solid fats and shortenings, such as butter, lard, and Crisco; meat fat, salt pork fat; coconut oil
SOUPS	Fat-free soups; homemade cream soups; consommé		Canned cream soups; canned soups made with butter or hydrogenated oils; cream soups made with unknown ingredients
BREAD, CEREALS, AND BAKERY PRODUCTS	White, whole-grain, rye, Italian and French breads; English muffins; breads made without added fat; hard rolls; homemade cakes, pastries, waffles and pancakes made with polyunsaturated oils; all cereals, hot and cold (check on labels); rice; melba toast; matzo; pretzels; spaghetti and macaroni; barley; angel food cake mix	Egg noodles	Butter rolls, egg breads; commercial biscuits, muffins, doughnuts, sweet rolls; cheese breads; prepared cake mixes; all commercially prepared baked goods unless you are sure they do not contain saturated fats, whole milk, cream, etc.

DESSERTS AND SWEETS	Gelatin desserts; ice milk; fresh and canned fruits; jams, jellies, sugar, honey; most prepared pudding mixes when made with skim milk; water ices; marshmallows, gumdrops; nonhydrogenated peanut butter; cocoa powder; walnuts, pecans, almonds, peanuts, pistachio nuts	Coconut and coconut oil; whole milk puddings; milk sherbets; filberts; cashews; macadamia nuts
BEVERAGES, SNACKS, AND CONDIMENTS	Tea, coffee (no cream), bottled drinks; all herbs, condiments, and spices; cocoa made with skim milk; wine, beer, whiskey	Potato chips and other deep-fried snacks

Cholesterol Content
of Some Foods

Food *	Amount †	Cholesterol (Milligrams)
Brains	2 ounces	1,700
Butter fat	3½ ounces	280
Buttermilk (skim)	1 cup	5
Cheese (Cheddar)	1 ounce	27
Cheese (Mozzarella, partially skim)	1 ounce	18
Cheese (Parmesan)	1 tablespoon	5
Cream, heavy	1 tablespoon	20
Crab meat	3½ ounces	161
Clams	3½ ounces	114
Egg yolk	1	250
Fish	3½ ounces	70
Ice cream	1 cup	53
Ice milk	1 cup	26
Kidney	2 ounces	250
Liver	3½ ounces	300
Lobster	3½ ounces	85
Meat (lean)	3½ ounces	94
Milk, skim	1 cup	7
Milk, whole	1 cup	30
Oysters	3½ ounces	200
Poultry	3½ ounces	75
Scallops	3½ ounces	53
Shrimps	3½ ounces	150
Sweetbreads	3 ounces	396
Veal	3½ ounces	90
Yogurt (low-fat)	8-ounce carton	17

(Figures from U.S. Department of Agriculture *Composition of Food* and A.M.A., Department of Foods and Nutrition)
* Meats, poultry, and fish are cooked weight.
† 3½ ounces are approximately 100 grams.

Approximate Composition
of Common Food Fats

		Cholesterol (Milligrams)	% Polyun- saturates	% Monoun- saturates	% Saturates
OILS:	Coconut	0	0	8	92
	Cocoa Butter	0	5	34	61
	Corn	0	58	31	11
	Cottonseed	0	59	16	25
	Olive	0	7	81	12
	Peanut	0	31	46	23
	Safflower	0	78	12	10
	Sesame	0	43	43	14
	Soybean	0	63	21	16
	Sunflower	0	53	15	12
FATS:	Butter (1 tablespoon)	30	4	37	59
	Lard (1 tablespoon)	13	10	52	38
	Crisco	0	26	49	25
	Regular hydrogenated shortening	0	7	70	23

	% Cholesterol	% Polyunsaturates	% Saturates
MARGARINE:			
Fleischmann's (stick)	0	27	20
Mazola (stick)	0	30	22
Promise (stick)	0	48	17
Fleischmann's (tub)	0	36	20
Mazola (tub)	0	37	23
Promise (tub)	0	63	15

Table of Equivalents

60 drops = 1 teaspoon
3 teaspoons = 1 tablespoon
2 tablespoons = ⅛ cup or 1 liquid ounce
4 tablespoons = ¼ cup or 2 fluid ounces
8 tablespoons = ½ cup or 4 fluid ounces
16 tablespoons = 1 cup or 8 fluid ounces
1 cup = ½ pint
2 cups = 1 pint
4 cups sifted all-purpose flour = 1 pound
4½ cups sifted cake flour = 1 pound
2 cups granulated sugar = 1 pound
2⅔ cups confectioners sugar = 1 pound
2⅔ cups brown sugar = 1 pound
4 tablespoons flour = 2 ounces or ¼ cup
1 pound walnuts or pecans in shell = ½ pound, shelled
1 cup shelled walnuts or almonds = ¼ pound
1 cup shelled pecans = ⅓ pound
4 cups grated cheese = 1 pound
3 tablespoons cocoa plus 1 tablespoon oil =
    1-ounce square bitter chocolate
Juice of 1 medium lemon = about 3 tablespoons of juice
Apples: 1 pound = 3 medium apples; 2¾ cups pared
                 and sliced; or 1¾ cups sweetened
                 sauce
Lemons: 1 pound = about 4 medium lemons
Oranges: 1 pound = 2 3-inch oranges; ⅔ cup juice or
                 2 cups orange sections
Carrots: 1 pound = 4 medium cr 6 small; 3½ cups
                 grated; 2½ cups diced
Peppers: 1 pound = 5 or 6 medium; 3½ cups chopped
Onions: 1 pound = 4 to 5 medium yellow onions; 2 to 2½
                 cups chopped (relax about the size of
                 onions—half an onion more than
                 called for can do whatever you are
                 cooking nothing but good)

Table of Calories *

FOODS	CALORIES	FOODS	CALORIES
Acorn squash		Baking powder, 1 teaspoon	5
Boiled, pulp only, ½ cup	39	Bamboo shoots, raw, whole,	
Raw, 1 pound	152	½ pound	18
Almonds		Banana, 1 medium (3 to a	
Shelled, ½ cup	424	pound)	85
Salted, 12–15	93	Barley, dry, ½ cup	354
Slivered, 1 ounce	176	1 tablespoon	44
Anchovies, 1 ounce	50	Bass, striped	
Anchovy paste, 1 teaspoon	7	Raw, 1 pound	173
Apples		Flesh only, 1 pound	445
Raw, 1 medium	80	Beans, dried white, cooked,	
Pared, 1 pound	200	½ cup	113
Apple juice, canned, ½ cup	58	Bean sprouts	
Applesauce		Raw, ½ pound	80
Canned, 1 cup	185	Canned, 4 ounces	22
Low-calorie, 1 cup	100	Beef (all lean cuts)	
Apricots		Chuck	
Fresh, 3 whole	54	Cooked, 3 ounces	270
Canned, 4 medium halves	105	Ground, 4 ounces	315
Dried, 10 small halves	99	Flank, raw, 1 pound	653
12 ounces	890	Corned, ¼ pound	380
Apricot nectar, canned, ½		Dried, 2 ounces	115
cup	68	Hamburger, 3 ounces	185
Apricot preserves		Round, 3 ounces	197
Low-calorie, 1 tablespoon	22	Filet mignon, 3 ounces	248
Regular, 1 tablespoon	51	Beets	
Artichokes		Raw, 1 pound	78
Uncooked, untrimmed,		Canned, ½ cup	38
1 pound (number of		Belgian endive	
calories depends		Raw, ½ pound	31
on freshness)	40–225	Trimmed, cut, ½ cup	4
Frozen, hearts, 5 or 6	22	Blueberries	
Asparagus		Fresh, ½ cup	46
Raw, 1 pound	66	Frozen, ½ cup	120
6 spears	25	Bluefish, raw, ½ pound	267
Canned, 1 cup	45	Borscht, prepared, 8 ounces	72
Frozen, 4 ounces	26	Bovril, 1 teaspoon	11
Baby foods, pureed fruits,		Brandy, 86 proof, 1 fluid	
7½-ounce jar Approx.	150	ounce	70
Bacon (Canadian)		Bread	
Fried, 1 ounce	79	French, 1 slice (1 ounce, ¾	
Uncooked, 1 ounce	42	inch thick)	78
Bagel, 3 inches	165	Rye, 1 slice	60

* Compiled from U.S. Department of Agriculture handbook *Composition of Foods* and information supplied by food manufacturers and processors.

FOODS	CALORIES	FOODS	CALORIES
Bread (*Continued*)		Catsup, 1 tablespoon	18
White, ½-inch-thick slice	65	Cauliflower	
Whole wheat, ½-inch-thick		Raw, whole, 1 pound	48
slice	60	Boiled, ½ cup	14
French, 1 pound	1,315	Frozen, 10-ounce package	60
Italian, 1 pound	1,252	Celery	
Bread crumbs, dry, grated,		Raw	
1 cup	400	Untrimmed, 1 pound	58
1 tablespoon	25	1 large stalk	7
Breadsticks, 1 piece	10	Chopped, ½ cup	10
Broccoli		Cheese	
Raw, 1 pound	89	Cottage, low-fat, ½ cup	92
Boiled, ½ cup	20	Farmer, 4 ounces	159
Frozen, 10-ounce package		Cream, 4 ounces	390
Chopped	82	Parmesan, grated, 1 table-	
Spears	79	spoon	26
Brook trout, raw, 1 pound	224	Cheez-ola, 1 ounce	90
Brussels sprouts		Countdown, 1 ounce	42
Raw, untrimmed, 1 pound	155	Sapsago, grated, 1 table-	
Frozen, 10 ounces	102	spoon	38
Boiled, ½ cup	37	Cherries	
Bulgur, dry, 1 cup	803	Fresh sweet, ½ cup	50
Burgundy wine, 3 fluid		Canned, ½ cup	84
ounces	60	Bing, water-packed, ½	
Butternut squash		cup	63
Raw, 1 pound	171	Chestnuts	
Boiled, 4 ounces	46	Fresh	
Cabbage		In shell, 1 pound	713
White		Shelled, 4 ounces	220
Raw, 1 pound	86	Chicken	
Shredded, cooked, 1 cup	30	Broiler	
Red, raw, 1 pound	111	Raw, 1 pound	382
Candied fruit, 1 ounce	90	Cooked, ½ breast of 2½-	
Cantaloupe, ½ melon 5		pound chicken	157
inches in diameter	60	Meat, cooked, ¼ pound	154
Cubed, ½ cup	24	Chicken broth, canned, 10¾-	
Capers, 1 tablespoon	6	ounce can	126
Caraway seed, 1 ounce	72	Chick-peas (garbanzos), dry,	
Carrots		½ cup	412
Raw		Chicory, raw, trimmed, ¼	
Untrimmed, 1 pound	112	pound	23
1 medium	21	Chili sauce, 1 tablespoon	16
Grated, ½ cup	21	Chives, fresh, ¼ pound	32
Boiled, ½ cup	22	2 tablespoons	6
Canned, ½ cup	24	Chow mein noodles,	
Casaba melon, fresh, 1		canned, 1 ounce	139
pound	61	Chutney, 1 tablespoon	53

FOODS	CALORIES	FOODS	CALORIES
Cinnamon, ground, 1 teaspoon	6	Curaçao, 1 fluid ounce	100
		Curry powder, 1 tablespoon	26
Cinnamon candies, 1 teaspoon	30	Dates	
		With pits, 1 pound	1,081
Clams		Pitted, ¼ pound	311
Raw, meat only, 4 medium	65	Chopped, 1 cup	488
Canned		Duck	
Drained solids, 4 ounces	111	Raw, meat only, ¼ pound	187
Chopped solids and juice, 4 ounces	66	Roasted, 1 large slice	209
		Duck sauce, 1 tablespoon	16
Clam juice, 1 cup	43	Egg Beaters, ⅛ cup (equivalent to 1 egg)	100
Cocoa, 1 tablespoon	27		
Codfish		Eggs, 1 whole: white, 15; yolk, 60	75
Raw, uncooked, 4 ounces	88		
Dried, salted, 4 ounces	148	Eggstra, ½ package = 1 egg	43
Coffee, liquid, 1 cup	2	Eggplant	
Consomme, Campbell's, 10¾-ounce can	86	Fresh, 1 pound	92
		Cooked, 1 cup	40
Corn		English muffin, 1	140
Cooked, fresh, ½ cup or 1 ear	83	Endive, Belgian, fresh untrimmed, ½ pound	31
Canned		Escarole, trimmed, ½ pound	46
Whole kernel, ½ cup	75	Fillet of sole or flounder, raw, ½ pound	180
Cream style, ½ cup	102		
Corn Chex, 1 cup	110	Finnan haddie, ½ pound	234
Cornflake crumbs, 2 tablespoons	80	Flour	
		All-purpose wheat,	
Cornflakes, 1 cup	112	1 cup	825
Cornmeal, 1 ounce	103	2 tablespoons	206
Cornstarch, 1 tablespoon	30	Corn, 2 tablespoons	104
Corn syrup, 1 tablespoon	58	French dressing, home recipe, 1 tablespoon	92
Crab meat			
Fresh, 1 pound	422	Fruit, frozen mixed, 5 ounces	141
Canned, ½ pound	229		
Cranberries, fresh, ½ pound	100	Garlic, 1 ounce	38
Cranberry juice, ½ cup	94	Gelatin	
Cranberry sauce		Dry, unflavored, 1 tablespoon	34
Homemade, ½ cup	200		
Canned, jellied, ¼ cup	184	Fruit, prepared, ½ cup	80
Crème de menthe, 1 fluid ounce	94	Low-calorie, prepared,	
		½ cup	10
Cucumber		⅜-ounce package	48
Raw, pared, 1 pound	46	Ginger, candied, 1 ounce	96
Pared and diced, ½ cup	10	Ginger root, 1 ounce	13
Unpared, 7½ by 2 inches	28	Gingersnaps, 1 small	14
Sliced, 3 slices, ⅛ inch thick	4	Graham cracker crumbs, 1 ounce	109

FOODS	CALORIES	FOODS	CALORIES
Grape		Lemon juice (*Continued*)	
Fresh, ½ pound	135	Canned, unsweetened, 1	
Whole, 20 grapes, ¾ inch		tablespoon	4
in diameter	54	Frozen concentrate, ½ cup	145
Canned, 4 ounces	87	Lentil	
Grapefruit, fresh, 1 pound	84	Dry, ½ pound	771
½ medium	50	Cooked, ½ cup	107
Grapefruit juice, ½ cup	48	Lettuce	
Gravy Master, 1 tablespoon	25	Bibb, 1 pound	47
Grenadine syrup, 1 fluid		Boston, 1 head, 4 inches in	
ounce	100	diameter	30
Haddock, fillet, raw, ½		Romaine, 1 pound	52
pound	180	Simpson, 1 pound	52
Halibut, raw, meat only, 1		2 large leaves	8
pound	454	Lima beans	
Ham, cooked, 3-ounce slice	125	Boiled, ½ cup	94
Hamburger roll, 1	116	Canned, 4 ounces	81
Herring		Dried, ½ cup	304
Canned		Frozen, cooked, 4 ounces	102
Plain, 4 ounces	236	Lime juice, fresh or bottled,	
In tomato sauce, 4 ounces	200	1 cup	64
Pickled, 4 ounces	253	2 tablespoons	8
Honey, 1 tablespoon	64	Liqueur, 1 fluid ounce	90
Honeydew melon, fresh,		Liver, raw	
1 pound	94	Chicken, 1 pound	585
2- by 7-inch wedge	50	Calves', 1 pound	635
1 cup, diced	55	Macaroni	
Horseradish, prepared, 1 ta-		Dry, 1 ounce	105
blespoon	5	Cooked tender, 1 cup	155
Ice milk, vanilla, ⅙ quart	135	Mackerel	
Jelly, 1 tablespoon	54	Raw, ½ pound	432
Kasha, 1 cup	760	Canned, ½ pound	424
Kidney beans, canned, 1 cup	230	Madeira wine, 3 fluid ounces	120
Kippers, 4 ounces	230	Mandarin orange, low-	
Kirsch liqueur, 1 fluid ounce	83	calorie, canned, ½ cup	32
Lamb leg		Maple syrup, 1 tablespoon	50
Raw, lean, 4 ounces	148	Maraschino cherry, 1 av-	
Cooked (79% lean, 21%		erage	8
fat), 4 ounces	369	Margarine	
Leeks, 3 medium	40	Regular, 1 tablespoon	102
1 pound untrimmed	123	¼ cup	413
Lemon, 1 medium	20	Diet, 1 tablespoon	50
Lemonade, frozen, 6-ounce		Marmalade, 1 tablespoon	51
can	430	Low-calorie, 1 tablespoon	4
Lemon juice		Marsala wine, 3 fluid ounces	124
Fresh, 1 cup	62	Mayonnaise, 1 tablespoon	100
1 tablespoon	4	¼ cup	400

FOODS	CALORIES	FOODS	CALORIES
MBT chicken broth powder, 1 package (0.19 ounce)	12	Parsley, chopped fresh, 1 tablespoon	1
Milk		Parsnips	
Buttermilk (skimmed), 1 cup	89	Raw, 1 pound	293
		Boiled, ½ cup	70
Evaporated skimmed, 1 cup	176	Pasta, cooked until tender, 1 cup	155
Skim (fluid), 1 cup	89	Peaches	
Skim (nonfat powder), 1 tablespoon	32	Fresh, 2 inches in diameter	35
Molasses, 1 tablespoon	50	Canned, 2 halves with 2 tablespoons syrup	79
¼ cup	200	4 ounces	51
Mushrooms		Frozen, 12-ounce package	300
Raw, untrimmed, ½ pound	62	Peanut butter, 1 tablespoon	93
Canned, 4 ounces	19	½ cup	739
Mustard, prepared, 1 teaspoon	8	Peanuts, roasted, 1 tablespoon	85
Navy beans, dry, ½ cup	321	Pea pods, Chinese, cooked, ¼ pound	49
Noodles		Peas, green	
Dry, 8-ounce package	880	Raw	
Cooked, 1 cup	200	In pod, 1 pound	145
Oatmeal		Shelled, 1 pound	381
Dry, 1 cup	250	Cooked, ½ cup	58
Cooked, 1 cup	130	Canned, ½ cup	69
Oil, salad or cooking, 1 tablespoon	125	Frozen, 10-ounce package	206
¼ cup	500	Peas, split	
Olives		Cooked, ½ cup	112
Green, 1 ounce	32	Dry, 1 cup	706
3 extra-large	15	Pears	
Ripe, 1 large	5	Fresh, medium-sized	100
1 supercolossal	16	Canned, 2 halves with 2 tablespoons syrup	85
Greek style, 4 ounces	307	Pecans	
Onion		Shelled, ¼ cup	178
Raw, 1 pound untrimmed	160	Chopped, ¼ cup	180
1 medium (4 to 5 per pound)	38	Peppers, green	
		Fresh, 1 large	22
Chopped, 1 tablespoon	4	1 pound	82
Boiled, ½ cup	30	Chopped, ½ cup	16
Dehydrated flakes, 1 ounce	99	Pickle, dill, 1 large	15
Orange, fresh, 2⅘ inches in diameter	63	Pickle relish	
		Sweet, 1 tablespoon	21
Orange extract, 1 teaspoon	14	Sour, 2 tablespoons	5
Orange juice		Pike, raw	
Fresh or frozen, ½ cup	55	Whole, 1 pound	104
Frozen concentrate, 6-ounce can	330	Flesh only, 1 pound	399

TABLE OF CALORIES / 421

FOODS	CALORIES	FOODS	CALORIES
Pimiento		Rice (Continued)	
Whole, 1 medium	10	White	
Diced, 4 ounces	31	Raw, ½ cup	359
Pineapple		Cooked, ½ cup	124
Fresh, 3-ounce slice	44	Rice Chex, 1 cup	103
Canned		Roll, Pillsbury Crescent	94
Chunks, ½ cup	64	Rum, 80 proof, 1 fluid ounce	65
Slices, 2	56	Salmon	
Crushed, ½ cup	94	Raw, ½ pound	480
Pineapple juice		Canned, 7¾-ounce can	310
Canned, unsweetened, ½		Smoked, ¼ pound	200
cup	74	Salt	
Frozen concentrate,		Table	0
6-ounce can	387	Lawrey's seasoned, 1 tea-	
Pine nuts, shelled, 2 ounces	313	spoon	1¼
Pork (lean)		Sardines	
Chop, cooked, 3 ounces		Fresh, ½ pound	360
without bone	230	Canned, drained, 3 ounces	166
Butt, roasted, 4 ounces	277	Sauce, Worcestershire, 1 tea-	
Port wine, ½ cup	150	spoon	4
Potato		Sauerkraut, 1 cup	32
Raw, 2½-inch diameter	95	Scallions, 6 small	25
1 pound	279	Scallops, raw, ½ pound	184
Boiled, 1 medium	92	Sea squabs, raw, 1 pound	374
Canned, 3–4 small	118	Sesame seeds, dry, whole, 1	
Pretzel, 1 ounce	111	tablespoon	35
Prune juice, canned, ½ cup	99	Shad, raw	
Prunes		Whole, 1 pound	370
Dried, uncooked,		Fillet, ¼ pound	193
4 medium	70	Shallots, peeled, 1 ounce	20
12 ounces	870	Sherry, dry, 3 ounces	84–120
Cooked, 1 cup (17 or 18)	295	Shrimps, raw, cleaned, 1	
Radishes, raw, 4 small	6	pound	413
Raisins, diced, seedless,		Smelts, raw, whole, 1 pound	244
½ cup	236	Soy sauce, 1 tablespoon	22
1 tablespoon	29	Spinach	
Raspberries		Fresh	
Fresh, ½ pound	126	Untrimmed, 1 pound	85
½ cup	41	Trimmed, 1 pound	118
Frozen, 10-ounce package	277	Chopped, 1 cup	14
Red snapper, raw		Frozen, chopped, 10-ounce	
Whole, 1 pound	219	package	69
Meat only, ¼ pound	105	Strawberries	
Rice		Fresh, 1 cup	53
Brown		Frozen, 10-ounce package	310
Raw, ½ cup	374	String beans	
Cooked, ½ cup	135	Raw, 1 pound	128

FOODS	CALORIES	FOODS	CALORIES
String beans (*Continued*)		Vanilla extract, 1 teaspoon	8
Cooked, 1 cup	25	Vanilla pudding mix made	
Canned, 1 pound	82	with skim milk, 1 cup	260
Frozen, 9-ounce package	58	Veal	
Sugar		Raw	
Brown, 1 ounce (2 table-		Lean and fat, 4 ounces	265
spoons)	106	Rump, 1 pound (with	
Granulated, 1 ounce (2 ta-		bone)	573
blespoons)	109	Cooked	
1 cup	872	Lean and fat, 4 ounces	245
Confectioners, 1 cup	366	Loin, with bone, lean, and	
1 tablespoon	23	fat, ½ pound	1,312
Summer squash		Scaloppine, 3 ounces	185
Raw, 1 pound	89	V-8 juice, ½ cup	22
Cooked, ½ cup	19	Vermouth, dry, 3 fluid	
Frozen, 1 pound	95	ounces	90
Sweet potato, raw, 1 pound	419	Vinegar, 1 tablespoon	2
Swordfish, raw, 1 pound	535	¼ cup (2 ounces)	8
Tangerine, 1 medium, 2½		Walnuts	
inches	35	Shelled, 2 ounces	356
Tapioca, dry, 1 tablespoon	35	4 to 8 halves	50
Tartar sauce		Chopped, 4 tablespoons	196
Regular, 1 teaspoon	26	Water chestnuts, peeled, 4	
Low-calorie, 1 teaspoon	10	ounces	96
Tomato juice, ½ cup	22	Watercress, ½ pound	40
Tomato paste, canned, 6-		½ cup (trimmed)	3
ounce can	138	Watermelon	
Tomato puree, canned, 1		Fresh, 1 pound	54
cup	98	1 piece 4 by 8	
Tomato sauce, canned, 8-		inches with rind	115
ounce can	75	Diced, 1 cup	42
Tomatoes		Wax beans	
Fresh, 2½-inch diameter	35	Raw, 1 pound	108
1 pound	98	Canned, 1 pound	68
Canned, 14½-ounce can	95	Frozen, cut, ½ pound	64
Trout, rainbow, raw, 1		Wheat Chex, 1 cup	165
pound	885	Wild rice, uncooked, ½ cup	288
Tuna fish		Wine, dry, white, 3½ fluid	
Canned, drained, 4 ounces	190	ounces	60–70
Raw, 1 pound	603	Yeast, dry, 1 ounce	80
Turkey		1 tablespoon	25
Raw, with bones, 1 pound	722	Yogurt, low-fat	
Cooked, ¼ pound	210	Plain, 4 ounces	70
Cooked, diced, 1 cup	257	Vanilla, 4 ounces	98
Turnips		Zucchini	
Raw, 1 pound	117	Uncooked, 1 pound	73
Boiled, diced, ½ cup	18	Boiled, ½ cup	9

Index

Notes

	RECOMMENDED
MEATS *	BEEF: Eye, top and bottom round; flank steak; fillet; lean ground round LAMB: Leg, well trimmed PORK: Lean loin; trimmed ham steak; Canadian bacon VEAL: Scallopine; loin chops; rump or shoulder; leg; eye roast
POULTRY	Young chickens, preferably skinned; turkey (white meat); Cornish hen; squabs
FISH AND SHELLFISH	All fish, fresh, dried, frozen, smoked; fish canned in soybean or cottonseed oil or water
EGGS	Egg whites: unlimited. Up to 3 egg yolks per week
DAIRY PRODUCTS	Skim milk, dry and liquid; low-fat cottage cheese; skim milk buttermilk; canned evaporated skimmed milk; special low-fat cheeses; low-fat yogurt; farmer cheese; sapsago; ice milk
FRUITS AND VEGETABLES	All fruits; all vegetables raw or cooked in polyunsaturated fats
FATS AND OILS	Safflower, corn, cottonseed, soybean, sunflower oils; mayonnaise and homemade salad dressings made with polyunsaturated oils; special polyunsaturated margarines
SOUPS	Fat-free soups; homemade cream soups; consommé
BREAD, CEREALS, AND BAKERY PRODUCTS	White, whole-grain, rye, Italian and French breads; English muffins; breads made without added fat; hard rolls; homemade cakes, pastries, waffles and pancakes made with polyunsaturated oils; all cereals, hot and cold (check on labels); rice; melba toast matzo; pretzels; spaghetti and macaroni; barley; angel cake mix
DESSERTS AND SWEETS	Gelatin desserts; ice milk; fresh and canned fruits; jams, jellies, sugar, honey; most prepared pudding mixes when made with skim milk; water ices; marshmallows, gumdrops; nonhydrogenated peanut butter, cocoa powder; walnuts, pecans, almonds, peanuts, pistachio nuts
BEVERAGES, SNACKS, AND CONDIMENTS	Tea, coffee (no cream), bottled drinks; all herbs, condiments, and spices; cocoa made with skim milk; wine, beer, whiskey

* Limit the meat portion to 4 to 6 ounces uncooked.
Beef, lamb, and pork should be served no more than 4 times a week.